Strategic Management for Voluntary Nonprofit Organizations

The voluntary nonprofit sector is now involved in all aspects of people's lives, from the cradle to the grave. The management of these organizations has never been of more interest and has been changing rapidly, with well-meaning amateurs being replaced by highly committed and professional leaders.

With one in every six employees in the service sector now working in the voluntary sector, *Strategic Management for Voluntary Nonprofit Organizations* examines arguments for and against whether voluntary organizations should now be more businesslike and considers how many organizations have responded to this challenge.

A unique collection of case studies presents important examples of how some voluntary organizations have developed, and the challenges they have faced, whilst other pedagogic features include review and discussion questions and an extensive bibliography.

Strategic Management for Voluntary Nonprofit Organizations provides an original insight into the theory and practice of strategic management for voluntary nonprofit organizations, for both practitioners and students of voluntary sector management.

Roger Courtney was the Chief Executive of a voluntary nonprofit organization for sixteen years and is now a freelance consultant in the voluntary nonprofit sector. He has published widely on the subjects of managing voluntary organizations, fundraising and homelessness.

Routledge Studies in the Management of
Voluntary and Non-Profit Organizations
Edited by Stephen P. Osborne
Aston Business School, UK

The Management of Non-Governmental Development Organizations
An introduction
David Lewis

Financial Management in the Voluntary Sector
New challenges
Paul Palmer and Adrian Randall

Strategic Management for Voluntary Nonprofit Organizations
Roger Courtney

Also available in the 'Management of Voluntary and Nonprofit Organizations'
series from Routledge Research:

1 Voluntary Organizations and Innovation in Public Services
Stephen P. Osborne

2 Accountability and Effectiveness Evaluation in Nonprofit Organizations
Problems and prospects
James Cutt and Vic Murray

3 Third Sector Policy at the Crossroads
An international nonprofit analysis
Edited by Helmut K. Anheier and Jeremy Kendall

4 Public–Private Partnerships
Theory and practice in international perspective
Edited by Stephen P. Osborne

Strategic Management for Voluntary Nonprofit Organizations

Roger Courtney

Routledge
Taylor & Francis Group

LONDON AND NEW YORK

First published 2002
by Routledge
2 Park Square, Milton Park, Abingdon, Oxon, OX14 4RN

Simultaneously published in the USA and Canada
by Routledge
270 Madison Ave, New York, NY 10016

Transferred to Digital Printing 2006

Routledge is an imprint of the Taylor & Francis Group

© 2002 Roger Courtney

Typeset in Garamond by Taylor & Francis Books Ltd
Printed and bound in Great Britain by TJI Digital, Padstow, Cornwall

British Library Cataloguing in Publication Data
A catalogue record for this book is available from the British Library

Library of Congress Cataloging in Publication Data
Strategic management for voluntary nonprofit organizations / Roger
Courtney.
  p. cm.
Routledge studies in the management of voluntary and nonprofit
  organizations
Includes bibliographical references and index.
1. Nonprofit organizations–Management. 2. Associations,
institutions, etc.–Management. 3. Voluntarism–Management. 4.
Volunteers. 5. Strategic planning.

HD62 .6.C686 2001
658'.048 dc21

12474236

ISBN 0–415–25023–4 (hbk)
ISBN 0–415–25024–2 (pbk)

Contents

List of illustrations   viii
The author   ix
Preface   x
Acknowledgements   xii

PART I
An introduction to the voluntary nonprofit sector   1

1   An introduction to strategic management in the
voluntary nonprofit sector   3

2   The growth and development of the voluntary nonprofit
sector   12

3   The rise of professional management in the voluntary
nonprofit sector   26

4   What is the voluntary nonprofit sector and how is
it different from other sectors?   36

PART II
**The development of different approaches to strategic
management**   55

5   The development of strategic management   57

6   What is an excellent organization? The Attributes of
Excellence School   73

7   Starting with the people: the Human Resources
    School   81

8   Post-modern perspectives on strategy   94

PART III
Strategy and the voluntary nonprofit sector   107

9   The development of strategic management in the
    voluntary nonprofit sector   109

10 How to measure success   121

11 Is strategic management effective?   139

PART IV
**Strategic analysis, formulation, choice and
implementation**   147

12 Strategic analysis: reviewing the organization   149

13 Strategic analysis: the external environment   171

14 Strategic formulation: creating the plan   179

15 Strategic formulation: basic choices   195

16 Strategic implementation: making it happen   210

PART V
Case studies   219

Save the Children Fund   221

Care In The Home (CITH)   230

World Wide Fund for Nature (WWF)   235

CARE   242

The Simon Community   246

Grameen Bank   255

Homeline   265

NSPCC   276

Oxfam   289

References   295
Index   316

Illustrations

Boxes

1.1	Definitions of strategy	7
2.1	Barnardo's	15
2.2	Amnesty International	19
2.3	Apex Trust	22
12.1	Typical list of stakeholders of a voluntary nonprofit organization	151
12.2	Investors In People standard	162
13.1	Examples of external changes for a cancer charity	175
14.1	Mission statements	181
14.2	Vision statements	183
14.3	Typical values in the voluntary nonprofit sector	187
14.4	The values of Voluntary Service Overseas (VSO)	188
14.5	The long-term aims of Centrepoint	190
14.6	Examples of performance indicators for services provided by a medical charity	193
15.1	Mergers in the voluntary nonprofit health field	203
15.2	Commercial piggybacking: Fundación Social	204
15.3	Matrix of strategic choices for voluntary nonprofit organizations	207
16.1	Examples of objectives for a faith-based training organization	214

Figures

4.1	The 'four overlapping circles' model of sectors	50
4.2	Types of organization in and around the social economy	52
10.1	General model of nonprofit effectiveness	133
10.2	A competing-values model of effectiveness criteria	134
10.3	The EFQM excellence model	136
12.1	Boston portfolio matrix	152
13.1	Environmental scanning	173
13.2	Issues impact analysis grid	173
13.3	Force field model	178
14.1	Strategic planning pyramid	189

The author

The author was born and brought up in Belfast. After obtaining a psychology degree and training as a community and youth worker, he set up and ran the Crescent Youth & Community Resource Centre in South Belfast, which eventually became Crescent Arts Centre. He became the Chief Officer of the Simon Community Northern Ireland in 1981, which by 1998 had expanded from two small rundown houses for people who are homeless, with three staff, to an organization with a turnover of over £2M, over 200 staff and accommodation projects for homeless people all over Northern Ireland.

Over this period, in parallel with the practical experience of managing a rapidly expanding organization, Roger Courtney gained a Diploma in Management Studies, a Master's in Human Resource Development, and an NVQ in Management at level 5. He is currently carrying out doctoral research on strategic management in the voluntary nonprofit sector.

Since 1998, Roger Courtney has been working as a freelance writer and consultant in the voluntary nonprofit sector, mostly in Ireland. He specializes in strategic planning, fundraising, governance, quality, human resource development and evaluation work.

He is the author of several books about fundraising, a book on new approaches to managing voluntary organizations and a guide to mentoring, as well as a number of publications on homelessness.

Roger Courtney was awarded an MBE in 1996 for his work with homeless people.

Preface

The two main reasons for writing a book are, first, to make the author rich, and second, to make the author famous (or infamous). In the unlikely event that this book doesn't manage to achieve either or both of these two objectives, there probably needs to be a further justification for inflicting the book upon an unsuspecting public – and in this instance I think there are two. The first is personal, in the sense that when it becomes clear to me that something is important but I am ignorant about it, I get a terrible desire, first of all to read everything I can about the subject, and then to try and write something down to make sense of what I have read. So, in the mid-1980s, when I was responsibe for managing a rapidly expanding voluntary nonprofit organization, I became increasingly aware of the need to have in place planning and management systems that would help ensure clear focus and direction for the organization. I therefore introduced a simple strategic planning process, based more upon intuition than knowledge. As the organization expanded I began to read more and more (much of it contradictory) about strategic management, mostly books that applied to the private sector or to the public and nonprofit sectors in the USA, but very little that related to voluntary nonprofit organizations in Europe. As I continued to try to make sense of what I was reading and apply what seemed to be appropriate to my organization, I also began to put down in writing how I understood the relevance of the theory for the world of voluntary nonprofit organizations in which I had spent my whole career.

When I began working freelance with a wide range of voluntary nonprofit organizations on their strategic development, and at the same time undertook further academic study and research, my realization that the only serious books in this area to date have been American was reinforced. This provided a further spur to write a book that would explain the theory and practice of strategic management for voluntary nonprofit organizations, both for leaders of organizations and for those studying the management of voluntary nonprofit organizations in the hope of eventually becoming the leaders of the future.

The result is not one of those 'one-best-way' guides to strategic management. It accepts that there are many different perspectives and theories to consider, and readers should draw on what is useful. I hope, however, that through sharing this journey with me the reader will develop a better understanding of the various approaches to strategic management and where these approaches come from, and that this will inform their decisions about the most appropriate models and approaches to help make their own organization more effective in changing the world.

Roger Courtney

Acknowledgements

I am very grateful to the various voluntary nonprofit organizations which helped me compile appropriate case studies and examples for inclusion in the text; to those others with which I have worked over the last four years for having the confidence in me to help guide their strategic management processes; to Dr Arthur Williamson, Stephen P. Osbourne and Professor Joyce for comments on earlier drafts; to the staff at Routledge for their help and support; to my own family for their tolerance in putting up with me while I worked on the book; and to my wife in particular for undertaking the inspiring task of checking the references.

Part I

An introduction to the voluntary nonprofit sector

1 An introduction to strategic management in the voluntary nonprofit sector

Chapter outline

This chapter provides a brief overview of the topic of strategic management in the voluntary nonprofit sector. It briefly explores the nature and significance of the sector in the UK and the definitions of strategy, strategic planning and strategic management. How to use this book is explained at the end of the chapter.

Learning objectives

When you have completed this chapter you should understand:

*   the significance of the voluntary nonprofit sector in the UK;
*   why the voluntary nonprofit sector has begun adopting strategic management models and tools;
*   the basic arguments about the use of these models and tools in the voluntary nonprofit sector;
*   the diversity of definitions of strategy;
*   the relevance of some of the definitions of strategy for the voluntary nonprofit sector;
*   Mintzberg's explanation of the different approaches to strategy;
*   the difference between strategy and planning;
*   the difference between strategic planning and strategic management;
*   how to use this book.

Introduction

Recent research has highlighted the significance of the voluntary nonprofit sector in contemporary society (Salaman and Anheier 1994). Far from being a marginal aspect of life in most countries, the voluntary nonprofit sector pervades almost all aspects of society from the cradle to the grave, and is a major player in the economy.

In the USA, for example, employment, at over 7 million people (full-time equivalents) in the voluntary nonprofit sector,* represents 6.8 per cent of the total workforce and 15.4 per cent of those employed in the service sector. In Europe the figures are smaller but still significant. In Germany (1 million people), France (0.8 million people) and the UK (0.9 million people), employment in the voluntary nonprofit sector is around 4 per cent of total employment and 10 per cent of employment in the service sector. Japan, which has a lower percentage, still represents 1.4 million employees in the voluntary nonprofit sector. To put this into perspective, while there are 2 million employees employed by the six largest companies in Europe and the USA (Daimler-Benz, General Motors, Hitachi, Fiat, Alcatel-Alsthom and Unilever), there are 11.8 million employed in the voluntary nonprofit sector in the countries mentioned above.

In relation to the expenditure of the voluntary nonprofit sector as a proportion of Gross Domestic Product (GDP), the USA is the highest at 6.3 per cent, followed by the UK at 4.8 per cent and Germany, France and Japan all around 3–3.5 per cent. However, the percentage growth in the contribution of the voluntary nonprofit sector between 1980 and 1990 is 15.8 per cent in France, 11 per cent in Germany and 12.7 per cent in the USA, so the significance of the role of the voluntary nonprofit sector is growing rapidly.

The terminology to describe the voluntary nonprofit sector varies from country to country, as do the areas of work in which the sector plays a significant role. While education, research, health, social services, culture and recreation are the main areas in which the voluntary nonprofit sector plays a significant role, regardless of country, the balance between these varies between countries for a variety of historical, cultural and political reasons. For example, in the UK and Japan the role of the voluntary nonprofit sector is most significant in education; in the USA and Germany, health, especially voluntary nonprofit hospitals, is the dominant area for the sector; in France and Italy, social/human services dominate the sector; and in Hungary, with a much lower proportion of GDP and employment in the voluntary nonprofit sector, culture and recreation are the predominant areas where the sector plays a major role. As we shall see, the nature of the voluntary nonprofit sector also changes over time. In the UK, for example, the development of the National Health Service after World War Two resulted in voluntary hospitals becoming part of the statutory service.

In the UK there are estimated to be 200,000–240,000 voluntary nonprofit organizations (Kendall and Knapp 1996). This figure rises to 378,000–418,000 if a broader definition of the sector is used which includes recreational clubs and organizations; primary, secondary and higher education; trade unions; and professional and business associations. As mentioned above, it is estimated (Kendall and Knapp 1996) that the sector in the UK employs 390,000 people, or 946,000 if you use the wider definition above – i.e. nearly one-tenth of all jobs in the UK service sector, not to mention the army of part-time volunteers. The total turnover of the sector in the UK is estimated at £10 billion, or over £26 billion if the wider definition of the sector is used.

As highlighted in Chapter 2, the voluntary nonprofit sector has very old roots indeed, long preceding the public sector as the main provider of human services such as education and hospitals to the population. It has experienced various periods of substantial growth under different political regimes and ideologies. The last thirty years in particular have seen a huge growth in the sector as a result of an increasing scepticism about the ability of governments or the private sector to provide services in a way that will adequately meet the needs of the population.

With this expansion have come changes in the expectations of how voluntary nonprofit organizations should be run. External organizations such as funding and regulatory bodies have been increasingly holding voluntary nonprofit organizations to account for the funding they receive and how it is used. Those with leadership responsibilities in the sector themselves have also increasingly recognized what is required to rise to the challenge of managing nonprofit organizations in the twenty-first century. They have also recognized that they are being forced to compete for funds and volunteers, not only with other voluntary organizations but with the private sector as well, as private companies increasingly bid for contracts to deliver human services that were previously provided by the public sector.

In rising to this challenge, voluntary nonprofit organizations have looked for models and tools that will help them to manage and develop their organizations in a way that is true to their mission and values. Some of these tools and techniques have been in specialist areas like marketing, finance, human resources or information technology, for example. But there has also been a need to find appropriate ways to enable voluntary nonprofit organizations to address some of the most fundamental questions about the purpose of the organization, what it is trying to achieve and how it is going to determine and achieve its mission and goals.

These fundamental questions fall clearly into the concept of strategy, determining 'the direction and scope of an organization over the long-term, ideally which matches its resources to its changing environment and in particular its markets, customers and clients so as to meet stakeholder expectations' (Johnson and Scholes 1993).

The concept of strategy has had long use in diplomatic and military history (see Chapter 5) and since the 1960s has been developed extensively to help private sector organizations to address the same questions, even if for a different purpose – in the case of the private sector, primarily to increase profitability.

The adoption of techniques which have been developed particularly for the private sector is not without controversy, however. There has been a long-standing concern amongst some people that voluntary nonprofit organizations have been becoming increasingly like businesses and have therefore been losing their distinctive identity and values as the boundaries of the sectors become increasingly blurred. For some, strategic management is just another commercial technique being foisted on an unwilling sector which is losing its soul.

For others, however, strategic management has provided a useful set of tools and techniques to draw on and adapt to enable them to be more focused, to create a stronger sense of unity and direction, to understand the external environment better and to manage more effectively the development of the organization.

In the voluntary nonprofit sector there is perhaps a tendency to create a simple caricature of strategic planning or strategic management in the private sector in order to refute its relevance for the voluntary nonprofit sector. The history of management fads in the private sector (Micklethwaite and Wooldridge 1996) makes this easy to do. In reality, as we shall see, there is a wide range of perspectives, models and tools which can be described under the heading of strategic management, many of which are in conflict with other strategic management approaches. They have, however, increasingly provided a useful cookbook for many voluntary nonprofit organizations from which to choose and adapt any of the recipes to suit their own purposes, with often-positive results.

Defining strategy

One of the difficulties about the area of strategic management is the language, not to say jargon, that is often used, much of it inconsistently. The basic concept of strategy is no exception. Many definitions of strategy that have been developed for use in the private sector emphasize features that are alien to the culture and language, not to say purpose, of the voluntary nonprofit sector. However, many other definitions are equally as applicable to the nonprofit sector.

Box 1.1 gives a number of definitions given by key writers in the field which are as relevant to the voluntary nonprofit sector.

Henry Mintzberg (1994) has shown that part of the problem in defining the concept of strategy is that the word is used in a number of different ways. In common language and dictionary definitions, strategy is normally thought of as a *plan*, although sometimes these are merely *ploys*, i.e. tactics or manoeuvres. The definition of strategy as 'plan' suits the traditional design and planning schools (see Chapter 5) well, which focus on intended strategies, but 'strategy' can also be used in a number of other senses. Strategy can be viewed as a *pattern* of actions that have consistency and consequences, whether they were planned or intended or not. This perspective may perhaps be seen more clearly in hindsight, or by an outsider. Here emergent strategies are crucial.

Strategy can also be seen as *position*, in the sense of the niche that the firm occupies – the fit of the firm to its environment, or its place in the product-market domain. And lastly, strategy can be viewed as *perspective*. In this sense strategies are 'abstractions which exist only in the minds of interested parties'. Strategy in this respect is to the organization as personality is to the individual. These different understandings of the concept are not necessarily

Box 1.1   *Definitions of strategy*

Strategy is the determination of the basic long-term goals and objectives of an enterprise, and the adoption of courses of action and the allocation of resources necessary for carrying out these goals (Chandler 1962).

Strategy is defined by decisions an organization makes that determine or reveal its objectives, purposes or goals; create the principal policies and plans for achieving its aims; define the range of businesses or services the organization is to pursue; identify the kind of economic and human organization it is or intends to be; and specify the nature of the economic and non-economic contribution to be made to the organization's shareholders or trustees, employees, customers and communities (Andrews 1971).

Strategy can be seen as a key link between what the organization wants to achieve – its objectives – and the policies adopted to guide its activities (Bowman and Asche 1987).

[Strategy is a] disciplined effort to produce fundamental decisions and actions that shape and guide what an organization is, what it does, and why it does it (Bryson 1988).

Strategy relates to the patterns/plans that integrate an organization's major goals/policies and action sequences into a cohesive whole (Quinn 1988).

Strategy is the pattern of organizational moves and managerial approaches used to achieve organizational objectives, and to pursue the organization's mission (Thompson and Strickland 1990).

[Strategy is a] decision or series of decisions made by or on behalf of an organization or organizational sub-unit which determines its medium to long-term objectives, priorities and overall direction; and which repositions the organization into its changing external environment, including competitive pressures and the availability of key resources (Public Services Management 1991).

Strategy provides the stability of consistent direction and orientation while permitting the flexibility to adapt to changing circumstances (Craig and Grant 1993).

Strategy is the direction and scope of an organization over the long term, ideally which matches its resources to its changing environment and in particular its markets, customers and clients so as to meet stakeholder expectations (Johnson and Scholes 1993).

conflicting but rather complementary, emphasizing different aspects of strategy that each need to be considered.

This helpful taxonomy of Mintzberg makes it possible to separate the concept of strategy from that of planning, which is important because an organization has a strategy, which can be perceived, whether or not it engages in any form of formal planning. Quite a lot of planning that takes place is also not strategic. It is often more operational or action planning.

Reflecting on some of the weaknesses of the classic early schools of strategy, Mintzberg *et al.* (1998) suggest that 'strategic planning' should have been called 'strategic programming' and promoted as a process to 'formalise, where necessary, the consequences of strategies already developed by other means'.

There has also been a change in the terminology over the last two decades, used in practice from the traditional 'Strategic *Planning*', as 'a disciplined effort to produce fundamental decisions and actions that shape and guide what an organization is, what it does, and why it does it' (Bryson 1988), towards the idea of 'Strategic *Management*' as 'the process of strategic change' (Bowman and Asche 1987) or as 'the process of making and implementing strategic decisions', 'strategic decisions' being those 'that determine the overall direction of an enterprise and its ultimate viability in light of the...changes that may occur in its...environments' (Quinn 1980).

Using the term strategic *management* to denote the whole process of innovation, strategic analysis, formulation and implementation emphasizes the continuous nature of the process and makes it much more likely that any strategies which are decided on will actually be implemented; and the term will generally be used throughout this book.

How to use this book

To understand better the use of strategic planning models and techniques in the voluntary nonprofit sector this book follows the following structure:

Part I

Chapter 1 introduces the topic; outlines the significance of the topic for the voluntary nonprofit sector; and explores various definitions of strategy. Chapter 2 describes the origins and the changing nature of the voluntary nonprofit sector, to indicate the internal and external factors that have led voluntary nonprofit organizations to adopt 'new managerial' approaches to management. Chapter 3 looks at the development of the voluntary nonprofit sector over the past ten years and the contract culture in particular. Some of the arguments for and against adopting such approaches are also introduced. Chapter 4, in order to address the relevance of models and techniques developed in the private sector for the voluntary nonprofit sector, explores ways that the voluntary nonprofit sector has been defined, both internally in terms of classification systems, and externally in relation to its relationships with other sectors. The suggested differences and similarities between the private and voluntary nonprofit sectors are explored.

Part II

Chapter 5 explores the development of the concepts of strategy and strategic planning from their early military and diplomatic uses to the development of theories and schools of strategic planning designed as an aid to the private sector, which achieved considerable hegemony and consensus during the 1960s and 1970s. The chapter also considers the increasing criticisms of the traditional schools of strategic planning voiced particularly in the 1980s. Chapter 6 describes an alternative approach to the traditional strategic planning schools which became enormously popular following the publication of Peters and Waterman's book *In search of excellence* in 1982, with its case study approach to 'excellent' organizations to determine the attributes of excellence, which was then emulated in a variety of geographical areas and sectors. The chapter concludes with a discussion of the value and relevance of this approach. Chapter 7 examines the Human Resources School of organizational development, which was also increasingly popular in the 1980s (and remains so), and its implications for strategic management. Chapter 8 explores a number of other post-modern critiques of traditional strategic planning/management theory and analyses the implications of these critiques for the development of strategic management theory.

Part III

Chapter 9 brings together the discussions about the voluntary nonprofit sector and strategic management with an exploration of the development of the theory and empirical evidence in relation to strategic management in the voluntary nonprofit sector. In particular, it describes the development of the literature on strategic planning and strategic management in the voluntary nonprofit sector and research evidence in relation to its prevalence in national voluntary nonprofit organizations in the UK. Chapter 10 explores the various different approaches to defining organizational effectiveness. Chapter 11 examines the evidence for the effectiveness of strategic management.

Part IV

Chapter 12 examines the tools and techniques that have been developed to analyse the internal environment of organizations; and Chapter 13 examines those that have been developed to examine the external environment of organizations. Chapter 14 outlines the classic approach to strategic formulation which has achieved significant consensus in the literature on strategic management. Chapter 15 explores the basic configurations of strategic options open to voluntary nonprofit organizations that have been suggested in the literature. Chapter 16 explores the various tools and techniques of strategic implementation relevant to the voluntary nonprofit sector.

Part V

The final section provides a variety of major case studies of voluntary nonprofit organizations which can be used to explore the issues highlighted throughout the book. Each case study suggests a number of questions for discussion or individual reflection.

If you are hoping to develop a better understanding of the voluntary nonprofit sector you should read Chapters 1–4 and 11 and some of the case studies in Part V. If you want to understand some of the theory behind strategic management, where it came from and some of its critiques, you should read Chapters 5–8. If you want to develop an understanding of, and be able to use, some of the basic models and techniques of strategic management that have been applied to voluntary nonprofit organizations, you should read Chapters 12–16.

Summary

This introductory chapter has highlighted the significance of the voluntary nonprofit sector, which now impacts on almost all aspects of our lives. The growth of the sector has been mirrored by increasing expectations of the management of the sector, by funders, beneficiaries and the public. This has resulted in the increasing professionalization of the management of voluntary nonprofit organizations, including the adoption of strategic management.

The chapter has also highlighted the range of meanings given to the word 'strategy', and the need to distinguish between the concept of strategy and that of planning.

Questions

1   Why is the voluntary nonprofit sector important?
2   Is the voluntary nonprofit sector the same regardless of country? If not, what are the factors that make it different?
3   How would you define strategy, and why?
4   Does a strategy have to be deliberate?
5   Is the definition of strategy for a voluntary nonprofit organization different to that for a for-profit company?
6   What is the difference between strategic planning and strategic management?

Suggested reading

Jeremy Kendall and Martin Knapp (1996) *The voluntary sector in the UK*, Johns Hopkins Nonprofit Sector Series, Manchester University Press.

Henry Mintzberg (1994) *The rise and fall of strategic planning*, Prentice-Hall.

Lester M. Salaman and Helmut Anheier (1994) *The emerging sector – an overview*, Johns Hopkins University Press.

Note

*   The definition of the voluntary nonprofit sector used in the Johns Hopkins study excludes religious congregations, political parties, co-operatives, mutual savings banks and mutual insurance companies. See Chapter 4 for a detailed discussion of how the sector can be defined.

2 The growth and development of the voluntary nonprofit sector

Chapter outline

To illustrate the growth and changing nature of the voluntary nonprofit sector, this chapter explores the origins and development of the nonprofit sector in the UK and the factors that have led to the changing role of the sector in response to changing needs and expectations.

Learning objectives

When you have completed this chapter you should understand

- the historical importance of the voluntary nonprofit sector;
- the extent to which most of the social institutions, such as hospitals and universities, were pioneered by the voluntary nonprofit sector;
- the important role of religion in the development of a variety of human services;
- the reasons for the development of the welfare state and its impact on the voluntary nonprofit sector;
- the growth of campaigning organizations in the 1960s and 1970s;
- the impact of the political move to the right in the UK and USA and the desire to reduce the role of the state.

Introduction

The voluntary nonprofit sector has very ancient antecedents, providing welfare for people in need on a not-for-profit basis for many centuries, and has gone through a number of previous periods of substantial growth (Marshall 1996; Hudson 1995; Davis Smith 1995; Owen 1964; Kendall and Knapp 1996). Kendall and Knapp go so far as saying that 'it is impossible to chart the development of UK society without frequent allusions to the pivotal role that voluntary organizations have played in changing ideologies, values, responsibilities and policies' (1996).

Mutual Aid and Friendly societies have been active in the UK at least since the first century AD (Gosden 1973), and probably one of the oldest schools in the world was founded by St Augustine in the sixth century.

The thirteenth century has been described as 'the golden age of small associations of piety geared much less towards the practice of sacraments than towards liturgy and good works' (Le Bras, quoted in Davis Smith 1995). In England some 500 hospitals were founded during the twelfth and thirteenth centuries (Rubin 1988).

By the medieval era, the Roman Catholic Church had come to occupy a central position in the delivery of formal philanthropy, under the auspices both of religious orders and of the secular clergy. The physical expression of this role was seen in the development of almshouses, doles and elementary education.

Two more secular strands of philanthropy can be seen at this time: one primarily rural, the other primarily urban. First, the feudal responsibility of the aristocracy towards those who lived on their rural estates.

> A lord was bound by personal obligations embedded in customary land law to ensure that at least the basic essentials of life were provided for any of his tenants who suffered exceptional hardship.
>
> (Chesterman 1979)

Second, the development of guilds and livery companies in the fourteenth century. Although they existed primarily for the benefit of their members engaged in the particular trade, they also became involved in a range of other philanthropic activities, including schools, bridges, monuments, almshouses and doles for local paupers (Chesterman 1979). The influence of the guilds waned by the end of the sixteenth century; however, the livery companies of London have remained significant supporters of philanthropy to this day.

The Protestant Reformation led to a significant reduction in the role of the Catholic Church and the development of another strand of philanthropy based on a more Puritan ethic, evangelical faith, and an individual work ethic. The expression of this ethic can be seen in the response to the increase in the landless underclass and the increase in the number of almshouses and hospitals, but more particularly in the creation and support of workhouses, work programmes, houses of correction, apprenticeship schemes, schools and universities (Chesterman 1979). These developments were as much an expression of self-interest by the elite as they were altruistic philanthropy, as the landless poor appeared to the elite to be posing a major threat to social order and stability (Williams 1989).

This was also the period of the creation of the Poor Law, which, in line with the Puritan ethic, tried to delineate clearly between the deserving and the undeserving poor. The workhouse provided the deterrent against 'vagrancy and idleness', enabling philanthropy to be focused on the really deserving poor (Jordan 1959).

The relevant legislation in the UK (the statute of Elizabeth), which to this day defines what is, and is not, charitable, dates back to 1601. It finally removed the role of ecclesiastical courts in enforcing charitable use and established roving commissioners to investigate the administration of charities (Davis Smith 1995), an important initial step in making charities accountable.

The eighteenth century saw a more tolerant age develop, and a series of reforms to the Poor Law system. It has even been described as the 'golden age of philanthropy' (Rodgers 1949), with the philanthropy of merchants increasing significantly with the increase of their wealth. This form of philanthropy has been described as the 'richesse oblige', in contrast to the noblesse oblige which still operated in many rural areas.

The eighteenth century also saw the development of associative philanthropy, as societies and associations developed to promote a range of philanthropic causes. Mutual aid through friendly societies also appears to have increased significantly during this period (Kendall and Knapp 1996).

It is possible to identify four main phases in the development of the provision of voluntary aid in Britain since 1800. The first of these phases has been described as the 'last phase of paternalism' where, in addition to religious provision, paternalism and patronage based on the relationship between landed aristocracy and gentry and those beneath them was administered by charity through the Poor Law system at local parish level. The Industrial Revolution and the rise of the industrial and commercial classes led to the old systems of patronage being swept away and a philosophy of laissez-faire and self-help created a desire to put in place systems that would further distinguish between the deserving and the undeserving poor.

Philanthropy in the nineteenth century was influenced by a number of important factors:

- the Industrial Revolution increased enormously the number of urban poor crammed together in insanitary and crowded conditions;
- the French Revolution had created the fear among the British elite that a similar revolutionary situation may arise in Britain;
- evangelical sects and movements with a strong moral tone became increasingly popular;
- the role and number of middle-class women were changing significantly. With domestic servants, philanthropic activities provided an acceptable role in society for many of these women.

These factors created four main strands in nineteenth-century philanthropy:

- A tightening-up of the Poor Law and almsgiving to ensure that the position of the 'idle poor' in receipt of relief was not better than that of the lowliest labourer (Hill 1970).

- The development of a wide range of evangelical and moral societies, some intent on improving the moral behaviour of the population, such as the Society for the Suppression of Vice and the strong temperance and Sabbatarian movements; others reflecting a more charitable ethos of middle-class ladies to help the poor (but which, according to Williams (1989), was not necessarily received with the desired response, as the recipients often felt an 'irritation with the moralizing cant of the relief workers, and resentment at providing a hobby for the Evangelical middle class whose women were precluded by custom from gainful employment').
- The development of great social reform movements, such as the anti-slavery movement.
- The establishment in urban areas which had expanded substantially with the Industrial Revolution of working-class organizations such as friendly societies, burial clubs and trade clubs.

The second half of the nineteenth century has been seen as the heyday of British philanthropy (Davis Smith 1995). The average middle-class household was spending more on charity than on any other household item except food (Prochaska 1990). The income of some London charities was more than that of many nation-states (Owen 1964). However, the proliferation of charitable activity sometimes created problems of duplication. Prochaska (1988) reports that, in parts of London, four or five visiting societies besieged poor households each week. Others have suggested, however, that the level of giving was highly localized (Thane 1982).

The social surveys of Charles Booth (1889), founder of the Salvation Army, and Seebohm Rowntree (1901) demonstrated that despite the apparent economic benefits of the Industrial Revolution and the expansion of the British Empire, and the extensive philanthropy of the latter part of the nineteenth century, large numbers of people were still living in abject poverty – a fact confirmed by the Royal Commission on the Poor Laws and Relief of Distress. As a result there were increasing calls for greater intervention from the state, led by various socialist groupings, including the Fabian Society.

The founding of Dr Barnardo's homes in 1871 by evangelist Thomas Barnardo (see Box 2.1) was typical of this period.

Box 2.1 *Barnardo's*

Thomas John Barnardo was born in Dublin in 1845. As a young man, he joined an evangelical church called the Plymouth Brethren and planned to become a medical missionary in China. In 1866, he travelled to London and began training as a doctor, but the poverty and

---

squalor he saw affected him so deeply that he realized he had work to do there and dedicated himself to work with destitute children.

In 1871 he opened a home for orphaned boys at Stepney Causeway, offering them shelter, clothes, food and some work training, and in 1876, with his wife, he opened the Village Home for Girls in Barkingside, Essex. This was a collection of 70 houses circling a green providing homes, run by 'cottage mothers', for about 1,000 girls, based on similar homes in France and Germany.

As his undertakings grew, so did the need for money. Barnardo was a tireless and persuasive fundraiser, an energetic speaker and writer, and an expert in public relations.

More homes, schools and training centres were opened. The 'Babies' Castle' was set up in Kent and an infirmary for sick children in Stepney. A boys' garden city was started in Essex and a naval training school in Norfolk, together with homes for disabled children.

An emigration programme for youngsters began in 1882. Most went to Canada after careful selection, preparation and training, and continued to receive support from the organization. By the time of Barnardo's death in 1905 about 18,000 children had emigrated. This programme continued until 1967.

At about the same time, Barnardo, in recognizing the importance of a 'family' upbringing rather than life in an institution, extended the practice of boarding out children with families, which was already being done by the Poor Law Authorities.

Residential homes were an important part of Barnardo's service until after the Second World War, when the philosophy gradually changed. It was increasingly realized that keeping families together was important and, where that was not possible, children would generally be better off in a foster family rather than a children's home. By 1966, as Barnardo's work expanded around the UK, more than half the children Barnardo's worked with lived at home with their families. To reflect this, Barnardo's changed its name from 'Dr Barnardo's Homes' to 'Dr Barnardo's'. The last traditional children's home closed in the 1980s, and the charity changed its name to 'Barnardo's' in 1988.

For many years, Barnardo's resisted the idea of adoption (which became legal in 1926) and clung to the idea that it was itself a surrogate family. But as the climate of opinion gradually changed, Barnardo's became a registered adoption society in 1974 and began to concentrate on older children with disabilities or emotional difficulties – children sometimes described as 'hard to place'.

As the social policy context, and awareness of the needs of children and young people, changed, Barnardo's carried out a number of strategic reviews in 1984, 1989 and 1995 which re-focused Barnardo's programmes on work with those children, young people, families and communities in greatest need, including responding to the particular social needs of which people were becoming increasingly aware like HIV/AIDS, sexual abuse, disability and youth homelessness.

With a turnover in excess of £100M, Barnardo's currently has over 300 programmes around the UK, working with children, young people, families and communities on a diverse range of programmes, and has been working hard to shake off its original Victorian image of a provider of children's homes for orphans.

The 1940s and 1950s – The welfare state

The third phase, the emergence of Statutory Social Services, was promoted by the Liberal Party which came into power in 1905 after a long period of opposition, and introduced a series of limited legislative reforms to provide some minimum standards outside the poor relief system.

In comparison with some of the early religious providers of voluntary nonprofit services, the welfare state and the comprehensive provision of services for those in need by the government or public bodies is a very recent invention, primarily of the twentieth century, mainly following the upheaval of World War Two. During this period, the perceived weaknesses of the voluntary nonprofit sector, such as particularism, amateurism, paternalism and insufficiency (Salamon 1987), were put under the spotlight. In particular, the limitations of philanthropic organizations in trying to deliver comprehensive services, such as education and health, in an integrated and consistent manner across the country were recognized.

Serious concern was expressed about the state of health of men conscripted into the army during World War One and the quality of the health care available. The UK Minister of Health, Bevan, described voluntary hospitals prior to the setting up of the National Health Service as 'a patch-quilt of local paternalisms' and an 'enemy of intelligent planning' (Davis Smith 1995).

The voluntary nonprofit sector's role in the management of hospitals was almost entirely removed by the establishment of the National Health Service in 1946, despite Conservative opposition. Universal secondary education was introduced in 1944, retaining at least a residual role for the voluntary sector. The Labour government of 1945–51 implemented most of Beveridge's recommendations in relation to the creation of a welfare state, including a minimum income.

With the loss of some voluntary services, such as hospitals, to state control, the future role of the voluntary sector was not clear and the twenty years that followed World War Two have been described as 'marking time' for the voluntary nonprofit sector (Wolfenden 1978). Indeed some supporters of the welfare state, including Crossman and Abel-Smith, although not Beveridge himself (as can be seen from his own book about the sector, *Voluntary action* (1948)), assumed that the voluntary nonprofit sector and their aura of middle-class patronage would wither on the vine as the hegemony of the state grew (Osborne 1996). However, this did not happen. The voluntary sector carved out a new if altered role for itself (Davis Smith 1995). As Cole (1945) argued:

> It is a great mistake to suppose that as the scope of state action expands, the scope of voluntary social service necessarily contracts. Its character changes in conformity both with changing views of the province of state action and with the growth of the spirit and substance of democracy.

The 1960s and 1970s – Growth in voluntary nonprofit organizations

The 1960s and 1970s represented a new phase of 'creativity, ingenuity and energy' in the development of the voluntary sector, with a very substantial increase in the number of voluntary nonprofit organizations in most countries of the world (Salamon and Anheier 1994), as new needs were identified, which were not being adequately responded to by the public sector.

There was also a rising disenchantment with the state's welfare bureaucracies (Wolfenden 1978; Hadley and Hatch 1981; Deakin 1995) and their ability to meet needs effectively and efficiently. There was an uneasy consensus between the Right, politically, who have traditionally supported charitable activities, and who viewed the 'voluntary spirit as the life-blood of democracy', and the Left, who saw the new campaigning organizations like Shelter, the Child Poverty Action Group, CND, Amnesty International (see Box 2.2), as well as a host of feminist, environmental, human rights and other radical organizations, as companions in the task of bringing about social justice and a truly participatory democracy (Hain 1975). The Left also recognized that philanthropy was also often used as an expression of social control by dominant status groups, effectively blocking social progress (Williams 1989; Wolch 1990; Beckford 1991; Kendall and Knapp 1996).

> What really excited reformers in the 1960s however was the way in which voluntary care could extend and influence state welfare. Self-help groups, for example, by increasing public participation – and above all increased participation by the 'consumers' of welfare and their carers – identified 'real' needs, to which the state had then to respond. Voluntary agencies were also able to pioneer new techniques and methods of care because, unlike their official counterparts, they had not always to ensure equity or to consider possible political objections.
>
> (Lowe 1993)

Box 2.2   *Amnesty International*

The beginning

In 1961, London lawyer Peter Benenson read about a group of students in Portugal who were arrested and jailed for raising a toast to 'freedom' in a public restaurant. This incident prompted him to launch a one-year campaign called 'Appeal for Amnesty 1961' in the London *Observer*, a local newspaper.

The 'Appeal for Amnesty' called for the release of all people imprisoned because of peaceful expression of their beliefs, politics, race, religion, colour or national origin. Benenson called these people 'prisoners of conscience'. His plan was to encourage people to write letters to government officials in countries which had prisoners of conscience, calling for their release.

The campaign grew enormously, spread to other countries, and by the end of 1961 the organization Amnesty International had been formed.

Amnesty International was founded on the principle encapsulated in the UN Universal Declaration of Human Rights, that people have fundamental rights that transcend national, cultural, religious and ideological boundaries. It worked to obtain prompt and fair trials for all prisoners, to end torture and execution, and to secure the release of prisoners of conscience. (Prisoners of conscience, as Amnesty International defines them, are people imprisoned solely because of their political or religious beliefs, their gender, or their racial or ethnic origin, and who have neither used nor advocated violence.)

Amnesty International's earliest activity was individual letter-writing on behalf of prisoners of conscience. After the organization had investigated a prisoner's case and determined that he/she was indeed a prisoner of conscience, it would 'adopt' this prisoner. People in the group would write many letters to officials in the prisoner's country asking for his/her release. They would also, if it was safe to do so, contact the prisoner's family and offer help.

This worked well, probably because people involved with Amnesty International felt a bond with individual prisoners, whose names, cases and families they grew to know, far more than they could have with a set of statistics on a country's human rights record. It also established Amnesty International's early focus on individuals, not countries or political systems. Amnesty International members work on behalf of individuals, not to change political systems.

After a while, though, individuals grew restless, wanting to do more than just write reams of letters, few of which were ever answered. During the late 1960s, members who wanted to be more active at the local level began to form what were then called Adoption Groups, and in the 1980s were renamed Local Groups, to focus additional efforts on an adopted prisoner and specific country or issue campaigns. They also helped increasingly with publicity, education and fundraising at the grassroots level, and reached out to churches, schools, businesses, professional organizations and trade unions. This activity brought in new members and resources, spurring the organization's growth.

Change of strategy

In the late 1960s, after some mistakes and consequent bad publicity, Amnesty International adopted the rule that people in the organization were to work on cases only outside of their countries, as experience had indicated that some people were not sufficiently impartial about cases in their own countries. They would either believe a story about a human rights abuse without checking it out, or refuse to believe it without verifying that it was actually false. Since the impartiality and accuracy of Amnesty International (or any human rights organization) is the source of its reputation and ability to influence events, this was a serious problem. Also, relatively few countries tolerated human rights activism sufficiently to allow an internal activist to work without interference or threats to his freedom and safety.

However, most of the early principles and types of work remain unchanged, and the organization has grown to over 1 million members in over 150 countries.

Despite these early mistakes and setbacks, and growing international opposition by human rights abusers, Amnesty International's various methods and activities were frequently successful. In 1977 Amnesty International was awarded the Nobel Peace Prize for its work.

The 1980s – new period of growth and heightened awareness

Many early members of Amnesty International were lecturers in higher education, but during the early 1980s the number of student groups grew tremendously. Because their membership changed rapidly, these groups did not adopt prisoners, but instead worked on country campaigns, organized publicity, and wrote letters on behalf of adopted prisoners for other groups. In many cases a campus group would team up with a local adoption group to organize human rights events and get out letters for their adopted prisoner.

In the mid-1980s a number of prominent musicians and artists adopted Amnesty International as a special cause, giving the profits from concerts or even from entire tours. This brought about tremendous growth and new visibility for the organization. It also increased Amnesty International's budget tremendously. New staff were hired and new regional offices opened all over the world.

To Amnesty International, the individual prisoners are the important thing; they do not work to change systems of government. However, by UK law they are not eligible for charitable status.

Amnesty today – still volunteer-based

Volunteers still carry out most of Amnesty International's work. They write letters to governments that are abusing the human rights of those who hold opposing viewpoints, whether through imprisonment, harassment, threats, physical mistreatment, torture, 'disappearances' or politically motivated murder. They staff tables at public events, passing out information to the public on prisoners of conscience and human rights issues. They organize demonstrations, write press releases and found letter-writing groups.

The relationship between the voluntary nonprofit and statutory sectors was sometimes uncomfortable, particularly when voluntary agencies publicly criticized the statutory sector. The Seebohm Committee, set up by the government to review the provision of social services, acknowledged that

> [a] certain level of mutual criticism between local authority and voluntary organizations may be essential if the needs of consumers are to be met more effectively and they are to be protected from the misuse of bureaucratic and professional power in either kind of organization.

The 1970s represented an important shift in the relationship between the voluntary nonprofit and statutory sectors in Britain, as the voluntary nonprofit sector became an increasing tool of Government policy, particularly with the development of programmes to combat the serious problem of unemployment. Through these programmes, very large amounts of Government funding were channelled through voluntary nonprofit organizations in order to deliver Government objectives in relation to employment and training. By 1988, 20 per cent of all Government funding to the voluntary nonprofit sector in the UK came from the Manpower Services Commission, particularly through its Community Programme (Deakin 1995).

The case study in Box 2.3 highlights an organization which expanded rapidly and broadened its remit on the basis of Government funding available through the Manpower Services Commission, and which faced total collapse when the funding scheme was withdrawn. The major case study in Part V about CITH (see page 230) also highlights an organization which was initially established to manage a Government scheme to help the long-term unemployed and which faced major strategic questions when the scheme was closed, and had to identify a completely new role for itself.

Box 2.3   *Apex Trust*

Apex Trust was founded in 1965 by Neville Vincent, chairman of Bovis Holdings, a leading construction company. The work of the Trust was based on the belief that

> [i]f an ex-prisoner can be found a job which, first, provides him a reasonable standard of living for himself and his family, and second, fulfils his own idea of himself and thus engages his self respect, the responsibility of his eventual return to prison will be diminished.

From the two pilot programmes set up in Pentonville and Wormwood Scrubs Prisons, Apex Trust identified a special need for a service for 'white collar' offenders and sex offenders. The success of the programme resulted in a request from the Courts and the Probation Service for a similar service in other parts of the country. In 1978, the Trust extended its services to all offenders, including those under supervision of the Probation Service, and introduced employers from industry to provide job search advice and support to serving prisoners.

In 1980, Apex opened its first regional office in Leeds, and in 1981, Apex became a limited company with charitable status. Eleven centres for unemployed people specializing in services to offenders were established through funds from the Manpower Services Commission (MSC) and, during 1986–7, the Trust further expanded, delivering twenty new MSC programmes for the unemployed (not only offenders). This included centres in Merseyside, Sunderland, Leeds and London. In 1988, a new development programme was established in Scotland, which eventually became the basis of the independent organization Apex Scotland.

In January 1992, with the complete change in government funding of employment programmes, Apex Trust went into administration and a campaign was launched to raise funds to save the organization. The securing of £300,000 through intensive fundraising and the returning to the Trust's original goals, i.e. focusing entirely on the employment

---

needs of (ex-) offenders, resulted in Apex emerging from administration in July 1992.

Godfrey Allen was appointed Chief Executive of the Trust in 1995 and has been taking the organization forward to meet the employment needs of (ex-) offenders, and, as he sees it, the requirements of an increasingly competitive and quality-driven voluntary sector.

The Trust now provides services in the following areas:

- Information and advice
- Assessment and guidance
- Pre-vocational training
- Enterprise advice, training and support
- Job search advice, training and support.

Partnerships have been established with four probation services. Work with prisoners has continued in two young offenders' institutions and two prisons. The Trust has also developed innovative joint ventures between itself and a diverse range of agencies in different sectors, including the Federation of Small Businesses, Federation of Black Housing Associations, Rotary Clubs, Institute of Personnel & Development, and Trade Unions. In all cases, it has focused on building public awareness of the economic and social case for ex-offender employment as a cost-effective way of reducing crime and unemployment. In 1996, Apex secured funding from the National Lottery Board to establish an enterprise development programme in rural Bedfordshire.

It is interesting to note that the Wolfenden committee, established in 1978 to look at the future of the voluntary nonprofit sector, had very little to say about the management of voluntary nonprofit organizations. Clearly, at that stage, the thinking on strategy and management that was so prevalent in the private sector had had little impact on the voluntary nonprofit sector in the UK. Wolfenden suggests, however, that such organizations should 'earn and deserve a reputation for the maximum amount of straightforward efficiency' and that there

> is more to be done than is done at present, in self-criticism, keeping up-to-date, monitoring performance, studying how far users and consumers are satisfied with what they receive. We are not asking that they should be perpetually pulling themselves up by their roots to see how they are getting on. But we do suggest that once every five years or so each and every voluntary organisation should engage in a deliberate self-examination about its aims, purposes, successes, failures, and, especially, possibilities for redirection of its activities.
>
> (Wolfenden 1978)

There is therefore the start of some strategic thinking in Wolfenden, if only on a once-every-five-years basis.

The 1980s and 1990s – The shift to the right

From the beginning of the 1980s, the expansion of the sector was further promoted by a fundamental shift in political and economic ideology, labelled 'Reaganism' in the USA and 'Thatcherism' in the UK. This ideology emphasized the primacy of the market. It argued that smaller government is better government and that services or industries that are run publicly are inevitably inefficient (a view that had been suggested as early as 1968 in the Fulton report in the UK; Fulton 1968). This resulted in the transfer of many former public functions to the private sector on the one hand, and to the voluntary nonprofit sector on the other.

Summary

This chapter has highlighted the crucial role of the voluntary nonprofit sector (although not described as such at the time), and of religious institutions in particular, in attempting to respond to the various needs of the population well before the concept of the public sector was conceived. It has also highlighted the inadequacy of voluntary nonprofit sector provision to provide universal services and the resulting creation of the welfare state. The changing role of the sector, particularly in the 1960s and 1970s, to identify and meet new needs as well as to campaign for policy changes is outlined, as well as the important role of local government and the Manpower Services Commission in the development of the sector in this period. Disillusionment with the public sector in the 1980s and the divestment of direct services, previously managed by the public sector, to be run by voluntary nonprofit and private providers of services on a contractual basis, is also analysed.

Questions

1   What role did religion play in the historical development of the voluntary nonprofit sector?
2   Historically has the voluntary nonprofit sector developed differently in urban and rural areas?
3   To what extent was the public sector created to compensate for the weaknesses in the voluntary nonprofit sector?
4   Why did the voluntary nonprofit sector not wither away with the development of the welfare state?
5   Why was there a significant growth in the nonprofit sector in the 1960s and 1970s?

6 To what extent was the growth in the voluntary nonprofit sector a product of becoming an agent of government?

Suggested reading

Justin Davis Smith 'The voluntary tradition: Philanthropy and self-help in Britain 1500–1945' and Nicholas Deakin 'The perils of partnership: The voluntary sector and the state 1945–1992', both in J. Davis Smith, C. Rochester and R. Hedley (eds) (1995) *An introduction to the voluntary sector*, Routledge.

Jeremy Kendall and Martin Knapp (1996) *The voluntary sector in the UK*, Johns Hopkins Nonprofit Sector Series, Manchester University Press.

For a US perspective:

Peter Dobkin Hall (1994) 'Historical perspectives on nonprofit organisations', in Robert D. Herman and Associates (eds) *The Jossey-Bass handbook of nonprofit leadership and management*, Jossey-Bass.

3 The rise of professional management in the voluntary nonprofit sector

Chapter outline

This chapter explores the development of the 'new managerialism' in the voluntary nonprofit sector from the 1980s on, and the arguments for and against the adoption of professional management approaches in the voluntary nonprofit sector.

Learning objectives

When you have completed this chapter you should be able to understand:

*   the reasons for the growth and changing role of the voluntary nonprofit sector in the 1980s;
*   the impact of the contract culture and increased expectations of accountability in the changing nature of voluntary nonprofit organizations;
*   the role of local authorities in the UK in relation to the development of the voluntary nonprofit sector in the 1980s;
*   the impact of increasing competition in encouraging voluntary nonprofit organizations to emulate the private sector;
*   the rise of the 'new managerialism' in the voluntary nonprofit sector;
*   the arguments for and against the use of professional management methods in the voluntary nonprofit sector.

Introduction

With the transfer in the 1980s of substantial functions previously run by government agencies (particularly the provision of social care services) to voluntary nonprofit organizations came major changes in what was expected of those organizations, and in the relationship between the public and voluntary nonprofit sectors (see Smith and Lipsky 1993; Kramer 1992; Lewis 1996; Deakin 1996; Gann 1996; Rochester 1995). This in turn started to have a very major impact on how these organizations were managed.

The main factors influencing this 'Flood' (Hudson 1995) away from the public sector towards the voluntary nonprofit sector were described by Hudson as the following:

- a political philosophy that believed state-run organizations are neither efficient nor responsive to people's changing needs;
- the consequent separation of the functions of the purchaser (to specify standards and desired outcomes) and the provider (to deliver services efficiently and effectively, responding quickly to changes in the external environment) – what Osborne and Graebler (1992) describe as separating rowing from steering;
- a desire to give local managers greater control over the management of their organizations;
- tighter control over public expenditure coinciding with increased social need;
- a belief that competition between suppliers can lead to efficiency gains, even though the notion of competition in the provision of basic services is deeply uncomfortable, particularly to professionals in these services (Hudson 1995).

Gann (1996), also writing in the context of the UK, reinforces the importance of most of these external factors and adds several additional ones, as follows:

- a reduction in the amount of 'untied' funds available to local authorities;
- a shift towards project- or programme-based funding of development work by national government through local authorities (e.g. through Economic Development Corporations, Urban Programme, City Challenge and Single Regeneration Fund schemes);
- an increased secularization of society, while much voluntary work continued to be provided by religious groups;
- an increased emphasis on the use of modern management techniques in local government (see also Joyce 1999), leading to similar expectations of voluntary nonprofit organizations funded through contracts by local authorities (e.g. in the use of monitoring and evaluation, staff appraisal, strategic and development plans, etc.) (Gann 1996).

The major case study in Part V about CITH highlights some of the issues facing an organization which receives most of its income through contracts with one statutory body. The major case study in Part V of the NSPCC highlights an organization founded on the basis of Victorian philanthropy, which has adapted to the contract culture and is now frequently contracted by statutory social services to provide childcare services to children at risk of abuse.

Some people have suggested that the contract culture has resulted in statutory organizations becoming increasingly managerial and controlling, and to voluntary nonprofit organizations becoming more like the statutory bodies they are in contract with and whom, in some cases, they replaced as primary providers of welfare services.

> There is a danger that voluntary organisations that take on mainstream services will become more and more like the statutory service providers they were meant to replace. Maria Brenton, in her study of nonprofits in the United States and the Netherlands, suggests: 'the process of development of the voluntary sector to the role of monopoly or major provider with the aid of state funds seems inevitably to follow a path similar to that taken by our statutory services – the path toward professionalisation and bureaucracy.'
>
> (Taylor 1992)

This difference of view is very relevant to the general discussion of whether voluntary nonprofit organizations should adopt professional management approaches and techniques.

Government departments and agencies that fund voluntary nonprofit organizations have been increasingly holding the organizations accountable, through monitoring and evaluation processes, for the outcomes of that funding. These monitoring and evaluation processes often impose a framework, similar to the management approach which is dominant within the statutory body itself and which emphasizes the articulation of goals, objectives, outcomes, performance indicators and budgets, as well as the establishment of monitoring and control mechanisms.

The development of contractual relationships between voluntary nonprofit and public sector organizations has also led to the position where certain voluntary nonprofit organizations, particularly those that are in a contractual relationship with statutory bodies, are considered as 'public bodies' in relation to particular statutory requirements such as the Human Rights Act 2000. This has already resulted in these bodies (housing associations, for example) being required to carry out the 'Best value' processes, initially only a requirement on statutory bodies. 'Best value', the Labour government's successor to Compulsive Competitive Tendering (CCT), requires the adoption of a strategic management approach involving the organization's stakeholders.

An alternative perspective is that the introduction of competition for contracts and funding is pulling voluntary nonprofit organizations into the culture of the for-profit sector rather than that of government. Voluntary nonprofit organizations are increasingly required to compete against other voluntary nonprofit organizations, as well as public and private sector organizations, for attention, funds, people (staff and volunteers) and commercial contracts (Clutterbuck and Dearlove 1996) and are therefore required to demonstrate that they are as effective and efficient as private companies. Gutch (1992) argues that contracting will result in voluntary nonprofit organizations becoming larger, more professionalized and more like private companies, with a reduced influence of management committees, volunteers and service-users.

These views may not be as far apart as they appear, as the public sector itself has taken on board much of the new managerialism (Pollitt 1990; Joyce 1999), also known as 'market-based public administration' (Lan and Rosenbloom 1992) and 'entrepreneurial government' (Osborne and Graebler 1992), with the encouragement of government, government advisors from the private sector, and large consultancy firms. In turn, these statutory bodies are requiring voluntary nonprofit organizations funded by them, and particularly those they contract with, also to adopt these new managerial approaches.

A recent study of UK local government (Flynn and Talbot 1996) suggests that not only did the majority of local authorities engage in formal strategic planning, but also that it was perceived as providing a wide range of benefits.

A study of strategic management challenges facing the voluntary nonprofit sector in the UK by Aston University (Lubelska 1996) suggests that

> [b]oundaries are definitely blurring between voluntary organizations and the private sector...while the contracting-out of central and local government services...has resulted in voluntary organizations becoming more like local authority operations...voluntary sector managers these days are running organizations that are businesses and public bodies at one and the same time.

Impact of local government

The importance of changes in local government, in particular, in transforming the voluntary nonprofit sector in the UK, stressed by Gann (1996), is supported by the analysis of Deakin (1995) which locates the changes clearly within the ideology of Thatcherism. He argues that an alliance had developed between some Labour-led local authorities and radical left-wing voluntary nonprofit organizations, which shared an ideology opposed to that of the Conservative government. These 'urban left' local authorities provided significant support, financial and otherwise, to various 'constituencies of the disadvantaged', including women and ethnic minorities, as 'a means of politicisation, mobilising new constituencies of support' (Gyford 1985). These local power bases were a major irritation to the government, which set about systematically destroying them by a combination of cuts and the centralization of power to Westminster. This strategy was largely successful. In the words of Deakin (1995): 'By the end of their second term (1987) the Conservative government had in substance won the battle with local authorities.'

The Conservative government of that time had its own vision of the role of the voluntary nonprofit sector in Britain, which was very different from that of the radical groups funded by some Labour-led local authorities. The Conservative agenda for the voluntary nonprofit sector, based on a return to perceived Victorian values, was to reactivate philanthropy – the responsibility of individuals, rather than the state, to be 'active citizens' and support those in need, who are considered to be deserving of that support. The government encouraged individuals, including wealthy business leaders, to support charitable activities financially as well as giving their time and skills.

However, there were also major critics of this philanthropic approach to social welfare. According to Salamon (1987), charity can 'create a self-defeating sense of dependency on the part of the poor since it gives them no say over the resources that are spent on their behalf'. Hall (1989) recalls the 'indignities – what I would call the offensive social contempt – which have always gone along with a system of welfare which depended only on private patronage'.

Changing expectations of voluntary nonprofit management

The other element of this agenda was to improve the standards of management in the voluntary nonprofit sector. This was seen to be important if the responsibility for delivering many services was to be taken away from the mainly Labour-led local authorities and given to the voluntary nonprofit sector. The strategy was to apply lessons from the 'new managerialism' which had developed in the private sector during the 1960s and 1970s, and was also starting to have a major impact on the public sector in Britain and the USA (Osborne and Graebler 1992; Pollitt 1990).

The Handy report, *Improving the effectiveness of the voluntary sector* (Handy 1981), highlighted the need for the development of these management skills, if the sector was to take on an expanded role. In response to this 'rising star of management in the voluntary sector' (Bruce and Leat 1993), umbrella agencies, training organizations, education institutions and private companies like IBM and the National Westminster Bank supported and developed programmes for managers in the voluntary nonprofit sector to improve their management skills.

Many people in the voluntary nonprofit sector took enthusiastically to this managerial approach which created what Drucker (1990) called a 'management boom' in the sector, and many senior managers came into the sector from outside (Leat 1995). However, as Knight (1993) has acknowledged, 'resistance to management was deep rooted'. Amongst some, there was 'a pervasive worry that management would be a Trojan horse, infiltrating alien systems and practices and undermining the perceived autonomy, cherished values, core identities and distinctive working methods of individual organisations and the sector as a whole' (Batsleer 1995). As

Handy states (1988): 'To many in the voluntary nonprofit sector, organisation means management, and management reeks of authoritarianism, of capitalism, of business and bureaucracy.'

Many voluntary nonprofit organizations in this period questioned the need for a managerial approach. 'Why can't we manage ourselves on the basis of our obvious stock of goodwill, flexibility, commitment and natural ability?' (Billis 1984).

Mason (1984) is particularly scathing about the idea that voluntary nonprofit organizations should become more like their private sector counterparts:

> Folklore says that management expertise resides permanently in the business sector, and that only the transfer of management knowledge from business to the other sectors will improve the latter. Becoming more 'businesslike' is a code phrase for improving management in both voluntary enterprises and government...the business sector has no monopoly on effectiveness...no more than government has a monopoly on bureaucracy or the voluntary sector on good intentions. All organisations are simply vehicles we human beings assemble to help us get to where we think we want to go. ...Running a business like a voluntary enterprise would be as disastrous as running a voluntary enterprise like a business.

Drucker (1990) suggests that ' "management" was a very bad word in voluntary nonprofit organisations. It meant "business" to them, and one thing they were not was a business, indeed most of them believed that they did not need anything called "management" '.

Handy (1988) argued, however, that voluntary nonprofit organizations needed to be more business-like, and that, when they are thinking about management issues, voluntary nonprofit organizations

> would be foolish to throw the baby out with the bathwater because of an 'ideological fanaticism'. While renouncing many of the assumptions which underlie the management of businesses they should not ignore the fact that they themselves are organisations made up of people and that there are things known about the way that people interact with each other or with organisations which are likely to hold true in their world as well as in that of business. ...Voluntary organisations are not businesses, but they do have clients, they provide services and they have to finance themselves in one way or another. It makes just as much sense to ask a voluntary organisation what its strategy is as it does to ask a business. It is not sinful to be businesslike.

He warns of the danger, both of 'strategic delinquency' in the sector, where it is more important to stand for something than to achieve; and 'strategic seduction' where an organization without clear goals follows whatever funding is available (Handy 1988).

Lyons (1996) suggests that the objections to the strategic management of voluntary nonprofit organizations are of four main types:

1   Strategic management is a business idea, a business technique that is designed to improve profitability and enshrines a set of values that undermines the essential values of voluntary nonprofit organizations.
2   Strategic management is an aid for, and indeed might be said to mandate, competition which is a value and an orientation hostile to the voluntary nonprofit sector which is about collaboration and partnership.
3   Strategic management is a method of control that contradicts the commitment of the voluntary nonprofit sector to participation, and to giving voice and power to the disadvantaged.
4   Strategic management is too elaborate and too time consuming for small voluntary nonprofit organizations that operate in a survival mode, living from one month or one year to the next.

Lyons argues that none of these arguments stands up to scrutiny and that strategic management is as important, if not more important, for the voluntary nonprofit sector as for the private sector. Leat (1995) also addresses this issue and provides a useful summary of the positions of those who are for and those against the use of for-profit management models. The objections of the 'against' camp include the following:

- they will destroy the distinctiveness of voluntary nonprofit organizations;
- voluntary nonprofit organizations will lose their commitment to their traditional values (see also Jeavons 1992, and Hailey 1999);
- they are incompatible with the internal values and relationships in voluntary nonprofit organizations;
- they encourage competition between organizations, thus reducing the sector's ability to meet the needs of those it supposedly serves (Young 1989; Bush 1992);
- they emphasize demand as opposed to need;
- they are at odds with the ethos and practice of volunteering;
- the role of trustees is marginalized;
- private sector management has a spurious credibility that needs to be challenged;
- they devalue the skills and achievements that the voluntary nonprofit sector has built up over many years;
- they will result in a failure to promote internal candidates for management positions;
- they create a spiralling increase in salaries;

- they create the need for expensive management training and use of external management consultants.

Leat (1993) also suggests the main arguments in favour of using for-profit management techniques in the voluntary nonprofit sector include the following:

- they create a new discipline of efficiency and cost effectiveness in the voluntary nonprofit sector;
- they raise the status and recognition of the voluntary nonprofit sector;
- they increase confidence in the voluntary nonprofit sector, especially amongst funders;
- they will give voluntary nonprofit organizations new concepts and tools to improve management and performance;
- they increase the learning across sectors.

Landry *et al.* (1985) analysed the failure of many radical left-wing voluntary nonprofit organizations in England in the 1970s and showed how many had collapsed precisely because they had done what Handy described, in failing to use basic management models and techniques that are important regardless of the sector. Landry concluded that

> one crucial function of management…is the clarification of organisational goals and the continuous development and monitoring of strategies to achieve these goals. The problem of how to clarify objectives, create a strategy to carry them out and find the means to make them happen, is one that few radical organisations recognise explicitly. Most just muddle through. This lack of strategic clarity can only be a recipe for disaster, as the history of failure in this sector over the last few years plainly demonstrates.
>
> (Landry *et al.* 1985)

Ten years later, the approach to management in the voluntary nonprofit sector had changed enormously. Batsleer (1995) described this change as follows:

> The last two decades have seen the emergence of a recognisable 'culture of management' in the voluntary sector. Even small community projects have begun to use the language of business plans, strategic choice, quality outcomes, mission statements and competing stakeholders. There has been much 'dancing with the enemy', despite the persistent anxiety that too large a dose of managerialism might lead to the loss rather than the enhancement of core values and identities.

Others (Klausen 1995; Harris 1997) have addressed the issue at a sub-sectoral level. Rather than arguing that strategic management tools and models are not appropriate for the voluntary nonprofit sector as a whole, they argue that, while it may be suited to larger, bureaucratic, professionized service-delivery voluntary nonprofit organizations, it is not appropriate to smaller mutual aid bodies centred on volunteers, where it may be dysfunctional and detrimental to the organization's image. However, community-based planning approaches, drawing on many of the strategic planning models, have also become increasingly popular. In a case study of two volunteer-managed nonprofit organizations, Harlow (1998) argues that such nonprofits can indeed benefit from strategic management.

Despite a wide range of initiatives in the UK to enhance the development of a management culture in the voluntary nonprofit sector, particularly over the last ten years, the systematic research literature, especially up to 1995, has been described as 'thin' (Batsleer 1995; Leat 1995). The tendency, in terms of research work, has been to focus on policy-related issues in the sector rather than look at organizational and management issues, with some notable exceptions (Davis Smith 1995). Mel Moyer, a voluntary nonprofit management theorist from the USA, argues:

> Historically management scholars have tended to neglect those organisations that are not companies, that are not profit-seeking, that are not large, that have high ideological content, that offer services rather than products, and that are led by women. There is one enterprise which combines all these analytically awkward features; and given their cumulative selective perception, management scholars have overlooked it almost entirely. It is the voluntary organisation.
>
> (Moyer, quoted in Mason 1984)

However, in the 1990s, particularly the second half, there have been important attempts to begin to bridge this gap in the UK, both with edited volumes (Batsleer *et al.* 1992; Osborne 1996; Billis and Harris 1996; and Davis Smith *et al.* 1995) and individual publications (Hudson 1995; Hind 1995; Clutterbuck and Dearlove 1996; and Courtney 1996), not to mention individual journal articles.

In Chapter 9 the development of the theory and practice of strategic management in the voluntary nonprofit sector is explored in detail.

Summary

This chapter has focused on developments in the last two decades of the twentieth century which have encouraged voluntary nonprofit organizations to adopt the 'new mangerialism' and, in particular, strategic management. It has explored the extent of the influence of both the public sector, including local government, as funder and evaluator of such organizations; and the private sector, where much of the work on strategy has originated, in pushing or helping (depending on your perspective) voluntary nonprofit organizations to adopt this approach. Some of the arguments for and against 'new managerial' approaches in the voluntary nonprofit sector, or in parts of it, have been explored.

Questions

1   Should the voluntary nonprofit sector have agreed to take over functions that were previously the preserve of the statutory sector?
2   What role did local government play in the changing nature of the voluntary nonprofit sector?
3   To what extent did a professionalized approach to management flow from the private sector or the public sector to the voluntary nonprofit sector?
4   Is the commercialization of the voluntary nonprofit sector inevitable?
5   To what extent have the boundaries between the sectors become blurred? Give examples of blurred boundaries.
6   To what extent are the culture and values of the voluntary nonprofit sector changing? And is that a good or bad thing?

Suggested reading

Nicholas Deakin 'The perils of partnership: the voluntary sector and the state 1945–1992', and Julian Batsleer 'Management and organisation'; both are in J. Davis Smith, C. Rochester and R. Hedley, (eds) (1995) *An introduction to the voluntary sector*, Routledge.

Nigel Gann (1996) *Managing change in voluntary organisations: A guide to practice*, Open University Press.

Jane Lewis 'What does contracting do to voluntary agencies?', and Nicholas Deakin 'What does contracting do to users'; both are in D. Billis and M. Harris (eds) (1996) *Voluntary agencies: Challenges of organisation and management*, Macmillan.

And for a US perspective:

Steven Rathgeb Smith and Michael Lipsky (1993) *Nonprofits for hire: The welfare state in the age of contracting*, Harvard University Press.

4 What is the voluntary nonprofit sector and how is it different from other sectors?

Chapter outline

In considering the value of strategic management to the voluntary nonprofit sector it is important to be clear exactly what the sector is (if indeed it is a sector) and how homogenous or diverse the sector is and therefore the extent that different management approaches are required for different parts of the sector. The extent that it is the same as or different from the private sector will also give an indication of whether the voluntary nonprofit sector requires different management approaches from the private sector. This chapter therefore attempts to define the nature and scope of the voluntary nonprofit sector. In particular the attributes that have been put forward to distinguish the voluntary nonprofit sector from both the public sector and, more particularly, the private sector will be investigated. How organizations within the voluntary nonprofit sector can be categorized will also be explored.

Learning objectives

When you have completed this chapter you should understand:

- the difficulties in defining, and the different labels applied to, the voluntary nonprofit sector;
- the huge diversity of the voluntary nonprofit sector;
- the different ways of classifying the voluntary nonprofit sector;
- the way the boundaries of the voluntary nonprofit sector are defined for the purposes of this book;
- the perceived differences between the voluntary nonprofit and private sectors;
- the arguments for and against the nature and significance of the differences between the sectors;
- an alternative approach to framing organizations other than simply by sector.

Difficulties of terminology

As the voluntary nonprofit sector is such a diffuse and varied one, ranging from tiny local neighbourhood groups to multi-million-dollar international agencies, the student of the voluntary nonprofit sector faces serious difficulties in defining clearly the territory that is to be explored. Even finding agreement on an acceptable expression to describe the sector (if indeed it is a sector) is problematic. In the UK the expression 'the voluntary sector' is frequently used, although seldom defined. However, the increased involvement of professional paid staff has raised questions about how appropriate the word 'voluntary' is to define the sector. Osborne (1996) distinguishes between 'voluntaryism', as the societal principle of voluntary action, 'volunteerism', which he views as individual action without personal benefit (i.e. by volunteers), and 'voluntarism', which he relates to organized voluntary action which may or may not involve any significant number of volunteers.

In the UK the expression 'the charitable sector' is also used. However, those organizations which have charitable status within the definition of 'charitable' in accordance with the statute of 1601 are a particular sub-set of the larger voluntary nonprofit sector. Many organizations, like Amnesty International (see Box 2.2 on page 19), that are not-for-profit and would be accepted by the public as part of the voluntary sector, do not have charitable status. Indeed in Scotland and Northern Ireland there is no register of charities that have officially been given charitable status by the Charity Commissioners or their equivalent. Charitable exemption from certain tax liabilities is granted instead by the Inland Revenue. What is deemed to be charitable also changes over time. For example, it was only relatively recently that promoting racial harmony, tackling unemployment or protecting the environment were considered to be charitable by the Charity Commissioners.

In both the UK and the USA the expression 'the third sector' is sometimes used to describe the sector that exists for a social purpose and is neither the private nor the public sector (Hudson 1995), although the term 'third sector' gives no indication about any of the charateristics of the sector. 'The independent sector' is also sometimes used, but this can mean all organizations that aren't statutory, i.e. both the voluntary and the private sectors.

In the USA the term 'the nonprofit sector' (sometimes 'not-for-profit') is most commonly used, highlighting the key negative characteristic: that such organizations by definition may not distribute a profit to members, or others with a beneficial interest. However, to define a sector by one characteristic alone, and in the negative, is not entirely satisfactory. Statutory bodies are also not permitted to distribute their profits, if any. Osborne (1996) therefore favours the term 'voluntary and non-profit organisations' (VNPOs). Peter Dobkin Hall (1994) prefers the 'private nonprofit sector'.

In France the concept of The Social Economy is commonly used to define not only not-for-profit associations that we would traditionally think of as being in the voluntary or nonprofit sector, but also other kinds of organizations such as cooperatives, where any profit is distributed to the members.

Internationally, particularly in Africa and South America, the concept of the Non-Governmental Organization, or NGO, is frequently used to define organizations which are for the public benefit, but are not public bodies. This is another example of defining something by what it isn't, rather than by what it is. Again internationally, because of the differences of culture, legal structures and definitions between different countries, the expression Civil Society Organizations is sometimes used, but like the French 'Social Economy' it tends to cover a very wide range of types of organization, including trade unions and cooperatives.

The concept of 'value-led organisations' (Hudson 1995) to cover the sector is very attractive and accords with Jeavons's suggestion that the distinctive characteristic of a nonprofit organization is that it gives 'expression to the social, philosophical, moral and religious values of their founders and supporters' (Jeavons 1992). Gerard (1983) and Paton (1992) also argue that 'voluntary action is essentially value-based' (see Chapter 14 for a detailed discussion of values in the voluntary nonprofit sector). However, increasingly organizations from all sectors may feel entitled, and have been encouraged, to consider themselves to be value-based organizations.

In the private sector, too, the concept of value has come to be used in the economic sense of economic value, i.e. as increasing the value of a product or service; and it may not be helpful therefore to define the boundaries of this 'loose and baggy monster' (Davis Smith *et al.* 1995) by adopting the designation of 'value-based' or 'value-led'.

Kendall and Knapp's (1995) conclusion that 'there is no single "correct" definition which can or should be uniquely applied in all circumstances' would be very difficult to dispute. For the purposes of this book, a combination of UK and US terminology has been adopted, and the terms 'voluntary nonprofit organizations' and 'voluntary nonprofit sector' are used throughout the book. Where these expressions are deviated from it will be for a particular reason that will be explained in the text.

As indicated above, it is important to be aware that what actually constitutes the voluntary nonprofit sector is different in different countries. For example, many of the US studies on strategic planning concern museums, universities, libraries and/or hospitals, none of which would be generally considered to be part of the voluntary sector in Britain. Because many of these institutions in the USA are considered to be voluntary nonprofit organizations, the basic texts on strategic planning for the voluntary nonprofit sector in the USA are also often equally directed at the public sector (Nutt and Backoff 1992; Bryson 1995), whereas in the UK the two sectors tend to be considered very separately when writing on management issues.

Classification: by function

If it is difficult to find an agreed expression to describe the voluntary nonprofit sector, then it is also very difficult to define the boundaries that are covered by the sector. If it is difficult to define the boundaries, then it is equally difficult to define and categorize what is within the sector, and therefore to develop an appropriate taxonomy.

One frequent approach to defining what makes up the voluntary nonprofit sector is to categorize organizations by function (Brenton 1985; Handy 1988; Nathan 1990; Gutch *et al.* 1990). William Beveridge, for example, who was the architect of the welfare state in Britain, distinguished between two forms of voluntary action: philanthropy and mutual aid. The service-providing function is probably the one that most people think of when they think of the voluntary nonprofit sector. Organizations in this category may provide support, advice, accommodation, information and/or particular programmes or activities for people in need. Prior to World War Two these service-providing voluntary nonprofit organizations were often the only place that a person in need could turn to for help. Kramer (1981), however, in his study of disability organizations in England, the USA, the Netherlands and Israel, argues that the provision of services is the least distinctive aspect of the voluntary nonprofit sector.

The mutual aid or mutual support (Handy 1988) function is one where a group of individuals who share a common need or interest get together to provide mutual support, advice and encouragement. This is what Brenton (1985) describes as 'self-help and exchange around a common need or interest'. This function has 'developed world-wide into a major social phenomenon' (Hasenfield and Gidron 1993). The most famous of these is probably Alcoholics Anonymous, but there is now a very large number of groups, particularly in the medical and psychosocial field. Community development is also a process of engendering mutual support and self-help. This has been described as the social solidarity category of voluntary nonprofit organization (Gerard 1983; Knight 1993). Harris (1993) argues along with Billis (1993) and Davis Smith (1995) that such voluntary associations for mutual aid are 'conceptually and organisationally distinguishable from the bureaucratic service-delivering agencies of the broader nonprofit sector' although there is a strong pull on them to become more like the service-delivering agencies. For these associations, according to Harris, 'organisation' is a matter of 'balancing competing interests, goals and values and of recognizing the motivations of volunteers' rather than formalizing or by 'adopting the management techniques and "rules of the game" of bureaucratic organisations' (Harris 1993).

Other writers have expanded on Beveridge's categories to include a number of additional functions. The pressure group function is one often identified with groups like Oxfam (see the major case study in Part V), Shelter, Liberty, Amnesty International (see Box 2.2 on page 19), the Child Poverty Action Group, and others. Most of the major case studies in Part V highlight important legislative changes that have come about, at least in part because of the lobbying and campaigning activities of voluntary nonprofit organizations. This campaigning or policy advocacy role involves 'the production of pressure on decision-makers in any sector to change policy and practices usually on behalf of some identifiable groups' (Kendall and 6 1994).

This is one of the areas where the law and practice on charitable status is controversial. Some campaigning organizations, such as Amnesty International, have been refused charitable status. Others, such as Oxfam, have received a number of warnings that they must desist from certain kinds of campaigning activity if they are not to lose their charitable status.

The individual 'citizen' advocacy function has been identified by Kendall and Knapp as a separate function (1995); others include it as a service-providing function or within a wider advocacy category including public as well as individual advocacy. In this role, organizations make representations on behalf of individuals to enable them to achieve their rights or otherwise obtain the services or resources that they require. This is common, particularly in the mental health and mental disability fields and in work with children. In some organizations the function is more about enabling individuals to advocate for themselves and achieve greater user control of services or resources.

Distinct resource and coordinating functions have been highlighted by Brenton (1985). Voluntary nonprofit organizations particularly involved in resource and coordinating functions are often intermediary bodies whose role is to help coordinate and support other voluntary nonprofit organizations, usually within a particular field. Such bodies 'act as a central catalyst or repository of expertise, information, research etc. on a specialist subject'. They frequently 'represent a membership of other voluntary bodies and seek to liaise between them and co-ordinate their activities, their public relations or their connections with Government' (Brenton 1985).

Knight (1993) also includes two further categories in his classification: mobilizing, where the purpose of the organization is to locate money or volunteers for causes; and creating, where the purpose is to express oneself through some form of creative arts in the company of others.

Classification: by control/resourcing

An alternative way of categorizing voluntary nonprofit organizations is by methods of control and/or resourcing (Kendall and Knapp 1995).

Gutch *et al.* (1990) distinguish between membership organizations which are essentially democratic in structure and those which are oligarchical, i.e. with a self-perpetuating group of trustees. However, it is one thing to define an organization by its legal status as a trust, or an unincorporated association with a membership structure. It is quite another to make assumptions about how these two different types of organizations work in practice. In particular, many organizations, with democratic membership structures according to their constitutions, operate in practice as self-perpetuating oligarchies.

Gerard (1983), from two major surveys of the sector in Britain, also distinguishes between organizations on the basis of management style and structure. He distinguishes between three different types: 'a hierarchical authoritarian approach'; 'a consultative approach with considerable delegation of powers'; and 'a fully participative approach'.

Hatch (1980) distinguishes between organizations that are primarily run by professional paid staff and those that are run mostly by volunteers. In the latter type of organization, he distinguishes between mutual aid organizations, highlighted above, which pursue members' interests, and those oriented towards non-members. In the professional staff organization category he distinguishes between those which are primarily statutory funded and those which are primarily funded from voluntary sources. While these are useful theoretical distinctions, they provide little useful practical guidance, because any organization may be at different points on any of the three dimensions:

1   proportion of paid staff to volunteers;
2   proportion of statutory funding to voluntary funding;
3   proportion of services/resources directed to members against those directed to non-members.

However, this could provide a useful theoretical three-dimensional model that would enable an organization to be located on each of the three axes.

A number of researchers (Chanan 1991; Ball 1989; Hatch 1980) have distinguished between three types of voluntary nonprofit organizations:

1   independent local organizations, which may be more oriented to a community development process than providing services, which, in the words of Kendall and Knapp (1995), makes them 'notoriously difficult to classify in terms of an "industry" or market since, by their very nature, conventional distinctions – between demand and supply sides, user and volunteer or process and output, for example – often conflict with underlying ideologies and operating principles';
2   organizations which are a federation of local groups with considerable local autonomy;
3   professional national voluntary nonprofit organizations which directly run local services.

Hasenfeld and Gidron (1993) distinguish particularly between self-help groups and professional human service organizations.

A self-help group can be defined as a group of individuals who experience a common problem, who share their personal stories and knowledge to help one another cope with their situation, and who simultaneously help and are helped. In addition, the group emphasises face-to-face interactions and informal and interchangeable roles. In contrast, human service organisations are characterised by career-oriented staff members, who need not personally experience the problems they address, distinct staff and client roles, a professionally based body of knowledge, and formal division of labour.

This distinction between more professionalized human service organizations and smaller mutual aid groups based around volunteer members is viewed by many to justify the two groups being seen to reflect two different sectors altogether, with the formal strategic management approaches that might be appropriate for the larger service bodies not being appropriate for the smaller community and other mutual aid groups (Klausen 1995; Harris 1997).

Smith and Lipsky (1993), considering the implications of the contracting culture in the USA, distinguish between three main types of voluntary nonprofit service agencies:

1   the traditional social services agency;
2   the more recent social services agency established to take advantage of Government funding/contracts especially in the fields of mental health and job training;
3   agencies founded in response to unmet neighbourhood or other community needs and which often commence life on a very shaky financial basis, run by volunteers or poorly paid staff, sometimes called the 'people's sector'.

Donnelly-Cox and O'Regan (1999), considering the resourcing of organizational growth and development in the voluntary nonprofit sector in Ireland, recognize that organizations are not static entities, but are constantly in flux. Drawing on open systems, resource-dependence and institutional theories and the well-known lifecycle model, they argue for a typology of three types of voluntary nonprofit organization: Emerging, Established and Institutionalized. The stage the organization is at will be reflected in resource issues (need legitimacy, organizational legitimacy, finance and human resources) and suggest, as organizations grow, where crises may occur over time.

All these categories are less than exhaustive. As Kendall and Knapp (1995) point out, local fundraising groups, which are autonomous but raise money for a particular cause, do not easily fit into these schemas. Organizations which are established to give grants to other organizations, either as a result of an endowment from a wealthy individual or individuals or as a result of ongoing support from a company or statutory body, also don't fit well into the categories suggested above.

Classification: by beneficiary

Blau and Scott (1962) distinguish between organizations on the basis of who benefits. In mutual aid organizations, for example, it is the members. In a medical charity it will be individuals with a particular medical disorder. For an animal charity it will be particular species of animals. For an environmental charity it will be the natural environment. For an umbrella agency it will be other voluntary nonprofit organizations. And so on.

Classification: by activity

Finally, attempts have been made to try to categorize the sector in terms of the field of activity. Salamon and Anheier (1993) have developed an International Classification of Non-profit Organizations (ICNPO) which identifies twelve groups of primary fields of activity:

- culture and recreation;
- education and research;
- health;
- social services;
- environment;
- development and housing;
- law, advocacy and politics;
- philanthropic intermediaries and voluntarism promotion;
- international activities;
- religion;
- business, professional associations and unions;
- those not classified elsewhere.

These categories are further broken down into twenty-six sub-groupings.

In the UK, the Charity Commissioners of England and Wales had a classification system that was put in place in the 1960s, following the 1960 Charities Act, which they felt was very inadequate for present-day purposes. They commissioned Aston Business School (ABS) to develop a new classification system. The Aston Business School team considered various existing classification systems including: the UK Standard Industrial Classification; the General Industrial Classification of Economic Activities; the UN's International Standard Industrial Classification; the National Taxonomy of Exempt Entities; and the International Classification of Nonprofit Organizations (ICNPO) mentioned above. The ABS team considered that, of these, the most useful was the ICNPO classification. However, they felt that only considering the field of activity limited the classification system, and they proposed a classification system which categorized organizations on three dimensions:

1   beneficiaries (i.e. individuals, institutions or the environment);
2   function (i.e. provision of services, provision of facilities, finance/resourcing, intelligence and development, and representation);
3   field of operation, using the ICNPO classification.

Boundaries of the voluntary nonprofit sector

In understanding the voluntary nonprofit sector, classifying voluntary nonprofit organizations is both important and useful, particularly for international comparison. It is also crucial in research into the appropriateness of different forms of management for different types of voluntary nonprofit organization. In Kendall and Knapp's (1995) view, 'there appears to be a consensus that the identification of appropriate criteria is virtually obligatory if progress is to be made towards the description and analysis of a meaningful construct', or, to put it another way, to create 'islands of meaning' (Zerubavel 1991), cognitive devices that group together objects to facilitate recognition and communication by developing a clear definition of the nonprofit sector, is crucial in trying to understand the sector. However, it does not help in establishing the boundaries of the sector, nor clarifying the difference between the voluntary nonprofit and other sectors.

To address the question of boundaries, Hatch (1980) identified three conditions for an entity to be in the voluntary nonprofit sector: formal; independent of government; and not profit-distributing. Brenton (1985) included these three in his definition, but added two others: self-governing (private); and for the public benefit. Johnson (1981) adds the requirement that at least some of the income should come from voluntary sources. Kendall and Knapp (1995) consider that significant consensus has been achieved around four key criteria which have been developed for international comparison purposes (Salamon and Anheier 1993). The four criteria are as follows:

1   An entity must be formal, in the sense of having a structure, a constitution and/or a set of rules, registered with the Charity Commissioners, a government body or an intermediate voluntary nonprofit umbrella body. This excludes informal family or friendship networks that exist and play a crucial role in supporting dependent relatives, etc.
2   An entity must be constitutionally and institutionally independent of Government and self-governing, with their own decision-making structures. The creation of quangos by statute which are technically independent of Government, but whose trustees are all government appointees and all, or nearly all, the funding comes from government, raises concerns about such bodies (Kendall and Knapp 1995).
3   An entity must be not profit-distributing and primarily non-business. An organization may make a profit, but the profit must be ploughed back into the business, it cannot be distributed to those who have an interest in the organization, such as trustees, members, officers, etc. This excludes most cooperatives and mutual benefit institutions such as the Automobile Association and building societies.
4   Finally, an entity must benefit to a meaningful degree from philanthropy or voluntary citizen involvement. This voluntary element may be

income from voluntary sources, the commitment of voluntary labour to carry out aspects of the work, or the involvement of volunteers as trustees, the latter of which has been described by the then chief executive of NCVO as the single most defining characteristic of the sector (Prashar 1991).

Potentially, however, political parties and sacramental (as opposed to service-providing) religious bodies could also be included under this definition, but are often excluded for the purposes of discussing the voluntary nonprofit sector.

Comparisons with the private sector

Of particular interest to the discussion of the relevance of professional management models and techniques is the extent of the differences and similarities between the voluntary nonprofit sector and the private sector. It was in the private sector where many of the strategic management models and tools were first developed during the late 1960s and through the 1970s, and which are now being used extensively in the voluntary nonprofit sector. An understanding of the differences between the two sectors will help to understand to what extent the voluntary nonprofit sector requires a different approach from those used in the private sector.

There have been various attempts to define the features of the voluntary nonprofit sector which distinguish it from other sectors, the private sector in particular. Mason (1984) suggests the following as distinctive features of the voluntary nonprofit sector: motivation; economy; board effectiveness; staff departments; directing professionals; creative/innovation; commitment/loyalty; survivability; strategy; employee satisfaction; optimizing customer service; consumer concerns; service knowledge; and women workers. Kendall and Knapp (1998) suggest: consumer choice; specialization; cost-effectiveness; flexibility; innovation; advocacy; and participation.

There have, however, been very few studies to determine whether there is any empirical basis for these claims of difference between the voluntary nonprofit and private sectors. One notable exception to this is Osborne's (1998) study of innovation in the UK voluntary nonprofit sector which demonstrated that only one-third of voluntary nonprofit organizations demonstrated any true innovation, despite the claims by both Mason and Kendall and Knapp, cited above, and therefore should not be claimed as a distinctive characteristic of the sector.

Paton and Cornforth (1992) and Leat (1993) examined a number of characteristics that have been put forward to distinguish the voluntary nonprofit sector from the private sector and that therefore have been used as a basis for arguing that the voluntary nonprofit sector needs to be managed differently from the private sector. They are described below.

Profit-making versus non-profit-making

The most common characteristic which is put forward as distinguishing the voluntary nonprofit from the private sectors is, as the name suggests, the fact that the voluntary nonprofit sector does not operate on the profit motive, while the private sector does. However, even this criterion is not quite as cut-and-dried as it might appear, because some voluntary nonprofit organizations do make a profit, intentionally or otherwise. In the UK, Guide Dogs for the Blind has, for example, made considerable profits year on year and has built up a very substantial reserve. On the other hand there are many private sector companies who do not make any profit. How profitability is defined in the private sector is also often problematic, with a wide variety of different measures being used to define success, including market share, return on capital invested, return on sales, and growth in sales revenue (Davis Smith 1992). Defining it in the voluntary nonprofit sector is even more problematic (see the discussion in Chapter 10).

Perhaps of more value is the concept of the non-distribution of any profits, as we have discussed. Voluntary nonprofit organizations may make a profit, but may not distribute this profit to anyone with a beneficial interest in the organization, such as staff, trustees, members, etc. In the private sector, profits may be distributed to shareholders. However, even in the voluntary nonprofit sector, there may be bonuses paid to certain staff, e.g. fundraising or charity shop staff, if the net income raised is over a certain amount.

Indicators of success

Of particular relevance to this current study, and linked to the issue of the lack of a profit motive, is the suggestion that a distinctive characteristic of voluntary nonprofit organizations is the lack of any clear indicators of success. As Drucker (1990) says about voluntary nonprofit organizations, 'What is the bottom line when there is no bottom line?' However, this view has been criticized (Anheier 2000) because, it is argued, the problem is not that voluntary nonprofit organizations do not have a bottom line, but that they have multiple bottom lines. Argenti (1965) has described this difficulty as 'the last unconquered peak in the study of management'. However, as mentioned above, it is not always entirely clear what the success indicators for a private company should be, and over what timescale should performance indicators be measured, and indeed many voluntary nonprofit organizations have put in place very well-developed performance indicators.

Multiple stakeholders

For some commentators the issue about lack of goal clarity in the voluntary nonprofit sector is caused by the multiple stakeholders that a voluntary nonprofit organization is expected to satisfy and be accountable to, compared with the equivalent private company. In Drucker's words (1990), 'it has to satisfy everyone; certainly it cannot afford to alienate anyone'. The argument is that the private sector only has to satisfy the customer and the shareholder; the voluntary nonprofit organization, on the other hand, has usually to satisfy multiple funders, individual, corporate and statutory, as well as regulatory bodies, customers, trustees, volunteers, staff, the media, the local community, etc.

It is the number and diverse nature of internal and external stakeholders and income sources that leads Anheier (2000) to suggest that the complexity of managing a voluntary nonprofit organization easily surpasses that of the equivalent sized for-profit firm. However, as Leat (1993) suggests, this argument is rather oversimplified, as private sector companies increasingly have had to become responsive to a wide range of different types of stakeholders, including staff, trade unions, individual and institutional shareholders, banks, directors, suppliers, statutory grant givers, regulatory bodies and the local community. As a result stakeholder analysis has become an important aspect of strategy-building in the private sector, despite its detractors (Argenti 1997), in order to satisfy its multiple constituencies. Although there are examples of voluntary nonprofit organizations which have a very wide range of stakeholders, and of private sector companies who appear to respond to a narrow range of stakeholders, there are also examples where this scenario can be reversed.

Resource acquisition/transactions

It has been suggested that the main difference between the private and voluntary nonprofit sectors is in relation to the resource acquisition activities in the two sectors (Moore 2000). Or, to put it another way, the difference is between the different form of transactions that take place in a voluntary nonprofit organization compared with a private company (Hudson 1995).

In the private sector there is a trading relationship where a customer purchases a product or service from the company and pays the price agreed. In the voluntary nonprofit sector the funding usually comes from government and/or private donations to pay for the product or, more usually, the service that the 'customer' receives. Instead of a two-way flow of resources, as in the private sector, there is a one-way flow of resources from funder to voluntary nonprofit organization to client. However, the reality is more complex than indicated. Many voluntary nonprofit organizations are heavily involved in trading activities where there is clearly a two-way transaction (Morales 1997; Mastrofski *et al.* 1994). Many beneficiaries of voluntary nonprofit organizations are required to pay for the service they receive, albeit at less than the commercial rate. Sponsors, too, are not only involved in a one-way transaction: they require a return on their investment in terms of branding, publicity, etc.

Culture and values

Others have concentrated on the issue of culture and values (Jeavons 1992). In particular it has been suggested that voluntary nonprofit organizations tend to be more participatory and egalitarian, with a greater commitment to equal opportunities. This is confirmed by research (Leat 1995) into the views of managers who have moved from the private to the voluntary nonprofit sector. The research found that these managers often experienced a significant culture shift, if not shock, in moving to organizations with an emphasis on participative decision-making, although the practice did not always match the rhetoric. Others argue that it is the voluntary nonprofit sector's focus on fundamental social values that makes it distinctive (Moore 2000).

However, it may be that, over time, this difference in culture and values is reducing because of an increased emphasis on participation and values in the private sector. For example, the message of the successful book by Collins and Porras on corporate strategy, *Built to last* (1994), is that for a company to be both globally competitive and locally effective it must cultivate and embed a deep sense of practical ethics that are driven at all levels by sound human values. Ohmae (1982) and Pascale and Athos (1981) argue that espousing these fundamental values is precisely the reason that Japanese firms have been so successful over the last thirty years. This perspective has been encouraged by various management theorists over the last fifteen years (Kanter 1989; Peters and Austin 1985; O'Toole 1986; Lawler 1986; Peters 1987). This is an interesting example of where the private sector may be moving more in the direction of the voluntary nonprofit sector (Clutterbuck and Dearlove 1996).

The general argument that the voluntary nonprofit sector has a stronger link with moral values has, however, been criticized (Marshall 1996) on the grounds that there is no evidence that activity in self-help groups and community organizations is any less self-interested than in the private sector (Richardson and Goodman 1983).

Cooperation versus competition

Another value that some argue is distinctive about the voluntary nonprofit sector is that of cooperation. The private sector is characterized by – almost defined by – competition (Porter 1980). This makes many voluntary nonprofit organizations, who don't see how they should be relating to other voluntary nonprofit agencies as 'competitors to be beaten', very suspicious of management theory.

However, the distinction between the two sectors is not as clear-cut as it might seem. Actual competition between voluntary nonprofit organizations for funds, volunteers and contracts is very common (Herman 1994). Many voluntary nonprofit organizations were set up to compensate for perceived weaknesses in another voluntary nonprofit organization. Private sector organizations have also realized that strategic alliances and cooperation are as important as competition in being successful, and have their own associations, strategic alliances, mergers and partnerships.

All these factors reduce the extent of the differences between the two sectors in relation to competition and cooperation. However, there probably does remain at least a difference in emphasis between voluntary nonprofit organizations which have a commitment to ensuring the needs of a particular client group are met, which may often be best done through collaboration with other nonprofit organizations and increasingly with organizations from other sectors (Butler and Wilson 1990), and the private sector where competitive advantage over (even the destruction of) other companies is the key to success (Porter 1980).

The nature of governance

The nature of governance in the private and voluntary nonprofit sectors has also been suggested as being a key difference between the two sectors. In the private sector the board will be made up, either partly or entirely, of paid full-time directors. In the voluntary nonprofit sector, the paid staff are generally not permitted by charity law to be members of the governing body, which is therefore made up of unpaid volunteers. There is evidence, however, that in the voluntary nonprofit sector the paid staff, and the Chief Executive in particular, often wield considerable influence on both the composition and decisions of the board (Cornforth and Edwards 1998).

In relation to the private sector, the 1992 Cadbury Report into governance in the private sector concluded that private companies in the UK needed to substantially increase the number of non-executive board members. In this respect, therefore, the private sector has been moving in the direction of the voluntary nonprofit sector in valuing the input and objectivity that non-executive board members can bring.

The above discussion indicates the complexity and diversity of the voluntary nonprofit sector and how difficult it is to create clear boundaries between sectors, particularly between the voluntary nonprofit sector and the private sector. It is possible to view the sectors as overlapping circles (see Figure 4.1)

However, there is an important question as to how many sectors there actually are. The general public, and, until recently, most of the modern social sciences, including economics, sociology and political science (Kendall and Knapp 1996), tended to think primarily about two sectors: the private and public sectors. Writers about the voluntary nonprofit sector tend to assume that there are three sectors: public, private and voluntary nonprofit. This, however, is not an uncontentious view. Organizational theorists often make a clear distinction between sectors represented by formal organizations and the informal sector made up of families and friendship ties, thus suggesting four sectors shown in Figure 4.1. Others

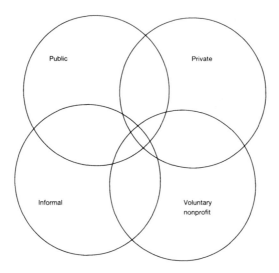

Figure 4.1   The 'four overlapping circles' model of sectors

have argued for a distinction to be made between the voluntary nonprofit sector and the mutual benefit/community nonprofit sector (Smith 1991).

Uphoff (1995), in exploring voluntary nonprofit organizations involved in world development, also distinguishes between not-for-profit service organizations or NGOs and mutual benefit membership organizations. However, he goes further and argues that NGOs operate much more like private sector organizations and should be considered a sub-set of the private sector, whereas mutual benefit membership organizations, including cooperatives, occupy space between the private and public sectors and should be considered as a separate 'collective action' or 'membership' sector. Others have argued that religious or sacramental bodies should be defined as a separate sector (Kendall and Knapp 1995). The case has been made for political parties to be distinguished as a sector (Kendall and Knapp 1995). There is also a case for including trade unions and business support organizations as a separate sector. A similar case can be made for recreational bodies, which don't easily fit into existing schemas.

The concept of sector is clearly a problematic one, because as we have seen there is neither a consensus about what a sector is, how many sectors there are, nor how they should be defined. However, this is also true of many concepts that are social constructs (Berger and Luckmann 1967), such as race. It is impossible to separate the language that we choose to use from our own values and contexts. It does not mean that using such concepts does not have value, but it does mean that it is important to keep the contingent nature of the concept in mind when it is being used.

The concept the 'voluntary nonprofit sector' will be used throughout the book in a descriptive sense. Following Osborne (1998), it does not assume any homogeneity in objectives or activities amongst voluntary nonprofit organizations. It is accepted that these are in fact extremely diverse. It also does not imply that the voluntary nonprofit sector is completely independent of the other sectors, because there is in fact considerable interdependence. And it does not assume that any particular organizational characteristics can be ascribed to an organization because it is in the voluntary nonprofit sector. It is accepted that these need to be addressed at sub-sectoral level and on the basis of empirical evidence.

Organizations are also dynamic entities which may, over time, move from one legal status to another depending on the legal, political, tax and financial framework in the country in which it operates at any particular time. We have already discussed the early schools, universities and hospitals in the UK that became incorporated into the statutory sector during the twentieth century, and the different balance that exists in the USA, for example, where many hospitals, museums and universities are seen as being in the voluntary nonprofit sector. The major case study in Part V of the Grameen Bank demonstrates the changing relationship that a particular organization can have with the various sectors and the difficulty inherent in the concept of sector.

Paton (1991), rather than trying to argue for a certain number of sectors, developed a more complex and dynamic model of organizations in which to try and fit various aspects of the social economy. Paton's model (see Figure 4.2) has two axes: the extent that the goals of the organization are social, i.e. for the public benefit or for private, i.e. personal, gain; and the size and degree of institutionalization and bureaucracy.

The above discussion has, at least, clarified the lack of consensus about boundaries and definitions in relation to the voluntary nonprofit sector. In terms of this book the focus will generally be on the more narrowly defined voluntary nonprofit sector, i.e. excluding cooperatives, business support organizations, trade unions, schools and churches (while including church-based human service organizations) unless otherwise specified.

Summary

This chapter has explored the difficulties in trying to define the voluntary nonprofit sector, even establishing an agreed name for the sector (if indeed it is a sector). The boundaries between the voluntary nonprofit sector and other sectors have been explored and the fact that these change with time and geography is acknowledged. The suggested differences between the voluntary nonprofit sector and the private sector in particular have been explored, and are seen to be not as clear-cut as is often suggested. The incredible diversity of the sector has also been acknowledged, and various ways of classifying the sector were discussed. Two models that recognize the complexity of the issues involved have been presented.

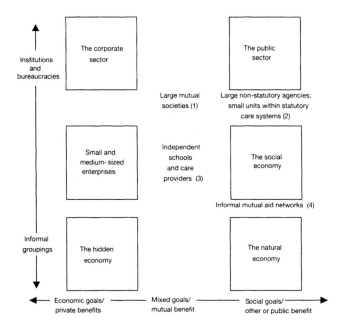

Figure 4.2   Types of organization in and around the social economy

Source: Paton (1991), as presented in Davis Smith (1995).

Notes
1   e.g. building societies, retail co-ops, the Automobile Association
2   e.g. large housing associations, Barnardo's, local authority centres, cottage hospitals
3   e.g. charitable public schools, nursing homes (private but professionally run)
4   e.g. baby-sitting circles, mother and toddler clubs

Questions

1   How would you define a sector, how many sectors do you think there are, and why?
2   What is the best term to define the voluntary nonprofit sector, and why?
3   What are the defining characteristics of a voluntary nonprofit organization?
4   What different ways are there to categorize the voluntary nonprofit sector, and which is most useful?
5   Should mutual aid and member-led groups be in a separate sector from large service-providing organizations?
6   What are the key differences between private sector and voluntary nonprofit organizations?
7   Is a strategic management approach appropriate for any or all types of voluntary nonprofit organization?

Suggested reading

Charles Handy (1988) *Understanding voluntary organisations*, Penguin.

Jeremy Kendall and Martin Knapp 'A loose and baggy monster: Boundaries, definitions and typologies', in J. Davis Smith, C. Rochester and R. Hedley (eds) (1995) *An introduction to the voluntary sector*, Routledge.

Jeremy Kendall and Martin Knapp (1996) *The voluntary sector in the UK*, Johns Hopkins Nonprofit Sector Series, Manchester University Press.

Stephen P. Osborne 'What is "voluntary" about the voluntary and non-profit sector?', in S.P. Osborne (ed.) (1996) *Managing in the voluntary sector – a handbook for managers in charitable and non-profit organisations*, International Thomson Business Press.

Rob Paton and Chris Cornforth 'What's different about managing in voluntary and non-profit organisations?', in J. Batsleer, C. Cornforth and R. Paton (eds) (1992) *Issues in voluntary and nonprofit management*, Addison-Wesley in association with the Open University Press.

Part II

The development of different approaches to strategic management

5 The development of strategic management

Chapter outline

This chapter explores the development of the concept of strategy, from its early origins in military and diplomatic contexts through the development of the various classic strategic planning schools in the 1960s and 1970s, as adopted extensively by the private sector; and introduces some of the critiques of the classic strategic planning schools.

Learning objectives

When you have completed this chapter you should understand:

* the origins of the concept of strategy;
* the development of prescriptive military and diplomatic theories of effective strategy;
* the development of scientific 'one-best-way' approaches to management;
* the development of the concept of strategy as applied to business;
* the ideas and critiques of the design school;
* the ideas and critiques of the planning school;
* the ideas and critiques of the positioning school.

Military and diplomatic origins

The word 'strategy' comes from the ancient Athenian position of *strategos* (Cummings 1993), which came about as a result of the reforms of Kleisthenes (circa 508BC). After leading a popular revolution against the Spartan-supported oligarchy, Kleisthenes created ten political and military sub-units headed by an elected strategos. The Athenian war council was made up of these ten strategoi, who because of their roles largely also controlled non-military politics.

Strategos was a combination of the word *stratos*, which meant 'army', or more accurately an encamped army spread out over ground, and the word *agein*, which meant 'to lead'. The emergence of the term paralleled the development of the complexity of military decision-making.

The *Concise Oxford Dictionary* defines strategy as 'the art of war' or 'a plan of action or policy in business or politics'. These two definitions probably give a good indication of where the concept of strategy came from and what the lay understanding of the word currently means.

Strategy as 'the art of war' is perhaps not the best definition to use in considering the idea of strategic planning and management as it relates to the voluntary nonprofit sector, but it is useful to be aware at least of the roots of some of the concepts that have developed since the earliest historians and poets began to 'collect the accumulated lore of these successful and unsuccessful life-and-death strategies and convert them into wisdom and guidance for the future' (Quinn 1988).

Some of the earliest writings on military strategy were by Sun Tzu, who lived three thousand years ago and whose work has been used to try to inform business leaders moving into the twenty-first century (Tzu 1963). Aineias the Tactician wrote the earliest surviving Western volume on military strategy, *How to survive under siege*, in the mid-fourth century BC. He was primarily concerned with how to deploy the available human and other resources to best advantage. In the first century AD, Frontinus defined strategy as 'everything achieved by a commander, be it characterised by foresight, advantage, enterprise or resolution'.

Early Greek historians, poets and philosophers wrote extensively about the military and diplomatic exploits of key figures. Epaminondas of Thebes was said to have brought together the two divisions of the army, the infantry and the cavalry, in a 'fruitful organisational blend'. His strategic principles included:

- economy of force coupled with overwhelming strength at the decisive point;
- close coordination between units and meticulous staff planning combined with speed of attack;
- knowledge that the quickest and most economical way of winning a decision is defeat of the competition, not at its weakest point but at its strongest.

Epaminondas was advisor to Philip of Macedon and under his guidance the Macedonian army was very successful, particularly under the control of Philip's son, Alexander the Great, famous for his contingency approach to strategy and whose battle strategies were said to have been replicated by Patton and Rommel in World War Two (Quinn 1988).

Socrates, like Clausewitz (see page 59), was aware of the analogy between warfare and business and the comparison between the duties of a general and a businessman, showing that both utilize plans to use resources to meet objectives.

In Europe, much was written about the military campaigns of Napoleon, who even wrote his own textbook *Maximes de Guerre* (in Phillips 1940), and Frederick the Great of Prussia, who introduced fundamental reforms of how an army should be organized. Machiavelli, considered by some to be the first real management thinker (Micklethwaite and Wooldridge 1996), also wrote extensively about strategy in *The prince*, applying many military concepts to the political and diplomatic arena. His writings too have been used to guide modern business leaders (Jay 1987). Machiavelli was very conscious of the difficulties of bringing about organizational change:

> It should be borne in mind that there is nothing more difficult to arrange, more doubtful of success, and more dangerous to carry through than initiating changes....The innovator makes enemies of all those who prospered under the old order, and only lukewarm support is forthcoming from those who would prosper under the new. Their support is lukewarm partly from fear of their adversaries, who have the existing laws on their side, and partly because men are generally incredulous, never really trusting new things unless they have tested them by experience.
>
> (Machiavelli 1950)

One of the greatest Western military thinkers was Karl von Clausewitz (1780–1831), writing in the aftermath of the Napoleonic Wars and drawing on the experiences of Napoleon in defeating forces often much larger than his own. In *On war*, Clausewitz (1984) proposed a number of principles of strategy to be used as building blocks in a particular situation. These included the following:

- Clearly defined, decisive and attainable objectives.
- Offensive action is necessary to achieve decisive results.
- Concentrate superior combat power at the critical time and place for decisive purpose.
- Economic expenditure of resources.
- Flexibility of manoeuvre to place the enemy at relative disadvantage.
- Unity of command.
- Security by measures to prevent surprise, preserve freedom of action, deny the enemy information.
- Surprise the enemy.
- Direct simple plans and clear concise orders to minimize misunderstanding.

The principles of Clausewitz were used by US Army Colonel Summers in 1981 to demonstrate the shortcomings of the US military operation in Vietnam (Summers 1981).

The two world wars in the twentieth century also provided enormous scope for military historians and strategists to analyse campaigns and try to draw out the lessons of both success and failure. Communist leaders in the person of both Lenin and Mao Tse-tung also wrote books about their own campaigns in order to educate others.

In more recent times many writers of business strategy have picked up on the sprit and sometimes the letter of these military maxims. James (1985) describes 'the military experience [as] a veritable goldmine of competitive strategies all well tested under combat conditions'.

What, then, can be learnt from these exponents of military and diplomatic strategy? One of the most important lessons, perhaps, is, like Clausewitz, to distinguish between strategy and tactics. Strategy is to do with achieving the overall political purpose; tactics are to do with particular ploys or activities put in place to try to gain advantage in a particular battle.

In the first book explicitly about strategy as it relates to business (Chandler 1962), its author makes clear that tactical decisions must be made about day-to-day problems that might threaten the smooth functioning of the organization and its ongoing viability. However, strategic decisions are oriented to the future and are concerned with the long-term health of the organization. In his seminal work in 1954, *The practice of management*, Peter Drucker also highlighted the importance of this crucial distinction between strategic and tactical decisions for modern business.

Quinn (1988) argues that the analysis of military–diplomatic (and sporting) strategies provides some important insights into the nature of formal strategies. First, he considers that the three main elements of successful military strategies are:

- the development of clear goals to be achieved;
- the setting of policies to guide or limit action;
- the sequence of actions (within the limits set) to achieve the goals.

Second, he suggests that effective strategies develop around 'a few key concepts and thrusts' which thereby provide cohesion and focus. Resources can then be allocated to ensure the success of these thrusts.

Third, strategies need to be able to deal with the unpredictable and even unknowable, because it is never possible to be sure what will happen in future and what your opponent(s) may do. Therefore it is necessary to build a posture which is both flexible enough and strong enough to deal with all possible eventualities.

Finally, there needs to be a number of hierarchically integrated and supporting strategies, which are coherent in themselves with their own goals and thrusts and which are also integrated into the overall strategy.

These and other maxims, ancient and modern, have been developed by a number of writers in what has been called the 'Attributes of Excellence School' (see Chapter 6).

Scientific management

With its antecedents in military strategy, it is perhaps no coincidence that the development of modern ideas of strategy and strategic planning for business began to develop shortly after World War Two. However, a scientific approach to management had already been taking shape prior to this, starting in 1776 with Adam Smith's *The wealth of nations* (Smith 1979), where he uses the terms 'manage', 'manager' and even 'bad management' in referring to those persons responsible for running joint stock companies. Charles Babbage, who invented an early form of computer, published a treatise in 1832 advocating a scientific approach to the planning and organizing of work. However, it was two particular individuals in the early part of the twentieth century who played a particularly important role in the development of the scientific approach to management, from their own experience in industry: Henri Fayol and Frederick W. Taylor.

Fayol, a Frenchman who became President and Director General of a mining company, articulated in *General and industrial management* (1916) five functions of management. These were: Planning; Organizing; Command; Coordination; Control. All would have made sense to the earlier military strategists discussed above, and have become part of the classic description of the role of a manager.

Taylor, an American and an engineer by profession, published a groundbreaking book in 1911 entitled *The principles of scientific management* which emphasized how better planning and organizing of work and training of staff could improve output. He advocated five basic principles:

1   Shift all responsibility to the manager for the planning and design of the work.
2   Use scientific methods to study each task and determine the most efficient and effective way that it can be carried out.
3   Select the best person to carry out the specified task.
4   Train the worker to do the job effectively and efficiently.
5   Monitor the worker's performance to ensure the work is being carried out according to the specification.

Taylor advocated the use of detailed time and motion methods to observe, analyse and standardize work, so that even small tasks are broken down and performed in the prescribed, most efficient manner. Taylor's work focused very much on the operational aspects of the company, at the level of the workers.

Ralph C. Davis (1928, 1951) built on this early work on the scientific approach to management and introduced the rational-planning perspective, which has had enormous influence on both the theory and practice of strategy ever since. Davis viewed the primary purpose of a company as providing economic service. He considered that no firm could survive if it doesn't provide economic value. This economic value is created by the activities members engage in to create the organization's products or services. It is these activities that link the organization's objectives with its results. It is the responsibility of management to group these activities together in such a way as to form the structure of the organization, and thus structure is contingent on objectives. This rational-planning perspective offered a simple model for designing an organization.

L. Urwick, an English engineer, provided a biographical account of all the key figures in the development of the scientific approach to management up to 1956, in *The golden book of management*, having outlined his own views in 'elements of administration' (as he described management). Interestingly he added 'forecasting' as one of the main elements of this fledgling science, and acknowledged that flexibility is required in planning.

This 'scientific' rational closed-system approach to the planning and organizing of work has had a profound effect on management methods up to and including the present day (e.g. in the development of 'Management By Objectives' and business process re-engineering initiatives). It describes well the approach of many current businesses, such as fast-food outlets. The approach has strengths in the context of a stable environment, a simple product, and where precision and standardization are paramount. However, the dehumanizing effect on human beings of being treated as parts of a machine has had major implications. The approach is also not appropriate when the environment is constantly changing, requiring the organization to adapt and change on a frequent basis; when the task is complex and requires the worker to use his/her brain to develop solutions; or when flexibility and cross-team working is required. It also sits uncomfortably in the voluntary nonprofit sector, which often requires flexibility and a high level of participation in decision-making.

Studies of military personnel and war-time manufacturing companies during and after World War Two also gave a major boost to all the human sciences, including a scientific approach to the study of management and organizations.

A famous study of a real organizational work setting by Elton Mayo (1945), known as the Hawthorne experiments, provided further evidence of the value of a scientific approach to studying work and workers, although not necessarily to the adoption of a mechanistic approach to the planning and organizing of work. These experiments began with a Taylorist perspective, to look at how to tackle the tiredness and boredom at work that results from the 'scientific' approach advocated by writers such as Taylor and Fayol. The research, as it developed, unexpectedly showed the importance of some very human factors in the working environment, in particular the influence of inter-personal and group relations. The study played a crucial role in the development of modern industrial psychology. Human resource perspectives on management and their impact on effectiveness are dealt with in detail in Chapter 7 of this book.

At around the same time as Mayo's experiments in the USA, Max Weber, a German sociologist, was examining the changes that were taking place in the industrial workplace and in society in general, and in particular the move towards specialization and standardization created by the 'scientific' paradigm, based on the analogy of a machine. He saw that what he called the bureaucratic approach had the potential to routinize and mechanize almost every aspect of human life, eroding the human spirit and capacity for spontaneous action.

Economic growth and the development of the strategic planning concept

The 1950s saw a major expansion in Western industrial economies and the globalization of many large companies. Long-term financial and management planning and control became a key feature of the 1950s (Greenley 1986) as these large firms tried to control what was happening, perhaps thousands of miles away.

From the work of Drucker (1964) in the USA, Management By Objectives (MBO) – where objectives are determined at the top of the organization and cascade down through the organization in a structured and systematic way – became very popular. This approach reflected the mechanistic paradigm articulated by Taylor, Fayol and others and the closed-system paradigm of organizational theory at that time (Robbins 1990).

The 1960s represented a move towards a more open-system perspective on organizations (Katz and Kahn 1966) and the beginning of modern strategic planning theory and practice.

The 1960s was also a period of substantial expansion of industrial economies, and saw the growth of national and multi-national companies into new markets and new products. How such companies should make such strategic decisions (e.g., which products? which markets?), in order to be successful, became a key question in the 1960s, and strategic planning became the key tool to use to try to answer these questions. Indeed perhaps *the* seminal work on strategic planning, *Corporate strategy* by H. Igor Ansoff (1965), Professor of the Carnegie Institute of Technology, was subtitled 'An analytic approach to business policy for growth and expansion', which is an indication of how bullish American industry was during this period, prior to the oil crisis of the mid-1970s and the rise of the Japanese and other Eastern economies.

The first use of the term 'strategy' to refer to business is by Chandler (1962) in his pioneering work *Strategy and structure*, which studied the evolution of management in big corporations in the USA. It was used again, in 1964, by Drucker in his seminal work *Management by results*. Indeed he has stated that he originally wanted 'strategy' in the title, but was dissuaded by the publishers because of the danger of misunderstanding.

The pioneers of strategy as applied to business in the 1960s and 1970s fall into three main overlapping schools, which remain extremely influential today despite their detractors. These are the Design School, the Planning School, and the Positioning School.

The Design School

The origins of the Design School can be traced back to two influential books written at the University of California (Berkeley) and at Massachusetts Institute of Technology (MIT): *Leadership in administration* by Philip Selznick (1957), and *Strategy and structure* by Alfred Chandler (1962). Selznick, in particular, introduced the idea of 'distinctive competence', highlighting the need to bring together the organization's 'internal state' with its 'external expectations' and argued for building policy into the organization's social structure, which later became known as implementation. The Design School is represented primarily by Ken Andrews and others from the Harvard Business School, first of all in its basic textbook *Business policy: Text and cases* (Learned *et al.* 1965) and then in one of the school's seminal works, *The concept of corporate strategy* by Andrews, first published in 1971. Here Andrews defined 'corporate strategy' as

> the pattern of decisions in a company that determines and reveals its objectives, purposes or goals, and defines the range of business the company is to pursue, the kind of economic and human organization it is or intends to be, and the nature of the economic and non-economic contribution it intends to make to its shareholders, employees, customers, and communities.

He went on in the same work to define it more simply as

> a rational decision-making process by which the organization's resources are matched with opportunities arising from the competitive environment.

Andrews stressed the crucial role of the Chief Executive Officer in corporate strategy as the organization leader, personnel leader and the architect of organization purpose. He summarized the four responsibilities of the Chief Executive Officer as:

1   securing the attainment of planned results in the present;
2   developing an organization capable of producing both technical achievement and human satisfaction;
3   making a distinctive personal contribution;
4   planning and executing policy decisions affecting future results.

Andrews distinguished clearly between the formulation of strategy, which involves matching external opportunity with corporate capability and attaches estimates of risk to each option, and its implementation. He summarized the four main components of strategy as:

1   market opportunity;
2   corporate competence and resources;
3   personal values and aspirations;
4   acknowledged obligations to people in society other than shareholders.

In these last three components of strategy Andrews was well ahead of his time, foreshadowing key themes which play a key role in management thinking in the 1990s on core competencies, business ethics, corporate responsibility and stakeholders. These concerns also reflect some of the particular values and interests of the voluntary nonprofit sector.

Andrews also recognized the importance of having the appropriate organizational structure in order to coordinate activities; organization processes which are directed towards the kind of behaviour required by organization purpose; and top management leadership. In relation to evaluating possible strategies he suggested ten questions to help judge a strategy:

1   Is the strategy simple and identifiable, and has it been made clear either in words or in practice?
2   Is the strategy in some way unique/distinctive?
3   Does the strategy fully exploit domestic and international environmental opportunity?
4   Is the strategy consistent with corporate competence and resources, both present and projected?
5   Are the major provisions of the strategy and the programme of major policies of which it is comprised internally consistent?
6   Is the chosen level of risk feasible in economic and personal terms?
7   Is the strategy appropriate to the personal values and aspirations of the key managers?
8   Is the strategy appropriate to the desired level of contribution to society?
9   Does the strategy constitute a clear stimulus to organizational effort and commitment?
10 Are there early indications of the responsiveness of markets and market segments to the strategy?

In summary he suggested that, regardless of the size of the organization, the essential elements of the strategic management process are the same:

1   Participation by key individuals in the identification of problems and strategic opportunities.

2   Inclusion of personal preferences, organization values, and corporate capability in the analysis.
3   The marshalling of accurate and relevant data on further market growth.
4   The recognition of financial constraints with respect to capital sources and projected return.

Mintzberg (1994) summarized the main features of the Design School as follows:

- strategy formulation should be a controlled, conscious process of thought;
- responsibility for the process must rest with the Chief Executive Officer: that person is *the* strategist (i.e. the 'Architect');
- the model of strategy formation must be kept simple and informal;
- strategies should be unique: the best ones result from a process of creative design, based on distinctive (now called 'core') competencies;
- strategies must come out of the design process fully developed;
- the strategies should be made explicit and, if possible, articulated, which means they have to be kept simple;
- once these unique, full-blown, explicit, and simple strategies are fully formulated, they must then be implemented.

To the lay person, however, the lasting overt legacy of the Design School is probably the SWOT analysis (Strengths, Weaknesses, Opportunities and Threats) which analyses the strengths and weaknesses of the firm and the threats and opportunities of the external environment, and which tries to produce an appropriate fit of the organization to its environment. SWOT analysis has become one of the most frequently used strategic planning tools (see Chapters 12 and 13).

Despite its enduring influence there have, however, been a number of important critiques of the Design School. These are summarized by Mintzberg *et al.* (1998) and include the following:

- it denies the importance of incremental or emergent strategies;
- by arguing that structure always follows strategy it denies the importance of existing competencies and therefore of structure on strategy;
- the importance of other players as well as the Chief Executive in formulating strategy;
- articulating strategy during periods of uncertainty can lead to blinkered thinking and 'premature closure';
- like other rational approaches the issue of creativity and innovation is not addressed. Great strategies tend to be those that redefine the nature of the market and the business, not just follow logically from the analysis.

Mintzberg *et al.* do, however, suggest that the approach of the Design School can be particularly valuable in particular circumstances where:

- one brain can, in principle, handle all of the information relevant for strategy formulation and that brain is able to have full, detailed, intimate knowledge of the situation in question;
- the relevant knowledge must be established before a new intended strategy has to be implemented – in other words, the situation has to remain relatively stable or at least predictable;
- the organization must be able to cope with a centrally articulated strategy, i.e. to defer to a central strategist.

The Planning School

At the same time as Harvard was publishing its original textbook on corporate strategy, Igor Ansoff at the Carnegie Institute of Technology was publishing his classic work, *Corporate strategy* (Ansoff 1965). The Planning School, as those who became associated with Ansoff's ideas came to be known, had many similarities with the Design School. However, Ansoff did not believe that the process could be kept simple and informal, and proposed a complex model of strategic planning. The Planning School also put much greater emphasis on setting formal objectives, rather than the Design School's stress on the concept of values.

Mintzberg, in *The rise and fall of strategic planning* (1994), summarizes the three basic premises of the Planning School:

1 Strategy formation should be controlled and conscious as well as a formalized and elaborated process, decomposed into distinct steps, each delineated by checklists and supported by techniques.
2 Responsibility for the overall process rests with the Chief Executive in principle; responsibility for its execution rests with the staff planners in practice.
3 Strategies come out of this process fully developed, typically as generic positions, to be explicated so that they can then be implemented through detailed attention to objectives, budgets, programmes and operating plans of various kinds.

The particular model that Ansoff developed in the first edition of *Corporate strategy* has a number of key features.

First, the strategic options for growth and expansion are potentially various combinations of new and existing products and new and existing markets. Ansoff developed a matrix of the various possibilities, to show that there are only four basic strategic options, as follows:

- sell existing products in existing markets;
- sell new products in existing markets;
- sell existing products in new markets;
- sell new products in new markets.

The Ansoff matrix, as this became known, has also been adapted for use in the voluntary nonprofit sector (Courtney 1996).

Second, he stressed the importance of recognizing different levels of decisions: strategy; policy; programme; and standard operating procedure. The level of uncertainty and risk decreases as one moves down this list, and therefore can be delegated accordingly down the organization. All but the first (strategy) also reduce the requirement to make an original decision each time a decision is required. They thus create consistency of action – what Ansoff calls 'economies of management'. Ansoff also recognized the necessity of cascading decisions down through an organization from the aggregate to the specific.

Ansoff proposed the importance of 'gap analysis', which he described as follows:

> The procedure within each step of the cascade is similar. (1) A set of objectives is established. (2) The difference (the 'gap') between the current position of the firm and the objectives is estimated. (3) One or more courses of action (strategy) are proposed. (4) These are tested for their 'gap-reducing properties'. A course is accepted if it substantially closes the gap; if it does not, new alternatives are tried.
>
> (Ansoff 1965)

Ansoff also argued for the importance of the concept of 'synergy' which has become of crucial importance in modern business thinking. He described it as the 2+2=5 factor, which helped explain the basic notion of 'fit' in the design of organization strategy. He defined it as any 'effect which can produce a combined return on the firm's resources greater than the sum of its parts'.

The closely related Design and Planning Schools inspired the development of a large number of one-best-way strategic planning models and 'how-to' publications, which tended to have a number of common features. These features were as follows:

- strategy as a rational decision-making process;
- a thorough analysis of the competitive environment;
- a thorough analysis of the organization's resources and distinctive/core competencies (i.e. what it does specifically well);
- the setting of clear goals/objectives;
- the evaluation of different strategic options;
- a hierarchy of objectives;
- effective implementation.

The Positioning School

Michael E. Porter, a professor at Harvard, in his seminal work *Competitive strategy* (1980), used economic perspectives to analyse strategy and argued that the profit available in a particular industry was strongly affected by competition. This competition could be analysed using five key factors:

1   The rivalry amongst existing firms in the industry.
2   The threat of new entrants to the industry, depending on how easy or difficult it is to enter the industry.
3   The bargaining power of buyers (are they few or many?).
4   The bargaining power of suppliers, including labour (are they few or many?).
5   The threat of substitute products.

To Porter, then, the purpose of formulating competitive strategy 'is to find a position...where the company can best defend itself against these...forces, or can influence them in its favour' (Porter 1980).

Unlike the Design and Planning Schools, which put no limitation on the type of strategies that an organization can adopt, Porter argued that there are basically only three generic strategies to deal with these five forces. These are:

- overall cost leadership, i.e. producing more cheaply than your rivals;
- differentiation, i.e. producing a product or service that is seen as unique;
- focus on a very particular market segment or geographical area and meeting their specific requirements better than 'competitors who compete more broadly'.

From Porter's perspective, strategists do not so much design strategies but rather select them from a list of generic strategies.

Porter's second major work, *Competitive advantage* (1985), reinforced the message of his previous book but added a number of concepts that have played a crucial role in business thinking.

He stressed the importance not only of gaining competitive advantage but also of making this advantage sustainable over the long term, usually by continual improvement. In relation to voluntary nonprofit organizations, however, the lack of a profit bottom line and identifiable competitors led to the suggestion that Porter's concept of 'competitive advantage has no direct analogue in not-for-profit organisations' (Goold 1997). However, it has been adapted for use by nonprofit organizations (see Oster 1995; Lindenberg 2001).

Arguably one of Porter's most important ideas, however, was that of the value chain, i.e. the sequence of activities which are strategically relevant because they are what enables the firm to provide value for the buyer. These activities may fall into a number of different categories, which he separates into *Primary* and *Support*.

Primary: inbound logistics (inputs/supplies); operations (the transformation of these inputs into final products); outbound logistics (storage and distribution); marketing and sales; service (e.g. maintenance).
Support: procurement; technology development; human resource management; firm infrastructure (e.g. planning, finance, legal, quality management).

Porter's concept of the value chain played an important role in the development of both total quality management and business process engineering. These initiatives were particularly influential in the 1980s and early 1990s.

Bruce Henderson (1979), founder of the Boston Consulting Group, was cynical about the traditional strategic planning prevalent in the late 1970s and early 1980s. He believed that socio-biology provided important clues to understanding the behaviour of firms. Henderson viewed modern business as the product of selection brought about by natural competition and that it owes more to intuition, expediency and chance than it does to 'an integrated strategy' (1984). Whittington (1993) describes this as the 'evolutionary' perspective, which says that the best businesses are selected by the competitive forces of the market. Such evolutionist theorists doubt the capacity of organizations to achieve deliberate adaptation to the environment, as opposed to Darwinian selection by the environment. Whittington sums up this perspective as follows: 'The construction of grand long-term strategies may be so much vain distraction; managers would do much better to get down to the modest business of making sure that what they do now is done as efficiently as possible.'

The Boston Consulting Group, however, developed a number of strategy models and tools that have been used by companies all over the world in the last twenty years. The most famous of the models and tools developed by the Group is the Boston Matrix for Portfolio Analysis. This is used to assess existing products, services or businesses and determine what a company's strategy should be in relation to each (i.e. invest, harvest, or divest), depending on its relationship to market share and market growth (see Chapter 12 for a more detailed discussion of Portfolio Analysis).

Mintzberg *et al.* (1998) criticize the Positioning School on a number of fronts, including the basic criticisms of the Design and Planning Schools, because it is based on similar predispositions (separating thinking and doing; the leader as the strategist, etc.). The other criticisms include the following:

- the focus is too narrowly on economics, ignoring political, social and cultural factors;
- there is a bias towards the big stable established companies;

- what industry to which any particular company belongs is not as clear in practice as it is in reality, and the definition of an industry is constantly changing;
- the strategy process is a rational number-crunching one rather than a process of experimentation and learning;
- there is no place for engendering commitment and energy in the Positioning School;
- the focus on generic strategies tends to go against companies developing unique innovative strategies;
- the evidence is that there is more difference between companies in the same industry than between different industries (Rumelt 1991; McGahan and Porter 1997).

Challenges to the rational strategy schools

The general consensus, in relation to the analytical rational approaches to strategy, began to be challenged in the mid-1970s. These challenges were:

- at the theoretical level, reflecting alternative perspectives on organizations that were being developed, including post-modernism, contingency theory, social constructionism, political and cultural perspectives;
- at a practical level as a result of both the first oil crisis, when the failure of planners to predict the crisis and the resultant problems experienced by firms whose strategies were formulated with, as it turned out, an erroneous set of assumptions about fuel prices; and the relentless success of Japanese companies without the use of any apparent strategic planning methods.

The result was a shift of focus. In the words of Craig and Grant (1993), 'Strategy became concerned less with *planning* the corporation and more with positioning the firm to make a profit.' Diversification was a common thrust in this period, whereby firms could limit the damage caused by incorrect assumptions about external factors in relation to one particular product or market.

Summary

This chapter has explored the origins of the concepts of strategy and strategic planning, from its early military and diplomatic use, through the development of a 'scientific' approach to management, to the three classic, and still influential, approaches to strategic planning in the private sector, the Design, Planning, and Positioning Schools. The importance of each of these Schools and the critiques that have been made of each have been explored.

Questions

1   Do military and diplomatic strategies have any relevance for today's voluntary nonprofit sector?
2   In what ways are the scientific approaches of Taylor and Fayol still relevant today?
3   What are the weaknesses of the Design and Planning Schools?
4   How relevant is Porter's five-factor industry analysis to the voluntary nonprofit sector?
5   What factors are most important for a voluntary nonprofit organization in assessing its existing portfolio of programmes?

Suggested reading

Henry Mintzberg (1994) *The rise and fall of strategic planning*, Prentice-Hall.
Henry Mintzberg, Bruce Ahlstrand and Joseph Lampel (1998) *Strategy safari: A guided tour through the wilds of strategic management*, Prentice-Hall
J.I. Moore (1992) *Writers on strategy and strategic management*, Penguin.

6 What is an excellent organization?

The Attributes of Excellence School

Chapter outline

This chapter explores the development of the ideas of the Attributes of Excellence School, which has its roots in some of the early military and diplomatic writings on strategy. The influential ideas of Tom Peters and others are explored, along with similar approaches in Japan, Europe and Britain. The critiques of this kind of approach will also be examined, as will its relevance for the voluntary nonprofit sector.

Learning objectives

When you have completed this chapter you should understand:

- the prescriptive ideas of Peters and Waterman in the USA, which have been unusually influential for a business publication;
- the relevance of the Peters and Waterman approach for the voluntary nonprofit sector;
- suggestions of the attributes of excellence in the public sector;
- the use of the Peters and Waterman case study approach in relation to European companies by Heller;
- the interest in what has made Japanese business so excellent;
- the use of a similar approach in Britain, which recognizes some of the dilemmas and balances that are required;
- the limitations to this prescriptive maxims approach.

The USA

In the 1980s a number of influential writers developed arguments against the traditional rational approaches to strategic management represented by the Design, Planning and Positioning Schools, and developed alternative approaches articulating prescriptions based on those characteristics perceived to exist in examples of successful companies.

In the early 1980s, having studied 43 successful American businesses,

Peters and Waterman (1982) published *In search of excellence*, which suggested that the key to corporate success lay not in using a mechanistic approach to strategic planning, but in installing a number of principles or attributes in a company. The book proved to be enormously popular, selling in unusually large numbers around the world.

The attributes of excellence that Peters and Waterman felt were decisive were as follows:

- stick to the knitting – build on the business you know well (core competencies);
- close to the customer – listen to what the customer wants and reward meeting the customer's needs;
- productivity through people – foster attitudes whereby people perceive themselves as belonging to an extended family;
- autonomy and entrepreneurship – encourage initiative and risk-taking;
- empower people to make decisions – to not blame failure;
- hands on, value driven – leaders articulate the company vision and values;
- bias for action – try out ideas emphasizing a fast trial-and-error action;
- simple form, lean staff – simple flexible structures, with small headquarters and decentralized decision-making;
- simultaneous loose–tight properties – tight control of finance and core values and a high emphasis on initiative and risk-taking.

Peters and Waterman, with many others, viewed the external environment as changing too rapidly to predict what is going to happen in the future, and they therefore stressed the need for non-rational trial-and-error approaches that allow flexibility – and thus the future – to emerge. Despite their enormous success in achieving extensive sales of the book, however, Peters and Waterman's research methods, choice of companies and generalizations have been criticized (Carroll 1983), and many of the 'vanguard' companies stumbled not long afterwards (Aupperle *et al.* 1986), some to return later.

The voluntary nonprofit sector

Bryson (1995) states, after examining the Peters and Waterman excellence criteria, that it 'is easy to see how these criteria might apply to many single-function public authorities and to many nonprofit organisations'. Diana Leat, looking at the similarities and differences between the voluntary nonprofit and private sectors, argues that the nine attributes in *In search of excellence* reflect the ideology, if not always the practices, of the voluntary nonprofit sector.

First, many non-profit organisations display a bias for action – for getting on and doing things rather than talking or thinking about it.

Second, non-profits emphasise their concern for the wishes and needs of their customers; this is what in many respects provides them with their *raison d'être*.

Third, autonomy and entrepreneurship are an important part of the ideology of the non-profit sector which prides itself on being a source of innovation.

Fourth, people are typically seen as the key resource of the non-profit organisation. Many have no other resource and even those with a substantial income are still likely to emphasise the importance of involving staff and volunteers in the work of the organisation.

Fifth, non-profits also stress the importance of a hands-on value-driven approach; values are at the core of the organisation's mission and hands-on knowledge and involvement are considered crucial.

Sixth, for various reasons, non-profits display a strong tendency to 'stick to the knitting' – so stay close to the business they know best.

Seventh, although it is debatable whether many non-profits could be described as displaying a simple form, they are likely to display lean staff; 'lean staff' may be due to lack of income and/or because a large paid staff and high expenditure on 'administration' are frowned on as an unnecessary diversion of charitable resources.

Finally, many non-profits have simultaneous loose–tight structures, strongly emphasising core values, but allowing workers considerable freedom within that. As noted above, the emphasis on core values stems from their centrality to mission and, for some, to charitable status.

(Leat 1993)

These principles have also been adapted for use by voluntary nonprofit organizations in their approach to fundraising (Courtney 1995).

Although Leat's reflection on Peters and Waterman's principles as they relate to the voluntary nonprofit sector could be challenged, they do reflect an interesting trend in the development of management theory as it relates to the private sector, which is that, arguably, it has been moving away from its top-down rational mechanistic centralized approach towards an approach which is much more in keeping with the traditional ethos of the voluntary nonprofit sector, represented by an emphasis on vision, values, innovation and participation. Warren Bennis foresaw this change in approach in the mid-1960s, and described it as the 'death of bureaucracy' (Bennis 1966).

The public sector

Various attempts have been made to suggest equivalent excellence criteria for the public sector (Bryson 1995; Sipel 1984; Osborne and Graebler 1992). Sipel suggests: action orientation; closeness to citizens; autonomy and entrepreneurship; employee orientation; values; mission, goals, and competence; structure; and political relationships. Osborne and Graebler suggest: catalytic; community owned; competitive; mission-driven; results-oriented; customer-driven; enterprising; anticipatory; decentralized and market-oriented.

Europe

Robert Heller (1997) reflected a concern amongst British and other European managers that all the companies researched by Peters and Waterman were based in the USA, and therefore that the solutions promoted may not be appropriate in a European setting. Heller also had the advantage of hindsight in seeing most of Peters and Waterman's 'excellent' companies doing rather badly in the subsequent decade and a half. In looking at successful European companies, Heller argued for the following ten principles or 'arenas of corporate renaissance':

1   devolving leadership – without losing control or direction;
2   driving radical change – in the entire corporate system, not just in its parts;
3   reshaping the culture – to achieve long-term success;
4   dividing to rule – winning the rewards of smallness while staying or growing large;
5   exploiting the 'organization' – by new approaches to central direction;
6   keeping the competitive edge – in a world where the old ways of winning no longer work;
7   achieving constant renewal – stopping success from sowing the seeds of decay;
8   managing the motivators – so that people can motivate themselves;
9   making teamwork work – the new indispensable skill;
10 achieving total management quality – by managing everything much better.

Japan

One of the most significant phenomena in the 1980s was the global success of Japanese companies, which do not use Western approaches to strategic planning and management. This led to a number of attempts to explore what Western business leaders could learn from companies in Japan. Pascale and Athos (1981) looked at 34 Japanese companies over six years and concluded that vision was a key component of Japanese management that was missing from the USA. The tendency in the USA, as they saw it, was to emphasize strategy, structure and systems, whereas in Japan the emphasis was much more on style, shared values, skills and staff.

Ouchi (1981) developed his Theory Z as to how American businesses could meet the Japanese challenge. He argued that American business needed to refocus its corporate culture from technology to people: that commitment to people is the most important organizational philosophy. American managers, he suggested, would have to act in ways that are publicly uncomfortable, emphasizing the values of:

- personal trust;
- intimacy – in the sense of personal concern;
- the subtlety of personalities and relationships;
- team rather than individual responsibility;
- learning many functions rather than one;
- moulding business and social life;
- long-term employment;
- investing in training.

He argued that decision-making should become a participative and collective activity.

In 1982, Ohmae, in his reflections on the success of Japanese business, emphasized the importance of the intuitive and creative over the analytical:

> Successful business strategies result not from rigorous analysis but from a particular state of mind. In what I call the mind of the strategist, insight and a consequent drive for achievement, often amounting to a sense of mission, fuel a thought process which is basically creative and intuitive rather than rational. Strategists do not reject analysis. Indeed they could hardly do without it. But they use it only to stimulate the creative process, to test the ideas that emerge, to work out their strategic implications or to ensure the successful implementation of the 'wild' ideas that might otherwise never be implemented properly. Great strategies, like great works of art or great scientific discoveries, call for technical mastery in the working out but originate in insights that are beyond the reach of conscious analysis.
>
> (Ohmae 1982)

Imai (1986) argues that the unique Japanese approach to incremental continuous improvement, he calls it *Kaizen*, is a key difference between the Western and Japanese approaches to management, and the main cause of Japanese success.

It is interesting to note that the qualities of Japanese companies which various writers judge to have made them so successful are those values which some writers have suggested are the distinctive qualities of the voluntary nonprofit sector.

Britain

In the 1980s, Goldsmith and Clutterbuck (*The winning streak*, 1984) had also developed a set of guiding principles, which were indicated by analysing successful British companies. As with Peters and Waterman's work, some people criticized their ideas for being too simplistic and prescriptive. In light of these criticisms and the experience of the following decade, a second edition was published (*Winning streak – Mark II*, 1997) which, along with Collins and Porras (1994) who stressed the need to get away from the 'tyranny of the OR' (the idea that people have to constantly choose between two seemingly contracdictory ideas or forces), emphasized the need to create balance between a number of different polarities:

- control versus autonomy;
- long-term strategy versus short-term urgency;
- evolutionary versus revolutionary change;
- pride versus humility;
- focus versus breadth of vision;
- values versus rules;
- customer care versus customer count;
- challenging versus nurturing people;
- leaders versus managers;
- gentle versus abrupt succession.

The new book highlighted companies that had failed to maintain a balance as well as those which had been successful, and added a number of case studies from both the USA and Sweden, as well as from the UK. This is similar to the approach suggested by Bolman and Deal (1991) who argue that dysfunctional patterns in an organization are due to the inadequate resolution of the major structural dilemmas that all organizations face, namely:

- differentiation versus integration;
- gaps versus overlaps;
- underuse versus overload;
- lack of clarity versus lack of creativity;
- excessive autonomy versus excessive interdependence;
- too loose versus too tight structures;
- diffuse authority versus over-centralization;
- goal-less versus goal-bound;
- irresponsible versus unresponsive.

In his own study of companies, Quinn (1980) found that what happened in practice bore little resemblance to a grand strategy worked out in its entirety in advance. The processes adopted tended to be 'fragmented, evolutionary and largely intuitive'. Real strategy, from Quinn's perspective, evolves from a consensus amongst top management. Like Peters, Heller,

Goldsmith and Clutterbuck and others, Quinn suggests a number of key principles as being important. However, Quinn considers the military–diplomatic (and sporting) maxims distilled from history, highlighted on page 60, to be the principles which are crucial in guiding strategic development in modern business. These principles include the following:

- clear decisive objectives;
- maintaining the initiative;
- concentration (on those things that determine superiority);
- conceding selected positions;
- flexibility;
- coordinated and committed leadership;
- surprise;
- security;
- communications.

Simon (1947) had already become disenchanted with the use of classical principles as a basis for managing organizations, well before the recent enthusiasm for describing the attributes of excellent organizations. He suggested that most classical principles were nothing more than proverbs and many contradicted one another. Pascale (1990), criticizing the simplistic formulae in Peters and Waterman's *In search of excellence*, argues that 'simply identifying attributes of success is like identifying attributes of people in excellent health during the age of the bubonic plague'. Mintzberg *et al.* (1998) are also cynical about the value of maxims generally. With a touch of irony, they suggest their own maxims, as follows:

- most maxims are obvious;
- obvious maxims can be meaningless;
- some obvious maxims are contradicted by other obvious maxims; so
- beware of maxims.

However, the Attributes of Excellence School has played an important role in the development of the Quality Movement, sometimes called TQM (Total Quality Management) or Continuous Improvement, and in the creation of various useful models and tools, highlighted in Chapter 12, such as the EFQM Excellence Model (and the Baldridge Quality Award in the USA). In the voluntary nonprofit sector it has spawned the development of various generic and specific quality frameworks which suggest standards that voluntary nonprofit agencies need to comply with if they are to be effective. These include the Joseph Rowntree standards and PQASSO in the UK, the Charities Review Council of Minnesota, and National Charities Information Bureau Standards in Philanthropy in North America.

Summary

With increasing disenchantment with complex detached strategic planning, Peters and Waterman's book *In search of excellence* was hugely successful, selling an extremely large number of copies (for a business book) around the world. They suggested that, by studying successful US companies, they were able to distil key characteristics of a successful company which others could follow. Many of these principles feel closer to the management of many voluntary nonprofit organizations than many traditional 'taylorist' private companies, where the emphasis is on command and control. Similar studies were carried out in Europe and a similar approach has been adopted to try to understand Japanese business success. Some of the later approaches avoid the 'one best way' approach and suggest balances need to be struck between various competing principles. However, the whole Attributes of Excellence approach has been criticized on both practical and theoretical grounds.

Questions

1   Are prescriptive maxims useful in helping an organization to become excellent? If so, which maxims would you say are most useful?
2   Are the maxims that are relevant to the private sector also relevant to the voluntary nonprofit sector? Give examples.
3   Why was Peters and Waterman's book *In search of excellence* so popular?
4   Is good management about finding a balance between competing values and prescriptions?

Suggested reading

Robert Heller (1997) *In search of European excellence*, HarperCollins.
Richard Pascale (1990) *Managing on the edge*, Viking Penguin.
Tom Peters and Robert Waterman (1982) *In search of excellence: Lessons from America's best run companies*, Harper & Row.

7 Starting with the people
The Human Resources School

Chapter outline

This chapter addresses the role of people in the process of managing and developing organizations. It explores the various theories of human motivation in relation to work that have been increasingly influential in the management of organizations generally, and is particularly relevant in supporting the kind of management that many voluntary nonprofit organizations aspire to. The importance of human resources in a resource-based view of strategic management is also highlighted.

Learning objectives

When you have completed this chapter you should understand:

- traditional approaches to motivation;
- what motivates staff in work;
- the main ideas of the Human Resources School;
- suggested differences in staff motivation between voluntary nonprofit and for-profit organizations;
- the significance of people in the resource-based view of strategy.

Introduction

An alternative frame (Bolman and Deal 1991) to the traditional mechanistic one adopted by the classic strategy schools from which to view the issue of the management and development of organizations is the Human Resources School. Organizations are made up of people (staff and volunteers) with their own visions, needs, values and views. Voluntary nonprofit organizations, in particular, exist to serve human needs (not the reverse). How the staff and volunteers within voluntary nonprofit organizations view work, the organization and the future are crucial to the strategic development of the organization.

Different approaches to management and effectiveness are influenced by different perspectives on human motivation which, according to Steers and Porter (1983), is the force that energizes (causes people to act); directs behaviour towards specific goals; and sustains behaviour until goals are achieved.

Traditional approaches to human motivation

The early writers on scientific management emphasized the 'command and control' aspects of management. The assumptions underlying these approaches were that

- the average human has an inherent dislike of work and will avoid it if they can;
- most people have to be coerced, controlled, directed and threatened with punishment to get them to make an effort in the direction of the organization's goals;
- the average human dislikes responsibility and has little ambition, prefers to be directed and wants security first and foremost.

On the basis of this theory, which assumes that organizations are like machines (Morgan 1986), and therefore that the people are like parts of the machine, effectiveness can best be measured by time and motion studies and *per capita* productivity.

Skinner (1938), from his work on learning in animals, developed the concept of instrumental conditioning, by which behaviour can be conditioned by the provision of positive and negative reinforcement. Hammer (1974) developed the reinforcement theory for the modern workplace and suggested rules for managers applying operant conditioning techniques – i.e. providing rewards – in the workplace. Charles Handy in his book *Understanding voluntary organisations* is particularly scathing about this view of managing people:

> Motivation has come to mean getting other people to want what you want them to want. Pigeons have been starved and then taught to dance for food. To treat pigeons like that is distasteful; to do it to humans and then to dignify it with names like reinforcement theory is akin to calling murder a form of genetic weeding.
>
> (Handy 1988)

Humanistic approaches

McGregor's Theories X and Y

McGregor (1960) described these mechanistic instrumental theories of human behaviour collectively as Theory X. In contrast he argued (along with Maslow 1970, who developed the concept of a hierarchy of needs – see page 84), that as organizations provide for the physiological and safety needs of their employees, the employees will seek to satisfy higher needs. However, if no opportunity is provided to satisfy these higher needs, then the employees are likely to act in ways consistent with Theory X.

He proposed an alternative theory of human behaviour (Theory Y) which assumes that

- physical and mental effort at work is as natural as rest or play;
- controls and the threat of punishment are not the only ways of achieving the goals of the organization;
- people do exercise self-control and self-direction if they are committed to these goals;
- the average human being is willing to seek out and take responsibility under certain circumstances;
- many people are capable of exercising a lot of imagination, ingenuity and creativity in solving the problems of the organization;
- the way things are traditionally organized (based on Theory X), the average human being's brainpower is only partly used.

Hertzberg's motivators and hygiene factors

Hertzberg (1968) developed a two-factor theory based on his research with groups of engineers and accountants. He argued that the factors which create job satisfaction are different from the factors that create dissatisfaction. The 'motivators' which create satisfaction tend to be factors such as achievement, recognition, responsibility, opportunity for advancement, and interesting work. The factors which create dissatisfaction, or 'hygiene factors', tend to be pay, working conditions, type of supervision, relationships with co-workers, and company policies. This theory suggests that, if they want to increase the motivation of workers, companies need to tackle, and measure the satisfaction with, the softer needs issues such as making the work interesting, giving recognition and a sense of achievement. This approach has resulted in the development of many programmes to enrich jobs and regular staff audits to assess satisfaction with the motivation and hygiene factors.

Hertzberg's motivators and hygiene factors have not found universal support in subsequent research (Schneider and Locke 1971). Dunnette *et al.* (1967) have suggested that they are only applicable to white-collar workers.

Interestingly, for the voluntary nonprofit sector, Kohjasten (1993) compared motivation in the private and public sectors, using Hertzberg's model. He confirmed the importance of work achievements in the public sector as a motivator, but found that pay and job security were motivators, not just hygiene factors, in the private sector. This would suggest that a sense of work achievement is also likely to be an important motivator in the voluntary nonprofit sector. This is confirmed by a research study comparing the meaning of work to employees in the private sector and those in voluntary nonprofit sector in Ireland. This research found that, compared with those in the private sector, employees of voluntary nonprofit organizations:

- indicate a higher work centrality;
- identify more with the company/organization and the product/service;
- value more the society-serving aspect of their work;
- seek interesting work, to learn new things, good inter-personal relations, match between job and skills, autonomy of work, variety in work, and convenient working hours.

This study indicates a much greater importance of the human resource perspective on motivation in the voluntary nonprofit sector than the private sector.

Maslow's hierarchy of needs

Maslow's hierarchy of needs suggests that, when lower-order needs, such as physiological and safety needs, are met, the individual seeks fulfilment of higher-order needs, such as love and esteem, cognitive needs, and, ultimately, self-actualization. While appealing in theory, particularly to the voluntary nonprofit sector which sees its key role as responding to human needs, Maslow's hierarchy has found little support in subsequent research (Rauschenberger *et al.* 1980; Miner 1984). Others have argued that the concept of need is too vague to be measured and ignores the crucial impact of environmental influences (Salancik and Pfeffer 1978). Maslow's hierarchy of needs has, however, been influential in the voluntary nonprofit sector, particularly in relation to the beneficiaries of care services. One organization even incorporated it into their value statement (Courtney 1992).

Alderfer (1972) developed a variation of Maslow's theory which proposes three types of needs, characterized by the initials ERG: Existence needs, similar to Maslow's physiological and safety needs; Relatedness needs, which are met through social interaction, a key feature of Mayo's work; and Growth needs, to enable the individual to develop and achieve their potential. Unlike Maslow, the ERG theory does not presume that the three types of need are in a hierarchy. Alderfer suggests that we aspire to all three, and failure to achieve one can be compensated for by progress in another area. There has been little academic research into the evidence for or against the ERG theory of Alderfer.

Clearly, an organization that operates according to Theory Y, to Maslow's hierarchy of needs, or to Alderfer's relatedness and growth needs will tend towards a much broader power base, as do many voluntary nonprofit organizations – what Leavitt (1963) has called 'power equalisation' – and will value the participation of employees in organizational decision-making

(Schein 1988) and strategic management processes. It was this power equalization and desire for participation that managers who moved from the private sector to the voluntary nonprofit sector found so difficult (Leat 1995).

Likert's system classification

Likert (1967) developed a classification which is more refined than McGregor's Theories X and Y, breaking down organizations into four main types of system:

Series 1   Primitive authoritarian
Series 2   Benevolent authoritarian
Series 3   Consultative
Series 4   Participative

He argued that most firms are positioned at around 2.5 on this scale, while the research evidence supports the hypothesis that organizations using System 4, or moving closer to it, are obtaining better results in terms of productivity, quality and labour relations.

Odiorne (1987) argued that management is most effective when employees are integrated into the organization; i.e. their needs are being met while fulfilling organizational goals. He views the primary goal of management as being to create conditions whereby individuals can control their own work behaviour. Arguably voluntary nonprofit organizations, particularly those which are led by mutual aid and membership, are more likely to operate somewhere between Systems 3 and 4.

McClelland's achievement, power and affiliation theory

McClelland (1961) suggested that people tend to be motivated by different things. Some people are motivated more by a need for achievement, others by a need for power, and others still by a need for affiliation. His theory emphasizes the importance of understanding the particular motivation of each individual, rather than trying to apply a blanket solution to problems of motivation.

Adams's concept of social exchange

Adams (1965) developed the social psychology concept of social exchange to develop an equity theory of motivation in the workplace, whereby workers weigh up what it costs (what they have to give, materially and psychologically, to work in a particular job) and what they get out of it. These factors may be actual objective factors, such as hours and pay, or they may be perceived, such as status. Dissatisfaction arises, according to the equity theory, when workers perceive that the balance between benefits and costs is inequitable. This may occur, not as a result of a change in their own position, but as a result of what is perceived as better treatment of another group of workers (Martin and Peterson 1987; Perry 1993; Van Wijck 1994).

Vroom's expectation theory

Vroom (1964) argued that motivation is complex and highly subjective and depends significantly on what we expect. He used the concepts of: valence – how much the outcome of work is worth to the individual; expectancy – how much work is required to complete the work; and instrumentality – the expectation of what will be the result of carrying out the work. Mastrofski *et al.* (1994) found the concepts of Vroom's theory to be consistent with their work with police officers related to arrest productivity.

Schein's psychological contract

In concluding a discussion of motivation, E. H. Schein (1988) underlined 'the importance of the psychological contract'. He argued that whether people work effectively depends significantly on 'the degree to which their own expectations of what the organization will provide to them and what they owe the organization in return matches what the organization's expectations are of what it will give and get in return'. The nature of what is actually exchanged tends to include:

- money in exchange for time at work;
- social need satisfaction and security in exchange for hard work and loyalty;
- opportunities for self-actualization and challenging work in exchange for high productivity, high quality work and creative effort in the service of organizational goals.

Schein further stressed that the psychological contract is constantly renegotiated throughout the organizational career, as both the organization's and the individual's needs change. This can make the change process particularly difficult. A developing voluntary nonprofit organization, for example, that has had largely the same group of staff for a number of years, may have developed a particular unwritten psychological contract with staff which may include the idea that the staff have a job for life with the organization. With the loss of a major funding source, for example, and the need to make staff redundant, this break in the psychological contract may have a strong adverse effect on all staff, not just those being made redundant, because the psychological contract between the organization and the staff is being broken.

Locke's goal-setting theory

The goal-setting theory developed by Locke (1968) supports the active participation of staff (and volunteers) in strategic planning and objective setting. Research in relation to this theory (Locke *et al.* 1981; Erez and Arad 1986; Handy 1988) has shown considerable support for the theory that workers will achieve more if:

- they have clear challenging goals to achieve;
- they are involved in setting the goals themselves;
- they are provided with feedback on progress en route to the goal.

These findings support the inclusive strategic planning processes that involve staff and volunteers, as well as the board, in developing clear objectives for an organization and providing regular progress reports. Argyris (1964) argues that, when employees in an organization aren't given the opportunity to participate in defining their goals, they become passive and dependent, experiencing 'psychological failure'.

Hackman's job factors theory

Hackman and his colleagues (Hackman and Lawler 1971; Hackman and Oldham 1975, 1979) developed a more complex and refined model which shows the core job conditions that lead to critical psychological states and produce desirable outcomes. The core job dimensions, he suggests, are:

- skill variety – the job requires the performance of activities that challenge a variety of skills and abilities;
- task identity – the degree to which a job requires completion of a whole and identifiable piece of work;
- task significance – the degree to which the job has a substantial and perceived impact on the lives of other people, which may be one of the key reasons that motivation levels of those in voluntary nonprofit organizations tend to be higher than those found in other sectors;
- autonomy – the degree to which the job gives the worker freedom, independence and discretion in scheduling work and in determining how it will be carried out;
- feedback – the degree to which the worker gets information about the effectiveness of his or her efforts.

These five factors can create the situation where employees experience the meaningfulness of work, responsibility for outcome, and knowledge of the actual results of work activities. This can then in turn create high internal work motivation, high-quality work performance, high satisfaction with work, and low absenteeism and staff turnover. However, the success of the model depends on employees having the appropriate skills, being happy with the basic organizational context – the hygiene factors, and being motivated by challenge and growth.

Katz's time-in-job theory

Katz (1978) suggests that different factors will be important at different points in time. In the first six months in a job, task significance and feedback are important; from six months to five years, all the factors are important; after five years, pay and working conditions may become more important.

Group dynamics

Research on group dynamics, which started in the 1940s and reached a peak in the 1960s, has indicated that increased involvement and participation are desired by most people and have the ability to energize greater performance, produce better solutions to problems, and greatly enhance acceptance of decisions. It was found (McGrath 1984) that such group dynamics worked to:

- overcome resistance to change;
- increase commitment to the organization;
- reduce stress levels;
- generally make people feel better about themselves and their worlds.

However, Janis (1972), using the US Government's response to the Bay of Pigs situation in the early 1960s, has shown that, particularly in a group with a dominant leader, there is danger of a group descending into 'group think' where alternative perspectives on a problem are not voiced and poor decision-making can result.

Lawler's determinates of organizational effectiveness

Lawler (1986) links research into the needs and expectations of individual employees with the need for organizational effectiveness. He argues from a human resources perspective that there are five major determinates of organizational effectiveness: motivation, satisfaction, acceptance of change, problem solving, and communication; and that all of these can be positively affected by increasing the participation of the employees.

Lawler also argues that increased participation reduces the resistance to change which so often undermines an organization's efforts to implement strategic plans.

Various studies have shown that increased participation at work leads to significant improvements in both morale and productivity at the same time (for a review of the literature, see Blumberg 1968; Katzell and Yankelovich 1975). Increased participation may also lead to demands for other changes in the organization.

Strategic planning and participation

The early theories of strategic planning in the design and planning schools tended to emphasize the importance of a top-down scientific management approach, and in particular the role of the Chief Executive Officer in the planning process. As planning processes became more sophisticated, the increasing tendency in companies became to employ expert planners.

Mintzberg (1994), however, is particularly scathing about the detachment of planners from the operations of the company. He argues that it is precisely the 'soft' information that comes from a day-to-day hands-on involvement in the operational aspects of a company that is crucial to making strategic decisions. Mintzberg's emphasis on learning and visionary approaches to creating strategy requires the active involvement of managers who are crucial 'nerve centres' of information. He argues that managers must take active charge of the strategy-making process; in doing so, they must make use of their tacit knowledge; their intuitive processes must be allowed liberal rein; and they must have intimate contact with (not detachment from) the organization's operations.

Lewin *et al.* (1939), in a classic experiment comparing the impact of autocratic, democratic and *laissez-faire* leadership styles in boys' clubs, found that the democratic leadership style was preferred and produced a more positive group climate. Maier (1967) found that effective leaders are concerned with both the task to be performed and the group process, and they enlist the involvement of the group in the management of both. Bass (1970), in a series of experiments, showed that people were more productive and more satisfied when they operated their own plans instead of other people's. He suggested various reasons for this:

- Productivity and satisfaction are lower when planning for others because the sense of accomplishment is less when executing someone else's plan.
- There is less tendency to try to confirm the validity of another's plan by executing it successfully – less confidence that it can be done.
- There is less commitment to see that the plan works well.
- There is less flexibility and less room for modification and initiative to make improvements in an assigned plan.
- There is less understanding of an assigned plan.
- Human resources are not so well utilized.
- There are more communication problems and consequent errors and distortions in following instructions.
- There are competitive feelings aroused between planners and doers to such an extent that it appears that if the former 'win' the latter 'lose'.

For all these reasons, many of the recent texts on strategic planning and strategic management emphasize the value of wide participation in the processes of strategic analysis, formation and choice, in order to improve both the quality of the strategic decisions and the likelihood that plans will be implemented effectively.

This emphasis on wide participation, providing clear goals which clarify the positive impact that the work has on people, and on regular feedback, is particularly evident in the literature on planning and management in the voluntary nonprofit sector, and emphasizes the need to establish strategic management processes that actively involve the board, managers, staff, volunteers and other stakeholders, if they are to be committed to making any plan into a reality.

Grewe *et al.* (1989) promote a participative approach to planning, which they argue has benefits for the participants which are as important as the contents of the plan, because it promotes a common vision of the future and its implications for the organization, including any necessary changes, more effective group problem-solving skills, and recognition that continuous planning is a management necessity. As Hudson (1995) argues, 'participation and communication processes are particularly important in value-led organisations. People who believe in the cause want to know what other parts of the organisation are doing and they want to participate in decision-making.'

The Human Resources movement played an important role in the development of particular methodologies for bringing large numbers of people together in order to engage whole systems in creating rapid change (Bunker and Alban 1997). Some of these (Search Conference, Emery and Purser 1996, and Future Search, Weisbrod and Janoff 1995) have been used frequently as community development tools as for organizational development. The Strategic Planning Process of the ICA (Institute of Cultural Affairs, which operates in the USA and Canada), in particular, has been used extensively in the USA and Canada as a community development technique to involve large numbers of people in the community in a change process. It involves the six key steps (Spencer 1989) listed here:

1   Focus on the key issue, question or problem.
2   Map out a clear practical vision.
3   Analyse the obstacles to achieving the vision.
4   Set the strategic directions (brainstorm for overcoming obstacles).
5   Design the systematic actions/strategies to achieve the vision.
6   Draw up an agreed-upon time line for implementation.

Letts *et al.* (1998), in *High performance nonprofit organisations: Managing upstream for greater impact*, argue that investing in the development of the internal capacity of voluntary nonprofit organizations and not just in specific programmes is crucial to their success. In particular, they argue that investing strategically in human resource management is especially important.

Webster and Wylie (1988), from their research on the use of strategic planning techniques in the voluntary nonprofit sector, suggest that a wider level of consultation can also have another kind of impact. In particular they show that the wider the level of participation the less likely it is that there will be a 'major change outcome', as the process is likely to involve a process which will produce a compromise solution which is acceptable to all the participants.

Resource-based theories of strategy

There is, however, an even more fundamental perspective on the role of human (and other) resources in relation to strategy. Resource-based theories of strategy start from the perspective that the resources of an organization are the principal source of competitive advantage (Wernerfelt 1984; Peteraf 1993; Dierickx and Cool 1989; Kay 1994). Strategy should therefore start with a consideration of the distinctive resources of the organization, rather than the conventional view that resources should only be considered in assessing the organization's ability to implement the desired strategy.

The resource-based view distinguishes between those resources that are readily available to all organizations and those that are distinct or unique to a particular organization, and which therefore should be carefully analysed and nurtured. Various criteria have been suggested for determining that a particular resource provides competitive advantage:

- it already exists in the organization;
- it provides innovative capability;
- it proves a real advantage over other organizations;
- it is difficult to substitute for or imitate;
- the advantage will accrue to the organization;
- the resource has durability.

John Kay (1994) suggests that distinctive capabilities relate particularly to three resource areas:

1 innovation capability;
2 reputation, particularly for quality;
3 architecture, in the sense of the network of long-term relationships and contracts.

Hamel and Prahalad (1994) argue that three areas distinguish what they call core competencies:

1 they must make a real impact on how the customer perceives the organization and its services (or products);

2   they must be unique, or at least really special;
3   they need to be able to be extended to new services (or products).

More recently the importance of knowledge to organizations has come to the fore as being critical to the success of an organization. This knowledge may be in a patent or the particular practices of an organization, but it also may reside in the people in the organization. This is likely to be true in many voluntary nonprofit organizations where much of the knowledge is not routinized but resides in the heads of the trustees, staff and/or volunteers. This is also a danger, as the individuals with the knowledge in their heads may leave and take that knowledge with them. The organization needs to ensure that the distinctive knowledge that exists is retained and nurtured.

The significance of all this for the strategic management of organizations, particularly voluntary nonprofit organizations, is that the human resource requirements do not necessarily simply follow the determination of organizational strategy (Chandler 1962's 'structure follows strategy'), but that the people and their distinctive competencies within the organization are a vital asset to the organization, which should provide important clues to where the organization is likely to be most effective in future and therefore the organization's strategic direction.

Summary

This chapter has explored organizations and strategy from a human resource perspective, which coincides with the culture of many voluntary nonprofit organizations. This perspective emphasizes the positive role of people in an organization. Research which demonstrates the positive effect of participation and consultation on job performance and satisfaction has been highlighted, suggesting that more participative approaches to strategic management are also likely to be effective. The resource-based view of strategy has also been discussed which suggests that the distinctive or core competencies in an organization, many of which reside in the heads of its staff (and its volunteers), are crucially important in determining the most appropriate future strategy of an organization.

Questions

1   What are the key factors that motivate staff in voluntary nonprofit organizations?
2   Are the motivations of volunteers different from those of paid staff in voluntary nonprofit organizations?
3   Do comparatively poor salaries and working conditions matter in the voluntary nonprofit sector? If so why?

4 Are there limitations, or potentially negative consequences, to the involvement of staff and volunteers in the strategic management of voluntary nonprofit organizations?

5 Does the Human Resources School support or contradict the design and planning school's emphasis on developing a hierarchy of goals and objectives?

6 How should voluntary nonprofit organizations manage their knowledge?

7 List the distinctive or core competencies/capabilities/resources of a voluntary nonprofit organization that you know.

Suggested reading

Sheila Hayward (1996) *Applying psychology to organisations*, Hodder & Stoughton.
Edgar Schein (1988) *Organisational psychology*, 3rd edn, Prentice-Hall.
Peter Warr (ed.) (1996) *Psychology at work*, Penguin.

8 Post-modern perspectives on strategy

Chapter outline

This chapter explores further the criticisms of the traditional schools of strategic management and discusses a number of alternative perspectives, particularly the Learning and the Political Schools. The more pragmatic 'new modernist' approaches to strategy in the 1990s, which are closer to the values and culture of many voluntary nonprofit organizations, are also explored.

Learning objectives

When you have completed this chapter you should understand:

- the perceived weaknesses in the classic rational approaches to strategy;
- the importance of continuous learning and experimentation at all levels within an organization reflected in the Learning School;
- the bounded rationality of strategic decision-making and the importance of power and negotiation in the strategic choices that are made;
- the main characteristics of the pragmatic 'new modernist' approach to strategy being adopted in the 1990s.

Introduction

Mintzberg (1994) argues that, while planning is important, an overemphasis on detailed formal long-range planning can push out other processes that are equally important. In particular, the creation and development of powerful visions can become ossified into rigid strategic positions, without the flexibility to respond to change. Quinn came to a similar conclusion:

> [A] good deal of corporate planning I have observed is like a ritual raindance; it has no effect on the weather that follows, but those who engage in it think it does. Moreover, it seems to me that much of the advice and

instruction related to corporate planning is directed at improving the dancing, not the weather.

(quoted in Mintzberg 1994)

In the traditional top-down rigid planning approaches, the process of continuous learning can also be lost, pushed out by long-range forecasts, one-, three- or five-year planning cycles, etc., which allow for little flexibility. Both Mintzberg (1994) and Stacey (1993) argue for the crucial importance of learning (discovery, choice and action) in the continuous process of making strategic decisions. Mintzberg, indeed, argues that even the basic terminology surrounding strategy formulation is unhelpful. He sees it as much more of an art form, a craft like that of a potter. In crafting strategy (Mintzberg 1987), 'what springs to mind is not so much thinking and reason as involvement, a feeling of intimacy and harmony with the materials at hand developed through long experience and commitment. Formulation and implementation merge into a fluid process of learning through which creative strategies evolve.'

As well as various pitfalls to avoid in strategic planning, Mintzberg (1994) argues that traditional strategic planning is based on a number of fundamental and inter-related fallacies:

1   The assumption of detachment – that planners not involved in the operational aspects of the organization can successfully craft strategy. Mintzberg argues that they can't, as they don't have a real intuitive feel for the business. Carr (1996) argues that 'strategic planning failed in part because companies relegated it to its own department, where it became increasingly irrelevant to the real life and problems of the company'.
2   The assumption of quantification – that strategy can be driven by hard facts about the organization and its environment when strategy is about creating something new, which requires intuition based as much on 'soft' information.
3   The assumption of pre-determinism – that it is in any way possible to predict the consequences of any particular action.
4   The assumption of formalization – that the strategy-making process can be programmed by the use of systems rather than the vision and learning of those deeply involved in the business.

Harvey-Jones, a former Chief Executive of ICI, for example, has described the implementation of strategic planning at its height as follows:

In many organizations planning became the job and responsibility of an increasingly specialized planning department, who were divorced from the everyday business and sought to apply theoretical measures of a quantified type to the complexities of business decisions All too often in those days one was faced with plans produced by the staff that

seemed somewhat remote or at variance with one's own experience of
the actual behaviour of the market in which one was operating. But
another and even more worrying variant of the same problem arose
when the plans laid would have been helpful in a business sense, but
were not followed because of the illusive lack of commitment in a
decentralized organization.

(Harvey-Jones 1987)

Ohmae (1982) even compared the state of strategic planning at the
beginning of the 1980s with the kind of centralized planning of the Soviet
economy:

We have all witnessed the heyday of the giant enterprise, the days when
it seemed that big US companies, and later big European companies,
could really end up controlling the whole world. Something happened to
prevent it. There has been a marked decline in the ability of large corporations to cope with the changes that confront them. In these companies,
brains and muscles were separated, destroying the entire body's co-ordi-
nation. On the one hand there were the brains; on the other there was
the muscle – the people of the enterprise. They were there to make the
plan a reality, to carry out the brain's instructions....In effect, most large
US corporations are run like the Soviet economy. Many are centrally
planned for three to five years, with their managers' actions spelled out
in impressive detail for both normal and contingency conditions. During
the ongoing implementation process, each manager is 'monitored' on
how accurately he has been adhering to the agreed objectives. Long
study of communist and socialist regimes has convinced many observers
that detailed long-range planning coupled with tight control from the
center is a remarkably effective way of killing creativity and
entrepreneurship at the extremities of the organization.

(Ohmae 1982)

These quotes reinforce the suggestion that the failure of strategic planning in the late 1980s was caused by the area becoming top-down,
technique-ridden and divorced from the day-to-day management process.

Steiner (1979) argues that the problems were caused by:

- planning being delegated to planners, top management failing to spend
  time themselves on long-range planning;
- the process being over-formalized and driving out innovation;
- planning processes used not being regularly monitored and reviewed;
- top managers ignoring the plan in practice and making intuitive decisions;
- poor-quality goal-setting, and failure to use the plan as a framework for
  reviewing management performance.

The impact of this kind of rigid approach in practice, the lack of consistent evidence for its effectivenes, theoretical difficulties in supporting strategic planning and the increasing turbulence of the external environment, led, in the 1980s, to strategy falling down the agenda of private sector companies. In a 1996 survey of a hundred Chief Executives of top UK and US companies, 'Future Strategy' only ranked sixth on their agenda. Only fourteen put strategy on the top of their list.

Much of the focus in the difficult economic circumstances in the West in the early 1990s moved to cost-cutting programmes, such as re-engineering (Hammer and Champy 1993), downsizing, and delayering, what Hamel and Prahalad (1994) call 'corporate anorexia'. The consequence of this shift over a significant period, according to Kare-Silver (1997), was that the art of future planning and strategy was lost and the in-house skills were no longer there to revive it. Kare-Silver argued that much of the difficulty with strategic planning and management was the use of models and tools that were out of date, having been developed for a different era. This view is supported by a survey made by the Kalkas Group in 1995 of senior managers and CEOs in the UK and USA which showed a low opinion of popular strategic planning and management tools, and that a majority felt that some new model was required.

Stacey, Professor in Strategic Management at the University of Hertfordshire Business School, however, went further and argued (1993) that the fundamental assumptions underlying traditional strategic planning, based on cybernetics, the study of artificial or natural systems which store information and use feedback mechanisms to guide and control their behaviour, are fundamentally flawed. He argued that the system that managers have to cope with is too complex to allow them fully to intend the future strategic direction of their organization. In other words, the complexity of the system is such that new strategic direction can only emerge, which is close to Mintzberg's concept of crafting strategy.

The Learning School

Quinn's work, mentioned above on page 94, is often described as being in the Incremental or Learning School. Like the Attributes of Excellence School, adherents to the Incremental or Learning School are not convinced that the classical rational deliberate approaches to strategy formation represented by the Design, Planning and Positioning Schools represent the truth as to how strategy is actually developed in organizations.

It was actually research in the public sector, 'The science of muddling through' (Lindblom 1959), that initiated this school. Lindblom suggested that policy-making in the public sector is not a neat rational linear process, but a messy one in which policymakers struggle with making sense of a world that is too complicated. Key to this school is a descriptive rather than prescriptive approach. The adherents to this approach suggest that major strategic moves rarely occur as a result of a structured strategic planning process, but can rather be traced back to small actions or decisions by actors who may not even be senior in the organization. This suggests a definition of strategy as 'pattern' (Mintzberg 1994) rather than plan.

From interviews with the Chief Executives of large companies in the USA, Quinn (1980) concluded that planning did not describe how they formulated their strategies. In contrast, he coined the expression 'logical incrementalism', drawing on Lindblom, to describe the process where

> Real strategy tends to evolve as internal decisions and external events flow together to create a new, widely shared consensus for action among key members of the top management team. In well-run organizations, managers pro-actively guide these streams of actions and events incrementally towards conscious strategies...successful managers who operate with logical incrementalism build the seeds of understanding, identity and commitment into the very processes that create their strategies. By the time the strategy begins to crystallize in focus, pieces of it are already being implemented. Through their strategic formulation processes, they have built a momentum and psychological commitment to the strategy, which causes it to flow toward flexible implementation. Constantly integrating the simultaneous incremental processes of strategy formulation and implementation is the central art of effective strategic management.
>
> (Quinn 1980)

Quinn, however, in keeping with the approaches of the Design, Planning and Positioning Schools, views the senior managers and the CEO as the key actors in the strategy process.

Other writers have focused on the important role of innovation within an organization, what has been called 'internal venturing', or 'intrapreneurship' (Pinchot 1985) involving the initiatives and skills of people who act deep within the corporate hierarchy.

Strategic initiatives, according to Burgelman (1980), often develop deep in the hierarchy and are then championed, or given impetus, by middle-level managers who seek the authorization of senior executives. He stresses the importance of these individuals at the operational level in the organization who often initiate the first step in the innovative process. Previous work on corporate strategy had tended to ignore their role by focusing almost entirely on senior management, particularly the CEO.

In the Learning School, top management still has a crucial role in creating the environment where this internal venturing can flourish, where innovation could take place with the support of management, and where new corporate competencies can be developed.

Centralized strategic planning and the emergent learning perspectives, although often presented as being in opposition to each other, are not necessarily entirely contradictory. The central top-down umbrella strategy (Mintzberg and Waters 1997) may establish the space, support and culture within which bottom-up experimentation and learning can take place and enable strategies to emerge and become key strategies for the future (Anderson 2000). In the words of Eccles and Nohria (1997)

> Strategy is a messy combination of both these perspectives...rational, top-down 'strategic plans' *can* effectively set the context for individual action. But people in firms always pursue their own strategic agendas as well, and many of these autonomous initiatives can end up as an important part of firm-wide strategy. Formal plans must be flexible enough to accommodate these emergent actions, which typically rely on individual intuition, timing and circumstances.

While the rational prescriptive strategy schools are primarily about planning and control, this new emergent school is very much about learning at the individual, team and corporate level in an organization through experimentation and discovery (Bartlett and Ghoshal 1998).

Mintzberg (Mintzberg *et al.* 1998) has postulated a grassroots model of strategic formation. In this model, strategies grow like weeds in a garden: they are not cultivated like tomatoes in a hothouse. They can take root in all kinds of places, virtually anywhere people have the capacity to learn and the resources to support that capacity. Such strategies become organizational when they become collective, i.e. when the patterns proliferate, consciously or unconsciously, to pervade the behaviour of the organization at large. New strategies which may be emerging continuously tend to pervade the organization during periods of change, which punctuate periods of more integrated continuity. To manage this process is not to preconceive strategies but to recognize their emergence and intervene when appropriate.

Literature on organizations as learning systems goes back to the early 1960s with Cyert and March's *A behavioural theory of the firm* (1963) and was further developed in the 1970s, particularly by Argyris and Schon (1978) who put forward the concepts of single- and double-loop learning. Single-loop learning reflects the traditional approach to strategy where the only learning is how to take corrective action to ensure the implementation of agreed goals. Double-loop learning allows a much wider scope to learning which can result in fundamental changes to goals and values. They also suggest a third level, deutero-learning, which encourages enquiry into the learning system itself.

Building on the approach of Argyris and Schon, Peter Senge in his highly influential *The fifth discipline* (1990) argues that organizations that will truly excel in future will be 'the organisations that discover how to tap people's commitment and capacity to learn at all levels in an organisation'. He suggests that the key elements of the learning organization are:

- systems thinking – recognizing that organizations are complex systems;
- personal mastery – not only the development of particular work-related skills, but also the transformation of individuals so they accomplish things they really care about;
- mental models – the organization's driving and fundamental values and principles;
- shared vision – the co-creation of a shared vision of the future;
- team learning – the process of dialogue and discussion, to explore new ideas creatively and then narrow them down to choose the best alternatives.

Senge generated a new interest in the concept of the learning company. He considered that there are three key roles for a leader:

1 as a designer of the mission, vision and values of the organization and the structures and policies that create learning;
2 as teacher, in the sense of helping everyone gain new insights;
3 as steward, bringing stewardship for the people being led and stewardship for the wider mission of the organization.

In Senge's words, 'people's natural impulse to learn is unleashed when they are engaged in an endeavour they consider worthy of their fullest commitment', a perspective that would be endorsed strongly by the nonprofit sector.

Lampel, in Mintzberg *et al.* (1998), summarizes the main principles of the learning school as follows:

- organizations can learn as much, if not more, from failure as from success;
- a learning organization rejects the adage 'if it ain't broke, don't fix it';
- learning organizations assume that the managers and workers closest to the design, manufacturing, distribution and sale of the product often know more about these activities than their superiors;
- a learning organization actively seeks to move knowledge from one part of the organization to another;
- learning organizations spend a lot of energy looking outside their own boundaries for knowledge.

The Learning School perspective provides a useful counterbalance to the mechanistic approaches of the classic rational planning schools, and as such is a useful perspective for the voluntary nonprofit sector. However, there is also the danger of going too far in the other direction. The development of a large number of innovations and experiments can result in a lack of direction, without a clear vision. In a crisis, in particular, muddling through without a clear unified vision of the future can be a disaster. There is also the danger of strategic drift, where the organization, over time, moves away from an effective strategy towards a less desirable one, as a result of a series of small steps (e.g. following inappropriate funding opportunities: what Handy (1988) calls 'strategic seduction').

It is also important not to ignore the real issues of power and self-interest in an organization which may influence which innovations are promoted and which are not. Indeed the Learning School has been criticized for ignoring power issues and suggesting that a learning organization is 'a utopia to be ushered in through the pursuit of shared goals in a climate of collaborative high trust and a rational approach to the resolution of differences' (Coopey 1995), whereas 'what is deemed worth learning has already been selected, because only those in power learn the right things' (Gherardi 1999).

In the learning organization the legitimization of learning is determined by the criteria for organizational success (Garrick and Rhodes 1998). Staff are encouraged to identify with the goals of the organization and to give full commitment to learning to achieve these goals. This is a common aspiration of many voluntary nonprofit organizations. However, real learning may result in a questioning of the legitimacy, not only of these goals, but also of the dominant modes of thought and power structures in the organization. This is reminiscent of Argyris and Schon's double-loop learning (1978).

The Political School

A further difficulty with the rational structural approach to strategic management is that it ignores the power realities within organizations and therefore the realities of decision-making. A different perspective on organizations is that they are political structures whereby decisions are determined not by rational analysis but by negotiation between the various power blocs.

According to this paradigm (Cyert and March 1963; Bolman and Deal 1991), strategic decision-making within an organization is little to do with the rational strategic management theories and a lot to do with this power-brokering within the 'alive and screaming' political arenas within organizations. As Scottish sociologist Tom Burns (1961) has pointed out, most modern organizations promote various kinds of politicking because they are designed as systems of simultaneous competition and collaboration. People must collaborate in pursuit of a common task, yet are often pitted against each other in competition for limited resources, status and career advancement.

If strategic decision-making is purely about power-broking, then is there any value in any form of strategic planning as we normally understand it and is it appropriate for the voluntary nonprofit sector? Hudson (1995) argues that, in fact, strategy is particularly important in voluntary nonprofit organizations precisely because 'they are always coalitions of people with different aspirations that need to be integrated for the organisation to thrive'. Strategy planning can therefore be seen as the process of bringing the various stakeholders together to negotiate an agreed future for the organization. This can recognize the power of each of the stakeholder groups, but also promote an active participation of all stakeholders in a 'bounded rationality'.

The new pragmatism

With the availability of so many different approaches to strategy, all with their proponents and detractors, it is difficult for those with responsibility for the management and development of their organizations to make decisions about which approach is best. It is likely, however, that there is no one best way.

The Contingency School of strategic management may be helpful in getting away from an either/or dilemma between the traditional technocratic approach to strategic planning and the experimental emergent approaches of the post-modernists.

Ansoff and McDonnell (1990) show how different approaches to strategy can be appropriate in different situations, depending particularly on the extent of turbulence, novelty and complexity in the external environment. In a stable, relatively simple environment a traditional planning approach may be appropriate. In environments which are highly complex and discontinuous a more experimental, spontaneous, learning approach may be more appropriate. This enables the various approaches to strategic management to 'co-exist in tension with each other' (Joyce and Woods 1996) rather than one paradigm replacing another.

In the voluntary nonprofit sector it is likely that different kinds of voluntary nonprofit organizations with stable or turbulent environments may require different approaches. This may change over time, too. Even within a single voluntary nonprofit organization it may be that the approach to strategy in relation to resource acquisition, e.g. fundraising, may need to be much more akin to the traditional strategic approach and language (target markets, competitors, return on investment, etc.) of private companies because of the high level of competition for funds. However, in relation to the provision of human services to a particular client group in a particular geographical area, particularly where there is an element of mutual aid involved, the environment may be more stable with much less competition. In this kind of context, participation, collaboration, learning, capacity-building, internal negotiation, influencing, living the values, and incremental development are likely to be the key aspects of strategy development.

The increasing realization in all sectors of the value of a strategic management approach which avoids the rigid, linear, technocratic and top-down approaches of the past has led to the development of a range of 'new modernist' or pragmatic approaches.

Van der Heijden (1996), Professor of General and Strategic Management at the Graduate Business School, Strathclyde University, for example, argues for the importance of bringing people together to engage in 'the art of strategic conversation'. He suggests a process in which managers can share their own intuitive thoughts and ideas – their own visions and dreams – in a way that uses what has been learnt. They can explore various possible scenarios for the organization and allow a consensus to develop that will create a viable way forward for the organization that can be continually reviewed, and adapted or transformed as appropriate.

It has been argued that the best metaphor for this new approach is jazz (Perry *et al.* 1993; Vaill 1990; Kao, quoted in Micklethwaite and Wooldridge 1996). In contrast to an orchestra, where everyone plays exactly what is on the score to the strict direction of the conductor whose back is turned to the audience, a jazz group improvises around basic patterns, keys and rhythms. In jazz the emphasis is on participation, creativity, innovation and effective and immediate communication.

This re-invention of strategic planning as 'strategic thinking', 'strategic learning' or 'strategic improvising' resulted in a major resurgence of interest in strategy in the second half of the 1990s, coinciding with a major period of growth in the economies of the USA and the UK. In 1996, *Business Week* announced that 'strategic planning is back', explaining that there was a new interest in strategic planning in the boardrooms of the day. In a survey of global companies by Bain and Co. in 1998, more than 80 per cent of the companies were engaging in strategic planning, with a satisfaction level of over 95 per cent. Ninety per cent also have mission and value statements with a satisfaction level of 93 per cent.

Characteristics of the new pragmatic approach

While retaining much of what is best about the traditional approaches to strategic management, the key characteristics of the new, more pragmatic or 'new modernist' approach seem to be the following:

- wide participation of staff, trustees and volunteers in reflecting on strategic issues rather than a top-down approach (Hatten 1982; Bunker and Alban 1997);
- creating a continuous process of experimentation and learning (Senge 1990; Argyris and Schon 1978; Nonaka 1991; Burgoyne *et al.* 1994);
- participation of a wider range of stakeholders (Freeman 1984; Bryson 1995);
- recognition of the need to negotiate between the various sources of power, inside and outside an organization (Bolman and Deal 1991; Pfeffer and Salancik 1978);
- focusing on key strategic issues, or change challenges (Ansoff and McDonnell 1990; Edwards and Eadie 1994);

- taking into account a range of potential future external scenarios (Schwartz 1992; de Geus 1988; Van der Heijden 1996);
- creating strong motivating visions, i.e. strategic intent, which enables the organization and its people to 'live deeply in the future while gaining the courage to act boldly in the present' (Hamel and Prahalad 1994; Collins and Porras 1994);
- creating a clear value base for the ethical management of the company (Collins and Porras 1994; Jones and Pollitt 1998);
- strategic thinking as a continual process, not just an annual cycle (Taylor 1992);
- strategic processes which produce common-sense frameworks which will help managers make decisions;
- innovation, experimentation and creativity are encouraged and supported (Quinn 1980; Pinchot 1985; Burgelman 1988; Senge 1990).

This approach is very different from some of the traditional mechanistic top-down strategic planning approaches that have been heavily criticized, and is much more in tune with the culture and values of the voluntary nonprofit sector.

Summary

This chapter has explored many of the critiques of traditional top-down strategic planning approaches, often carried out by detached expert planners. In contrast, this chapter has explored a number of other approaches including the Learning and Political Schools. Recognition has been given to the fact that different approaches may be appropriate for different situations, even different parts of the same organization. Finally, the key characteristics of the 'new pragmatism' approach to strategic management are highlighted which reflect many of the values and culture of the voluntary nonprofit sector.

Questions

1 What are the weaknesses of the classic rational approaches to strategic management?
2 What are the best ways that an organization can develop a learning culture?
3 To what extent is the Learning School in conflict with the classic rational approaches?
4 To what extent is decision-making in an organization rational?
5 Where are the main power blocs in a voluntary nonprofit organization likely to be?

6   What are the main characteristics of the pragmatic 'new modernist' approach to strategic management?

7   To what extent does the pragmatic 'new modernist' approach to strategic management reflect the culture and values of the voluntary nonprofit sector?

Suggested reading

James C. Collins and Jerry I. Porras (1994) *Built to last: Successful habits of visionary companies*, Random House.

Gary Hamel and C. K. Prahalad (1994) *Competing for the future*, Harvard Business School Press.

Henry Mintzberg, Bruce Ahlstrand and Joseph Lampel (1998) *Strategy safari: A guided tour throught the wilds of strategic management*, Prentice-Hall.

Part III

Strategy and the voluntary nonprofit sector

9 The development of strategic management in the voluntary nonprofit sector

Chapter outline

This chapter explores the development of the use of strategic management models and techniques in the voluntary nonprofit sector from the 1970s to the present day and some of the constraints in its development in the sector. Research in the voluntary nonprofit sectors in the UK and the USA on the use of strategic management models and tools is highlighted.

Learning objectives

When you have completed this chapter you should understand:

- the factors that may constrain the development of strategic management in the voluntary nonprofit sector;
- the nature of the literature on strategic management in the voluntary nonprofit sector;
- some of the strategic management tools and techniques used by voluntary nonprofit organizations;
- the extent and nature of strategic management in national UK voluntary nonprofit organizations;
- key tools and techniques used by US voluntary nonprofit organizations.

Introduction

Around the time that strategic planning was starting to be perceived in the private sector with less than the enthusiasm it had become used to in the late 1960s and early 1970s, the voluntary nonprofit sector began to explore the potentialities of strategic planning models and techniques.

In 1976, Charles Hofer, a leading scholar in the field of strategic management, published a review of research on strategic planning and throughout remarked on the lack of research into 'nonbusiness organisations'.

However, with the increasing use of strategic management models and techniques in the voluntary nonprofit sector in the 1970s, literature on strategic planning in the nonprofit sector started to appear in the late 1970s, particularly in the USA. A range of publications and articles was produced which exhorted the sector to adopt the strategic planning and management techniques that have been used (successfully, they would argue) in the private sector (Firstenberg 1979; Keating 1979; Selby 1978; Steiner 1979; Drucker 1980; Greenberg 1982; Unterman and Davies 1982; Hatten 1982; Steiner *et al.* 1994). Karger and Malik (1975), for example, having demonstrated, as they saw it, the effectiveness of formal integrated long-range planning in the private sector, confidently predicted that 'future research will undoubtedly further emphasise the importance of such planning for both profit seeking and non-profit organisations'. Much of this literature reflected a preoccupation with the similarities and differences between the private (profit) and voluntary nonprofit sectors (Cyert 1975).

The timing of the development of literature on management techniques in the private and later the voluntary nonprofit sectors is interesting, and would suggest a time lag between the two of approximately fifteen years. The literature on strategic planning in the private sector developed in the mid-1960s and equivalent literature in relation to the nonprofit sector began in the late 1970s.

Unterman and Davies (1982), in their study of 102 voluntary nonprofit organizations in the USA and their boards of trustees, concluded that

> not only have NFP (not-for-profit) organizations failed to reach the strategic management stage of development, but many of them have failed to reach even the Strategic Planning stages that for-profit enterprises initiated 15 to 20 years ago.

Ayal (1986) suggested that the reason for the long time lag between the use of strategic planning techniques in the private sector and the nonprofit sector was the fact that

> [t]he mission for many nonprofit organisations is rather diffuse, and goals and objectives are multiple and more difficult to define; nonprofit organisations, more than the typical business firm, have multiple constituencies, frequently with conflicting goals. Resolution and decision making is usually 'political' in nature, and thus less amenable to formal planning; and leadership in many nonprofit organisations is volunteer, changes frequently, and though usually highly devoted, frequently lacks the time, staff, and other resources required for a proper strategic planning job.

Newman and Wallender (1978) identified a number of factors which have constrained the development of rational planning in voluntary nonprofit organizations. These are:

1 Service is intangible and hard to measure. This difficulty is often compounded by the existence of multiple service objectives (see also Kanter and Summers 1987).
2 Customer influence may be weak. Often the enterprise has a local monopoly and payments by customers may be a secondary source of funds.
3 Strong employee commitment to professions or to a cause may undermine their allegiance to the enterprise.
4 Resource contributors may intrude into internal management – notably fund contributors and government (see also Wortman 1981).
5 Restraints on the use of rewards and punishments result from factors 1, 3 and 4 above.
6 Charismatic leaders and/or the mystique of the enterprise may be important means of resolving conflict in objectives and overcoming restraints.

These very much reflect the discussion in Chapter 4 about the perceived differences between the for-profit and voluntary nonprofit sectors.

Others have pointed to the difficulties presented by the existence of multiple stakeholders in voluntary nonprofit organizations (McLaughlin 1986; Bryson 1995; Rochester 1995). O'Neill and Young (1988) highlight the particular need for 'people skills' as well as planning skills in the nonprofit sector.

In considering the differences between the private and voluntary nonprofit sectors (discussed extensively in Chapter 4), some writers and researchers have suggested that strategic management techniques are, indeed, relevant to the voluntary nonprofit sector, but need to be adapted to the particular circumstances and values of the sector (Steiner *et al.* 1994; Bryson 1995; Setterberg and Schulman 1991; Chauhan 1998; Kearns 2000; Lindenberg 2001). Others have gone further and suggested that the differences between the sectors mean that the 'generic concept of formal planning may have limited use for voluntary organisations which have value-based goals and missions' (Gerard 1983). Walker (1983) suggests that following a 'rational model of planning in the voluntary/non-profit sector may be dysfunctional as it may be subverted by those in the organisation committed to its ideological belief systems'.

Salipante and Golden-Biddle (1995) argue that the enduring nature of needs and the missions of voluntary nonprofit organizations make strategic planning approaches inappropriate because they imply that there is scope for substantial organizational change. Private sector organizations can change to producing very different products or services if they think it will be more profitable, but this is inappropriate for voluntary nonprofit organizations which are much more constrained by their founding documents and missions.

Fundamental differences with the for-profit sector, and that sector's own experiences, make it unwise for nonprofit leaders to adopt business organisations' externally focused approach to strategic change. Theories of organisational survival and punctuated equilibrium models of change and continuity, as well as the authors' research, suggest that planning aimed toward matching the organisation to changes in its environment has limited value...due to the relative constancy of societal needs and nonprofits' missions and the importance of society's demands for reliable, accountable performance, nonprofits should greatly value continuity...potential organisational change should be approached cautiously with a strong regard for traditionality.

(Salipante and Golden-Biddle 1995)

Other researchers have pointed to the changes that have taken place in the approaches to strategic management in the private sector, which have moved much closer to the ethos of the voluntary nonprofit sector in relation to values such as social responsibility, multiple stakeholders, ethical values, non-executive directors and participation, for example (see discussion of the new modernist, pragmatic approach to strategy discussed in Chapter 8).

However, as we have seen, there is extensive literature, particularly from the USA, which argues for the benefits of using strategic management techniques, originally developed in the private sector, in the voluntary nonprofit sector. The potential benefits from the use of strategic planning tools and techniques in the voluntary nonprofit sector have been summarized (Courtney 1996) as follows:

- opportunities are identified, evaluated and capitalized on;
- threats are identified, evaluated and avoided or, where they cannot be avoided, their impact can be minimized;
- contingency plans can be established for what to do in the event of a potential threat actually being realized;
- different scenarios can be explored, so an organization can be prepared for different eventualities;
- internal strengths and unique selling points are identified and built on;
- internal weaknesses are identified, and corrected, compensated for or the impact of them minimized;
- the purpose and direction of the organization is clarified so everyone is pulling in the same direction;
- the distinct culture/values/principles of the organization (i.e. 'the way we do things round here') is clarified and built on;
- clear, achievable objectives and standards are identified that people can work towards and know if they have been achieved;

- donors/funders can be given the opportunity to invest in the creation of a clear and positive vision of the future, and they know what their funding will achieve;
- limited material and financial resources can be targeted on clear priorities;
- the morale of trustees, staff and volunteers is likely to improve with clearer goals and achievements;
- the human resource strategy of the organization can be focused on achieving specific organizational goals;
- progress can be regularly and clearly monitored, because it is clear what the organization is trying to achieve.

While much of the early literature on strategy in the voluntary nonprofit sector challenged the sector to examine their approaches to management and planning and to adopt more professional management methods, it was not backed up with sound empirical evidence. It tended to make the assumption that the voluntary nonprofit sector could and should uncritically copy the models and techniques of the profit-making sector without an analysis of the appropriateness of the models and tools to the sector.

'How-to' literature

A body of 'how-to' literature on strategic planning in the voluntary nonprofit sector was also developed in the 1980s and 1990s which draws particularly on the techniques and models used in the private sector.

This 'how-to' literature in the voluntary nonprofit sector has demonstrated a considerable consensus in its use of relevant models and concepts, particularly SWOT analysis, environmental scanning, mission, vision, values, aims, objectives, performance indicators and key results areas.

Other techniques have been particularly adapted for use in the voluntary nonprofit sector (see Chapters 12 and 13), including the following:

- PEST (Jain and Surendra 1977);
- Ansoff's matrix (Courtney 1996);
- Porter's industry analysis (Oster 1995);
- Portfolio analysis of the Boston Consultancy Group (Gruber and Mohr 1982; Bryson 1995; Nutt and Backoff 1992; Lawrie 1994; Courtney 1996; Roller 1996; Bovaird and Rubienska 1996).

Other strategy tools have been developed for use in the public and/or the nonprofit sector (see Chapter 12). Bryson, Professor of Planning and Public Affairs at the University of Minneapolis, has highlighted (1988) three other techniques that are particularly useful in the public and nonprofit sectors:

1   mandate analysis, which looks at the written mandates that the organization has from legislation, constitutions, trust deeds, public policy documents, research reports, funding agreements, etc.;

2   stakeholder analysis (Freeman 1984), which explores the expectations of the organization's beneficiaries, funders, volunteers, staff, regulatory bodies, etc., and what needs to be done to meet these expectations;

3   identifying strategic issues that may have an impact on the ability of an organization to meet its aims and therefore requires urgent action (Bryson 1988; Nutt and Backoff 1992; Ansoff and McDonnell 1990; Edwards and Eadie 1994).

These tools and techniques are discussed in detail in Chapters 12 and 13 in the course of analysing the organization and its external environment. Some of the early publications that advised voluntary nonprofit organizations on how they should be planning and managing their own futures included: Wortman (1979); Hatten (1982); Ring and Perry (1985); Setterberg and Schulman (1985); Barry (1986); Bryson (1988); Koteen (1989); Nutt and Backoff (1992).

These are all American publications. A British guide to the literature on the management of voluntary nonprofit organizations, *Organising voluntary agencies* by Harris and Billis, published in 1986, makes no mention of strategic planning for the sector. The UK literature really only began to come into its own in the 1990s with the publication of the following, mainly by consultants working in the nonprofit sector in Britain: Web (1990); Barnard and Walker (1994); Lawrie (1994); and a number of books focused more broadly on voluntary sector management by practitioners and consultants working specifically in the nonprofit sector (Hudson 1995; Courtney 1996; Osborne 1996; Hind 1995).

The time lag (two decades) between a strategic planning approach being used by voluntary nonprofit organizations in Britain and in the USA is similar to the time lag before British private sector organizations would adopt the strategic planning approaches developed in the 1960s and 1970s by American writers such as Ansoff, Andrews and Porter, and indicates that much of the formative thinking in this area comes from academic institutions and business schools in the USA.

Research evidence

In a recent comprehensive review of the strategic planning research literature as it relates to voluntary nonprofit organizations (mostly in the USA), Stone *et al.* (1999) concluded that a number of key things are known about strategic management in the voluntary nonprofit sector, as follows:

Formulation

1   Many voluntary nonprofit organizations have not adopted formal strategic planning (Brown and Covey 1987; Crittenden *et al.* 1988; Jansson and Taylor 1978; Jenster and Overstreet 1990; Odom and Boxx 1988; Stone 1989; Tober 1991; Wolch 1990).
2   For those that do adopt formal strategic planning, primary determinants are organizational size, characteristics of the board and management, prior agreement on organizational goals and mission, and funder requirements to plan.
3   Principal outcomes of formal planning are changes in organizational mission, structure and board and management roles.
4   The relationship between formal planning and performance is not clear but seems to be associated with growth and with who participates in the process.

Content

5   The determinants of strategy are largely driven by characteristics of resource environments and existing funder relationships.
6   Little attention has been paid to determinants expressing changing demands for services or shifts in client needs.
7   Voluntary nonprofit organizations pursue both competitive and cooperative strategies, and the outcomes associated with each differ substantially.

Implementation

8   Exogenous turbulence affects organizational structure and the relationship between strategy and structure.
9   Important determinants of implementation activities are leader behaviour, the structure of authority, values and their interactions.
10 Inter-organizational systems or networks are critical to strategy implementation.

Use of strategic planning tools by UK voluntary nonprofit organizations

To find out to what extent voluntary organizations in the UK make use of strategic planning tools and techniques, the accountancy firm Clark Whitehill undertook a survey of members of the Association of Chief Executives of National Voluntary Organizations (ACENVO – now ACEVO). These therefore tended to be the larger voluntary nonprofit organizations, with the majority having an annual turnover in excess of £1M.

The research found that the vast majority (82 per cent) of respondents had a strategic, corporate or business plan, and another 15 per cent intended to prepare one during the next twelve months, which apparently contradicts the finding of Stone *et al.* (1999) that many voluntary nonprofit organizations have not adopted strategic management. The conflict may be the difference between voluntary nonprofit organizations in the USA (most of Stone *et al.*'s studies) and the UK (the ACENVO study). It also may reflect the difference in time, as Stone *et al.*'s studies were mainly undertaken in the 1980s whereas the ACENVO study was conducted in the 1990s, by which time the prescriptive literature on the value of strategic management in the nonprofit sector may have had more time to take effect.

The arrival of a new Chief Executive was the most common reason given for preparing a strategic plan (40 per cent), followed by request by trustees (22 per cent) and financial situation (20 per cent).

Not surprisingly, the Chief Executive took the lead in the preparation of the strategic plan in 89 per cent of cases, and trustees in 14 per cent. Almost half of the organizations also made use of a consultant, particularly to advise on the process and as a sounding board. In one-third of cases, however, the consultant actually wrote the plan.

Content of plans

The majority of plans included the following: strategic objectives; mission statement; financial plans/implications; detailed objectives; strategic priorities; and organizational values. A minority (between a quarter and a half) also included the following: vision statement; resource/skills needs; detailed action plans; competitive analysis; and critical success factors.

Strategic planning processes used

Respondents were also asked to indicate which strategic planning tools and techniques were used in preparation of the plan, how satisfied they were with each of them, and whether they would use them again. By far the most popular tool was SWOT (discussed in Chapters 5, 12 and 13) which was used in the vast majority of cases. On average, organizations using it were 'somewhat satisfied', and most would use it again. The second most common was gap analysis (one-third), discussed in Chapter 5, which received a satisfaction rating just over halfway between 'neither satisfied nor dissatisfied' and 'somewhat satisfied', although three-quarters would use it again. Third most common was cost–benefit analysis (30 per cent), which produced an even lower satisfaction rating, close to 'neither satisfied nor dissatisfied', although the majority said they would use it again. Fourth most used technique was PEST (environmental appraisal looking at the potential impact of Political, Economic, Social and Technological trends, discussed in Chapter 13). Satisfaction ratings for PEST were similar to cost–benefit analysis, and three-quarters would use it again. Other tools and techniques used were as follows:

Table 9.1   Other tools and techniques used in strategic planning

	Usage	*Satisfaction*	*Would use again*
Zero based budgeting	15	3.15	92
Scenario planning	14	3.75	75
Force field analysis	13	3.91	100
Portfolio analysis	11	2.44	78
Five forces analysis	11	3.33	56
Lifecycle analysis	8	3.14	86
Value analysis	8	3.71	57

This indicates that, of the less popular techniques, at least Scenario planning and Force field analysis could be made more use of. This is reinforced by the comparatively small number of techniques used, on average, by the voluntary organizations in the survey (an average of two) compared with the private sector (where the average was six).

The Mandate Analysis and Stakeholder Analysis techniques which have been adapted by Bryson (1988) specifically for the public and voluntary nonprofit sectors were not included in this survey.

Participation

The level of consultation in the preparation and drafting of plans was also interesting. The only groups consulted during the preparation and drafting stages by the majority of organizations were trustees, directors and senior managers. The level of consultation with 'all staff' was low (11 per cent in preparation and 6 per cent in draft stage), as was the consultation with funders (15 per cent in preparation, 12 per cent in draft stage).

The extent that the strategic planning processes were internally focused is particularly highlighted by the very low level of consultation with customers (13 per cent in preparation and 5 per cent in draft stage), clients (11 per cent in preparation and 8 per cent in draft stage), users (19 per cent in preparation and 12 per cent in draft stage) and supporters (8 per cent in preparation and 4 per cent in draft stage). These same groups were also a very low priority when it came to communicating the final plan.

This lack of participation by various stakeholders is despite the literature reviewed in Chapter 7 which suggests that participation enhances commitment to the goals agreed and that it is generally considered to be a particularly strong value in the voluntary nonprofit sector. This may indicate that, in adopting strategic planning techniques developed in the private sector, the voluntary nonprofit sector may also have adopted the lower emphasis on participation that has traditionally been a characteristic of the private sector. However, as noted, the culture of participation may be in the process of significant change in the private sector, as reported by many of the writers on management and strategy, particularly in the 1990s.

Impact of strategic planning

Asked about the impact of the plan on the organization's overall success, almost two-thirds of respondents felt that the plan and its implementation had a 'strong influence' on the organization's overall success (although, when asked, half of the CEOs stated that they referred to the plan only every three months or less often). Unsurprisingly, a similar fraction (two-thirds) felt that the time and money spent on the Strategic Plan was 'very worthwhile' and a further quarter felt that it was 'somewhat worthwhile'.

The Clark Whitehill study gives an interesting snapshot of strategic planning in some of the larger voluntary nonprofit organizations in the UK. It indicates that the various strategic management models, techniques and tools are now making a very major impact on the voluntary nonprofit sector (at least on national voluntary organizations) in the UK.

However, the study may also indicate two particular areas of concern. First, the level of consultation with non-managerial staff, customers, clients, users, funders, suppliers and supporters is very low, which is likely to reduce both the quality of the plan produced and the sense of ownership, and therefore the commitment to the implementation, of the plan. Second, the level of actual satisfaction with most of the tools and techniques is not particularly high. Indeed, none of the tools and techniques achieved a better rating than 'somewhat satisfied'. Despite this, most of the same tools and techniques would be used again, which may indicate the lack of alternative tools and techniques for use in the voluntary sector. However, Scenario Planning and Force Field Analysis, which were used by only a minority of organizations, received relatively high satisfaction ratings and could perhaps be made greater use of in the sector.

It would have been very interesting to know if there were any key differences in the organizations, or the processes they used, between those that felt the strategic planning work was 'very worthwhile' and had a 'strong influence' in the organization's overall success and those which had a more negative view.

Key factors for US nonprofits

In a survey of leaders of US voluntary nonprofit organizations (Katsioloudes and Butler 1996) conducted in the mid-1990s, the following were rated at the highest level of importance in strategic planning:

1　Review of the organization's mission and values.
2　Notification of all managers of broad long-term objectives.
3　Review and approval of the strategic planning document by the board.
4　Notification to all managers of specific short-term objectives.
5　Use of the plan as the basis for ongoing monitoring of organizational performance by senior management and the board.
6　Involvement of the professional staff in the strategic planning process.
7　Search for continuous improvement of internal activities.
8　Formulation of strategies by the management team and the employees involved in the strategic planning process.
9　Involvement of a strategic planning committee or ad hoc task group of the board in the strategic planning process.
10　Regular meetings with managers to discuss the overall strategic planning process issues.

Other issues such as performance appraisal, SWOT analysis, organization structure, use of external consultants, market research, financial projections and competitive analysis were considered of low importance.

Also looking at the USA, Szabat and Simmons (1996) carried out a survey of small to medium-sized nonprofit organizations in greater Philadelphia, together with a sample of grantmakers, to explore their attitudes to different elements of strategic planning and to discover what happened in practice. They found that both the organizations themselves and the grantmakers considered that six main elements of strategic planning were very important:

1　A strategic plan written in document form.
2　A clearly articulated and agreed upon mission/purpose.
3　An understanding of external trends, internal capacities and their impact on nonprofits.
4　Generally understood one-year initiatives.
5　A process to evaluate and modify a strategic plan.
6　Objectives, strategies and action plans.

However, in practice only the mission statement existed in the overwhelming majority of cases. Half had a written document, 42 per cent had initiatives, 30 per cent had objectives, strategies, action plans, while only around a quarter had external trends and internal capacities and evaluation process. The authors suggested that further research would be useful in those areas where there is a gap between perceived importance and actual practice and whether this is having an impact on the success of voluntary nonprofit organizations.

To conclude this analysis of the theory and practice of strategic management in the voluntary nonprofit sector, it is clear that strategic management tools and techniques that originated primarily in the private sector have

...aking significant inroads into the voluntary nonprofit sector in both ... and USA.

...it is not clear, however, is the extent to which these strategic management tools and techniques represent the classical top-down rigid strategic planning approaches used in the private sector in the second half of the 1960s and throughout the 1970s, and which came into disrepute in the 1980s, or whether the approaches now being used by the voluntary nonprofit sector reflect the current more inclusive and pragmatic approaches to strategic management now being recommended, which are closer to the culture and values of the voluntary nonprofit sector.

Summary

This chapter has highlighted some of the difficulties in applying strategic management approaches to the voluntary nonprofit sector, particularly the lack of a clear bottom line and the large number of stakeholders. The literature on strategic management in the voluntary nonprofit sector has been explored, much of it exhorting voluntary nonprofit organizations to adopt private sector strategic management techniques and outlining specific strategic planning frameworks. Research in the UK and the USA which analyses the experience of strategic management in the voluntary nonprofit sector has also been highlighted.

Questions

1. To what extent can strategic management tools and techniques be transferred from the private sector to the voluntary nonprofit sector?
2. What factors in a voluntary nonprofit organization make it more likely that it will adopt a strategic management approach?
3. What are the benefits of adopting a strategic management approach?
4. Why do you think there is so little literature or research into strategic management in the voluntary nonprofit sector in the UK?

Suggested reading

Michael Allison and Jude Kaye (1997) *Strategic planning for nonprofit organisations*, Wiley.

John Bryson (1995) *Strategic planning for public and nonprofit organizations* (2nd edn), Jossey-Bass.

Mark Lyons (1996) 'On a clear day...: Strategic management for VNPOs', in Stephen P. Osborne (ed.) *Managing in the voluntary sector – a handbook for managers in charitable and nonprofit organisations*, International Thomson Business Press.

Paul Nutt and Robert Backoff (1992) *Strategic management of public and third-sector organizations*, Jossey-Bass.

Sharon Oster (1995) *Strategic management for nonprofit organizations: Theory and cases*, Oxford University Press.

10 How to measure success

Chapter outline

The purpose of strategic management is often described as trying to make organizations more effective. This chapter explores the concept of organizational effectiveness and the various models that have been put forward, under three main headings: the rational–structural frame; the human resources frame; and emergent approaches. In relation to each model the discussion will try to clarify the concept, the conceptual and operational difficulties presented by these models, and examine whether there is a way forward in considering the concept of organizational effectiveness that is both academically sound (as far as any model or theory can be) and pragmatically useful in the voluntary nonprofit sector.

Learning objectives

When you have completed this chapter you should understand:

- the factors increasing the demand for measurement of performance;
- the difficulty in measuring effectiveness in voluntary nonprofit organizations;
- the rational goal approach to measuring effectiveness;
- value for money efficiency measures;
- the stakeholder approach;
- the various overarching models that are available.

Introduction

Every day we make judgements about the performance of organizations. We usually have no difficulty coming to a view as to whether organizations we know well are effective or not. It is important, too, for organizations themselves, not to mention their funders and users, to get a clear idea about the effectiveness of the organizations with which they are involved, or fund.

As highlighted in Chapters 2 and 3, the pressure on voluntary nonprofit organizations to account for their effectiveness has been increasing. Public bodies themselves are subject to increasing pressures to demonstrate 'value for money' or 'best value', and are in turn requiring substantial account- ability for funding received, often under a detailed written contract or service agreement detailing expected outcomes.

In the USA, this demand for increased accountability has culminated in legislation (the Federal Government Performance and Results Act of 1993) requiring a significant level of performance measurement and accountability. In Britain, the Government's 'Scrutiny' report (1990) and the 1992 Charities Act heralded a new level of accountability to be applied in the funding and regulation of voluntary nonprofit organizations.

Voluntary nonprofit organizations themselves, conscious of an increased demand for services and often fierce competition for contracts and funding, realize they need to be able to demonstrate to funders and potential funders the particular effectiveness of the organization (Lubelska 1996). Their concern is that, unless they take measuring organizational effectiveness seri- ously, voluntary nonprofit organizations will tend to be perceived as a 'kind of therapy: warm but illusory feelings of momentary comfort' (Matthews 1996).

The general public, too, has become more sceptical about voluntary nonprofit organizations generally, in the wake of particularly well-publicized scandals and accusations of unreasonably high administrative costs (see the major case study of the NSPCC in Part V). These are leading to an increasing demand for greater transparency, accountability and administra- tive efficiency and effectiveness.

It has been argued that the concept of effectiveness is at the heart of orga- nizational analysis and is the ultimate dependent variable in organizational research (Au 1996). As a result, for over forty years the academic community has been investigating the concept of organizational effectiveness, to try to clarify what it means and how it might be operationalized.

In the private sector the concepts of profit, return on investment, and share value have provided widely used measures of organizational success, which can be used to assess the effectiveness and efficiency of an individual firm. The single measure, profitability, can evaluate how well it is satisfying customer needs, as well as enabling firms from very different sectors to be compared. While the profit concept is far from free of controversy, and wider measures are increasingly being introduced (Kaplan and Norton 1992; Eccles and Nohria 1992; Meyer and Gupta 1994), at least these measures provide the private sector with commonly used indicators of effectiveness with which to assess their own organizations and make comparison with others in the same or different industries.

Because of the quasi-public nature of the services provided by voluntary nonprofit organizations, frequently at no cost to the consumers, the volun- tary nonprofit sector has no such agreed measures. Herman and Renz (1999) argue that the fundamental reason that developing a single measure of voluntary nonprofit organizational effectiveness is an impossibility is that the crucial exchange that voluntary nonprofit organizations help to enact is not measured in monetary terms but in moral or value terms. The key question for the voluntary nonprofit sector, therefore, succinctly put by Drucker (1990), is: 'What is the bottom line when there is no bottom line?' Or, put another way, is it possible to develop indicators of effectiveness for the voluntary nonprofit sector at organizational, industry, or sector level?

Achieving goals

The early explorations of the concept of organizational effectiveness tended to revolve around a rational, structural closed-system paradigm that postulates that organizations are rational goal-seeking entities that process inputs to create outputs to achieve these goals (Georgopoulos and Tannenbaum 1971; Gouldner 1971; Scott 1992). This model has been described as purposive–rational (Pfeffer 1982) and as the managed systems model (Elmore 1978). The origins of this approach can be traced back to the earlier proponents of scientific management.

March and Simon (1959) suggested the following principles underlying the rational model:

- Organizations have one or more formal goals.
- Those who decide what the organization will do choose activities aimed at achieving these goals, and they take steps to measure the effectiveness of these activities.
- When these measures indicate that progress towards goal achievement is unsatisfactory, 'problems' are defined for decision-makers.
- Decision-makers can follow rational procedures to solve these problems, gather information on causes, identify alternative solutions, estimate the relative costs and benefits of the alternatives, choose the optimum alternative, and evaluate the impact of its implementation.

The particular effectiveness models suggested within this paradigm have included *mission accomplishment* (Ford and Ford 1990; Sheehan 1996; Brudney and Golec 1997) and *goal attainment* (Green and Griesinger 1996; Byington *et al.* 1991; Glisson and Martin 1980; Schumaker 1980; Lillis and Shaffer 1977). From this perspective, the more that an organization achieves its mission or the goals that it has set itself, the more effective it is.

Unfortunately, despite the seeming logic of this approach, a range of conceptual and practical objections have been raised against it (D'Aunno *et al.* 1991; Hannan and Freeman 1977; Jenkins 1977; Reimann 1975; Scott 1977), as follows:

1   How do you know whether the goals were the right ones in the first place? Surely, the argument goes, to be properly effective the organization must be effective in tackling the need (in the case of voluntary

nonprofit organizations) not just in meeting the goals. These goals may have been set to be very easy to meet, or to address the least important need, or the need least difficult to meet, or may not benefit the intended beneficiaries at all.

2   The organization's activities may also have a range of other effects, positive and negative, which may be ignored by only focusing on the goals which were set.

3   The question also arises as to who sets the mission or goals: the founder? the board? the Chief Executive? the staff ? the funders? And in practice are they all pursuing the same goals for the organization? If not, then for the purposes of organizational effectiveness which, or rather whose, goals are the relevant ones? Are the official goals the same as the actual goals being pursued by all parts of the organization?

4   From a practical perspective, too, most mission statements and organizational goals are couched in very general terms, making it very difficult to provide any clear measure of success in achieving either.

5   There is also an issue of timescale, and this is equally true regardless of sector. In making the judgements about effectiveness in achieving the mission or goals, what length of time should be considered? Britain has often been accused of taking too short a view, compared with, say, the Japanese. It is suggested that, in the UK, short-term results are given most prominence to the detriment of the long-term. In the private sector, those firms that forgo profits in the short term may be much more profitable in the long term. For the nonprofit sector, too, there is a similar issue of what length of time should be considered reasonable to assess the effectiveness of an organization: a year? three years? five years? longer? Kanter and Summers (1987) argue:

> When immediate effectiveness measures set the standard for the organization, a tendency can arise to favor the short term over the long term – to maximize the score on indicators of today's performance. But very different criteria may be appropriate to the short, intermediate, and long runs.

They summarize well the weaknesses in the goal-attainment perspective. Voluntary nonprofit organizations are

> ... complex entities, the specification of whose goals is problematic. Organizations may have many goals, and they can be inconsistent, contradictory or incoherent; it is often unclear at what level or with respect to what units the goal should be measured...goals may even be a mystification.
>
> (Kanter and Summers 1987)

Value for money

Within the structural–rational paradigm, an alternative measure of effectiveness gained popularity, particularly during the Reagan and Thatcher years of the 1980s. This was also concerned with outputs, but was equally concerned with inputs and the relationship between the two. This is sometimes called cost-effectiveness, efficiency, or value for money. If two organizations had the same outputs, which organization produced them with the smaller amount of inputs? (See the CITH major case study in Part V, which highlights a voluntary nonprofit organization contracting with a Health Authority for services that are more expensive than those of other organizations, but, they argue, are of a higher quality.) However, problems remain similar to the above, of assessing outputs (or goal achievement), and the outputs may not be the same as the outcomes for the beneficiaries.

An emphasis on efficiency as opposed to effectiveness, some would argue, results in aiming for a low quality of service, particularly for beneficiaries of the services of voluntary nonprofit organizations who often cannot choose an alternative provider. In practice it is also probably impossible to find even two voluntary nonprofit organizations that provide the same quantity and quality of a specific service to enable valid comparisons to be made.

Economy

An approach closely aligned with that of cost-effectiveness or efficiency is an emphasis on economy. In assessing economy the important consideration is the cost of the various inputs, and particularly whether the cost could be, or could have been, reduced. Unlike the efficiency approach, no comparison is made with the number or quality of outputs or outcomes.

Equity

It has also been argued from a voluntary nonprofit perspective (Osborne and Tricker 1995) that measures that focus only on effectiveness as outputs/outcomes or efficiency ignore the value base of many voluntary nonprofit organizations which emphasize equity as much as the other two dimensions. In their view, any measure of voluntary nonprofit effectiveness needs to also contain a measure of equity (Savas 1977), i.e. the extent to which the service meets the expectations or needs of those in greatest need, or of those who tend to be socially excluded because of gender, ethnicity, disability, sexual orientation, etc. This usually requires significant monitoring of beneficiaries to assess the extent that equity has been promoted.

Measuring internal processes

Particularly where it is not possible to develop goal attainment output or outcome indicators, some researchers favour the development of internal process measures of organizational effectiveness other than efficiency or economy. 'Processes' can include all the activities that translate the input resources into outputs and eventually outcomes. It can include management, financial, quality, human resource, and administration policies, systems and procedures, management – any activity that is involved in carrying out the work of the organization.

The development of benchmarking arrangements provides organizations with comparative organizations against which they can compare particular processes (usually organizations which are considered to be particularly advanced in the area that the original organization wishes to improve in). This can enable an organization to consider how these processes can be improved. Letts *et al.* (1998) suggest that benchmarking is one of the four key areas that voluntary nonprofit organizations need to address in order to develop their capacity to become high-performing organizations. Lindenberg (2001) high-lighted the difficulty in adapting traditional top-down benchmarking processes in a particular voluntary nonprofit organization, at the same time reporting that methods that mixed project manager self-rankings, self-improvement plans and high levels of participation had the greatest success.

In addressing internal processes, the organization can measure the extent that it is 'doing things right'. However, this approach has been criticized by those who point out that there is no way of knowing whether these internal processes, even carried out exceptionally effectively, will actually lead to the organization being effective externally in the achievement of its goals and the provision of services to its beneficiaries (Porter 1997). It may be doing things right, but is it doing the right things?

Compliance with values

In light of the suggestion that it is their basis in values that makes voluntary nonprofit organizations distinctive, and the increasing importance placed on all kinds of organizations addressing the question of organizational values, John Hailey (2001) has suggested that voluntary nonprofit organizations should develop measurable, clear and precise indicators of key organizational values. He suggests, for example, in relation to NGOs involved in overseas development, assessing the capacity of voluntary nonprofit organizations to do the following:

- promote internal learning;
- engage in genuine participation in planning, monitoring and evaluation processes;
- be accountable and transparent in their dealings with the community;
- have local legitimacy and be embedded in local society.

Hailey (2001) goes on to give some examples of what the specific indicators might look like. He recognizes that there are voluntary nonprofit agencies that concentrate on living their values, but their level of performance is low, and suggests that other forms of indicators should not be jettisoned, but that indicators of compliance with stated organizational values should complement other kinds of financial and social indicators.

Resource acquisition

A second general approach that has been developed is the system–resource approach (Seashore and Yuchtman 1968) which is based more on an organic open systems or population ecology approach than the goal-attainment model. The system–resource approach argues that all organizations need to be adaptable and acquire resources from outside in order to survive. Its ability to acquire these resources is therefore an appropriate measure of effectiveness in sustaining their own functioning.

Survivability is therefore the ultimate measure of effectiveness in this model. However, as Kanter and Summers (1987) point out, 'Survival may also be unrelated or even negatively related to impact.' Particularly in the voluntary nonprofit sector, where some would say the main job of voluntary nonprofit organizations is to do themselves out of a job by eradicating the social problem they were set up to deal with (see the quote by the founder of Save the Children Fund on page 222), survival may well not indicate effectiveness. Meyer and Zucker (1989) have commented on the persistence of voluntary nonprofit organizations despite low performance, precisely because of a lack of measures of success or failure.

The resource-acquisition model has some attractions to the voluntary nonprofit sector, which is constantly aware of the need to obtain funding from statutory, private and charitable sources as well as volunteers from the general public. However, as a measure of effectiveness it tells us little about how the money is used, i.e. what effect the resources had on the beneficiaries. Perhaps an organization has an effective fundraising and PR machine, but achieves little with it.

Although it is theoretically possible to compare the resources acquired by one voluntary nonprofit organization against another, it makes little sense to try to compare the resource acquisition of Oxfam, or a children's hospice, with that of a neighbourhood residents' association or an unpopular cause such as a wet house for alcoholics with a mental health problem.

There are also likely to be a range of other properties that are required for an organization to sustain itself, which are much more difficult to measure, such as morale, adaptability and cohesion (Quinn and Rohrbaugh 1983).

The danger is that if the adaptability and resource acquisition functions become dominant in an organization's strategic thinking, it can lead to the sort of strategic delinquency in which an organization cynically pursues any potential funding source regardless of the mission or values of the organization or any assessment of needs.

Decision–process model

Seashore (1983) proposes a further model, the decision–process model, in which the effective organization is the one which 'optimised the processes for getting, storing, retrieving, allocating, manipulating and discarding information'. However, the organization might be excellent in the information–decision function, but provide a poor service to its beneficiaries, quantitatively or qualitatively. It is also difficult to see how such a model might be operationalized, or how organizations might be compared.

Stakeholders

It is clear that there are many different perspectives on organization effectiveness. In relation to any single organization there will be a range of internal and external stakeholders who will have different values, different reasons for being involved in the organization, and therefore very different perspectives on what might constitute success or organizational effectiveness (Kanter and Summers 1987). Indeed, research has shown (Herman and Renz 1997) that stakeholders often differ markedly in their judgements of the effectiveness of the same voluntary nonprofit organization.

Bigelow *et al.* (1996), in reviewing the literature on voluntary nonprofit strategies, argue that in the voluntary nonprofit sector institutional pressures from funders and other stakeholders are particularly strong and therefore the management of stakeholders through some form of 'corporate political strategy' is particularly important for voluntary nonprofit organizations. Strategies that ignore the intrusive nature of these multiple stakeholders are likely to be inadequate. This has led writers in the field down three parallel channels:

1   the multiple constituency approach;
2   the political approach;
3   the more post-modernist, social constructionist, contingent and symbolic frame approaches.

Multiple constituency approach

In the multiple constituency approach, the diversity of perspectives of the various stakeholders (clients, funders, board members, volunteers, staff, etc.) is recognized (particularly that of the dominant coalition) and is used positively to define the criteria with which the organization will be evaluated. This can then create a rich framework of indicators of effectiveness (Connoly *et al.* 1980; Bluedorn 1980; Zammuto 1984; Kanter and Brinkerhoff 1981; Tsui 1990; D'Aunno 1992).

Herman and Renz (1998) argue that 'given the nature of NPOs the multiple constituency model must be part of any approach to understanding their effectiveness'. The model also provides a useful theoretical underpin-ning for practices such as social auditing (Gonella *et al.* 1998), which has been defined as 'a means of assessing the social impact and ethical behaviour of an organization in relation to its aims and those of its stakeholders', and which has been championed in the UK by the New Economics Foundation and taken up by a significant number of socially-minded private sector companies (although few in the top 100 UK companies), as well as voluntary nonprofit organizations (Raynard and Murphy 2000). Social auditing is discussed further in Chapter 12. Other similar approaches are constituency accounting, developed by Gray (Dierkes and Bauer 1973); and ethical accounting (Pruzen and Thyssen 1990).

A similar, although single-stage, approach has become known as the reputational or participant satisfaction approach, and seeks the views of various stakeholders on the effectiveness of the organization (Jobson and Schneck 1982; Herman and Tulipana 1985; Smith and Shen 1996).

Political approach

The weakness of the previous approach is that it provides no way of determining the particular weight that should be given to any particular constituency or group of stakeholders. It assumes that it is possible to integrate the various different perspectives, which may in fact be in conflict with each other, and indeed may be mutually exclusive.

In contrast, the political approach (Perlmutter and Gummer 1994) starts from the bases of limited resources, conflicting priorities, unequal power, and the formation and dissolution of coalitions. Organizations, as viewed through the political frame, are seen as 'alive and screaming' political arenas that house a complex variety of individual group interests.

There is some research evidence to support the importance of this frame for the voluntary nonprofit sector. Heimovitics *et al.* (1993) found that effective executives in the voluntary nonprofit sector, particularly when faced with external issues, are more likely to employ a political frame as part of a more complex multi-frame perspective than executives who are identified as not effective. They also found in a later study (1995) that effective executives were more likely to accept responsibility for executing a political dimension to leadership, such as coalition building.

Bolman and Deal (1991) summarize the five main propositions of the political perspective as the following:

1 Organizations are coalitions composed of varied individuals and interest groups.
2 There are enduring differences among individuals and groups in their values, preferences, beliefs, information and perceptions of reality. Such differences change slowly, if at all.
3 Most of the important decisions in organizations involve the allocation of scarce resources: they are decisions about who gets what.

4   Because of scarce resources and enduring differences, conflict is central to organizational dynamics, and power is the most important resource.
5   Organizational goals and decisions emerge from bargaining, negotiation and jockeying for position among members of different coalitions.

Gummer (1990, quoted in Au 1996), suggests that social services is

> ...mainly a political arena in which money is tight and there are no commonly accepted rules for how resources should be allocated. Resources often go to those organizations skilled at competing for them, but not necessarily to those which deliver the most effective services. Furthermore, goals of a social welfare organization often reflect the interests of those powerful factions within and beyond the organization, rather than as products of rational choices themselves. As a result, effective organizations are those which can survive and adapt to these political dynamics while at the same time are able to exploit the environment for the scarce resources that they need.

From this political perspective the existence of conflict about priorities is the norm for any organization, and not necessarily a bad thing. As Heffron (1989) argues:

> ...a tranquil, harmonious organization may very well be an apathetic, uncreative, stagnant, inflexible, and unresponsive organization. Conflict challenges the status quo, stimulates interest and curiosity. It is the root of personal and social change, creativity and innovation. Conflict encourages new ideas and approaches to problems, stimulating innovation.

The political frame is a useful counterbalance to the rational–structural perspective as to how in practice organizational goals are determined, usually following a process of negotiation and bargaining between the various coalitions, internal and external to the organization. Understanding the relative power positions of each of these various stakeholders (often easier to do in hindsight) can often provide a salutary dose of reality to the process of determining organizational goals, the methods to achieve them and how achievement will be measured.

Contingency approach

D'Aunno (1992) argues that the approach to the concept of organizational effectiveness should be dependent on the particular context of the organization, i.e. that the definition of effectiveness is contingent on a range of internal and external factors which need to be considered before agreeing the measures of effectiveness in a particular organization. It is not therefore possible to agree any global criteria of effectiveness that can be applied either to all organizations or to any particular organization in advance of considering the external and internal factors which may influence the criteria of effectiveness appropriate to that particular organization.

Social constructionist approach

The social constructionist approach (Pfeffer 1982), derived from institutional theory, takes this argument a step further and holds that definitions and assessments of effectiveness have meaning, but that the meaning is (a) created by the individual or organizational actors involved; (b) specific to the context in which it was created; and (c) capable of evolving as the actors continue to interact (Forbes 1998).

From this perspective, according to Quinn and Rohrbaugh (1983):

> ...effectiveness is not a concept but a construct. A concept is an abstraction from observed events, the characteristics of which are either directly observable or easily measured. Some concepts, however, cannot be so easily related to the phenomena they are intended to represent. They are inferences, at a higher level of abstraction from concrete events, and their meaning cannot easily be conveyed by pointing to specific occurrences. Such higher-level abstractions are sometimes identified as constructs, since they are constructed from concepts at a lower level of abstraction. The problem is that no-one seems to be sure which concepts are to be included in the construct of effectiveness, or how they are to be related. The highly abstract nature of the construct and the lack of agreement as to its structure accounts for a major portion of the confusion in the effectiveness literature.

This post-modernist perspective, like the political and contingency ones, does not necessarily help in developing ways of defining or measuring the concept of organizational effectiveness, but it puts the discussion into a wider framework. The questions that arise from these post-modernist perspectives are more to do with who is asking the questions about organizational effectiveness and why. What are the power relationships? What is the meaning each of the players give to the concept? And how does this relate to the meanings that are important to the other constituencies?

From this discussion of alternative approaches to measuring organizational effectiveness, it can be seen that these emergent frameworks – multiple constituency, political, contingency and social constructionist – are complementary to each other and provide a wider perspective on the concept of organizational effectiveness which is particularly useful from a theoretical perspective. Together they suggest that

...criteria for evaluating organizational effectiveness cannot be produced by some objective apolitical process. They are always normative and often controversial, and they are as varied as the theoretical models used to describe organizations and the constituencies that have some interest in their functioning.

(Scott 1992)

The symbolic frame

The symbolic frame is more interested in exploring organizational myths, symbols, culture and rituals that legitimize the organization internally and externally. In this view, the concept of organizational effectiveness is a myth created through organizational ritual to help legitimize the organization internally and externally. In common with the social constructionist perspective, what an event means is more important than what actually happened – the same event can have completely different meanings for different people. In the symbolic frame, events and activities in an organization are inevitably ambiguous and uncertain. The greater the uncertainty the harder it is to use rational analysis and decision-making, and therefore the participants (actors) tend to create symbols and ritual to resolve confusion, increase predictability and provide direction, helping the participants to find meaning and order (Bolman and Deal 1991). In relation to organizational effectiveness, the symbolic frame sees this as a powerful and useful myth.

Ceremonial criteria of worth...are useful to organizations: they legitimize organizations with internal participants, stockholders, the public and the state. The incorporation of structures with high ceremonial value...makes the credit position of an organization more favourable. Loans, donations, or investments are more easily obtained.

(Meyer and Rowan 1991)

Unfortunately, the utility of these essentially post-modernist approaches in relation to measuring organizational effectiveness has been described as more on revealing problems associated with defining and measuring the concept in a rational manner than on providing solutions to these problems.

Overarching models

The various approaches and models discussed above are not necessarily conflicting. Various attempts have been made to develop an overarching model that can encompass a number of these different approaches. Kushner and Poole (1996), having reviewed the literature on organizational effectiveness, suggested a general model of voluntary nonprofit effectiveness with five key elements: constituent satisfaction, resource acquisition effectiveness, internal process effectiveness, goal attainment and organizational effectiveness.

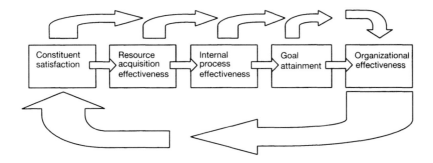

Figure 10.1 General model of nonprofit effectiveness

Source: Kushner, as presented in Kushner and Poole 1996.

Production of welfare model

Kendall and Knapp (1998) favour the economist's production of welfare model (Knapp 1984) as their starting point for addressing organizational effectiveness, which has many similarities to the model of Kushner and Poole (1996). This rational–structural model, described by Osborne and Tricker (1995) as 'an excellent framework of service delivery in human services', clearly distinguishes between inputs, process, outputs, outcomes and impact on the policy framework. This model shows how the four Es (Economy, Efficiency, Effectiveness and Equity), discussed above, relate to each part of the service production process (inputs, activities and outputs).

In building on the production of welfare model, Kendall and Knapp also suggest building into any indicators of effectiveness the distinctive features of the voluntary nonprofit sector. In particular they suggest the additional performance domains of choice/pluralism, social capital/participation, advocacy and innovation, all of which would be neglected by most traditional models. They recognize, however, the difficulty that can exist in trying to operationalize concepts like advocacy, choice and innovation.

Competing-values model

Quinn and Rohrbaugh (1983) developed a spatial model (Figure 10.2) by using multivariate techniques on a range of criteria used by theorists and researchers to evaluate the performance of organizations. The axes of the model are internal–external and flexibility–control. The four quadrants contain the human relations model (flexible/internal), the open system model (flexible/external), the rational goal model (external/control) and the internal process model (internal/control).

The debate over models of organizational effectiveness may indicate the development of a British school, represented by Kendall and Knapp and

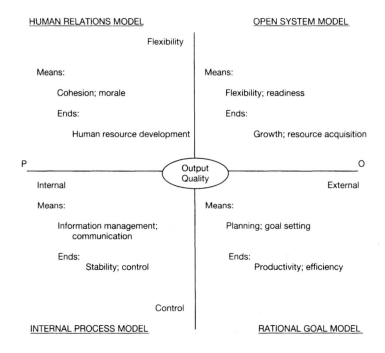

HUMAN RELATIONS MODEL   OPEN SYSTEM MODEL

Flexibility

Means: Means:

 Cohesion; morale   Flexibility; readiness

Ends: Ends:

 Human resource development   Growth; resource acquisition

P   Output Quality   O

Internal   External

Means: Means:

 Information management;   Planning; goal setting
  communication

Ends: Ends:
  Stability; control   Productivity; efficiency

Control

INTERNAL PROCESS MODEL   RATIONAL GOAL MODEL

Figure 10.2 A competing-values model of effectiveness criteria

Osborne and Tricker at Aston Business School in Birmingham, supporting the more rational–structural model of the production of welfare model from which measures of performance can be developed; and the more subjective social constructionist school which has particular prominence in the USA, led by Herman *et al.* at the Bloch School of Business and Public Administration, University of Missouri in Kansas City.

Balanced scorecard

Another overarching framework which tries to encompass a number of the models above is the balanced scorecard, developed by Kaplan and Norton (1996). This has been used extensively by private sector companies around the world looking for a broader approach to organizational effectiveness than the narrow financial indicators.

The balanced scorecard model, which can be used for the development of strategy as well as for measuring its impact, comprises four main areas against which to develop objectives, measures, targets and initiatives:

1 the customer – concerned with outputs and outcomes (goal attainment, multiple stakeholder and reputational models);

2   learning and growth – concerned with both a human resource develop-
    ment model and an internal process model;
3   internal business processes – concerned with an internal process model;
4   financial, which includes resource acquisition, economy and efficiency
    models, and a goal attainment model (even if the goal is not to incur a
    deficit).

One of the founders of the balanced scorecard approach (Kaplan 2001) has
reviewed some of the uses of the model in the voluntary nonprofit sector,
and argues that

> The balanced scorecard has enabled the nonprofit organizations to
> bridge the gap between vague mission and strategic statements and
> day-to-day operational actions. It has facilitated a process by which
> the organization can achieve organizational focus, avoiding the
> pathology of attempting to be everything to everybody. The measure-
> ment system has shifted the organization's focus from programs and
> initiatives to the outcomes the programs and initiatives are supposed
> to accomplish.

Applying the balanced scorecard to the voluntary nonprofit sector has
presented some difficulties (Bozzo 2000), particularly for small voluntary
nonprofit organizations (Cutt 1998). However, Murray and Balfour (1999),
having reviewed a range of systems for evaluating performance improvement, suggest that the balanced scorecard does show promise if combined
with another system (he suggests the Canadian Comprehensive Auditing
Foundation System: see the discussion in Chapter 12 on social auditing).

A similar approach to the balanced scorecard is known as the triple
bottom line, in which success means being economically viable, environmentally sound and socially responsible.

European Excellence Model

The European Excellence Model has been developed by the European
Foundation for Quality Management (EFQM) and promoted by the British
Quality Foundation and various quality centres around the UK.

This model has now been used extensively for continuous improvement
by a large number of private sector companies and a few voluntary
nonprofit organizations. It is similar to the Baldridge Quality award framework in the USA.

The EFQM framework contains nine elements, five of which are described
as enablers (leadership, people, policy and strategy, partnership and
resources, processes) and four results areas (people results, customer results,
society results and key performance results).

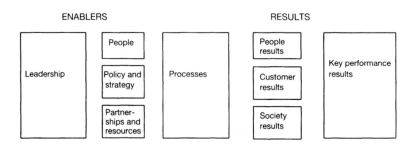

Figure 10.3   The EFQM excellence model

Source: Excellence in view, Quality Standards Task Group 2000a.

© EFQM. The EFQM Excellence Model is a registered trademark

Enablers

1   Leadership – how leaders set the direction of the organization and encourage and enable people to achieve the right results.
2   Policy and strategy – how the organization sets out what it wants to achieve and the way it will do it.
3   People (staff) – ensuring that staff and volunteers have the required knowledge and skills and are motivated, supported and rewarded.
4   Partnerships and resources – working with partners and the organization's resources in ways that achieve the target results.
5   Processes – designing and managing ways of working so that products and services are delivered efficiently, effectively and to the standard that meets customers' needs and expectations.

Results

6   Customer results – what the organization is achieving for its external customers (in other words, anyone who receives products or services from the organization, e.g. service users, customers, beneficiaries, members, funders, the general public, other services, stakeholders and targeted groups).
7   People results – what the organization is achieving for its staff and volunteers.
8   Society results – how the organization is viewed by and impacts on the society and community of which it is a part, over and above its core purpose (since, for most voluntary organizations, having an effect on the community is one of the reasons for their existence).
9   Key performance results – how well the organization has achieved what it planned to achieve.

These nine areas are further subdivided into 32 sub-criteria, each of which generates a set of scaled questions.

One of the positive advantages of the EFQM model is that the results of one organization can be compared with those of another in the same or a different industry or sector. It is also a fairly comprehensive framework that can incorporate most of the elements of the various models discussed above.

The link between use of the European Excellence Model and traditional measures of business performance has been described as inconclusive (Ghobadian and Woo 1994), and concern has been expressed that the model has been used so extensively with so little research evidence for or against its efficacy.

Because of the plethora of quality models on offer, The National Council for Voluntary Organizations (NCVO) in Britain established a major review of quality models in the mid-1990s with a view either to adapting one of them for general use by the voluntary nonprofit sector or the establishment of a new voluntary nonprofit quality model. The conclusion of this project after substantial consultation was that, of all the models, the EFQM model could be most suitably adapted for use by the voluntary nonprofit sector. The project has now also produced some useful materials for voluntary nonprofit organizations wishing to use the Excellence framework (QSTG 2000b).

Summary

An underlying assumption is that strategic management is designed to make organizations become more effective. This chapter has explored what is meant by the concept of organizational effectiveness. It has explored the rational goal-based approaches: input, process and output models that emphasize economy, efficiency, effectiveness and equity; and resource acquisition approaches and their limitations. Alternative perspectives which recognize that effectiveness is defined by different stakeholders in a different way according to their own interests, meanings and values, have also been explored. Finally a number of overarching models which try to incorporate different models have been discussed.

Questions

1   To what extent is measuring the achievement of an organization's stated goals or objectives a reasonable measure of success?
2   Is income generation a reasonable indicator of success?
3   How important is it for voluntary nonprofit organizations to demonstrate value for money, and how can this be done?
4   How can the effectiveness of an organization's internal processes be measured?

5   How can an organization's adherence to its values such as equity be measured?
6   Who are likely to be the stakeholders of a voluntary nonprofit organization, and how can their perspectives on the effectiveness of a voluntary nonprofit organization be measured?

Suggested reading

Rosabeth Moss Kanter and David V. Summers (1987) 'On doing well while doing good: Dilemmas of performance measurement in nonprofit organizations and the need for a multiple-constituency approach', in W. W. Powell (ed.) *The nonprofit sector: A research handbook*, Yale University Press.

Vic Murray and Bill Tassie (1994) 'Evaluating the effectiveness of nonprofit organisations', in Robert D. Herman and Associates (eds) *The Jossey-Bass handbook of nonprofit leadership and management*, Jossey-Bass.

Stephen P. Osborne (1996) 'Performance and quality management in VNPOs', in S. P. Osborne (ed.) *Managing in the voluntary sector – a handbook for managers in charitable and nonprofit organisations*, International Thomson Business Press.

11 Is strategic management effective?

Chapter outline

In this chapter the difficulties in determining the relationship between the extent an organization has engaged in strategic management and organizational effectiveness will be explored. The evidence of the impact of strategic planning/management on organizational performance is examined, both from private and voluntary nonprofit sector perspectives.

Learning objectives

When you have completed this chapter you should understand:

- the difficulties involved in defining effectiveness;
- the evidence for the effectiveness of strategic management in the private sector;
- the evidence for the effectiveness of strategic management in the voluntary nonprofit sector;
- the need for further research in this area.

Introduction

From the discussion above, there are clearly different perspectives on the concepts of strategy and strategic management: different academics, consultants and practitioners advocate a diverse range of models, tools and techniques to help organizations become more successful (in whatever way success is defined). What most organizational leaders want to know, however, is whether any of it actually works. What is the evidence for the success of organizations and companies who have adopted any of the techniques and models advocated?

Effectiveness in the private sector

It is one thing to expound a particular approach to the management and development of companies, but it is quite another to prove that this will in fact make an organization more effective – will improve its performance. Most significantly, within five years two-thirds of the 'excellent' companies in the sample used by Peters and Waterman had slipped from the USA's top company listings, though some did return later (O'Toole 1986).

Assessing the evidence on the success or otherwise of strategic planning models and techniques in relation to any sector is somewhat problematic for a number of reasons.

1   How should success be defined? Even in the private sector there is a range of options for how performance can be measured:

- pre-tax profits;
- long-term asset growth;
- return on capital invested;
- earnings per share;
- increase in share price;
- profit margin;
- net asset turnover;
- solvency;
- liquidity;
- market share (Thompson 1997).

It is hard to find agreement on universal criteria to assess organizational performance in the private sector (Smith 1992). Agreement in the voluntary nonprofit sector is likely to be even harder to come by.

2   What planning activities are being assessed? Every organization's planning processes will be different. How does a researcher create comparable and control organizations for research purposes?
3   How can causation, as opposed to simple correlation, be demonstrated? That is, even if an organization is successful on key results indicators and has well-developed strategic planning processes, that does not prove that it was the planning that caused the success. It may indeed be that only successful organizations can afford to employ consultants and planners to develop sophisticated strategic planning processes, or both things may be the result of a third factor altogether.

Mintzberg (1994) concludes that 'the assumption that the final number on some bottom line has an identifiable and therefore measurable relation to some process the organisation happens to use – one among hundreds – would appear to be, if not extraordinarily arrogant, then surprisingly naïve'.

However, various studies have attempted to assess the link between formal strategic planning and financial performance in the private sector. The results of a range of studies in the 1970s and 1980s on the relationship between strategic planning and financial performance have been described as 'inconclusive' (Bresser and Bishop 1983), and 'inconsistent and often contradicting' (Pearce *et al.* 1987).

Despite early studies that seemed to indicate very positive correlations (Thune and House 1970; Ansoff *et al.* 1970; Herold 1972; Karger and Malik 1975), for every study in the 1980s that produced positive findings (Armstrong 1982; Robinson 1982; Frederickson 1984; Welch 1984; Bracker and Pearson 1986; Rhyne 1986; Rule 1987; Robinson and Pearce 1988) which indicated there is an association between strategic management and profitability, there was another study that seemed to indicate no correlation (Klien 1981; Kudla and Cesta 1982; Robinson and Pearce 1983; Whitehead and Gup 1985; Gable and Topol 1987; Rhyne 1987).

In 1983, Pearce and colleagues (Pearce *et al.* 1987) studied ninety-seven small US manufacturing companies and examined the relationship between strategy and performance using subjective evaluations of return on assets, return on sales, sales growth and overall performance. They found that planning formality was consistently linked to performance and concluded that 'increased emphasis on formal strategic planning activities appeared to be an effective method of achieving improved financial performance'.

Greenley (1986) reviewed nine previous studies which had looked at manufacturing firms in the UK and the USA. He reported that five of them had found a relationship between the use of strategic planning and performance; the other four did not find such a relationship.

Boyd (1991), who reviewed forty-nine journal articles and book chapters, concluded that the correlations were 'modest' and that the overall effect of planning on performance '[was] very weak'.

More recent studies, however, using more sophisticated definitions of planning, suggest that a strategic planning process that adheres to the key elements of the conventional strategic management paradigm (including the development of mission statements, long-term goals, action plans and controls) does seem to support organizational performance, although the formalization of these processes in plans and manuals does not (Miller and Cardinal 1994).

Waalewijn and Segaar (1993) argued that in small companies profitability is associated with the extent that the company has progressed through the various phases of strategy development, i.e. financial planning, forecast-based planning, environmental planning, and integrated strategic management.

More recently, Pekar and Abraham (1995) have shown that return on investment grows as strategic management sophistication grows. They conclude that 'the important question is no longer "shall we adopt a strategic management process?"; now the questions are "what type of process is most appropriate? and how do we successfully implement and manage this process?" '

Several studies have looked at the impact of strategic planning on companies with different types of external environment. These studies have suggested that comprehensiveness of strategic planning does have a positive relationship with performance in stable industries, but a negative relationship in dynamic industries (Fredrickson 1984; Fredrickson and Mitchell 1984; Fredrickson and Iacquinto 1989; Powell 1992; Miller and Cardinal 1994).

Anderson (2000), in a study of three separate industries, explored the impact of both strategic planning and autonomous actions nurtured and supported by managers, reflecting the Learning School. This study showed that in all three industries strategic planning has a positive relationship with economic performance. Autonomous actions only had a significant effect in the dynamic computer sector, not in the more stable banking and food industries. The interaction between the two was also important, showing that organizations that adopted both approaches simultaneously achieved higher levels of performance than organizations that embraced only one of the approaches.

Evidence in the voluntary nonprofit sector

As the ultimate measure of organizational success, there has been a significant number of studies which have attempted to operationalize the concept of effectiveness in the voluntary nonprofit sector as a way of assessing the impact of particular organizational characteristics. A number of these studies have focused on the impact of the boards of voluntary nonprofit organizations (Bradshaw *et al.* 1992; Murray *et al.* 1992; Siciliano and Floyd 1993; Green and Griesinger 1996).

However, of central concern here is the use of measures of effectiveness to assess the impact of strategic planning/management. Because of the difficulties in determining criteria to assess effectiveness in the voluntary nonprofit sector, the studies that have taken place have used a number of different methods or factors to assess their relationship to organizational effectiveness. These have included the following:

- income generation (Cameron 1982; Crittenden *et al.* 1988);
- financial strength, in terms of free reserves as a proportion of turnover; financial efficiency (Siciliano 1997; Van de Ven 1980; Glisson and Martin 1980);
- reputation/satisfaction (as effective) with funders (Szabat *et al.* 1996; Green and Griesinger 1996);
- satisfaction (as effective) with CEO/staff (Siciliano and Floyd 1993);
- assessment by experts (Green and Griesinger 1996);
- assessment (as effective) with all stakeholders (Herman and Renz 1997; Crittenden *et al.* 1988);
- community acceptance (Van de Ven 1980);
- goal attainment (Glisson and Martin 1980; Byington *et al.* 1991; Schumaker 1980; Cameron 1982; Sheehan 1996);

- service or membership growth (Odom and Boxx 1988; Jenster and Overstreet 1990; Crittenden *et al.* 1988; Bradshaw *et al.* 1992).

Impact of strategic planning on effectiveness

There have been a number of anecdotal case studies of the impact of strategic planning and management in particular organizations and sections of the voluntary nonprofit sector, particularly in the USA. A number of these have related to church organizations (Kohl 1984; Wasdell 1980; Coghlan 1987), hospitals (Bart and Tabone 1998), and a professional association (Ayal 1986). There has been a profile of ten diverse 'excellent' nonprofit organizations (Knauft *et al.* 1991), case studies of three very diverse nonprofit organizations (Steiner *et al.* 1994), and a case study approach to three different types of nonprofit organization (Chauhan 1998). These all demonstrate how various strategic planning and management techniques have been used beneficially in specific organizations and subsets of the voluntary nonprofit sector.

What is missing from the literature on strategy in the voluntary nonprofit sector, however, is the rigour of academic empirical research (even with all the methodological difficulties of interpretation). As Singh (1996) has found, 'very few empirical studies have been conducted in the general area of strategic planning effectiveness in either public or nonprofit human service organisations'. Stone and Crittenden (1993) describe it as a 'noticeable gap' in the literature. Lubelska (1996), in a review of strategic management challenges in the UK voluntary nonprofit sector, concluded:

> We need much more research into strategic management in the sector. We need to study the links between process and outputs and outcomes and how this relates to the organisation's type, size, etc. We need to know what strategies work – to assess success. We need to ask – what stops an organisation from being effective? What can be done about it? We need to know when, where and how to apply global success factors from other sectors. We need to know to what extent *general* good practice measures apply across the whole of the sector to achieve performance and to what extent *specific* factors are more important.

There have, however, been several attempts to study strategic planning and its outcomes more widely in the voluntary nonprofit sector in the USA.

Webster and Wylie (1988) tried to examine the content of plans in terms of recommended organizational changes. However, they did not assess the extent to which recommendations were implemented or the impact of the process on organizational performance.

Van de Ven (1980) studied childcare community projects and showed that those that used a formal programme planning model had significantly higher levels of efficiency and community acceptance than those that did not.

Odom and Boxx (1988) found that planning sophistication, categorized as informal, operational, and long-range planning, was positively related to church growth rate in terms of Sunday school attendance, total additions and baptisms.

Crittenden *et al.* (1988) also studied religious organizations and concluded that the select use of individual strategic planning elements, particularly having a formal written planning process in place, was sufficient in many cases to maintain stakeholder satisfaction, which in turn ensured a continued flow of resources.

Siciliano (1997), in a study of 240 YMCA organizations, showed that, regardless of size, those organizations that used a formal approach to strategic planning had higher levels of financial and social performance than those with less formal processes.

Jenster and Overstreet (1990) attempted to correlate strategic planning with selected measures of organizational performance of particular credit unions studied in the research. They concluded that formal planning is related to multiple institutional performance measures: that credit unions that plan were found to have significantly greater goal clarity, more effective communications, more timely and effective decision-making and higher growth rates, although they report that their research findings did not enable them to assess the strength of the relationship or the extent to which strategic planning 'caused' the better performance (a problem identified earlier when looking at research in the private sector).

Crittenden (2000), in a three-year study of fifty-one voluntary nonprofit social service organizations in the USA, found that organizations with little strategic direction and without a clear funding strategy were more likely to demonstrate poor or faltering financial performance.

Kearns (1996) highlights many of the weaknesses in the literature on strategic planning in the voluntary nonprofit sector and concludes that

> We should make the effort to assess the extent to which strategic planning actually affects organizational behaviours and the extent to which those behaviours achieved the desired results. The effort must begin with research on the actual content of strategic plans. But we must go further to obtain information on the extent to which recommendations in a formal planning document are actually implemented and the extent to which those actions achieved the desired result: What was the intended purpose of the strategic plan and what recommendations were made? When does implementation break down? To what extent did the implementation of recommendations achieve the desired effect on organizational performance?

Summary

This chapter has highlighted some of the difficulties in carrying out research into strategic management and organizational effectiveness. It has explored some of the conflicting evidence for the effectiveness of strategic management in the private sector, including a number of increasingly sophisticated studies. The limited research on the effectiveness of strategic management in the voluntary nonprofit sector has also been analysed and found to indicate a positive relationship. The need for further research in this area has also been highlighted.

Questions

1   What measures of effectiveness does the private sector use, and to what extent are they unambiguous?
2   To what extent has the effectiveness of strategic management been proved in the private sector?
3   Is strategic management more effective in certain kinds of environments than others; and if so, which?
4   What measures of effectiveness can be used by voluntary nonprofit organizations?
5   To what extent has the effectiveness of strategic management in the voluntary nonprofit sector been proved?
6   Might strategic management be more effective in some voluntary nonprofit organizations or external environments than others?

Suggested reading

D. P. Forbes (1998) 'Measuring the unmeasurable: Empirical studies of non-profit organisation effectiveness', *Nonprofit and Voluntary Sector Quarterly* 27(2): 159–82.
J. I. Siciliano (1997) 'The relationship between formal planning and performance in nonprofit organisations', *Nonprofit Management and Leadership* 7(4).
Melissa Stone, Barbara Bigelow and William Crittenden (1999) 'Research on strategic management in nonprofit organisations: Synthesis, analysis, and future directions', *Administration and Society* 31(3).

Part IV

Strategic analysis, formulation, choice and implementation

12 Strategic analysis
Reviewing the organization

Chapter outline

The strategic management process can be broken down into three main activities: strategic analysis, strategic formulation, and strategic implementation. This chapter explores some of the ways that the board and staff of voluntary nonprofit organizations might review themselves as part of their strategic analysis. Review tools that have proved useful in other sectors, as well as a number of tools that have been specifically designed for the voluntary nonprofit and public sectors, will be examined.

Learning objectives

When you have completed this chapter you will understand:

- the importance of carrying out an internal review;
- some of the common tools for carrying out an internal review;
- some of the limitations of the various tools of internal analysis.

Introduction

The rubber band theory of how organizations develop suggests that if an organization can clearly articulate where it is now, as well as have a vision of where it wants to go, the vision will catapult the organization from where it is now towards its vision. In this section, ways of defining where an organization is at present will be examined.

Unlike the situation of a decade ago, organizations can now choose from a range of useful frameworks designed for the board and staff of voluntary nonprofit organizations to review their organizations. Alternatively they can use some of the more general well-tested tools and techniques (some of which have already been mentioned in this book) that are available as a result of previous thinking and practice in other sectors about strategic planning.

Internal review tools and techniques

The following are some of the models and tools that have been developed by strategic planning practitioners and writers over the last thirty years to help evaluate organizations and their internal environment.

Mandate analysis

Mandate analysis has been developed by Bryson (1995) for use specifically in the public and nonprofit sectors. According to the *Concise Oxford Dictionary*, a mandate is 'support for a policy or course of action'. Mandate analysis is a process of exploring the written documents that exist in support of the mission of the organization. Mandates for a voluntary nonprofit organization might include the following kinds of documents:

- UN Declarations of Rights;
- International legislation or policy documents;
- government legislation or policy documents;
- government statements;
- election manifestos;
- regional or local government policy documents;
- research reports;
- evaluations of the organization's work;
- the organization's constitution or founding document;
- quotes about the organization's work by significant individuals.

These documents can be used by the board and staff to explore the fundamental bases for the organization's mission, to understand the extent and nature of the need that the organization is concerned with, and to reflect on the distinctive competencies of the organization. These are all important in considering the appropriate strategies for the future.

Stakeholder analysis

One of the most powerful and relevant techniques that can be applied in the voluntary nonprofit sector is stakeholder analysis, also developed by John Bryson (1995) for public and voluntary nonprofit sector organizations from the work of Freeman (1984). 'Stakeholders' are all those who are affected by the activities of the organization or who have expectations of the organization. Stakeholder analysis is not only concerned with internal analysis, as the stakeholders will include both internal and external players, who will have views about both the internal aspects of the organization and the implications of changes in the external environment. However, stakeholder analysis is invaluable in assessing the views of internal and external stakeholders about the current state of the organization.

Typically the first step in the process is for the board and staff to identify exactly who these stakeholders are in relation to the organization and to prioritize them in relation to their importance to the organization.

The second step is to determine what the needs and expectations of each of the most important stakeholders are in relation to the work of the organization. The board and staff of the organization can do this by engaging in thoughtful guesswork, but a much more valuable approach is to ask the key stakeholders directly what they think and expect of the organization and how it is currently doing. This is central to Social Auditing, and is often part of an evaluation process. It is also a crucial part of quality management initiatives.

The third step involves deciding on which of those actions will help the organization to fulfil the expectations and aspirations of the stakeholders.

Box 12.1 contains a common list of stakeholders for nonprofit organizations.

Box 12.1   *Typical list of stakeholders of a voluntary nonprofit organization*

- Beneficiaries/service-users/clients
- Members
- Statutory funders
- Individual or corporate donors
- Staff
- Volunteers
- Board of management
- Agencies who refer clients or to whom the organization refers clients
- Regulatory bodies
- The general public

Portfolio analysis

This technique was developed by the Boston Consulting Group, normally considered to be in the Positioning School (discussed in Chapter 5). It is a way of evaluating the programmes that an organization currently runs in preparation for deciding what place they have in the organization's future plans (see Figure 12.1).

The model has been adapted for use by the nonprofit sector (Bryson 1995; Nutt and Backoff 1992; Courtney 1996; Bovaird and Rubienska 1996; Gruber and Mohr 1982) using different dimensions, e.g. social value (Gruber and Mohr 1982), tractability and stakeholder support (Nutt and Backoff 1992), demand for (and capability to deliver) the service (Courtney 1996).

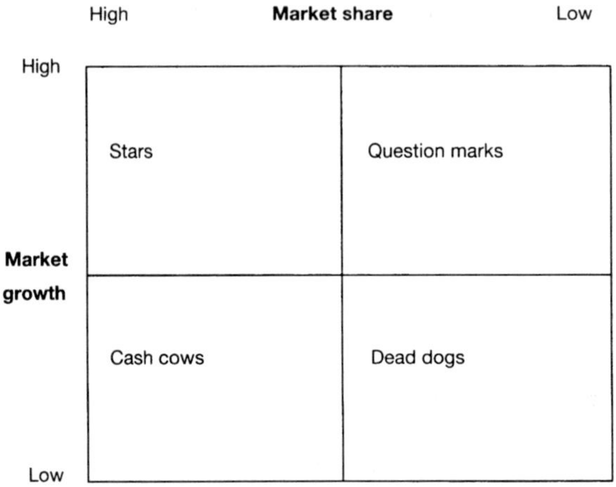

High   **Market share**   Low

High ┌───┐
     │   │
     │   Stars   Question marks   │
     │   │
Market
growth
     │   Cash cows   Dead dogs   │
     │   │
Low └───┘

Figure 12.1   Boston portfolio matrix

In its simplest form, portfolio analysis involves allocating each programme of the organization to one of the following categories:

Rising Star   the kind of innovative programme that is generating increasing interest from the public and funders
Cash Cow   a popular programme that receives significant support and funding
Question Mark   a programme that needs re-evaluating to see in which of the other categories it best fits
Dog   a programme that is clearly past its sell-by date and should be cancelled

On the basis that most products and services, including those provided by the voluntary sector, follow the lifecycle of a normal distribution curve (Hudson 1995), at any point in time it is likely that any service is likely to be at one of the following stages:

1   growth stage (Rising Star) and needs to be invested in;
2   mature stage (Cash Cow) and currently requires little attention;
3   in decline (Dead Dog) and should probably be wound up;
4   unclear what category the activity should fall into (Question Mark) and therefore in need of further investigation.

The Boston Matrix has been criticized (Slatter 1980; Seeger 1991;Whittington 1993; Ohmae 1982; Baden-Fuller and Stopford 1992; Kare-Silver 1997) on the grounds of:

- being too simplistic in taking the two key categories of the Design School (external environment and internal capabilities), selecting only one dimension of each and dividing each programme simply into 'high' and 'low';
- basing too much emphasis on cost, ignoring differentiation;
- having a too-narrow emphasis on market share and market growth;
- not providing any real tools to determine what strategy would lead to competitive advantage;
- depending on industry boundaries, which in fact are hard to define;
- depending on being able to see where a product or organization is in its lifecycle.

Others have tried to rectify these criticisms by developing more complex models.

MacMillan (1983), for example, developed a much more sophisticated three-dimensional matrix which considers programme attractiveness internally and externally, competitive position (i.e. the capacity to deliver the programme), and alternative coverage (i.e. extent of competition from other agencies).

Strengths and Weaknesses

The SW (Strengths and Weaknesses) assessment of a SWOT analysis, although used frequently in a variety of contexts, is still a straightforward and invaluable way of bringing out views of what an organization is currently good and bad at doing. This enables the organization to build on its unique strengths so that the strategy eventually adopted reflects what the organization does particularly well. It also enables the organization to develop strategies to work on, or manage the things that it currently does less well, or, indeed, to withdraw involvement in those areas and leave it to others who will do it better.

The kinds of strengths that a voluntary nonprofit organization might have include the following:

- a well-known name and image (brand capital);
- significant financial reserves (financial capital);
- effective income generation (financial capital);
- strong user participation (social capital);
- a high level of expertise in relation to the service/user group (knowledge capital);
- strongly committed and motivated staff and volunteers (human capital);
- well-known people associated with the organization (human capital);
- the extensive use of volunteers (human capital);
- strong collaborative relationships with other organizations in the nonprofit, private and/or public sectors;

- the ability and flexibility to develop new programmes quickly in response to need.

However, even the ever-popular SWOT analysis has been the subject of criticism (Haberberg 2000) for:

- being too imprecise;
- failing to evaluate the strategic importance of any of the suggested strengths or weaknesses;
- assuming a static external environment;
- providing no assistance in assessing products or services that might become a strength in the future if only they were developed a bit further.

The resource-based view of strategy which has become popular in the 1990s has a number of useful insights which help elaborate on the simple technique of looking at internal strengths and weaknesses as part of a SWOT analysis.

It distinguishes between resources which are the basic inputs/assets of the organization, e.g. buildings, equipment, technology, finance, staff, etc. – the basic units of analysis; and capabilities, also sometimes called 'distinctive competencies' (Kay 1994) or 'core competencies' (Hamel and Prahalad 1994), which are the distinctive ways that the organizational resources are coordinated and configured in teams or bundles of resources to exploit the organization's unique characteristics in achieving its objectives (Grant 1997).

It would be very rare that an organization's success was based on a single resource or even several individual resources. The resource-based view is therefore concerned with how various resources are organized in synergy to create a successful organization. Grant suggests a model of strategic analysis using the resource-based view, which can be adapted for use by the board and staff of voluntary nonprofit organizations.

1 Identify and classify the organization's resources. Appraise strengths and weaknesses relative to other organizations. Identify opportunities for better utilization of resources.
2 Identify the organization's capabilities. Ask what the organization can do more effectively than other organizations. Identify the resources inputs to each capability, and the complexity of each capability.
3 Appraise the potential of resources and capabilities to meet need and/or generate resources.
4 Select a strategy that best exploits the organization's resources and capabilities relative to external opportunities.
5 Identify resource gaps which need to be filled. Invest in replenishing, augmenting and upgrading the organization's resource base.

Grant (1997) recognizes, however, the main problem in appraising capabilities: the difficulty in maintaining objectivity. He suggests that organizations fall victim to 'past glories, hopes for the future, and wishful thinking' which lead the organization to assume that it is better than other organizations in key areas, when in fact it is not. Obtaining an objective view from key stakeholders, as suggested above, can be a useful counterbalance to this tendency.

Creating distinctive capabilities is not just a case of assembling a team of resources. Capabilities involve complex patterns of coordination between people and other resources, and such coordination requires the development of organizational routines (Nelson and Winter 1982), regular and predictable patterns of activity made up of a sequence of coordinated actions. These routines need to be learnt and embedded through repetition. The development of these routines can lead to organizational efficiency, but there is also often a trade-off with flexibility. A turbulent external environment usually requires a flexible response from an organization. It can be difficult to make rapid changes to deeply embedded organizational routines.

The language of competitive advantage is not one that is often used by voluntary nonprofit organizations. However, in the fields of fundraising or competing for contracts from a local authority, or in recruiting volunteers, it is hard not to recognize that the organization is competing with other organizations, voluntary nonprofit and otherwise. In these circumstances, voluntary nonprofit organizations have no choice but to maximize the potential of their resources and capabilities, and this in a way that is sustainable for as long as possible. According to the resource-based view, this sustainability is based on four key factors.

1 Durability – the extent to which internal resources are sustainable, i.e. they do not depreciate. An expensive mobile screening unit for a medical charity may depreciate relatively quickly, for example. An organization's reputation may be much more durable. The skills of particular trustees or staff may be lost when they retire or move to another organization. This is a good example of where the capabilities of trustees or staff need to be embedded in a way that is not lost when personnel changes.

2 Transparency – the extent to which other organizations can assess the capability advantage an organization has, and can replicate it. Many activities of voluntary nonprofit organizations are public and relatively easy to replicate. Therefore an organization that gets 'first mover' advantage in developing a new kind of fundraising activity, for example, often does not have it for long, as other organizations can see the success and easily emulate it. Many fundraising activities, therefore, often have a short lifecycle.

3 Transferability – the extent to which the resources and capabilities of one organization can be acquired or developed by another organization. A

new children's charity, for example, cannot easily develop the reputation of Save the Children, Barnardo's or the NSPCC. But they could develop the capacity to engage in a direct mail campaign (which is often outsourced). Geographical location can also be a significant factor in transferability.

4   Replicability – the extent to which the distinctive resources and capabilities of a successful organization can be replicated by internal development. Some capabilities may be relatively easy to replicate by training a member of staff or trustee, for example. Others may be much more difficult to replicate, such as good decision-making by the board or an organization's ability to motivate staff and volunteers.

Evaluation

One of the most common ways for the boards of voluntary nonprofit organizations to review their progress is to carry out an evaluation. In some cases it is an evaluation carried out or commissioned by a core funder. The UK Government's 'Scrutiny' initiative has resulted in major external evaluations of many voluntary nonprofit organizations every five years. Oster (1995) suggests that 'outside evaluations are especially helpful in nonprofits'.

Whether it is the initiative of the organization and is entirely controlled by the organization, one entirely imposed by a funder, or some negotiated compromise, evaluation is frequently the first step in and trigger to the move towards a more strategic approach to the management and development of the organization.

Evaluation has been defined (Weiss 1998) as 'The systematic assessment of the operation and/or outcomes of a programme or policy, compared to a set of explicit or implicit standards, as a means of contributing to the improvement of the program or policy.'

Evaluations may be carried out to:

- test a new programme idea;
- make mid-course corrections to a programme;
- choose the best of several alternatives;
- decide whether to continue, or continue funding, a programme;
- decide whether to expand, contract, divest, mainstream or end a programme.

However, as Weiss points out, evaluations are also sometimes instigated:

- as a PR exercise for the organization – to make it look good;
- to justify further funding to an external funder;
- to duck responsibility for taking a difficult decision, e.g. to close the programme or remove a problematic member of staff;
- to postpone a decision.

Evaluations can be carried out in many different ways and focus on different aspects of the organization, depending on who has commissioned the evaluation and who is carrying it out and their particular interests and skills. It has been suggested that the evaluation of a voluntary nonprofit organization funded by a government department should cover the following areas, in addition to providing a general description of the organization:

1   Aims and objectives of the organization

- how these can contribute towards the attainment of departmental policy objectives, partnership approaches, use of volunteers;
- whether the current activities of the organization are in line with its aims and objectives;
- relevance of aims and objectives to assessed need in the organization's field of interest;
- the strategic direction of the organization.

2   Effectiveness of services
Some effectiveness issues which might be considered are:

- consumer satisfaction, feedback from service users and professional partners;
- quality standards, existence of and adherence to standards in organizational and professional activities;
- relevance to need, evidence of effective targeting of resources;
- consumer participation, extent to which service users are involved in decisions about issues affecting them;
- methods of redress for service users, existence of complaints and representation procedures;
- non-service activities, effectiveness in influencing, promoting and advocating the interests of the user group.

3   Effectiveness in meeting objectives

- regional and local planning processes;
- ability to set and meet targets;
- evidence of progress and achievements;
- systems of review;
- the organizational culture, e.g. communication, participation, consultation.

4   Efficient and effective use of departmental grant

- staff salaries, volunteer costings, terms and conditions of service;
- administrative and secretarial support;
- use of buildings, vehicles and equipment;
- cost of services;

- financial strategies and resourcing within the organization.

5   Adequacy of organizational systems for meeting need and monitoring efficiency and effectiveness

- management of information systems;
- systems for self-monitoring and review;
- employment practices, staff monitoring and support;
- commitment to total quality approaches;
- financial accounting and audit;
- policies and procedures, including equal opportunities and non-discriminatory practice, health and safety policies and procedures, and child/vulnerable person protection policies.

Criticisms about the appropriateness of a general professional management approach being applied to mutual aid community groups and the particular difficulties involved in establishing performance indicators for community development type activities have been addressed by some useful work in Scotland and Northern Ireland. The Voluntary Activity Unit commissioned papers on the evaluation of organizations and local-based organizations involved in community development ('Measuring community development in Northern Ireland') which provide some very helpful suggestions as to how community development can be evaluated. It is suggested that the key dimensions that should be measured fall into two main categories:

Community empowerment

1   personal empowerment
2   positive action
3   development of community organizations
4   power relationships and participation

Quality of life

5   economic development
6   social development
7   environmental development
8   community safety
9   community satisfaction
10 long-term viability of the community

Social auditing

The concept of social auditing, developed by the New Economics Foundation in England alongside the similar approaches developed in Scandinavia and Canada, puts the evaluation of organizations within the context of the needs and expectations of all its stakeholders. It provides a framework whereby the extent to which an organization is making progress towards meeting these needs and expectations can be regularly assessed by establishing key performance indicators and putting in place a social book-keeping system that assesses progress towards achieving performance targets and involves stakeholders in reviewing the performance indicators.

Social auditing is based on the following eight principles:

1   Inclusive – any accounting process must reflect the views of all stakeholders, not only those who have historically had the most influence over the evolution of the organization's formal mission statement.
2   Comparative – the performance of the organization must be compared over time, or with external benchmarks drawn from the experience of other organizations, statutory regulations or societal norms.
3   Complete – no area of the organization's activities can be deliberately or systematically excluded from the assessment.
4   Regular and evolutionary – an organization's 'social footprint' cannot be assessed in any one-off exercise. Issues vary over time, as do the composition and expectations of key stakeholder groups.
5   Embedded – the organization must develop clear policies covering each accounting area, as well as procedures that allow the accounting to be regularized and the organization's awareness and operationalization of policies and commitments to be assessed and influenced through audit.
6   Communicated – disclosure of information must be routed in meaningful dialogue, not just consultation by publishing a document.
7   Externally verified – external verification of the social audit ensures accountability and legitimacy, in the same way as a financial audit.
8   Continuous improvement – the approach must identify whether the organization's performance has improved over time in relation to its values and objectives and those of its stakeholders and support future improvement.

The key stages of the social auditing process are as follows:

Planning

- establish commitment and governance procedures
- identify stakeholders of the organization
- define and review objectives, policies and values

Accounting

- identify issues upon which performance is assessed
- determine scope of process
- identify indicators of performance

- collect information
- analyse information, set targets and develop improvement plan

Auditing and reporting

- prepare reports
- audit the reports
- communicate results and obtain feedback

Embedding

- establish and embed systems for continuous improvement

ACEVO, the Association of Chief Officers of Voluntary Organizations in Britain, established a study (Raynard and Murphy 2000) into social auditing with voluntary nonprofit organizations (the SAVO project) to test the applicability of the Social Audit methodology in UK voluntary nonprofit organizations. The study was carried out by the New Economics Foundation. The conclusions of the thirteen case studies of organizations which participated in the study included the following:

- Social auditing is a very useful tool in improving the accountability of voluntary nonprofit organizations and building trust with stakeholders.
- It can assist with the development of social objectives, strategic planning, evaluation, building trust in stakeholder relationships, and the demonstration of accountability and transparency.
- There are a number of particular strengths of the process:
    - the emphasis of stakeholder dialogue as opposed to straight consultation;
    - an opportunity to examine their social objectives and assess performance against these;
    - the emphasis on developing indicators that were stakeholder-led in order to assess performance;
    - the verification of the process and outcomes – this process encouraged organizations to be open about their performance in the final report;
    - the emphasis on communicating the results in a meaningful way to external audiences, including specific stakeholder groups;
    - the emphasis on setting meaningful and measurable next steps for continuous improvement.

The report suggests that the social auditing process could be developed further in relation to internal management and leadership processes and can learn from the EFQM Excellence model and Investors In People in these areas (see page 161).

The experience of the participating groups also suggests that including all stakeholders on all issues at once can be too much to do effectively, and it might be better to focus on a smaller number of stakeholders or issues each year with a view to ensuring that all stakeholders and areas are covered over a period of time. The resource limitations of the organization, both financially and in terms of time, can also be a barrier.

The project also found that stakeholders were sometimes not sufficiently well briefed to make informed judgements and, therefore, part of the process may need to involve building the capacity of stakeholders to contribute to the process. To be effective, too, the social audit recommendations need to be fed into the organization's planning systems and then effectively implemented.

With the development of social auditing, and of a number of similar approaches in Scandinavia and Canada in particular, and criticism that some of the social auditing reports in the private sector are so much PR gloss with little real substance (Doane 2001), the need for quality standards for such ethical accounting, auditing and reporting processes has become apparent. To address this, an organization called AccountAbility has developed a quality framework, *Accountability 1000 standard*, as a foundation standard in social and ethical accounting, auditing and reporting (AA 2000).

Investors In People audit

The Investors In People (IIP) framework may also be useful in assessing the extent that the organization has a clear vision that staff and volunteers understand, that there is a framework to assess and meet the training and development needs of the trustees, staff and volunteers in helping them to achieve this vision, and that there is a process to evaluate the extent that the training actual achieves the purpose for which it is designed. Through a questionnaire to be answered by the trustees, staff and volunteers, the IIP audit explores the key areas, as shown in Box 12.2.

The results of the IIP audit questionnaire enable the organization to draw up an action plan to address any weaknesses in any of the areas above. This action plan can then be integrated into the organization's strategic plan.

However, an IIP audit relates to the organization's internal processes as they relate to the development of staff in achieving organizational goals. It does not assess other aspects of the organization, e.g. financial, impact on users, public awareness, etc.

European Excellence Model

The EFQM Business Excellence Model, discussed in detail in Chapter 10 in relation to measuring effectiveness, was not particularly designed for the voluntary nonprofit sector (nor, indeed, was IIP in the previous section). However, the Quality Standards Working Group established by the

Box 12.2   *Investors In People standard*

Principles	Indicators	Evidence
Commitment An investor in people is fully committed to developing its people in order to achieve its aims and objectives.	1. The organization is committed to supporting the development of its people.	Top management can describe strategies that they have put in place to support the development of people in order to improve the organization's performance. Managers can describe specific actions that they have taken and are currently taking to support the development of people. People can confirm that the specific strategies and actions described by top management and managers take place. People believe the organization is genuinely committed to supporting their development.
	2. People are encouraged to improve their own and other people's performance.	People can give examples of how they have been encouraged to improve their own performance. People can give examples of how they have been encouraged to improve other people's performance.
	3. People believe that their contribution to the organization is recognized.	People can describe how their contribution to the organization is recognized. People believe that their contribution to the organization is recognised. People receive appropriate and constructive feedback on a timely and regular basis.
	4. The organization is committed to ensuring equality of opportunity in the development of its people.	Top management can describe strategies that they have put in place to ensure equality of opportunity in the development of people. Managers can describe specific actions that they have taken and are currently taking to ensure equality of opportunity in the development of people. People confirm that the specific strategies and actions described by top management and managers take place and recognize the needs of different groups. People believe the organization is genuinely committed to ensuring equality of opportunity in the development of people.

Planning An investor in people is clear about its aims and its objectives and what its people need to do to achieve them	5. The organization has a plan with clear aims and objectives which are understood by everyone.	The organization has a plan with clear aims and objectives. People can consistently explain the aims and objectives of the organization at a level appropriate to their role. Representative groups are consulted about the organization's aims and objectives.
	6. The development of people is in line with the organisation's aims and objectives.	The organization has clear priorities which link the development of people to its aims and objectives at organizational, team and individual level. People clearly understand what their development activities should achieve, both for themselves and the organization.
	7. People understand how they contribute to achieving the organization's aims and objectives.	People can explain how they contribute to achieving the organization's aims and objectives.
Action An investor in people develops its people effectively in order to improve its performance.	8. Managers are effective in supporting the development of people.	The organization makes sure that managers have the knowledge and skills they need to develop their people. Managers at all levels understand what they need to do to support the development of people. People understand what their manager should be doing to support their development. Managers at all levels can give examples of actions that they have taken and are currently taking to support the development of people. People can describe how their managers are effective in supporting their development.
	9. People learn and develop effectively.	People who are new to the organization, and those new to a job, can confirm that they have received an effective induction. The organization can show that people learn and develop effectively. People understand why they have undertaken development activities and what they are expected to do as a result.

		People can give examples of what they have learnt (knowledge, skills and attitude) from development activities.
Evaluation An investor in people understands the impact of its investment in people on its performance.	10. The development of people improves the performance of the organization, teams and individuals.	The organization can show that the development of people has improved the performance of the organization, teams and individuals.
	11. People understand the impact of the development of people on the performance of the organization, teams and individuals.	Top management understands the overall costs and benefits of the development of people and its impact on performance. People can explain the impact of their development on their performance, and the performance of their team and the organization as a whole.
	12. The organization gets better at developing its people.	People can give examples of relevant and timely improvements that have been made to development activities.

National Council for Voluntary Organizations in England (NCVO) which undertook a major review of the issue of quality in the voluntary nonprofit sector in Britain and the whole range of models that are currently available, concluded that the EFQM Excellence Model represents the best overarching model for voluntary nonprofit organizations to use to assess their organizations and put in place measures to improve the quality of what they do. The Excellence Framework provides a very powerful assessment process to enable organizations to see to what extent the commitment to meet user and stakeholder needs and expectations is being delivered and to encourage continuous improvement. The key areas involved in an EFQM assessment are as follows:

Enablers

- leadership
- policy and strategy
- people
- partnerships and resources
- processes

Results

- customer results
- people results
- society results
- key performance results

Like IIP, the Business Excellence Model assessment process is supported by a self-assessment questionnaire. The NCVO Quality Standards Working Group, working with the British Quality Foundation, has developed very useful materials to help nonprofit organizations carry out assessments under the Excellence model (*Excellence in view*, Quality Standards Task Group 2000a; and *Self-assessment workbook: Measuring success*, Quality Standards Task Group 2000b).

PQASSO

This framework (the Practical Quality Assurance System for Small Organizations) has been developed specifically for smaller voluntary nonprofit organizations by The Charities Evaluation Service in Britain. It provides twelve suggested quality standards and types of evidence at three different levels (depending on the development stage of the group or organization). The standards are as follows:

Planning for quality

The organization defines clearly for its stakeholders its long-term purpose, and its plans for the medium and short term. It sets clear priorities and targets for its activities that are designed to meet the needs and expectations of its stakeholders, and it reviews its progress.

Governance

The organization ensures that it governs itself effectively and responsibly. It demonstrates accountability to the appropriate people and bodies, and the board of trustees has the skills and information it needs to achieve its mission.

Management

The management of a quality organization is appropriate to the organization's needs. Managers carry out all legal and financial responsibilities and are accountable to the organization's funders and other stakeholders. Managers carefully plan the development of the organization and promote effective communication.

User-centred service

The organization recognizes and values its users, and builds good relationships with them. It includes them in designing, delivering, reviewing and assessing services in order to meet their needs. Users are encouraged to make a positive contribution to the organization.

Staff and volunteers

The organization recruits and manages the right people to work as staff and volunteers to the benefit of the organization and its users. The organization values its staff and volunteers and the contribution they make towards achieving its aims.

Training and development

Trustees, staff and volunteers are supported in gaining appropriate skills and knowledge to meet their responsibilities. Training and other learning opportunities are seen as an essential part of individual and organizational development. Training and development supports the organization in achieving its objectives.

Managing money

The organization systematically attracts and generates money to support its work, and manages its funds effectively and prudently. It exercises financial control, and accounts for all its money within a framework of law and good practice.

Managing resources

The organization manages its resources effectively, efficiently and ethically. Managers ensure there are enough resources for the planned level of activities. Premises and information resources are managed so that targeted users have the best possible access to services.

Managing activities

The organization identifies its core activities, and develops appropriate processes and standards to deliver and improve them. Staff and volunteers are well informed about the processes and standards.

Networking and partnership

The organization works with other organizations in a variety of ways, locally and nationally. It is more effective through sharing information, providing complementary services, joint working and influencing change.

Monitoring and evaluation

The organization collects and analyses relevant information appropriately and systematically and uses it to help trustees, managers and staff to evaluate and improve the organization and its activities.

Results

The organization achieves its planned results, and learns from its experiences. Its results show improvements over time and compare well with similar organizations, providing value for money for users and other stakeholders.

The PQASSO manual provides detailed descriptions at each level of the types of evidence that should be in place to comply with the relevant standard. It therefore provides a useful way of assessing the current state of the organization as well as providing an important improvement tool.

Voluntary sector code of practice

Although not strictly a framework to review voluntary organizations, this code, developed by the Joseph Rowntree Foundation, provides a useful list of policies and practices that voluntary nonprofit organizations ought to have in place under the following headings:

1   Effectiveness
2   Accountability
3   Standards
4   User involvement
5   Governance
6   Voluntary action
7   Equality and fairness
8   Staff management

The working group which devised the code recommended that voluntary organizations adopt a series of commitments (the numbers in brackets denote to which of these eight headings the commitments refer). Organizations agree to:

- State their purpose and keep it relevant to current conditions (1).
- Be explicit about the needs that they intend to meet and how this will be achieved (1).
- Manage and target resources effectively and do what they say they will do (1).
- Evaluate the effectiveness of their work, tackle poor performance and respond to complaints fairly and promptly (1 and 2).
- Agree and set out for all those to whom they are accountable how they will fulfil these responsibilities (2).
- Be clear about the standards to which they will work (3).
- Be open about their arrangements for involving users (4).

- Have a systematic process for making appointments to their governing body (5).
- Set out the role and responsibilities of members of their governing body (5).
- Have clear arrangements for involving, training, supporting and managing volunteers (6).
- Ensure that their policies and practices do not discriminate unfairly or lead to other forms of unfair treatment (7).
- Recruit staff openly, remunerate them fairly and be a good employer (8).

Minnesota principles of nonprofit excellence

The Minnesota Council of Nonprofits has developed a set of 87 principles and practices of nonprofit excellence, which covers the following areas:

Mission and values

- mission
- programme service and quality
- values
- commitment to diversity, accessibility and social justice

Governance

- board responsibilities
- board composition
- conduct of the board
- conflict of interest

Human resources

- employees and volunteers

Financial management

- financial accountability
- external financial arrangements

Charitable fundraising

- fundraising activities
- donor relationships and privacy
- acceptance of gifts
- employment of fundraising personnel

Public accountability and communications

- public access
- communication of information

Public policy and advocacy

- public policy advocacy
- promoting public participation

Information and technology

- information systems
- technology

Partnerships and alliances

- objectives
- structure

Like the Joseph Rowntree standards described in the previous section, it is possible for an organization to assess itself against these standards to identify current strengths and weaknesses and determine areas for future improvement to be included in the strategic plan.

All the tools and techniques highlighted here enable the board and staff of a voluntary nonprofit organization to clarify the organization's current position – what it is good, and not so good, at – and therefore begin to identify priorities for the future.

Research on evaluation models

Murray and Balfour (1999) examined 19 systems for reviewing a voluntary nonprofit organization, available in North America, including the following:

- the Balanced Scorecard;
- the Drucker Foundation 'self improvement tool';
- the Balridge National QualityAward (similar to the EFQM Excellence model);
- the ISO 9000 quality assurance framework;
- the 'high performance non-profit organizations' system of Letts *et al.* (from *High performance non-profit organizations: Managing upstream for greater impact*, 1998);
- the outcome funding system of the Rensselaerville Institute;
- the American Institute for Philanthropy 'charity rating guide';
- the United Way 'outcome funding' approach;

- the Canadian Comprehensive Auditing Foundation's 'framework for performance reporting'.

Murray and Balfour concluded that there is inadequate research on the impact of any of the models considered. However, the Balanced Scorecard combined with the Canadian Comprehensive Auditing Foundation's 'framework for performance reporting' showed most promise. The others that were rated highly were the 'high performance non-profit organizations' system of Letts *et al.*, the outcome funding system of the Rensselaerville Institute, and the United Way 'outcome funding' approach.

Summary

This chapter has explored a range of tools and techniques that have been used to help voluntary nonprofit organizations analyse their internal environment. These tools include methods developed for the voluntary nonprofit sector such as evaluation, mandate and stakeholder analysis, social auditing and quality frameworks such as PQASSO, and the Joseph Rowntree and Minnesota frameworks. They also include tools that are frequently used in the private sector, such as Strengths and Weaknesses (usually part of a SWOT analysis), portfolio analysis, the EFQM Excellence model and Investors In People.

Questions

1   What is mandate analysis? Use it to determine the key mandates of a voluntary nonprofit organization you know.
2   List the distinctive or core competencies of a voluntary nonprofit organization you know.
3   List the key stakeholders of a voluntary nonprofit organization you know and what you think they expect from the organization.
4   What criteria would you use to assess that a particular programme in an organization is a 'Dead Dog' and should be ended?
5   What are some of the 'Rising Star' issues in the voluntary nonprofit sector?
6   What criteria should be used to evaluate a voluntary nonprofit organization?

Suggested reading

John Bryson (1995) *Strategic planning for public and nonprofit organizations* (2nd edn), Jossey-Bass.

P. C. Nutt and R. W. Backoff (1992) *Strategic management of public and third-sector organizations: Theory and cases*, Jossey-Bass.

Sharon Oster (1995) *Strategic management for nonprofit organizations*, Oxford University Press.

13 Strategic analysis
The external environment

Chapter outline

Voluntary nonprofit organizations do not exist in a vacuum, but in a changing (in some cases turbulent) external environment which can have profound implications for the organization and its future. This chapter explores the tools and techniques used by voluntary nonprofit organizations to analyse the external environment in which they operate and the implications of that environment for future strategy.

Learning objectives

When you have completed this chapter you should understand:

- the importance of understanding trends in the external environment before making strategic decisions;
- ways of scanning and analysing the external environment and its potential impact.

Introduction

Voluntary nonprofit organizations exist in a complex, often dynamic and uncertain environment. At any one time, while one aspect of the environment may be relatively stable, another may be in a perpetual state of flux. The success of any organization depends on how it interacts with this external environment, and this in turn depends on developing a clear understanding of what is happening in the external world.

Pettigrew and Whipp (1993), in a three-year study, found that environmental assessment at the top of an organization, involving all functions through networks and task forces, etc., was one of five key success factors in the highest-performing companies they studied.

Voluntary nonprofit organizations are also not only passive players blown about by changes in the external environment, they are often very active in the fields of education, advocacy and campaigning – actually trying to influence the external environment. (See the major case studies of Save the Children, NSPCC, Oxfam, WWF and the Grameen Bank in Part V.)

A number of useful tools and techniques have been developed to enable organizations to analyse what is going on in this environment: several of them are examined in this chapter.

Opportunities and Threats

Mention has already been made of SWOT analysis, and the final two parts of the acronym refer to the Opportunities and Threats that may exist for an organization in the external environment. It can be a very powerful and simple technique to ask the key stakeholders in an organization, especially board members, staff and volunteers, to look outside the organization and suggest what trends or changes in the external environment might constitute opportunities for the organization to take advantage of in future, or alternatively what might constitute threats to the organization's achievement of its vision and which the organization may need to try to avoid or to manage.

The criticisms of SWOT mentioned in previous chapters also apply to the external aspect; for example, SWOT analysis doesn't indicate how important each of the factors that are suggested might be, or how likely they are to happen or what the impact would be if they did happen.

Environmental scanning

Another method that has been developed to analyse the external world is known as environmental scanning, and is rather akin to a submarine echo sounder which detects other craft or objects that might be relevant to the mission of the submarine, and shows them up on a radar screen. Environmental scanning makes a judgement as to how imminent or distant the potential impact is by its closeness to the centre of the radar screen, and how big the impact might be by the size of the image on the screen (see Figure 13.1).

Scenario analysis

A third useful technique is scenario analysis (Schwartz 1992; Heijden 1996) whereby a number of different plausible future scenarios are generated and the potential impact on the organization's future are considered, as well as an assessment being made of the likelihood of each scenario coming true. This enables the organization to avoid strategies becoming derailed because assumptions about the future turn out to be unreliable.

Such scenario planning provides the organization with the opportunity to develop its plans in ways that will take most advantage of the possibilities provided by the most positive scenarios, and also to devise strategies to deal

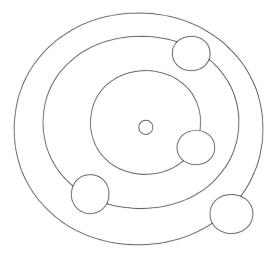

Figure 13.1   Environmental scanning

with the more negative scenarios in case they come about. This avoids the limitations of strategies that are frequently developed on the basis of only one set of assumptions about the future and also enables the organization to track some key features in the external environment to provide an early warning that a particular scenario may be developing.

Issues impact analysis grid

With concern about the limited usefulness of simply listing the external factors which might impact on the organization in future, Peters (1993) developed an issues impact analysis grid so that each external factor could be assessed against the likelihood of occurrence and the impact if it did occur. This enables an organization to give most attention to those external factors which are most likely and/or might have the greatest impact. An impact analysis matrix is presented in Figure 13.2.

Extent of impact:

	High	*Medium*	*Low*
Likelihood:			
High	Priority action	Action	Monitor effects
Medium	Action	Contingency plan	Track
Low	Contingency plan	Track	Track

Figure 13.2   Issues impact analysis grid
Source: Adapted from Peters 1993.

PEST

Another common technique for exploring the external environment is to analyse these external trends under a specific series of headings:

- Political
- Economic
- Social
- Technological

In PEST analysis, the various trends in each area, and what the potential impact of each might be on the organization, are explored. This can be done in a participative way, as brainstorm or focus groups with organizational stakeholders, including board members and staff, by expert research of the relevant literature, or by using the Delphi technique to enrol experts to refine the external analysis over a series of stages to achieve consensus. The PEST framework has also been adapted as PESTLE, to include Legal and Environmental issues.

Other issues that are likely to be of particular importance to the voluntary sector might include:

- changing needs;
- changing attitudes (the public, funders, users);
- funding.

An alternative acronym that might be a more appropriate mnemonic for this complex environment is PLANET DEFOE:

Public policy
Legislation
Attitudes
Need
Expectations (of users and other stakeholders)
Technology
Demography
Economy
Funding
Other organizations
Environment

See Box 13.1 for an example of an analysis of external trends by a voluntary nonprofit organization.

Box 13.1   *Examples of external changes for a cancer charity*

Cancer

- Breast cancer deaths decreasing
- Cancer to overtake heart disease as no. 1 killer
- Lung cancer overtaking breast cancer
- Increasing research into cancer (causes, cures, prevention)
- Life expectancy and quality of life of people with cancer increasing
- More awareness of cancer – people can talk about it
- Increased awareness of men's cancers
- More overweight people – increase in cancers
- Genetic developments (ethical issues)
- Research progress in future (progress in drug treatments)
- Development of digital mammography
- Development of colon/rectal screening
- Increasing young girls' smoking – increase in women's lung cancer

Demographics

- People living longer (higher expectations)
- Increased percentage of elderly in the population

Health Service

- Increasing use of voluntary organizations to deliver services
- Increasing waiting times in NHS for detection and treatment
- Specialization of medical services
- Ageism in health services
- Impact of healthy living centres

Attitudes

- Younger generation are:
  - more proactive about their health
  - less likely to put up with poor service
- Patients more empowered/taking more control and want choice
- Increasing acceptance of complementary therapies
- Changing attitudes towards charities (increasing awareness of waste, administration and overlap)
- More awareness of gender issues

IT

- Internet – wider access to information
- On-line charitable donations
- A lot of conflicting information available to the public

Funding/fundraising

- Increased competition for funds and volunteers
- Greater accountability for donations (admin costs)
- Tighter statutory financial regime

Organizational mapping

For all organizations, one of the most important issues is to consider which other organizations exist that are involved in similar work, and how they might impact on the work of the organization. For voluntary nonprofit organizations it is likely to be important to avoid overlapping services and for each organization to have its own distinctive contribution to make. This distinction might be based on the specific geographical area being served, the particular client group, the distinctive nature or quality of the service provided, or indeed on cost, e.g. the provision of a service free of charge to individuals who cannot afford the normal cost of that service, or providing a service at a much lower cost than other organizations.

Opportunities for collaboration are also crucially important to many voluntary nonprofit organizations in achieving their visions of social change.

For all these reasons it can be very useful to carry out an organizational mapping exercise which compares the organization with each of the other organizations that might be considered to be similar. The comparison should clarify both the similarities and the differences.

In developing a future strategy, this analysis of other players can help in enabling an organization to focus on those things in which it has a distinctive role to play, and perhaps to adapt or withdraw from services which overlap with other agencies.

Although 'competition' is often an uncomfortable concept in the voluntary nonprofit sector, Porter's competitive strategy concepts can be relevant to the voluntary nonprofit sector in considering the impact of other organizations, particularly for organizations heavily involved in fundraising and those trying to obtain or keep contracts with statutory bodies. Lindenberg (2001), however, found problems in trying to apply Porter's framework to a particular international voluntary nonprofit organization, meeting resistance from both cultural and mechanical/conceptual perspectives. Managers in the organization found the language of market and competition problematic, and, for example, found it difficult to know where to place donors.

Oster (1995), however, has adapted Porter's model for the voluntary nonprofit sector. She suggests the following forces as being relevant to the voluntary nonprofit 'market':

- relations among existing organizations;
- the threat of new entrants;
- the threat of new substitutes (competition from alternative services);
- the number and power of the user group;
- the power of the funding group, which typically increases with the proportion of revenues;
- the power of the supplier industry, especially the staff and volunteers, for voluntary nonprofit organizations.

Although the meaning and relevance of Porter's industry analysis framework for the general voluntary nonprofit sector has been described as 'dubious' and 'not very useful' (Goold 1997), Oster describes in some detail how the future strategies of voluntary nonprofit organizations can be very significantly affected by the following factors:

- other organizations moving in and providing a better or cheaper service;
- the development of substitutes, e.g. the development of fostering rather than children's homes (see the Barnardo's case study on pp. 15–17);
- the power of funders: for example, to grant or withhold a service contract which could result in the destruction or contraction of the organization;
- the power of users: for example, organizational members of an umbrella voluntary nonprofit agency may have considerable power to determine the future of the agency.

Force field analysis

Another useful technique that can be adapted to a number of different situations is Force field analysis, which was developed by Kurt Lewin (1957). This technique is used to determine the strength of those factors which support change against those which inhibit or oppose change. In considering the external environment, it can be useful to look at the organization's mission or its particular aims or objectives, and to suggest those factors which will support the achievement of the mission, aims or objectives and those which might prevent or inhibit their achievement (see Figure 13.3).

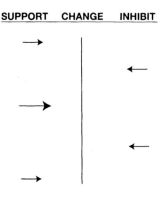

SUPPORT   CHANGE   INHIBIT

Figure 13.3   Force field model

Summary

This chapter has highlighted the importance of understanding the changing external environment in making strategic decisions. It has explored a number of tools and techniques that can be used to help analyse this external environment, including Opportunities and Threats (from SWOT analysis), PEST, PLANET DEFOE, environmental scanning, scenario planning, organizational mapping, and force field analysis.

Questions

1   What external trends are likely to affect most voluntary nonprofit organizations in the next five years? How many of them can be described under the headings Political, Economic, Social and Technological?
2   What factors are likely to drive and inhibit the achievement of an organization's mission?
3   Considering one organization you know, list the organizations that are similar and describe the similarities and differences with the organization you know.
4   Which areas of work within the voluntary nonprofit sector do you think it would be easy for a new organization to enter? Which would be difficult?

Suggested reading

John Bryson (1995) *Strategic planning for public and nonprofit organizations* (2nd edn), Jossey-Bass.
P. C. Nutt and R. W. Backoff (1992) *Strategic management of public and third-sector organizations*, Jossey-Bass.
Sharon Oster (1995) *Strategic management for nonprofit organizations: Theory and cases*, Oxford University Press.

14 Strategic formulation
Creating the plan

Chapter outline

In this chapter the classic strategic planning framework used by a large number of voluntary nonprofit organizations to develop and describe their strategic direction will be explored. The theory behind each element of the framework and how they are interrelated will also be explored.

Learning objectives

When you have completed this chapter you will understand:

- the structure of a classic strategic planning framework;
- the purpose of, and difference between, mission, vision and values;
- the relationship between values and culture;
- the purpose of, and difference between, aims, priorities and objectives.

Introduction

Once the organization and its external environment have been analysed, it is then possible for the board and staff of a voluntary nonprofit organization to begin putting together a framework for making decisions about the future development of the organization. In doing so it is important to use the needs and expectations of the stakeholders, the changing trends in the external environment, developments with the other key players, and the distinctive or core competencies of the organization to help form the backdrop to the plan. But crucially the plans need to be formed from a clear and inspirational sense of mission, vision and values.

Mission

According to Collins and Porras, in their very successful book *Built to last: Successful habits of visionary companies* (1994), the first and most fundamental questions that any organization needs to ask in a changing world are: 'what do we stand for?' and 'why do we exist?' They argue that encapsulating the answers to these questions in a statement of purpose or mission which taps into the intrinsic motivations of the people in the organization is crucial to the creation and development of an enduring and successful organization.

Such a mission statement which 'captures the soul of the organization' is even more important for voluntary nonprofit organizations, which are not driven by making a profit but by some particular sense of purpose or mission. Drucker, who is very clear that 'the mission comes first' (1990), quotes a private-sector CEO who served on various voluntary nonprofit boards, and who said 'The businesses I work with start their planning with financial returns. The nonprofits start with the performance of their mission.' Knauft *et al.* (1991) in *Profiles of excellence* argue that a 'clear, agreed-upon mission statement' is one of the four primary characteristics of successful voluntary nonprofit organizations.

Sitting down with the key players in an organization and its key external stakeholders, to explore the various answers to the basic question of what the purpose of the organization is, can be a very salutary experience as it is discovered how different the answers to that question can be, even in an apparently united organization, and immediately raises some of the key strategic issues for the organization. It is also a very powerful question, as very quickly it gets to the heart of what motivates each person to commit themselves to give their time, energy and money to the organization.

The end product of these discussions should be a clear, concise and motivating statement of purpose (a mission statement) which covers all aspects of the organization's work.

Oster (1995) argues that a mission statement serves three main purposes.

1   It describes the boundary of the organization.
2   It motivates staff, volunteers and donors, and creates a sense of unity and focus for all stakeholders.
3   It helps in the process of evaluation of the organization.

Drucker (1990) argues that a mission statement should be based on three things:

1   the things that the organization does well – its strengths or competencies;
2   where the organization can make the biggest difference in tackling the needs;
3   what the people in the organization really believe, i.e. what they are really committed to.

Examples of the mission statements of some voluntary nonprofit organizations are given in Box 14.1.

Box 14.1   *Mission statements*

'To promote the values of the Universal Declaration of Human Rights and to work world-wide for the release of prisoners of conscience, fair trials for political prisoners and an end to torture, extrajudicial executions, disappearances and the death penalty.' (Amnesty International Mandate)

'We take the lead in challenging discrimination of any kind and in consistently improving the quality of life of people with a learning disability.' (Mencap)

'To represent UNICEF in the United Kingdom, to support its work for the promotion of children's rights world-wide and to help meet children's needs by building awareness, implementing programmes and raising funds.' (UNICEF)

'The National Childbirth Trust offers information and support in pregnancy, childbirth and early parenthood. We aim to give every parent the chance to make informed choices. We try to make sure that our services, activities and membership are fully accessible to everyone.' (NCT)

'To ensure that no young person is at risk because they do not have a safe place to stay.' (Centrepoint)

'To provide counselling and advice for children and young people in trouble, need or danger by means of free confidential helpline services.' (Childline)

'To provide guide dogs, mobility and other rehabilitation services that meet the needs of blind and partially sighted people.' (Guide Dogs for the Blind Association)

'To challenge blindness by empowering people who are blind or partially sighted, removing the barriers they face and helping to prevent blindness.' (RNIB)

'To end cruelty to children.' (NSPCC)

'VSO enables men and women to work alongside people in poorer countries in order to share skills, build communities and promote international understanding and action, in pursuit of a more equitable world.' (VSO)

'To improve the quality of life of the most vulnerable children and young people.' (NCH Statement of Purpose)

Examination of the mission statements quoted in Box 14.1 demonstrates that mission statements can serve a number of purposes. They can:

- highlight commitment to core values (e.g. Amnesty International's commitment to the Universal Declaration of Human Rights);
- clarify the target group of beneficiaries (e.g. Centrepoint's 'young people at risk');
- highlight the changes that it wants to see in relation to the target group of beneficiaries (e.g. NSPCC's 'end cruelty to children');
- clarify the means that the organization uses to achieve its objective (e.g. Childline's 'to provide counselling and advice');
- clarify the geographical boundaries of the organization's work (e.g. UNICEF UK's 'in the UK').

Very often an organization begins with a clear sense of a distinctive mission, but over time, with changes in trustees and staff and incremental decisions to develop new or innovative services, or to serve new groups of beneficiaries, a process of 'strategic drift' takes place which gradually takes the organization away from the distinctive mission. Around the original core of uniqueness, 'encrustations' (Porter 1997) are added incrementally. Like barnacles, however, Porter suggests these need to be removed to reveal the underlying strategic positioning. The challenge, in his view, is to refocus on the unique core and to realign the organization's activities with it.

Although the process of strategy development is primarily about looking to the future, Porter argues that the organization's history can be particularly instructive. He suggests that organizations should ask themselves the questions 'What was the vision of the founder?' and 'What were the features that made the organisation successful in the first place?' He suggests that it is possible to re-examine the original strategy to see if it is still valid, although he recognizes that it may need to be implemented in a modern way, consistent with today's technologies and practices. He suggests that this sort of thinking may 'lead to a commitment to renew the strategy and may challenge the organisation to recover its distinctiveness' (Porter 1997).

Vision

Alongside developing a mission statement, many voluntary nonprofit organizations now also produce a vision statement. This is a statement of the state of affairs that the organization would ideally like to see if its work was successful.

Mintzberg (1994) argues that 'many of the great strategies are simply great visions…only when we recognise our fantasies can we begin to appreciate the wonders of reality!' Bennis, a leading writer on leadership, defines leadership entirely in terms of vision, as 'the capacity to create a compelling vision and translate it into action and sustain it' (Bennis and Nanus 1985).

Mary Parker Follett, one of the great (and neglected) early writers on management, who took a much more human view of management than either Taylor or Fayol, argues that 'the most successful leader of all is one who sees another picture not yet actualised' (1941).

Bryson (1995) argues that an organization should have a vision for the future which:

- clarifies the organization's direction and purpose;
- is relatively future-oriented;
- reflects high ideals and challenging ambitions;
- captures the organization's uniqueness and distinctive competence as well as desirable features of its history, culture and values;
- is short and inspiring;
- is widely circulated;
- is used to inform organizational decisions.

Pascale and Athos (1981), having explored the success of Japanese companies, argue for the value of the Japanese approach to vision statements which are 'dynamic, vivifying *modus operandi* rather than pallid or generic statements of corporate intent'.

Rice (1997), exploring the changing external environment for volunteer administrators in voluntary nonprofit organizations, argues that these administrators must help voluntary organizations to think more systematically about the future, and advocates a process of strategic visioning to enable staff, volunteers and trustees to respond more effectively to change and increase the organization's ability to survive and succeed in a rapidly changing environment.

Examples of the vision statements of some voluntary nonprofit organizations are given in Box 14.2.

Box 14.2   *Vision statements*

'A world in which
    I make decisions about my life and get the help I need
    I do the things I want with everyone else in the community
    I am safe from prejudice and fear
    I have the opportunity to reach my potential with the support which enables me to do this.'
        (Mencap, through the eyes of someone with a learning disability)

'That the right of all children to develop to their full potential be honoured, as an essential contribution to world development, world peace and a civilised society.' (UNICEF)

'The National Childbirth Trust wants all parents to have an experience of pregnancy, birth and early parenthood that enriches their lives and gives them confidence in being a parent.' (NCT)

'To become the leading national provider and voice for young people at risk of social exclusion and homelessness within the next five years.' (Centrepoint)

'Guide Dogs for the Blind Association wants a world in which all people who are blind and partially sighted enjoy the same rights, opportunities and responsibilities as everyone else.' (Guide Dogs for the Blind Association)

'A world where people who are blind or partially sighted enjoy the same rights, responsibilities, opportunities and quality of life as people who are sighted.' (RNIB)

'Our vision for children is a society where all children are loved, valued, and able to fulfil their potential.' (NSPCC)

'NACRO's vision is of a socially inclusive society which is far less damaged by crime and where human rights and dignity are universally respected. It is a society where resources are used constructively, fairly and effectively to reduce crime and where offenders are dealt with in ways most likely to stop offending, repair relationships and encourage re-integration.' (NACRO)

'To work for a world in which all humans respect and live in harmony with members of the animal kingdom.' (RSPCA)

Most of the vision statements quoted in Box 14.2 provide inspiring statements of how the organization wants the world they are concerned with to look at some unspecified point in the future. Two of the vision statements have particularly interesting features. The Centrepoint statement is also a vision for the organization, i.e. 'to become the leading national provider...'; and the Mencap vision statement is written from the viewpoint of one of its target group of beneficiaries, i.e. a person with a learning disability.

Values

The third element of a fundamental statement of what an organization is about is often a statement of values, principles or philosophy which underpins the whole work of the organization. Thomas Watson Jr, a former CEO of IBM, observed in 1963:

Consider any great organisation – one that has lasted over the years – I think you will find it owes its resilience not to its form of organisation or administrative skills, but to the power of what we call beliefs and the appeal these beliefs have for people.

Peters and Waterman argued that shared values are one of the seven key elements of an excellent company, and devoted a whole chapter to them in *In search of excellence* (1982). Collins and Porras (1994) also state that one of the key principles of a successful company is the existence of a core ideology that 'gives guidance and inspiration to people inside the company'.

Bryson (1995) argues that only strategies that are consistent with the philosophy, core values and culture of an organization are likely to succeed. He also argues that clarifying its values will enable an organization to maintain its integrity, by turning down opportunities which might damage this integrity. Hudson (1995) suggests that, while organizations in other sectors may have values, voluntary nonprofit organizations must really cherish their values.

Values are the articulation of the desired culture of the organization, 'how things are done around here'. Culture has been defined by Cooke and Rousseau (1988) as 'the shared beliefs and values guiding the thinking and behavioural styles of members'; and by Smircich (1983) as:

the social and normative glue that holds an organisation together...the values or social ideals and the beliefs that organisation members come to share. These values or patterns of belief are manifested by symbolic devices such as myths, rituals, stories, legends and specialised language.

All organizations have a culture, regardless of whether they have a statement of values or not. Indeed, different parts of an organization may reflect different cultures. The values and culture of people involved in finance or fundraising in a voluntary nonprofit organization may be different, for example, to those providing human services, community development or campaigning. Young professional staff may have different values to older, more traditional volunteers or trustees. This diversity, as well as being a rich source for dialogue, can sometimes give rise to conflicts within organizations. At least identifying the differences, and the reasons for them, can help to clarify, if not resolve or transform, them.

It is also important to distinguish between values in theory and values in practice (Argyris and Schon 1974) and to identify and try to narrow the gap between the two. There is considerable evidence that publicly espousing a particular value or view is likely to result in behaviour which is more consistent with that value or view than if there had been no public espousal of the view. However, there are many organizations with charters or statements of values or beliefs that bear little relationship to how the organization actually works and deals with customers/clients in practice. This can result in cynicism, both internally and externally.

Bartlett and Ghoshal (1989) argue that culture, what they call 'organisational psychology', can be 'developed and managed just as effectively as the organisational anatomy and physiology', although many major change programmes which have attempted to change the fundamental culture of an organization have shown how difficult this can be. It has been suggested that it takes at least five years to change the fundamental culture of an organization.

It is important to put in place processes to assess the extent that these values are being applied in practice, and, therefore, to help ensure that they are values in practice as well as values in theory. This can be done, for example, through induction and training, the good example of leaders ('the actions and behaviour of senior managers are vital as examples and statements of commitment': Bartlett and Ghoshal 1989), regular referral to the values (e.g. equal opportunities, confidentiality, quality, health and safety), and adopting policies and strategies for implementing those values.

The distinctive culture and values of an organization often tend to derive initially from the influence of a charismatic leader, usually the founder, who defines the basic beliefs, values and patterns of behaviour that epitomize good citizenship (Schein 1992). These may be important many years after the leader has gone. Often such a strong sense of vision and values forms the basis of an entrepreneurial strategy (Mintzberg and Waters 1997) which is very much in the control and direction of one person. Many successful organizations are the result of the strong sense of vision and values of a powerful founder. However, the environment, or key parts of it, needs to be open in some way to this vision, otherwise the organization would not survive or develop. When this strong sense of vision and values becomes accepted by a group of people, usually the trustees and staff of an organization, it can be described as an ideological strategy (Mintzberg and Waters 1997). Though the trustees and staff of voluntary nonprofit organization are often committed to changing the world, they can also be very resistant to pressures to change from outside.

Although much of the literature on culture and values is about the positive aspects of organizations having and living up to these shared values, as Hamel (2000) has pointed out there is also a dark side. Organizations may be faced with a rapidly changing external environment, including changing attitudes of funders, service-users and/or the public, which strongly conflicts with the traditional values of the organization.

Many older voluntary nonprofit organizations, for example, were founded on Victorian values of charity and philanthropy (the case study of Barnardo's would be a good example of this: see Box 2.1 on page 15). Much of the current philosophy around social care is based on the concepts of rights, empowerment, integration and equal opportunities, often giving rise to conflict between professional managers (who increasingly have been appointed to voluntary nonprofit organizations from outside) and long-serving trustees who feel a strong desire to remain true to the historic principles of the organization and of the founder. This conflict can be particularly strong where relatives, descendants or friends of the founder (even the founder him/herself) are still on the board of management.

Hamel (2000) has argued that, when values are 'endlessly elaborated, overly codified and solemnly worshipped', they can become the manacles that shackle the organization to the past. (See the major case study in Part V about the Simon Community.)

The importance of values is not a new phenomenon in relation to organizations. Chester Barnard, as far back as 1938, recognized that all acts of individuals and organizations are interconnected and interdependent, and he argued (in the language of the times) that 'the distinguishing mark of the executive responsibility is that it requires not merely conformance to a complex code of morals but also the creation of moral codes for others' (Barnard 1938).

Some of the mission and vision statements already quoted include statements of key values. For voluntary organizations which are, by definition, value-led it is particularly important to be concerned with not only what it does but also how it does it. Some organizations base their values on universal declarations of rights, such as the International Rights of the Child or the UN Declaration of Human Rights. Most, however, develop their own, some of which may be rights-based. Some, on the other hand, may be very general in scope and others may be very specifically focused on the concerns of the particular organization. The headings of typical statements of values in the voluntary nonprofit sector are shown in Box 14.3.

Box 14.3   *Typical values in the voluntary nonprofit sector*

Accountability/probity/efficiency	Learning
Challenging discrimination	Openness
Compassion	Partnership
Confidentiality	Putting the needs of the users first
Diversity	Quality/excellence
Dynamism/innovation	Respect
Effectiveness	Sustainable development/
Empowerment	self-reliance
Equal opportunities/equality	Teamwork/working together/
Equal right to achieve potential	partnerships
Inclusion	Trust
Integrity	Valuing people

A actual example of a statement of values (from Voluntary Service Overseas) is shown in Box 14.4.

Box 14.4 *The values of Voluntary Service Overseas (VSO)*

VSO

- values the individual and believes in the equal right of all to realize their potential
- believes in countering disadvantage by practical action, person to person
- values action motivated by and responding to the needs of others, both through work abroad and through voluntary activity by supporters at home
- believes in promoting sustainable development and increasing self-reliance
- values and respects diversity of culture
- values two-way partnerships which openly share costs and benefits
- values the learning and friendship which result from people living and working alongside each other, in pursuit of shared goals

---

The mission, vision and values statements discussed in this chapter provide the pinnacle of a pyramid through which the strategic plan of the organization can be cascaded. Each level becomes more specific and closer in time than the one above, but also provides the means of achieving the level above. The classic model of strategic planning, therefore, might look something like Figure 14.1.

Long-term aims

Mission, vision and values statements by their very nature tend to be aspirational, long term and broad. To give the strategic plan a coherent framework there is commonly a number (usually between four and ten) of long-term aims (sometimes called strategic objectives) which cover each of the main activities (sometimes called critical success factors) that the organization will need to engage in if it is to make progress towards achieving its mission and vision. These long-term aims typically cover the main types of activities and programmes that the organization may carry out on behalf of, or with, its beneficiaries, but they may also include the support services which ensure that the organization is efficiently administered, that the trustees, staff and volunteers are appropriately trained, and that sufficient income is raised. Sometimes the core aims are included in the mission statement.

In some strategic plans the aims are stated as general activities, such as: 'To run a youth centre for disadvantaged young people.' For others, this

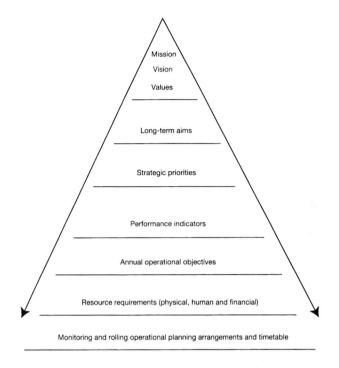

Figure 14.1   Strategic planning pyramid

approach is not visionary enough, because, to continue the example, as long as the organization runs some kind of youth centre for disadvantaged young people this aim has been achieved. Some long-term aims are therefore like miniature vision statements which focus on the long-term situation that the organization would like to see achieved. The long-term aim in the case of the youth centre in the example might therefore be: 'That all disadvantaged young people in the town have access to an excellent youth centre that meets their cultural, recreational and informal education needs.'

Collins and Porras (1994), in their influential book *Built to last: Successful habits of visionary companies*, argue that organizations should create what they call 'B'Hags' (Big Hairy Audacious Goals). These provide real challenge and motivation for all those involved in the organization. This is consistent with Hamel and Prahalad's (1997) concept of stretch – the sense of real ambition which creates a consistency of effort and purpose over the long term. Working to acquire the resources needed to achieve the goals is as important as managing the resources in the organization. Hamel and Prahalad argue that the problem with many larger, older organizations is that they are complacent and have lost the original sense of ambition or stretch, and are often overtaken by new smaller organizations which have a hunger or ambition to achieve audacious goals. (See the major case study in Part V on the Simon Community, and on the development of the Community in London in particular.)

As an example, the key long-term aims of Centrepoint (Centrepoint actually calls them key objectives) include aims in relation to both their work with young people and their internal needs. They are shown in Box 14.5.

Box 14.5   *The long-term aims of Centrepoint*

- To be the service of choice for young people at risk
- To be the major voice for young people at risk
- To be the employer of choice for professional staff and volunteers who have a commitment to working with young people at risk of homelessness or social exclusion
- To secure the future of Centrepoint through effective financial management and building reserves
- To achieve appropriate standards of excellence across the organization

---

Strategic priorities

All of the above concepts (mission, vision, values and long-term aims), which form the top half of the strategy pyramid, are not time-bounded. They are all visionary or idealistic. It is important, however, for an organizational plan to have some more specific goals that the organization can work towards achieving within the period of the strategic plan (often three or five years).

One useful step in this direction is to establish some key priorities for change, or main thrusts under each long-term aim, that the organization will focus on over the three or five years of the plan.

For example, in relation to the hypothetical youth centre for disadvantaged young people in the previous section's example, a priority might be 'to double the number of disabled young people using the centre', or 'to achieve and maintain Investors in People'. These should not be goals that can easily be achieved within the first year of a plan, but should require work throughout the period of the plan.

Performance indicators

This is one of the most important and difficult aspects of strategic planning, as can be seen from Chapter 10 on 'How to measure success'. Voluntary nonprofit organizations are often resistant to the idea that what they do can be reduced to measurable outcomes or outputs. There is often a concern that hard measures of performance can push aside the important soft issues. However, many voluntary nonprofit organizations have shown that, over a period of time, it is possible to produce a number of key measurable indicators to show the progress that the organization is making towards achieving its long-term aims.

Rapp and Poertner (1992) suggest six types of outcome related to what they call 'client status'. These are as follows:

1   The service-user's attitude towards themselves (level of self-esteem, etc.)
2   The service-user's level of knowledge about a particular issue
3   The service-user's use of a particular skill, e.g. cooking, debt management, social interaction, etc.
4   Changes in the service-user's behaviour, e.g. reduction in substance use/abuse, talking to parents, etc.
5   Changes in the service-user's status, e.g. from unemployed to employed, homeless to housed, or ill to well, etc.
6   Changes in the service-user's environment, e.g. provision of play facilities for children

Patton (1996) also includes a further type of outcome:

• Prevention, e.g. prevention of unplanned pregnancies, eviction, etc.

The performance indicators should ideally be final outcomes, e.g. how people's lives have changed as a result of the activities of the organization. However, these can often be difficult to measure, or it can be difficult to determine the extent to which it was the organization itself that brought about the change. Organizations often adopt intermediate outcomes, therefore, which may for example include more immediate outcomes for service-users, or the satisfaction level expressed by service-users with the services provided. Performance indicators often include outputs, i.e. ways of counting the extent of the service provided: e.g. the number of sessions run, the number of people who attended, etc.

United Way of America, a leading funder of voluntary nonprofit organizations in the USA, has developed a sophisticated outcome-focused approach to funding. In *Measuring program outcomes: A practical approach* (1996), a logic model is presented which is consistent with the approaches of Kushner and Poole and Kendall and Knapp, discussed above. The model has six key elements:

1   Inputs
2   Activities
3   Outputs
4   Initial outcomes
5   Intermediate outcomes
6   Longer-term outcomes

In the example of an education programme for expectant teenage mothers, the following outputs and outcomes are distinguished:

- outputs: the number of pregnant teenagers attending the programme;
- initial outcomes: teenagers' level of knowledge of prenatal nutrition and health, and the proper care, feeding of, and social interaction with infants;
- intermediate outcomes: teenagers follow proper nutrition and health guidelines during pregnancy, deliver healthy babies, and provide proper care, feeding and social interaction to their babies;
- longer-term outcomes: babies achieve appropriate 12-month milestones for physical, motor, verbal and social development.

Andrews *et al.* (1994) suggest that performance indicators (outcome measures) should comply with the following factors:

- applicability: addresses dimensions that are important for the service-users and the staff/volunteers working in the organization, but also enable the collation of data;
- acceptability: they are brief and user-friendly in terms of format and language;
- practicality: simple to score and interpret, minimal cost to collect and analyse, and require little training to collect;
- reliability: the method of collecting the information should produce the same result regardless of who is collecting it;
- validity: the indicator should measure what it is designed to measure and not something else;
- sensitivity to change: the indicator must be sensitive enough to detect the relevant changes that have taken place.

The performance indicators should be linked to the aims the organization has agreed. The hypothetical youth centre used as an example earlier in this chapter (see page 188) might, for example, have a long-term aim that 'All the staff and volunteers have received the training and accreditation they need in youth and community work to provide a professional youth work service.' The performance indicators might be:

- The percentage of staff and trainees who achieve a recognized youth work qualification at a particular level.
- The level of satisfaction of the young people using the centre with the professionalism of the youth work service provided.
- The level of satisfaction of staff and volunteers with the training received.

It is important not to create too long a list of performance indicators, as it can become difficult to regularly track and report on all of them. Every indicator does not have to be a perfect indicator of success, but together they should provide at least a good indication of whether the organization is making progress in the right direction. The important point is that at least once a year there should be a review against each indicator. With experience, annual targets for these indicators can be set which can then be integrated into the annual operational plan. Examples of the performance indicators for services provided by a medical charity are given in Box 14.6.

Box 14.6   *Examples of performance indicators for services provided by a*
           medical charity

- The number of people using the early detection service
- The number of men using the early detection service
- The number of people from areas of high deprivation using the service
- The extent that early detection clients are from all parts of the country
- The number of people using the genetics counselling service
- The satisfaction level of early detection clients with the service
- The number of cancers detected
- The number of other medical conditions detected that are referred on for treatment or further assessment
- The waiting time to get an appointment for early detection screening
- The time clients are kept waiting after their agreed appointment time
- The waiting time from screening to receiving the results

Summary

This chapter has explored the classic elements of a strategic plan and their relevance for the voluntary nonprofit sector. In particular the need for clear statements of mission, vision and values, as well as ambitious long-term aims and priorities, has been highlighted. The importance of measuring performance by agreeing indicators has been highlighted. A pyramid model of strategic planning has been presented.

Questions

1   What is the difference between a mission statement and a vision statement?
2   Write mission and vision statements for an organization you know.

3   To what extent should organizational values remain the same, or change over time?
4   Write the values that you think underpin an organization you know.
5   What is organizational culture and what is the relationship between organizational values and culture?
6   What is the difference between performance indicators and objectives?
7   Write performance indicators for an organization you know.

Suggested reading

Michael Allison and Jude Kaye (1997) *Strategic planning for nonprofit organisations* (2nd edn), Wiley.

John Bryson (1995) *Strategic planning for public and nonprofit organizations*, Jossey-Bass.

P. C. Nutt and R. W. Backoff (1992) *Strategic management of public and third-sector organizations: Theory and cases*, Jossey-Bass.

Sharon Oster (1995) *Strategic management for nonprofit organizations*, Oxford University Press.

15 Strategic formulation
Basic choices

Chapter outline

This chapter examines the concept of generic strategic options and various approaches that have been suggested for describing the choices open to voluntary nonprofit organizations and the circumstances in which it might be appropriate to adopt particular kinds of strategy.

Learning objectives

When you have completed this chapter you should understand:

- the difficulty of determining generic strategies;
- different ways of categorizing the strategic choices available to nonprofit organizations;
- different types of growth strategies for voluntary nonprofit organizations.

Introduction

Having explored the history and concepts of strategic planning, strategic formulation and strategic management in some depth, the question of the *content* of strategies, as opposed to the concepts, models and processes, has not yet been considered.

Some writers consider that it is not possible to talk about generic strategies. Every organization is different with different capabilities or competencies. The environment of each organization is also different. Does it therefore make sense to talk of generic strategies or configurations of strategy?

Generic strategies

Kearns (2000) argues that there are only basically three choices when deciding on an appropriate strategy: growth, retrenchment and stability.

However, within these options are a number of more detailed choices. For example, within the fundamental growth strategy are the options of concentrating on and expanding existing services and programmes (horizontally or vertically) by increasing the capacity to serve more users or expanding geographically; or to diversify into new, related or unrelated services (Kearns 2000).

Growth, according to Kearns (2000), can also happen in a number of different ways:

- by internal expansion, i.e. by expanding the existing organization;
- by setting up a joint venture, partnership or strategic alliance with another organization, or a consortium of organizations, which may be in the voluntary nonprofit sector or in the private or public sector;
- by merging with or taking over another voluntary nonprofit organization.

Crittenden (2000) has noted that growth options in voluntary nonprofit organizations are an infrequently researched topic.

Ansoff's matrix

Ansoff (1965) of the Planning School suggests that there are two key dimensions of strategy: the market, and product/service. Companies only have a limited number of options: market penetration, product/service development, market development and diversification. Ansoff's matrix has also been used as the basis for exploring the options that are available to nonprofit organizations (Courtney 1996), as follows:

- Extend existing services to cover a new target group of potential beneficiaries; sometimes called market extension. (This is similar to Kearns's description of horizontal integration concentration strategy. Osborne 1998 describes this approach to organizational change as expansionary.)
- Develop new services with the existing target group in the current geographical area; sometimes described as product/service development. (Osborne 1998 describes this approach as evolutionary; Kearns 2000 describes it as concentric diversification.)
- Develop new services with a new target group in a new geographical area (described by Osborne 1998 as total organizational change, and by Kearns 2000) as conglomerate diversification). Crittenden (2000) warns, however, that voluntary nonprofit service organizations need to stay focused in their product/service offerings and avoid adding numerous related or unrelated product/service offerings, as these can diffuse management's attention and make it more difficult to send a clear message to funding sources.

- Extend existing services to the current target group in existing areas. (Osborne 1998 describes this as a developmental approach.)
- Extend existing services to the current target group into new geographical areas.
- Develop new kinds of services in new areas.
- Reduce or close existing services (similar to Kearns's retrenchment strategy).
- Improve existing services (see Oster's account of quality leadership below).
- Wind up the organization.

In Osborne's study of innovation (1998), only the first three items listed above qualify as being innovative strategies, as they involve discontinuities over the past. The others are forms of organizational development, decline or stagnation.

Porter's generic strategies

In the Positioning School, Porter suggests that there are only three possible generic strategies:

- cost leadership: being the lowest cost producer in the industry;
- differentiation: developing unique products, relying on brand loyalty;
- focus: developing knowledge and competence in a narrow market segment.

Others (Miller 1992; Baden-Fuller and Stopford 1992; Gilbert and Strebel 1988), however, have criticized Porter's assertion that a company's strategy has to be just one of these three and cannot be a combination.

In the voluntary nonprofit sector, using an adapted version of Porter's five forces industry analysis (Oster 1995) discussed above, it is possible to suggest a number of similar generic strategies for nonprofit organizations, as follows:

- cost leadership: achieve the same objectives as other voluntary nonprofit organizations in the same field, but at a lower cost, therefore enabling the organization to compete more effectively for contracts. However, it has been argued that nonprofits are not well equipped to engage in a narrow efficiency competition with private companies (Frumkin and Andre-Clark 2000; Anheier 2000);
- quality leadership: provide a better quality of service for the users than other organizations;
- differentiation: provide a service that is unique, and develop a loyalty to that unique service and/or to the organization. Anheier (2000) argues that the complexity of voluntary nonprofit organizations makes them natural niche-seekers;

- focus: develop knowledge, credibility and competence in a very narrow area (geographical or type of beneficiary).

The differentiation and focus strategies are clearly very similar, and may be better seen as a single kind of strategy.

The major case study in Part V on Care In The Home discusses an organization that focuses on a very specific geographical area and type of service (domiciliary care), provides a high quality of service, but is more expensive than its competitors.

Miles and Snow's strategic types

Miles and Snow (1978) suggest four main strategic types, based on the rate at which companies change their products/services and markets. These types are as follows:

- Defenders: seek stability (see also Kearns 2000) by producing a limited range of products/services directed at a narrow segment of the potential market. They tend to defend their turf aggressively to keep out the competition, by efficiency measures, competitive pricing, creating relationships with key decision-makers, or concentrating on the high-price, high-quality end of the market. They tend to develop by market penetration and limited product development. Defensive strategies tend to be most appropriate when the external environment is stable. Osborne's study of innovation (Osborne 1998) describes this approach as being traditional as opposed to innovative or developmental.
- Prospectors: almost the opposite of defenders, their strength is in finding new products and market opportunities. The focus is on innovation, market research to identify gaps in the market, and flexibility. The Prospector strategy tends to be most appropriate when the external environment is dynamic/turbulent.
- Analysers: try to combine the strengths of both Defenders and Prospectors. They seek to minimize risk and maximize profit, but also to innovate. However, the innovation tends to be on the basis of products or services that have been tried out by Prospectors first. Analysers tend to follow Prospectors with a superior or a cheaper product. The strategy of the Analysers is most appropriate in a changing but not turbulent external environment.
- Reactors: these tend to be companies that, in Porter's words, are 'stuck in the middle'. It is not clear which kind of strategy they are following, if any, and they tend to react to the latest whim or change in the external environment.

Boschken (1988), in a study of US port authorities, demonstrated the applicability of Miles and Snow's typology to the public sector.

Acar's contingency-based framework

Nutt and Backoff (1992) suggest that only two of these strategies are in fact viable strategies – Defender and Prospector. Acar (1987) developed a contingency-based framework which suggests effective strategies for each of the possible environmental conditions. These are as follows:

- Custodian: this is similar to the Defender strategy of Miles and Snow. It assumes a stable environment and market. Custodians maintain the distinctive competencies of the organization and nurture historical markets. They tend to ignore competitive threats, limit risk as far as possible, and accept slow growth rates. They tend to seek protection from regulatory authorities.
- Stabilizer: appropriate where markets are seen as being stable with many aggressive competitors (a 'clustered–placid environment'). Each cluster in the market is recognized as having different characteristics, and the demand and market share can shift, requiring appropriate response in relation to that cluster through steps such as cost-cutting or efficiency measures.
- Developer: in a disturbed environment, Developers take action in response to moves from their competitors, often emulating their new products or services.
- Entrepreneur: in turbulent environments, Entrepreneurs seek to capture changing markets by aggressive action. Entrepreneurs read weak market signals, take risks, and innovate with new products and services, often leading to rapid growth and profitability.

Miller's archetypes of strategy formation

Danny Miller, at the University of Montreal's École des Hautes Études Commerciales and McGill University, developed a strategy framework based on four dimensions: innovation, market differentiation, breadth, and cost-control strategy. He suggests ten archetypes of strategy formation from his study of companies (Miller 1976, 1979), four of failure and six of success, including the following:

- Stagnant bureaucracy: where the previous placid environment has lulled the firm to sleep, unable to respond when major changes to the market or technology, etc., take place.
- Headless giant: where there is a set of businesses with weak central authority to provide guidance and direction.
- Aftermath: where a transformational strategy, a turnaround, is required but the new team has inadequate resources or experience.
- The dominant firm: well established, controlling key patents with strong traditional strategies, and immune from serious challenge.

- The entrepreneurial conglomerate: an extension of the kind of approach used by a visionary entrepreneur in starting a company.
- The innovator: a smaller firm with a simple structure and undiversified product line, with much product innovation.

In 1986, Miller suggested that there are four basic strategic configurations which are associated with particular organizational structures. These configurations are:

- Niche marketers: focus on a specific type of customer, service or geographical area. The structure tends to be simple, with little formalization or bureaucratization, dominated by a chief executive. This is a common scenario in the voluntary nonprofit sector.
- Innovators: invest in research and development, to constantly develop new services and products so as to stay ahead of other organizations in the field. The structure is often organic (Burns and Stalker 1961), and the organizations are sometimes called 'adhocracies' (Mintzberg 1979), having few rules or structures. Power tends to be decentralized.
- Cost leaders: tend to operate in relatively stable environments and to standardize the production of a product or service to deliver it at the lowest-possible cost. The structure tends to be a rigidly mechanistic (Burns and Stalker 1961) bureaucracy.
- Divisionized conglomerates: tend to operate unfocused, diversified strategies. The structure tends to be divisionalized and bureaucratic. Each division is responsible for one, or one group of, products or services and may be quite different from the others. There are various instances of voluntary nonprofit organizations that have developed a range of only tangentially related services aimed at diverse beneficiaries.

Nutt and Backoff's matrix

Nutt and Backoff, in their handbook on strategic management for public and nonprofit organization leaders (1992), recognize the importance of the political arena for public and voluntary nonprofit organizations. Their framework has two dimensions: the extent of pressure for action to tackle needs, and the need for external responsiveness and collaboration with other agencies. They suggest a positive and negative strategy that can be adopted in each segment of the matrix, as follows:

High pressure for action, but low external responsiveness required:

- Director strategy: assumes a moderate to high action orientation with a moderate accountability. Where the organization tries to operate with no accountability (a Dominator strategy), it tends to run into difficulties.

Low pressure for action, but high external accountability required:

- Accommodator strategy: in a stable environment this strategy demonstrates an adequate responsiveness to a particular constituency. When there is no real action the strategy can become one of Posturer.

Low pressure for action, and accountability required:

- Bureaucrat strategy: depends on routinized programmes and standardized procedures in a stable environment, to carry out modest action in relation to specific needs with limited accountability and little innovation. At its most negative the strategy becomes that of a Drifter, with little direction or accountability, and achieving little.

High pressure for action, and accountability required:

- Mutualist strategy: the most proactive of the archetypes, which is particularly appropriate to deal with a turbulent environment and respond to diverse and changing needs in an effective and collaborative way with other agencies. In response to calls for action to respond to a number of needs, the Compromiser strategy will try to play constituencies off against each other, often only responding to the needs of the most important or the most needy.

Rubin's strategy metaphors

Rubin (1988), from his study of public sector organizations, characterizes types of strategic actions as the following metaphors:

Saga: depicts an historical perspective focusing on the heroic exploits, achievements and traditional values of the organization to defend itself from change. Within the Saga orientation, Rubin suggested that three different strategies may operate:

- restorative strategies: bring the organization back to where it was before changes were imposed by the external environment;
- conservatory strategies: protect the values of individuals and particular organizational arrangements;
- reformative strategies: will modify existing policy and mandates which are no longer seen to be appropriate.

Quest: suggests leaders who focus their efforts and resources around a compelling vision and captures the sense of adventure and test of courage in search of something of value. Within the Quest metaphor, Rubin suggested there can be three kinds of strategy:

- the new agenda strategy: involves creating a coalition of people around a new agenda which deliberately brings together actors with different priorities;

- the grand vision strategy: develops a clear image of what the future state of the organization can become which attracts support around it;
- an alternative course strategy: designed to deal with a particular burning issue, and to focus attention on resolving this key problem.

Venture: an action that responds to particular opportunities or needs in the present or near future, particular in relation to emerging issues where the appropriate long-term response is not clear. The strategies may include:

- the target strategy: improves the organization's capacity before an emerging issue can be addressed;
- the trial strategy: involves short-term experiments and temporary arrangements to deal with an emerging issue;
- the compact strategy: involves short-term arrangements with other organizations concerned with the issue or need, which can be renegotiated later.

Parlay: used by organizations to exploit opportunities to position themselves for better opportunities. This can be useful when it is difficult to read the pattern of trends and events. It draws on Quinn's (1980) incremental approach where small actions may result in learning which will feed into further actions, etc. The strategies involved may include:

- a hedging strategy: where there are several likely future scenarios. Prioritization of programmes is deliberately avoided to give scope for action when the situation becomes clearer;
- a leveraging strategy: using the development of social contacts and networks that will build up social credit and goodwill that can be cashed in when required at a later date;
- an advancing strategy: uses a windfall opportunity to reduce risk.

Barry's nonprofit strategies

Barry (1986) is one of the few writers who has addressed the particular strategy configurations of voluntary nonprofit organizations. He has categorized them as follows:

- Large voluntary nonprofit organizations, in particular, often choose growth and diversification of funding sources as a way of gaining control over their environment. The major case studies in Part V of Save the Children, Barnardo's, Oxfam, Grameen and CARE, for example, all reflect this kind of combined expansion strategy.
- Nonprofit organizations may choose to team up with each other through mergers, collaborations, joint ventures, etc. The HIV/AIDS charities in Britain have recently gone through a period of merger, to ensure their long-term ability to survive in the context of a changing external environment (see Box 15.1).

Box 15.1   *Mergers in the voluntary nonprofit health field*

In the private sector there has been considerable evidence of consolidation taking place in various industries, through mergers and acquisitions. Until recently there has been little sign that the voluntary nonprofit sector would follow suit. However, in the health field in the UK, there have been significant moves towards mergers, particularly in relation to HIV/AIDS and cancer.

Following a period of financial difficulties caused by competitive contracting in the Health Service and a drop-off in public interest in HIV/AIDS, two key mergers have been taking place in the HIV/AIDS field.

In April 2000 the National AIDS Trust (NAT), a leading HIV charity, focused on policy and prevention, and Red Ribbon International, which has led the campaigning around World AIDS Day with the red ribbon, as well as other campaigning work, merged. The two organizations see combining the two campaigning/policy organizations (neither provide direct services to people with HIV) as a way of strengthening their ability to improve the lives of people with HIV and protect communities vulnerable to infection in the UK and developing countries.

In October 2000, two of Britain's leading HIV/AIDS organizations, the Terence Higgins Trust, which had already merged with a number of regional HIV/AIDS charities in the previous year, and London Lighthouse, joined forces to form a single organization, Terence Higgins Trust Lighthouse. The combined organization will have a turnover of £8M. They hope that merging will enable savings to be made of around £1.2M through efficiency measures and streamlining of activities. They also hope that, as a single entity, the two organizations will in the longer term be able to generate greater income in this difficult fundraising field.

The two organizations are complementary in their particular strengths. The Terence Higgins Trust has been traditionally strong in relation to campaigning, health promotion, direct marketing, major donors and corporate fundraising, while London Lighthouse is very well regarded by those who use their services, and has been effective in cause-related marketing and committee-led fundraising.

In the cancer field, the plethora of large cancer charities has been confusing for the public, who find it hard to distinguish the roles of the various charities and therefore to be confident that they are not unnecessarily duplicating services.

In 2000, Macmillan Cancer Relief and Marie Curie Cancer Care, two leading UK cancer charities, discussed merging, but decided against it because of doubts as to whether a combined organization would be

> more effective than two single organizations working apart. In 2001, the Cancer Research Campaign and Imperial Cancer Research Fund are engaged in talks about a possible merger, driven particularly by the medical research side, which believes a combined organization is more likely to find a cure for cancer. The impact on income generation of combining two very large fundraising operations is currently an open question.

- With financial constraints, voluntary nonprofit organizations may choose to downsize, or have it imposed on them.
- Voluntary nonprofit organizations may choose to focus on a particular area or issue and specialize in that area. The major case study of Care In The Home in Part V discusses a voluntary nonprofit organization which has chosen to focus its activities.
- Nonprofit organizations may use 'piggybacking' – developing an activity which is income-generating in order to subsidize an activity which needs resources (see Box 15.2 for an example of an organization that has very effectively developed piggybacking as an income-generation strategy).

Box 15.2   *Commercial piggybacking: Fundación Social**

Fundación Social, a Colombian foundation founded by a Jesuit priest in 1911, is committed to the elimination of the structural cause of poverty and the transformation of Colombian society. It was established to provide a sustainable source of funding for social development projects without relying on the government or any other source. Originally, Fundación Social was funded solely by the Caja Social de Ahorros, a savings fund generated by the workers who benefited from the fund's resources. The fund's profits were invested and the income used to support community self-help initiatives. Today, Fundación Social's revenue base continues to come from private companies that are owned by the foundation.

Unlike many successful businesses, the Fundación Social is not a business that has its own philanthropic foundation; it is a foundation that has its own group of businesses. The board of directors and the executive staff of these companies are the same as those of the foundation. With assets of more than US$2 billion, Fundación Social has fourteen for-profit companies and numerous social programmes serving some three million clients throughout Colombia.

The foundation's companies span the industries of finance, construction, health, recreation and communication. They are highly competitive

---

and growing, particularly those in the financial sector, laying to rest the myth that financial services geared to low-income populations cannot yield profits. The largest and most profitable is the original Caja Social de Ahorros, with thousands of small deposits from low-income individuals and families, whose profits are then invested and used for social development.

After reinvesting a portion of annual profits to conserve patrimony, compensate for inflation and keep its enterprises at the cutting edge, Fundación Social is left with approximately $4 million of its $35 million annual profits to support social programmes, which are integrated local development programmes in some of Colombia's most challenging areas. They tend to focus on the poorest sectors of society and generally use long-term, holistic, replicable strategies.

Fundación Social's success rests on a series of strengths that have important implications for replication:

- a relatively secure source of working capital social projects leveraged from an expanding market;
- a mechanism for supplying financial services to low-income people regularly denied access to credit and savings opportunities;
- competition from market forces, which makes the organization efficient and carries over into the social programmes to stimulate a focus on sustainability criteria;
- a large clientele of low-income individuals and families, which effectively disperses risk;
- a foothold, gained by operating in the market, from which to influence the market on behalf of poor people.

At the same time, there are several constraints to this approach. Capital is only available once the enterprise establishes a certain level of profitability, and the fourteen companies operate at different levels of profitability. As with any business, there is always risk of failure. It may be difficult to assemble a management team that combines business acumen and social commitment. And a precarious balance must be maintained between the financial health of the enterprise and the social investment.

Through this unique self-financing strategy, Fundación Social has broken the traditional approach that centred on projects in favour of a long-term, results-oriented, programme-support strategy.

* This case study was adapted by Horacio R. Morales Jr (1997) from Steven Pierce, 'Grassroots Development and the Issue of Scale: A Colombian Case', *Grassroots Development*, vol. 19, no. 2, 1995.

- Voluntary nonprofit organizations can seek contracts, especially in the Health and Social Services field. The NSPCC, for example, has developed extensive contracts with social services for a range of services over the past twenty years (see major case study on the NSPCC in Part V).
- Voluntary nonprofit organizations may choose to professionalize their activities by upgrading their staffing. This is very common after the first entrepreneurial phase of a voluntary nonprofit initiative that has been started by volunteers, sometimes supplemented by placements or trainees. As the organization develops, professional staff are appointed. (See, for example, the major case studies of the Simon Community and the NSPCC in Part V.)
- Voluntary nonprofit organizations can also deprofessionalize, using volunteers, peer education, community development strategies, etc.
- Voluntary nonprofit organizations can also decide to wind up if they believe they are no longer of value, or are not economically viable.

An interesting approach that bridges the voluntary nonprofit (or at least churches, as part of the wider voluntary nonprofit sector) and private sectors has been developed by Henry Mintzberg, one of the leading figures in modern thinking on strategy in the private sector, and Frances Westley, who had originally trained in the sociology of religion. Mintzberg and Westley looked at the strategies that the main world religions had used to survive over such a long time period despite enormous changes externally. They suggested three key types of strategy (in the sense of pattern rather than plan):

- Enclaving: involves the carefully controlled integration of learning from within the existing structures.

  The change is conceived in an enclave of the organisation. Rather than destroying the effort, the organisation tolerates it (however minimally), isolating it to avoid challenge to, or contamination of, the rest of its activities. At some point, however, whether because the movement has moderated its radicalism or the larger organisation finds itself in crisis and so has the need of the change (or perhaps, more commonly, both together), the change is accepted, legitimised, and then allowed to infuse the rest of the organisation and so effect a broader shift.

  (Mintzberg and Westley 1992)

- Cloning: involves the splitting-off of groups into separate organizations or units, allowing for the expression of a variety of interpretations and a range of innovations. There are many examples of voluntary nonprofit organizations that spin off new organizations, either in a new geographical area or from an emerging activity from within the organization. Kearns (2000) discusses divestment strategies for nonprofit organizations but assumes that they are only appropriate in negative circumstances requiring retrenchment. Many voluntary nonprofit organizations, however, adopt the positive strategy of developing new initiatives and, if they are successful, then floating them off as independent organizations.

- Uprooting: a way of trying to keep the original vision and enthusiasm fresh by preventing the organization becoming bureaucratized and safe, by plunging the organization, or part of it, into a new context. Mao Tze-tung's Cultural Revolution was an example of how Mao tried to revitalize the Revolution by literally uprooting large numbers of Chinese from their homes. As in this example, the question is 'At what cost?'

The founder of the Simon Community (see the major case study on the Community in Part V), which works with people who are homeless in Britain and Ireland, had a deliberate policy of occasional retrenchment which involved the closure of its houses for people who were homeless in order to provide the organization with a period of reflection on its vision and purpose.

The various models and taxonomies of strategic options suggest a complex matrix of strategic choices for voluntary nonprofit organizations (see Box 15.3).

Box 15.3   *Matrix of strategic choices for voluntary nonprofit organizations*

	Client group	Services	Geography
Retrench	Reduce, divest or close services to particular client group(s)	Reduce, divest or close particular services/activities	Reduce, divest or close services in a particular geographical area
Reduce costs	Reduce costs of services to particular client group(s)	Reduce costs of particular service(s)	Reduce costs of services in a particular geographical area
Maintain	Continue services to existing client groups	Continue existing services	Continue services in existing areas
Improve quality	Improve the quality of services to particular client group(s)	Improve the quality of particular service(s)	Improve the quality of services in particular area(s)

Experiment	Pilot service(s) to a new client group	Pilot new kind of service(s)	Pilot service(s) in a new geographical area
Quantitative expansion	Increase the number of clients served	Increase the extent of provision of particular service(s)	Increase the provision of services in a particular area
Expand boundary	Extend the boundary of particular client group(s)	Extend the amount of particular service(s) that is provided	Extend the boundary of the geographical area covered
Change strategy – switch to new related	Switch services to a related client group	Switch to delivering a related type of service/activity	Switch to delivering services in a related geographical area
Radical change strategy – switch to new unrelated	Switch services to an unrelated client group	Switch to delivering an unrelated type of service/activity	Switch to providing services in an unrelated area
Piggybacking	Develop fee-earning service(s) to a particular customer group to earn income to subsidize other programmes	Develop particular fee-earning service(s) to subsidize other activities	Develop fee-earning service(s) in a particular geographical area to subsidize other activities
Partnering	Develop a closer partnership with another agency in relation to particular client group(s)	Develop a closer partnership with another agency in relation to particular service(s)	Develop a closer partnership with another agency in particular geographical area
Unrelated expansion	Expand to provide services to an unrelated client group	Expand to provide unrelated types of service/activity	Expand to provide services in unrelated area(s)

Summary

This chapter has explored the difficulty of determining generic strategies, and asked whether it is even possible to talk about generic strategies. A variety of different possible ways of categorizing the generic strategic choices that voluntary nonprofit organizations face have been explored.

Questions

1   How many different generic strategies are there that voluntary nonprofit organizations can adopt? Are some more effective than others?
2   Is growth always a good thing for voluntary nonprofit organizations?
3   To what extent is innovation a good thing for voluntary nonprofit organizations?
4   Should voluntary nonprofit organizations always aim for survival?
5   Should voluntary nonprofit organizations divest/spin-off good projects that could be independent?
6   Should voluntary nonprofit organizations working in a similar field and geographical area merge?
7   What are the advantages and disadvantages of joint initiatives with other organizations?

Suggested reading

Kevin P. Kearns (2000) *Private sector strategies for social sector success*, Jossey-Bass.
Henry Mintzberg *et al.* (1998) *Strategy safari: A guided tour through the wilds of strategic management*, Prentice-Hall.
P. C. Nutt and R. W. Backoff (1992) *Strategic management of public and third-sector organizations*, Jossey-Bass.
Sharon Oster (1995) *Strategic management for nonprofit organizations: Theory and cases*, Oxford University Press.

16 Strategic implementation
Making it happen

Chapter outline

This chapter explores the various factors that ensure the strategy of a voluntary nonprofit organization, once it has been agreed, will actually be implemented effectively. In particular the chapter will explore the issues of organizational resources, physical, financial and human; operational planning; performance management; and structure.

Learning objectives

When you have completed this chapter you should understand:

* the key elements of successful strategic implementation;
* the importance of plans for each of the organization's resources to achieve the overall plan;
* the concept, and importance, of operational planning;
* the concept, and importance, of performance management;
* the importance of monitoring the implementation of the strategic plan;
* some of the options for organizational structure.

Introduction

For some voluntary nonprofit organizations, indeed for any organization, the greatest weakness in relation to strategic planning is probably in the implementation phase, or, rather, the non-implementation phase. All too often a one-off plan is drafted, even including many of the elements given above, but it then sits in a filing cabinet for a few years until someone, often an evaluator or a new chief executive or chair, comes along who thinks it is time for a new strategic plan, and so on. This is not only a problem of implementation. It is also a problem of formulation, because the plan does not include a number of elements that are key to ensuring that the plan is implemented and regularly revised to take into account changing circumstances. As Bryson (1995) states:

Creating a strategic plan is not enough. Developing effective programs, projects, action plans, budgets, and implementation processes will bring life to the strategies and create real value for the organization (or community) and its stakeholders.

However, as Stone *et al.* (1999) point out, there has been little actual research that has focused directly on implementation of strategic activities in the voluntary nonprofit context.

Bryson (1995) also points out the danger of implementation processes being too rigid, preventing adaptive learning taking place (see the Learning School, discussed in Chapter 8) when circumstances change or new knowledge becomes available internally or externally. As Mintzberg (1994) points out, realized strategies are (and should be) a mixture of what is intended and what emerges in practice.

Resource implications

One of the key criteria for an activity being strategic is that it requires the commitment of significant resources. One of the first of the crucial elements in strategic implementation, then, is consideration of the resource implications of the plan that has been drafted, i.e. to ask what resources will be required to ensure that the plan can be implemented fully. These resource implications are likely to include:

- physical resources, such as buildings, vehicles, equipment, furniture, etc., which may be purchased or rented/leased;
- human resources, such as the number and type of staff and volunteers (including trustees) required to carry out the plans; the skills and knowledge needed to implement the plan effectively; human resource policies and procedures which ensure that trustees, staff and volunteers receive the support and supervision they require, and that the appropriate salary and benefits structure are in place to ensure both that good staff stay and that the organization is able to recruit appropriate new staff; and an appropriate organizational structure to make sure the organization works effectively together (see the discussion on organizational structures later in this chapter);
- systems and procedures, such as administration, personnel, finance, training, quality, governance, etc.;
- financial resources, which are the costs of the other resources outlined above, and may be one-off capital costs, time restricted project costs, salaries, or annual programme or administration costs.

The ultimate aim of considering the resource implications of the strategic plan under the above headings is often to create a multi-year budget which will clarify the specific financial resources and ultimately the funding/fund-raising targets that will need to be set and achieved within the plan to ensure these resources are provided. Alternatively, it may result in a revision of the strategic plan in order to make the plan more realistic.

Bryson (1995) argues that budget decisions are critical to strategic implementation and often 'represent the most important and consequential policy statements that…nonprofit organisations make'.

Having developed a budget that puts a price tag on the strategic plan, the monitoring of this requires an appropriate financial management and reporting system (Oster 1995), yet, as Anthony and Young (1984) suggest, the financial controls in many voluntary nonprofit organizations are woefully inadequate.

The resource aspects of the annual operational plan are sometimes referred to, or included as part of, a business plan (see the definition of business planning later in this chapter).

The resource-based view discussed in Chapters 7 and 12 places resources at the heart of strategy and argues that resources don't simply follow strategy, as the organization's distinctive resources are central to the organization's success and around which the strategy needs to be built. The organization's distinctive resources will therefore be an important part of the review of the organization discussed in Chapter 12. Some of the organization's resources may reflect particular strengths or unique competencies which should help indicate where the organization's future strategy should lie.

Monitoring

Many strategic plans fail to be implemented simply because no framework was put in place at the beginning to monitor progress against the plan. At its simplest this requires the board of the organization to agree a timetable for reports to be produced which describe the progress that has been made in achieving the objectives under each aim/objective and at the same time reporting on each of the performance indicators. It is obviously important to indicate if an objective has not been achieved, and why, and a new timetable to be established for its achievement if the objective is still relevant.

This process of regular monitoring of progress against the strategic plan provides a key agenda item for the board, and ensures that its members remain focused on strategy rather than operational detail. It also enables the board to feel much more in control of the outcomes of the organization.

Depending on the nature of the plan and the changeability of the external environment, it may be appropriate for the board to consider a progress monitoring report quarterly, or every six months.

Rolling operational plan

The structure of the planning process recommended by Bryson (1995) and many others, which is outlined in Chapter 14 of this book, requires a further step to be included in the process to ensure that it is implementable. This is the process of drawing up the detailed operational or business plan for each year based on the agreed mission, vision, values, long-term aims and priorities contained in the strategic plan. Schofield defines such business planning as follows: 'business planning is about making strategic vision a reality and it does this by identifying the tasks which need to be completed and then allocating these tasks into particular organizational functions'. This process, which Koteen (1989) calls 'bite-sized management' and Bryson (1995) describes as 'action planning', usually begins in the middle of the previous operational plan year. In the middle of year one, therefore, the organization would begin the process of drawing up the year two operational plan. In the middle of year two the process of drawing up the operational plan for year three would begin.

The mission, vision, values and priorities, however, tend to remain largely the same each year, unless there is major change in the focus of the organization or external environment over the three years; yet typically the operational plan is created each year as it is rarely possible for an organization to be able to say exactly what it will be able to achieve over each of three years of a strategic plan. Plans that do try to do this tend to look very sparse in year three! It is therefore common to create these much more specific operational plans which usually clarify, one year at a time, the progress the organization intends to make that year towards achieving the organization's mission, vision, values and priorities.

The operational plan is normally based on creating objectives which are SMART:

Specific and Stretching
Measurable and Motivating
Achievable and Agreed
Realistic and Robust
Time-scaled and Timely

Examples of objectives for a faith-based training organization are given in Box 16.1.

The operational objectives are usually established under each long-term aim in the expectation that, taken together, the objectives will make an impact on achieving that aim and, therefore, ultimately on the mission of the organization.

Box 16.1   *Examples of objectives for a faith-based training organization*

Objectives for 2000–2001

- Agree with the churches a formal system for assessing skills training needs by October 2002
- Twenty young people to have completed the new youth work training programme by 31 March 2002
- Agree a training evaluation framework by October 2002
- Put in place a system for monitoring the training performance indicators by October 2002
- Produce an assessment of training needs by 31 March 2002
- Run one 'Effective Youth Work' programme by 31 March 2002

Managing individual performance

The strategic plan will also come to nothing if it does not become part of the daily work of each of the individual staff teams and members. In small organizations it may be enough to ensure that each of the objectives in the operational plan is allocated to a named individual. In larger organizations the cycle of performance appraisal or review with staff and volunteers usually relates to the operational planning cycle, so that targets can be set with individuals which will in turn achieve the operational objectives in the plan.

Where there is a performance management system that is based on the organization's strategic and operational planning cycles, the review of the performance of staff should take place at the end of the annual operational planning period so it is possible to discuss the contribution that the individual made towards the organization's operational plan in the preceding twelve months, and will make in the forthcoming twelve months.

The board also needs to consider the management of the chief officer, which should also be based on how well the aims and objectives have been achieved. The appraisal of the chief officer may be done by the chair, or by another board member with the relevant skills.

Commitment and motivation

It is clear from the discussion in Chapter 7 that ensuring the plan is implemented requires the commitment and motivation of the board, staff and volunteers. This commitment is only likely to be there if there is a high level of ownership of the plan. As Weisbrod (1988) says, 'people will support what they help to create'. This, in turn, will require ensuring that board members, staff and volunteers have all had a real opportunity to participate in the strategic planning process and put forward their own ideas. Experience would indicate that the earlier in the process the board members, staff and volunteers are involved, the more committed they are likely to be to implementing the final plan.

Similarly, involving other key stakeholders in the strategic analysis and formulation processes is likely to result in a much greater commitment and support from them in implementing the agreed strategy.

Structure

To deliver an organizational strategy there needs to be an appropriate structure through which the strategy can be delivered. Some of the issues that will influence organizational structure are as follows:

- The legal status of the organization. This will be particularly important in relation to the structure of the board or management committee, as well as the relationship between sub-units/affiliates/members and the central/parent organization.
- The size of the organization. An organization of six staff will be very differently structured from an organization with one hundred staff. In particular, larger organizations will require additional layers of management and the relevant policies and procedures for supervision and appraisal and team leadership, as well as specialist skills in particular functions such as finance and human resources.
- The level of collaboration or competition with other agencies.
- The complexity of the tasks that the staff/volunteers need to undertake. This will affect the amount of supervision that is required and therefore the span of control of any manager.
- The organization's geographical spread.
- The diversity of services provided and user groups served.
- The diversity of the different skills and knowledge that are required to carry out the various functions.
- The extent to which services are provided by permanent staff, or by volunteers or short-term placements, trainees, freelance consultants, etc.
- The financial stability of the organization, which will affect the ability to commit the organization to permanently contracted staff.

Any organization has a number of basic choices about the main structure of the organization. These include:

- Geographical structure: many international agencies, for example, have directors and offices, even separate organizations, in each country or region in which they have a presence. The nature of this relationship is often problematic. Depending on the organizational history, the need and demand for local control and the value of what is provided by the centre, the relationship can be:
    - a direct hierarchical relationship with strong central control;

- a looser relationship with greater autonomy, and perhaps a local advisory board;
- closer to a franchise, with considerable autonomy within the constraints of the franchise agreement, which must be met if the region wishes to be able to use the name and logo of the parent (Oster 1992 argues that this structure has significant advantages);
- complete autonomy, with no central control, and perhaps with a federal membership structure where the members collectively control the centre.
- Client group structure: where the organization serves very different kinds of client groups, the organization may be structured around the different groups; e.g. an organization that serves children and young adults may have separate children's and young adults' divisions.
- Services structure: alternatively, where the kinds of services provided are very different from each other, it may be more appropriate to structure around the different kinds of services; e.g. an organization providing services for the homeless may have separate hostels, long-term housing and campaigning divisions.
- Functional structure: where the structure creates a number of separate functional departments, e.g. finance, fundraising, human resources, communications, direct services. Boards sometimes mirror these functions by establishing sub-committees to oversee at least some part of them (finance is the most common instance of this).
- Process/project structure: much more fluid than the other structures and provides the flexibility to create project teams for various periods to respond to particular opportunities (or threats); e.g. an international relief agency may put together specific project teams with the right mix of skills to respond to a particular disaster situation.

It is important to recognize that the issue of structure is not a static one. Particularly for organizations that are growing, the issue of structure will regularly come to the fore, as structures need to adapt to meet the current requirements of the organization.

When an organization is small and situated all on one site, the structure can be simple, with all the staff or volunteers meeting regularly together as a team. Expansion of the number of staff or volunteers often leads to the creation of a new structure with additional managers and separate teams. This can create the silo effect, with departments tending to protect their own patch within the organization and engage in turf wars with other departments. Expansion into other sites can create further potential for conflict. Grossman and Rangman (2001) highlight some of the areas of difficulty when an organization has more than one site, including the following:

- How is income generated in the area of an affiliate (sub-office, region, etc.) allocated?

- How well does that affiliate comply with the quality standards and procedures established by the centre?
- Is the affiliate keeping within the mission of the organization and reflecting the appropriate image of the organization's name?
- Does the centre provide appropriate and valued services, commensurate with any affiliation fee?
- Is decision-making authority clear between the centre and the affiliate (often between a national board and a local one)?

Some major organizations that have had a devolved structure with independent affiliates have successfully transformed the organizational structure to create a much stronger and unified structure. Examples include the British Red Cross, the American Heart Association, the American Cancer Society, and the American Diabetes Association. Others have given greater devolved authority, even independence, to geographical regions.

The success of restructuring to create more centralized organizations probably reflects the success the national organizations had in winning the trust of the member organizations through a broadly inclusive decision-making process; member organizations were persuaded that the restructuring would increase resources available for local programmes and services (Standley 2001).

Ultimately it is vital that the adopted structure enhances the ability of the organization to deliver the agreed strategy. Clarity and simplicity of structure is probably the key. There has been an increasing awareness in the last decade that too many levels in an organization, and too complicated structures, only diminish the ability of the organization to be effective. All the teams and individual staff and volunteers need to be clear about the contribution they are required to make to achieve the agreed strategy. The structures should enhance the ability of individuals and teams to achieve the strategy.

Summary

This chapter has highlighted the importance of implementation in the strategy process. It has explored the key elements of the implementation of the strategic plan, and in particular the analysis of resource requirements and the drawing up of budgets, the monitoring of the implementation of the strategic plan, the performance management systems to connect the individual staff (and volunteers) with the requirements of the strategic plan, the importance of relevant organizational structures, and the importance of wide participation in the strategic planning process to gain commitment to implementing the strategic plan.

Questions

1 To what extent does the existing structure of the organization help determine the strategy? And to what extent does it work the other way round?
2 How should individuals be linked into the implementation of the strategic plan?
3 How can the process of drawing up the plan assist in ensuring that it is effectively implemented?
4 How can you ensure that an individual contributes to the achievement of the organizational strategy?
5 What factors should determine the structure of a voluntary nonprofit organization?

Suggested reading

Richard L. Edwards, John A. Yankey and Mary A. Altpeter (eds) (1998) *Skills for effective management of nonprofit organisations*, NASW Press.
Andrew Hind (1995) *The governance and management of charities*, Voluntary Sector Press.
Mike Hudson (1995) *Managing without profit*, Penguin.
Stephen P. Osborne (ed.) (1996) *Managing in the voluntary sector – a handbook for managers in charitable and non-profit organisations*, International Thomson Business Press.
Smith, Bucklin and Associates (1994) *The complete guide to nonprofit management*, Wiley.

Part V

Case studies

Introduction

Most of the following case studies are drawn from publicly available information, mainly annual reports and websites, with two exceptions (CITH and Homeline). They are designed to illustrate issues highlighted in the main text of the book. At the end of each case study, there are a series of questions for discussion or individual work.

Learning objectives

While the learning from each case study will be different, taken as a whole the case studies should enable the reader who has tried to answer the questions given at the end of each case study to understand:

- the different kinds of strategies that voluntary nonprofit organizations adopt, consciously or unconsciously;
- the difference between planned and emergent strategies;
- the potential implications of some kinds of strategy;
- the impact of a changing external environment;
- different phases of organizational development;
- the significance of the founder, both positively and negatively;
- the impact of the lobbying by voluntary nonprofit organizations in changing legislation and policy at national and international level;
- some of the difficulties of organizational change.

Case studies

The case studies are as follows:

Save the Children Fund	The Simon Community
Care In The Home (CITH)	Grameen Bank
World Wide Fund for Nature (WWF)	Homeline
	NSPCC
CARE	Oxfam

Save the Children Fund

Foundation

> All wars, just or unjust, disastrous or victorious, are waged against the child.
> Eglantyne Jebb

Save the Children was founded in 1919, as a response to conditions in Europe immediately following World War One. During the war, the Allied powers had enforced a blockade that had brought Germany and her allies to their knees, and continued this after the signing of the Armistice in order to force them to accept the Allies' terms for peace. A month after the signing of the Armistice, an election was held in the UK. The Conservative coalition's successful campaign was based around popular sentiment that wanted to 'squeeze Germany until the pips squeak'.

Meanwhile the populations of the Axis powers, especially in the cities of Berlin and Vienna, were devastated by the blockade. Children were especially affected by the food shortages which inevitably left them vulnerable to diseases like TB and rickets.

Not all people in the UK took a vengeful view of their former enemies. Throughout the war a group led by Dorothy Buxton had been reading and translating the European press for the *Cambridge Magazine*. These 'Notes from the Foreign Press' attempted to provide balance to the propaganda-driven UK newspapers.

At the beginning of 1919, Buxton and her associates set up the Fight the Famine Council in order to campaign for justice and compassion for the defeated nations. This organization's campaigning soon fell foul of the Defence of the Realm Act for publishing and distributing the leaflets *A Starving Baby* and *Our Blockade Has Caused This* without the permission of the government. Buxton's sister, Eglantyne Jebb, was arrested and fined for distributing copies of *A Starving Baby* in Trafalgar Square.

By this time, the Fight the Famine Council had decided that practical measures, as well as campaigning, were needed to alleviate suffering caused by the blockade and the aftermath of war. Buxton and Jebb were heavily involved in getting this fundraising venture off the ground. The Save the Children Fund, as Dorothy named it, was publicly launched at London's Royal Albert Hall in May 1919. It began a fundraising campaign to raise money to send to children in Europe in the areas devastated by war.

Jebb argued that the organization must be modern and business-like.

> The new charity…must be scientific; it must have the same clear conceptions of its objects and seek to compass them with the same care, the same thoroughness, the same intelligence as are found in the best commercial and industrial enterprises.

The new organization was successful in gathering donations very quickly. Initially, Save the Children allocated money to organizations working with children in Germany and Austria, and also in France, Belgium, the Balkans and Hungary, and with Armenian refugees in Turkey. It was not anticipated that it would be a long-lived organization and its first workers were employed on six-week contracts. In the immediate post-war period, however, Save the Children had to deal with emergency after emergency in Europe. Once it became clear that people were prepared to continue entrusting money to Save the Children, the organization's council began to look at ways of helping children to build longer-term futures for themselves, as well as giving temporary relief.

> [T]he work of the Save the Children Fund is constructive as well as palliative…our earnest endeavour is always to ensure that a just proportion of the money with which we are entrusted shall be devoted to works which will bear increase in permanently bettered conditions for children.
>
> (Lord Weardale, First President of Save the Children, 1922)

It was able to sustain its fundraising effort because its leaders were prepared to use the range of media available to them to raise money. Eglantyne Jebb, in particular, was a persuasive and committed leader, with many ideas about the welfare of children that were well ahead of her time.

Within a short period, Save the Children had become known as an effective relief agency, able to distribute food, clothing and money swiftly and at low cost. By 1921, when the world learnt of extensive famine in Russia, Save the Children was able to organize an operation to feed up to 650,000 people there at a cost of just a shilling (5p) each per week.

Claiming rights for children – the 1920s

Jebb was a committed internationalist and believed that international cooperation would make the work of her new organization more effective. Early in 1920 she oversaw the creation of the International Save the Children

Union, a combination of organizations from various countries which were working together to relieve child suffering in Europe.

Jebb planned an initiative that would ensure that the rights and welfare of children continued to be a major issue around the world. She was not the only person thinking along these lines, but her vision was a simple statement of rights that would have a claim on everybody dealing with children, not just the wealthy or the powerful.

> I believe we should claim certain Rights for the children and labour for their universal recognition, so that everybody – not merely the small number of people who are in a position to contribute to relief funds, but everybody who in any way comes into contact with children, that is to say the vast majority of mankind – may be in a position to help forward the movement.
>
> (Eglantyne Jebb 1923)

Jebb's *Declaration of the Rights of the Child* was adopted and promoted by the International Save the Children Union. Within a year it had been adopted by the League of Nations and had achieved lasting international significance. The present UN Convention on the Rights of the Child is derived at least partly from Jebb's original inspiration.

The Declaration had a major impact on Save the Children, which became increasingly focused on international child welfare. At Jebb's instigation, the *Record of the Save the Children Fund* changed its name to *World's Children* and became a journal focused on child rights and welfare issues around the globe. Regular summer schools for staff and supporters were held in Geneva, debating international questions of child welfare.

After 1923, the nature of the organization's work changed. With less emergency work to be done, and with the Declaration as its main focus, Save the Children became involved in carrying out and publishing research and books about working with children in different countries, and organizing conferences, as well as running pioneering projects in various countries in Europe.

In Hungary, Save the Children supported a school to give job training to unemployed young people. This institution relied on the principle of cooperation that was dear to Jebb. The children worked in teams, the more able helping the less skilled. Team leaders were able to deal with minor disciplinary matters and the children were given a say in the life of the school.

> All our wisdom in the work school comes from the children.
>
> (Julie Eve Vajkai, Save the Children, 1929)

Save the Children also attempted lasting solutions for resettling refugees. Special villages were constructed in Albania and Bulgaria where refugees had land, seeds and tools, and were given a chance to rebuild their lives.

It was during this period that work in the UK began. A recuperative school for children from inner-city areas was opened at Fairfield House in Kent. Save the Children also worked with young families of miners in poverty stricken areas of Wales and Cornwall.

Towards international working – the 1930s

Jebb died in 1929 at the early age of 52. At the time of her death, her ambitions for the future were based on extending the work of Save the Children outside Europe. Save the Children and the International Save the Children Union made efforts to turn her vision into a reality. In 1931, they organized a conference in Geneva into the condition of children in Africa. From this a report was published, and the Child Protection Committee was established which continued to lobby for the rights of children in Africa and Asia throughout the decade. The organization's first foray into direct work in Africa was a nursery school in Abyssinia (Ethiopia), which was set up in Addis Ababa in 1936.

> If we accept our premise, that the Save the Children Fund must work for its own extinction, it must seek to abolish, for good and for all, the poverty which makes children suffer and stunts the race of which they are the parents.
>   It must not be content to save children from the hardships of life – it must abolish these hardships; nor think it suffices to save them from immediate menace – it must place in their hands the means of saving themselves and so of saving the world.
>
> (Eglantyne Jebb 1927)

Despite the worldwide recession and a rapid fall in the Fund's income, the 1930s was a period of continued development and consolidation for Save the Children. In the UK, the Depression had highlighted the lack of any meaningful provision for pre-school education in the most depressed areas. The organization responded by setting up nursery schools in several of the worst-hit areas, including the first nursery school in Wales, at Merthyr. It also organized some research into the effects of mass unemployment on children; publishing *Unemployment and the Child: An Enquiry* in 1933. Based on the findings of the report, Save the Children campaigned for the protection of UK children's rights to adequate nutrition by the mandatory provision of school meals and milk in all counties of the UK. It continued this campaign until the principle was accepted in the Education Act of 1944.

The Italian invasion of Abyssinia/Ethiopia brought an end to all work in Africa. In Europe there were refugees from the Spanish Civil War. Save the Children was also part of the Inter Aid committee that organized the *Kindertransports* of Jewish refugees from Nazi persecution to Britain.

World War Two – the 1940s

War disrupted the work of Save the Children in Europe to the extent that the organization was forced to withdraw from projects in occupied Europe. In the UK, Save the Children worked on solutions to social problems caused by the war. Residential nurseries were set up to accommodate young children who had been evacuated from the cities. Day nurseries were set up for the children of parents working in wartime industries. And children's play-centres were set up in air raid shelters in the large cities.

Save the Children also began to establish Junior Clubs for older children in response to concerns for their safety and development, as many of them were playing unsupervised on bombsites. These clubs offered them a place to play and express themselves in safe conditions and with a responsible adult on hand, and, at one of these clubs, the Hopscotch in East London, a 'nursery play-group', was set up for younger children – the first playgroup in the UK and the start of a major area of work for Save the Children in subsequent years.

Overseas, planning for post-war work began in 1942 with the report *Children in Bondage* (Save the Children Fund/Longmans, London, 1943), which painted a picture of widespread violations of children's rights and consequent terrible suffering.

Even though most of the work was concerned with planning for the needs of children in Europe when the war ended, there were attempts to follow Jebb's vision of work in Asia and Africa. Save the Children supported a child welfare centre in Calcutta, and in 1945 a health centre was set up in Nigeria.

The post-war period was marked by the return to Europe of relief workers from the UK. By the autumn of 1946, Save the Children had 105 workers in the field. Work commenced with displaced people, refugees and concentration camp survivors and children in devastated areas of France, Yugoslavia, Poland and Greece.

A changed world – the 1950s

By the beginning of the 1950s the situation in Europe was beginning to return to normal. There were still many displaced families and children in Europe. Work continued in Germany, Austria, Italy and Greece throughout the 1950s, with extra Save the Children teams being sent to Austria in 1956 to help Hungarian refugees fleeing after the failed revolution.

Save the Children Fund continued to develop work outside Europe. In Malaya, the Serendah project worked with orphaned boys, offering them education, training and a safe place to live. Initial attempts to set up projects in Nigeria and Sudan did not last, but other work in Somaliland, Syria and the Lebanon was more successful.

In 1950 the Korean War began. In 1952 the first Save the Children workers arrived in Korea and were to stay for over twenty years, eventually

handing over projects to local organizations. Many children were left destitute by the war and large numbers of unaccompanied children were living
on the streets. Malnutrition and associated diseases were rife. By the end of
the 1950s, the majority of the organization's expenditure was going on work
in Asia instead of Europe.

In spite of its non-political, non-sectarian character and its philosophy of
international cooperation, Save the Children was sometimes affected by post-
war international politics. The drawing of the Iron Curtain meant that Save
the Children was compelled to withdraw from some of the areas in Eastern
Europe where it had been working, such as Poland, Yugoslavia and
Hungary, and it was forced to withdraw from some areas of the Middle East
following the Suez crisis of 1956.

New challenges – the 1960s

The 1960s were hailed as the 'development decade'. The ending of the colo-
nial period saw a new relationship between the West and the new
governments of the developing world, with Western governments prepared
to supply money and resources for development projects. In a relatively pros-
perous era, the public was prepared to donate more money to Save the
Children and other agencies and there was far more scope and funding available for long-term development projects as well as for response to
emergencies and disasters. As some long-running projects in Malaya and
Somalia were handed over to local management, new work such as the
Mwanamugimu project at Mulago Hospital, Uganda, was instigated. This
project worked with communities to teach mothers about nutrition.

> Announcing that, for the first time in the Fund's history, cash contribu-
> tions had passed the £1 million mark during the past financial year,
> Lord Boyd said that the Fund now had full medical and welfare teams in
> 17 countries and that its total help, including that in Great Britain,
> extended to 26 countries in Europe, Asia, Africa and the West Indies.
> Freedom from Hunger projects were beginning to show results in
> Korea, Morocco, Nigeria and the West Indies.
> (Save the Children 45th annual meeting, 1964)

Better welfare systems had not eradicated the social problems caused by
poverty and bad housing. Save the Children continued to work with children
affected by these conditions. Save the Children also believed that giving children in hospital a chance to play would have powerful therapeutic benefits
and would also reassure children frightened by this alien environment. In
1963, Save the Children started the first hospital playgroup in the UK.

Save the Children was again working with children denied basic rights by
conflict during the 1960s, including refugees from the Chinese invasion of

Tibet, children in Vietnam, and children on both side of the civil war in Nigeria.

Disaster and cooperation – the 1970s

During the 1970s Save the Children worked in emergency situations in Bangladesh, Ethiopia, Nicaragua, Honduras and the Sahel region of Africa. In some countries, such as Bangladesh and Honduras, a programme of development work and establishing long-term partnerships with local communities followed emergency work. In other areas, such as Ethiopia, Save the Children's existing presence made emergency work more effective.

One consequence of the experience of the Nicaraguan earthquake disaster was the foundation of the International Save the Children Alliance. The Save the Children International Union, founded by Jebb in 1920, had merged in 1946 with another body to become the International Union for Child Welfare. There were by now several Save the Children organizations in other countries, notably the long-standing operations in Norway, Sweden and Denmark and the USA. They decided to renew formal cooperation on issues of common interest. Later the Alliance played its part in the international cooperation to secure children's rights that led to the adoption of the UN Convention on the Rights of the Child in 1989.

In 1979, Save the Children launched the Stop Polio Campaign as part of an attempt to eradicate polio worldwide.

In the UK, the 'troubles' began in Northern Ireland, and Save the Children worked to secure the rights of young people from both communities. At the same time it began working on projects with the children of travelling people, and for unaccompanied children arriving from Vietnam.

HRH the Princess Royal became President of Save the Children in 1970, on the understanding that she would be a working President and not merely a figurehead.

A changing image – the 1980s

During the 1980s there were new challenges. Disasters again dominated the scene, with famine in Uganda as well as in Somalia. The most high-profile emergency was the famine in Ethiopia. Television coverage of scenes from Ethiopia sparked a renewed interest in Africa's problems, and a consequent rise in donations to Save the Children and a major increase in the organization's work around the world.

While disasters such as the Ethiopian famine of 1984 caught the public attention, they perpetuated negative and destructive stereotypes of the people of developing countries, creating an impression that they were dependent and unable to help themselves. One of Save the Children's initiatives at the end of the decade was to introduce a set of image guidelines which attempted to portray those with whom they work in every country with dignity and respect.

Alongside emergency work, Save the Children attempted on-going support for communities. This included healthcare, immunization and education projects. During the 1980s the spread of HIV/AIDS first came to the attention of the public and was accompanied by a great deal of prejudice and misconception. Save the Children has supported education, prevention and treatment for HIV/AIDS since the 1980s.

In the UK, work was gradually changing to a more community-based approach. Problems caused by poverty continued to affect many children in the UK. Pioneering projects with prisoners' children, work on equal opportunities in education, and Intermediate Treatment – an alternative to custody for young offenders – were also achievements of the decade.

Towards the new century – the 1990s

Children continued to be denied basic rights because of wars, including the Kurds in Iraq following the Gulf War, in Sudan, Somalia, Mozambique, Nicaragua, Colombia, Sri Lanka, Sierra Leone and Angola. The collapse of communist systems saw Save the Children once again working in Eastern Europe, and unfortunately again with children caught up in the conflicts in the Balkans. Save the Children also began campaigning for the rights of child soldiers and for the protection of children forced from their homes by war.

Save the Children's work in the 1990s also encouraged and helped young people to speak for themselves about their experiences, to express their views and to achieve positive change.

A fundamental shift in strategy came in 1996, in relation to work in the UK. This involved a withdrawal from the long-term provision of direct services in favour of innovative projects, research and policy work. The 1996/97 annual report highlighted this change in strategy as follows:

> Adapting to change has meant that Save the Children has taken a long hard look at how it organises itself and uses resources. This has included taking the difficult decision to move away from long-term direct service provision, towards a greater emphasis on innovative projects where we can develop best practice and learn lessons for wider implementation.

The eightieth anniversary of Save the Children, and the tenth anniversary of the UN Convention on the Rights of the Child, were both celebrated in 1999.

The new century, particularly with increasing globalization, has presented new challenges to Save the Children (Gnaerig and MacCormack 2001):

- how to respond to an ageing profile of supporters;

- what the campaigning focus should be, now that the UN Convention on the Rights of the Child has been adopted by most countries;
- how to become more effective and united as a global alliance, given complete national autonomy;
- how to resolve the debate between those who favour child sponsorship as a fundraising method and those who oppose it (usually strongly);
- how to maintain the traditional and deep sense of commitment of staff and volunteers while managing the political sophistication and technological complexities that will be required in the twenty-first century.

Questions

1   How many different strategies can be identified from the above description of Save the Children's development (see Box 15.3: Matrix of strategic choices)? In which decades were each of the strategies most dominant?
2   Do you agree that voluntary nonprofit organizations should be 'scientific' and as good as the best commercial and industrial organizations? If so, in what respects?
3   What are the pros and cons of Save the Children withdrawing from direct service provision in the UK in 1996?
4   What fundamental principles are suggested by the above description of Save the Children's work?
5   Write a mission statement for Save the Children which honours the past but looks to the future.
6   What performance indicators should Save the Children Fund use to evaluate progress in achieving its mission?
7   Jebb suggested that the purpose of Save the Children should be to put itself out of business. To what extent does the development of the organization show that, far from putting itself out of business, any effective organization continuously finds new needs to tackle?
8   If you were asked to give the organization advice on the key issues that they now face, what would that advice be?

Further reading

Save the Children Fund website: www.savethechildren.org.uk/.
International Save the Children Alliance website: www.savethechildren.net/.
Save the Children Fund 1996/7–1999/2000 annual reports.
B. Gnaerig and C. F. MacCormack (1999) 'The challenges of globalization: Save the Children', *Nonprofit and Voluntary Sector Quarterly* 28(4) Supplement.

Care In The Home (CITH)*

Background

CITH was established in a large city in the north of England in 1995 to:

- offer care-managed clients and their carers practical assistance with any aspects of personal caring which clients cannot manage without help;
- provide carers of clients with the opportunity to achieve some quality time for themselves through a home respite service.

CITH grew out of the work of a community house, run by a lay ecumenical Christian Community, in responding to local needs. The religious community had been running a government-funded scheme employing the long-term unemployed to provide local befriending and respite services to those in need in the area. With the ending of funding for the scheme, the religious community reviewed what kinds of services were needed in the area and could be provided. Following the review and some research, the need for domiciliary care services was identified and Care In The Home (CITH) was formally constituted as a company limited by guarantee with charitable status in July 1996.

The agreed key values of CITH were:

- empowering clients to reach their full potential by involving them in expressing their care needs;
- actively promoting equality, choice, dignity, respect and access to individual care and support, without prejudice to age, disability, sex, religion, political or ethnic orientation.

The local health authority agreed to contract CITH to provide domiciliary care services in its area. In 1998, CITH became formally approved as a domiciliary care provider in the wider health region, following the adoption of a set of standards for domiciliary care.

In 1999–2000, CITH was contracted to provide 365 core hours per week to care-managed clients. Of these hours, 355 were under the health authority's Elderly programme, and 10 hours were under the Physical Health and Disability programme. CITH is currently delivering 440 hours home care each week.

Care assistants, who must have at least two years of relevant experience, provide a range of services to meet the needs of clients, seven days a week between 7.30am and 10.30pm. Tasks include the following: washing, dressing, bathing (with appropriate aids), toileting, catheter care, changing urinary and colostomy bags, supervising a client taking medication dispensed from a medibox, teamaking, and serving prepared meals.

Subsequent to October 1999, CITH also provides a respite care service funded by a major charitable trust. Respite staff carry out duties five days a week between 9am and 11pm, including home sitting, assistance with reading and writing letters, teamaking, and small craft activities.

Since 1995, CITH has been successfully providing domiciliary care services on a contractual basis to clients of care managers in the health authority's area and, as a result, has expanded rapidly.

In light of this expansion, and of questions about the future of CITH because of the nature of short-term contracts and the health authority's concerns about the high costs of the care provided, the management committee of CITH decided to commission an evaluation to assess the organizational health of CITH and make recommendations which would ensure that the organization would be able to both honour and build on the work of the past and strengthen it to take on the challenges of the future.

The evaluation

Having gathered a range of information and comments from clients, carers, care managers in the health authority and staff within the organization, the evaluator summarized the key strengths and weaknesses of CITH as follows:

Strengths and weaknesses

Strengths

- The quality of service that is provided by the care assistants to clients and carers is very high. The quality of service was given a consistently high rating in a confidential survey amongst service users and those commissioning the service. This positive response from all those involved in the service is particularly indicative of the trust and positive relationships that have built up between staff and clients and the responsiveness to the needs of clients. The lack of complaints is a further indication of the excellence of the service that is provided.

- The health authority, the sole purchaser of CITH services, is very pleased with the quality of service provided by CITH and would like to see it extended.
- The health authority is also very happy with the communication with CITH. The coordinator and other staff are meticulous in ensuring that the health authority is informed of changes or other issues related to particular clients.
- The staff have a good understanding of the needs and services in the area and there is a sense of friendship and camaraderie between staff.
- The members of the management committee have shown a very substantial commitment to creating and developing the service.
- Because of her particular experience and skills, the coordinator has played a vital role in developing the service in a way that so exceptionally meets the needs of clients, carers and the purchasing agency.
- The care staff clearly demonstrate a high level of commitment, skill and sensitivity to their work with clients.

Weaknesses

COSTS

- The health authority considers that the cost per hour charged by CITH is high compared with other providers. This suggests a threat, in that the health authority may decide in future to save money by commissioning other providers instead of CITH or may establish a standard rate that all providers have to adhere to for similar services, which would be inadequate to enable CITH to meet its costs.
- Related to the above, the comparatively small size of CITH compared with other providers makes it difficult for CITH to spread the administration and management costs of the organization amongst a very large number of clients as other providers can do.

SINGLE PURCHASER

- CITH is completely dependent on one purchaser of a single service. This makes it very weak in terms of negotiating, and makes its future always uncertain, not knowing whether the health authority will renew its contract each year.

INCREASING BUSINESS CULTURE IN THE CARE SECTOR

- Domiciliary care has become a very competitive business, with both voluntary and private providers competing more and more aggressively for the same business. The culture and history of CITH as a local caring group makes it difficult for the organization to compete with multi-million-pound players in both the private and voluntary sectors.

GOVERNANCE

- The voluntary management committee, which grew out of a commitment to prayer, peace and service, played an absolutely vital role, in a very hands-on way, in developing the service. As the service has expanded and the pressures for a more businesslike approach have become increasingly evident, there has been an increasing need for the management committee to change and to adopt modern good practice in relation to governance, finance and strategy.
- Related to the above is the feeling amongst some of the current committee members of having run out of energy and perhaps that it is time to hand over to a new generation.
- There is little enthusiasm amongst the current committee members to expand CITH's services into other geographical areas so as to become less dependent on one purchaser.
- There is a lack of clarity about the role of the management committee and the office-bearers of the committee, and there is no mechanism for reviewing the skills required on the management committee and for bringing appropriate new members onto the committee. There is only one outsider on the management committee. All the other members are also involved in the religious community. There are no other members with particular current expertise in relation to domiciliary care provision, governance and management or accounting.
- There is a potential conflict of interest within the role of those CITH management committee members who are also committee members of the religious community, as the religious community is the landlord of CITH and charges a rent set by the religious community. The paid auditor of CITH is also involved in the religious community.

MANAGEMENT

- At staff management level, the undoubted focus on ensuring that clients receive a high quality of service has perhaps sometimes been at the expense of the business and management aspects of the organization. These aspects are barely mentioned in the coordinator's job description.
- There is no manager with specialist finance or personnel skills. There are no regular management accounts each month or quarter.
- Staff supervision and support, appraisal and team meetings are issues that need to be addressed.
- Contracts of employment are not up to date.
- How rotas are currently arranged is clearly raising a number of issues for staff, and these issues need to be addressed.
- The staff feel that there is a lack of back-up out of office hours.
- Aspects of the staff's terms and conditions are also currently problematic, particularly travel expenses.

STATISTICS

- There is little analysis of trends in the client group by age, gender or needs.

LONG-TERM FUTURE OF RESPITE CARE

- The respite service is funded by a major charitable trust for three years. The health authority was not involved in, or consulted about, the process of making an application to provide this service, and it does not know which of its care-managed clients are receiving respite care from CITH. The authority needs to be engaged in discussions as soon as possible about contracting the service, once the funding from the charitable trust ends.

LONG-TERM FUTURE OF CITH

- The coordinator, who has played an important role in developing CITH as a quality provider of domiciliary care services, has indicated her intention to retire. This has inevitably created a sense of uncertainty about the future, and highlighted the need to commission the current review in order to establish a clear sense of direction for the future.

Questions

1   What are the key strategic issues facing CITH?
2   What would you recommend to the management committee of CITH in relation to the key strategic issues, and why?
3   What recommendations would you make to ensure the organization has the internal capacity to face the challenges of the future?

Note

*   The name of the organization has been changed for confidentiality reasons.

World Wide Fund for Nature (WWF)

The beginning

The key figure in the foundation of WWF was the renowned British biologist, Sir Julian Huxley. The first Director General of UNESCO, Huxley had also helped found a scientific research-based conservation institution, now known as IUCN – The World Conservation Union. In 1960, Huxley went to East Africa to advise UNESCO on wildlife conservation in the area. He was appalled at what he saw and wrote three articles for the *Observer* newspaper in which he warned the British public that habitat was being destroyed and animals hunted at such a rate that much of the region's wildlife could disappear within the next twenty years.

The articles hit home, alerting readers to the fact that nature conservation was a serious issue. Huxley received a number of letters from concerned members of the public. Among these was a letter from businessman Victor Stolan, who pointed out the urgent need for an international organization to raise funds for conservation. Huxley contacted ornithologist Max Nicholson, Director General of Britain's Nature Conservancy, who took up the challenge with enthusiasm.

By spring 1961, Nicholson had gathered together a group of scientists and advertising and public relations experts, all committed to establishing an organization of the kind Stolan had suggested. Prominent among those experts was another ornithologist, Peter Scott, a Vice-President of IUCN, who was later to become the new organization's first chairman.

The group decided to base its operations in neutral Switzerland, where IUCN had already transferred its headquarters to a villa in the small town of Morges on the northern shores of Lake Geneva. The new organization, which planned to work closely with IUCN, was to share this villa.

IUCN welcomed the fledgling organization. 'Together', both parties agreed, 'we will harness public opinion and educate the world about the necessity for conservation.'

Meanwhile, Chi-Chi the panda had arrived at London Zoo. Aware of the need for a strong, recognizable symbol that would overcome all language barriers, the group agreed that the big furry animal with her appealing, black-patched eyes would make an excellent logo. The black-and-white panda has since come to stand as a symbol for the WWF movement as a whole.

WWF was officially formed and registered as a charity on 11 September 1961. The founders decided that the most efficient approach would be to set up offices in different countries. They therefore launched national appeals, which would send up to two-thirds of the funds they raised to the international secretariat in Morges (now known as WWF International), and keep the remainder to spend on conservation projects of their own choice.

WWF planned to work, wherever possible, with existing non-governmental organizations, and to base its grants on the best scientific knowledge available – a policy which has been adhered to ever since. Its first grants went to IUCN, the International Council for Bird Preservation (ICBP, now Birdlife International), the International Waterfowl Research Bureau and the International Youth Federation for the Study and Conservation of Nature.

The first National Appeal, with HRH The Duke of Edinburgh as President, was launched in the United Kingdom on 23 November 1961. On 1 December it was followed by an appeal in the United States, and, a few days later, one in Switzerland.

Since then, WWF has grown considerably. National appeals are now known as National Organizations. Twenty-four of these are affiliated to WWF International, while five organizations which operate under a different name are associated with WWF. Each national organization is a separate legal entity, responsible to its own board and accountable to its donors. WWF International itself is accountable to the national organizations, donors, and also to the Swiss authorities.

Most of the members of WWF International's board and committees are drawn from the boards and Chief Executive Officers of the national organizations. WWF also has programme offices throughout the world and representatives in many countries.

In its first three years, WWF raised and donated almost US$1.9 million to conservation projects. Much of this money was given by individuals.

Some of the early grants, such as those to IUCN and ICBP, were large. A substantial donation, for example, went to the Charles Darwin Foundation for the Galápagos Islands. WWF still funds projects in the Galápagos, and has helped the Ecuadorean government to establish the Galápagos National Park, control introduced species which threaten the islands' rare indigenous plants and animals, and set up research training and education programmes. The Galápagos Islands could now stand as an example of the way low-impact tourism can be integrated with research, development and conservation initiatives.

Many grants, however, were small. In 1962, WWF gave US$131 'to enable Mr E. P. Gee of Upper Shillong, Assam, to visit the Rann of Kutch to ascertain the total numbers and present trends of the population of Indian wild ass'. Mr Gee found 870 animals. By 1975, numbers had dropped to

400 and the wild ass seemed to be on the verge of extinction. So a rescue mission was launched, a wild ass sanctuary established, and by the mid-1980s the population had risen to an impressive total of well over 2,000. Other early grants went to provide a road grader and rotary mower for Kenya's Masai Mara Game Reserve, and to fund a survey of Costa Rica's few remaining white-bearded spider monkeys.

In 1969, WWF joined forces with the Spanish government to purchase a section of the Guadalquivir Delta marshes and establish the Coto Doñana National Park. This important wetland area, one of the last refuges of the Spanish imperial eagle and the Iberian lynx, is constantly threatened by schemes to increase local agricultural output and tourism. WWF still supports Coto Doñana, and is fighting proposals to drain the marshes and siphon off water to irrigate agricultural land along the coast and to expand tourist facilities.

The 1970s

From the very beginning, WWF was aware that people donated money to the organization because they wanted to give direct support to conservation.

In 1970, HRH Prince Bernhard of the Netherlands, then President of WWF International, launched an important initiative that was to provide WWF with the solid, independent financial base it needed. The organization set up a US$10 million fund, known as The 1001: A Nature Trust, to which 1,001 individuals each contributed US$10,000. Since establishing The 1001, WWF International has been able to use interest from the trust fund to help meet its basic administration costs.

When WWF helped the Indian government launch Project Tiger in 1973, the public was assured that its donations would go towards saving India's severely endangered tigers. Prime Minister Mrs Indira Gandhi set up a task force to carry out a comprehensive six-year tiger conservation plan, and the government put aside land for nine tiger reserves. India later added six more reserves. Nepal followed suit with three, and Bangladesh with one.

Two years later, WWF embarked on its first worldwide Tropical Rainforest Campaign, raising money and arranging for several dozen representative tropical rainforest areas in Central and West Africa, Southeast Asia and Latin America to be managed as national parks or reserves. Forest conservation has been an important WWF focus ever since. The organization's Forest Programme now supports 350 projects all over the world, in an effort to conserve not only tropical rainforests but also the forests of the temperate zones.

The 1970s was an exciting and active time. The launch in 1976 of an ambitious marine campaign, The Seas Must Live, enabled WWF to set up marine sanctuaries for whales, dolphins and seals, and to protect marine turtle nesting sites. The decade drew to a close with a campaign to Save the Rhino, which rapidly raised over US$1 million to combat rhino poaching, as trade in ivory and rhino horn was driving many species towards extinction. IUCN had created a body to monitor trade in wildlife and wildlife products, known as TRAFFIC (Trade Records Analysis of Fauna and Flora In Commerce) which opened its first office in the UK in 1976. With WWF's help, TRAFFIC has now grown into a network of seventeen offices on five continents, and has played a major role in persuading governments all over the world to increase species protection and strengthen wildlife trade controls.

All this activity meant that WWF had long outgrown its villa in Morges, and desperately needed new premises. In 1979, the accommodation problem was solved by an anonymous donation that enabled the organization to move to a modern office block in Gland, along the lake, halfway between Geneva and Lausanne.

The 1980s

By the end of the 1970s, WWF had grown from a small organization that concentrated on problems such as endangered species and habitat destruction, into an international institution involved in all manner of conservation issues. Perhaps the most important of these was the need to integrate development with conservation.

WWF marked the dawn of the 1980s by collaborating with IUCN and the United Nations Environment Programme (UNEP) on the publication of a joint World Conservation Strategy. Endorsed by the United Nations Secretary General, the Strategy was launched simultaneously in thirty-four world capitals. It recommended a holistic approach to conservation and highlighted the importance of using natural resources sustainably. Since the launch, fifty countries have formulated and initiated their own national conservation strategies, based on its recommendations. A simplified version, *How to Save the World*, was subsequently published in several languages.

Meanwhile, WWF continued to build up its popular support base. In 1981, when HRH The Duke of Edinburgh took over from John Loudon as President of WWF International, the organization had one million regular supporters worldwide. Fundraising efforts received a boost in 1983, with the launch of the Conservation Stamp Collection. Under this scheme, WWF, in collaboration with Groth AG, has worked with the postal authorities in more than 200 countries, helping them select threatened species to feature on official postage stamps. The programme has so far raised over US$13 million.

By 1986, WWF had come to realize that its name (the World Wildlife Fund) no longer reflected the scope of its activities. The WWF Network therefore decided to publicize its expanded mandate by changing its name from the World Wildlife Fund to the World Wide Fund for Nature. The United States and Canada, however, retained the old name.

As part of its Twenty-fifth Anniversary celebrations, WWF invited leaders from the world's five main religions to a two-day retreat in the historic Italian town of Assisi. After the retreat, the leaders issued declarations that conservation was a fundamental element in their respective faiths. This led to the formation of an international network that now includes eight religions, through which WWF and religious groups work together to achieve common aims.

WWF's status as a non-governmental organization with whom governments are happy to work means that it is well positioned to press for changes in government policy. In 1985, the organization helped bring about an international moratorium on whaling. Since then, a whale sanctuary has been established in the important Antarctic feeding grounds.

The fact that the organization has good relationships with governments has also enabled it to negotiate debt-for-nature swaps, under which a portion of a nation's debt is converted into funds for conservation. Debt-for-nature swaps have been made with a number of countries, including Ecuador, Madagascar, the Philippines and Zambia.

The 1990s

The 1990s began with the launch of a revised mission and strategy. The expanded mission reiterated WWF's commitment to nature conservation, and classified the organization's work into three interdependent categories: the preservation of biological diversity, promoting the concept of sustainable use of resources, and reducing wasteful consumption and pollution. The 1990 strategy aimed to decentralize WWF's decision-making, and to increase cooperation with local people.

The following year, building on lessons learned in the decade since the launch of the World Conservation Strategy, WWF, IUCN and UNEP joined forces again to publish *Caring for the Earth – A Strategy for Sustainable Living*. Launched in over sixty countries around the world, *Caring for the Earth* listed 132 actions people at all social and political levels can take to safeguard or improve their environment, while simultaneously increasing the quality of their life.

In 1990, WWF helped bring about an international moratorium on the ivory trade. And in 1992, it played a part in pressurizing governments to sign conventions on biodiversity and climate change at the United Nations Conference on Environment and Development – the Earth Summit in Rio de Janeiro. It is now working to ensure that those conventions are implemented in an effective manner.

The Rio Earth Summit alerted politicians and businesspeople to the urgency of the environmental crisis facing the modern world. Since the conference, WWF has been working to build stronger relationships with the business community. In the UK, for example, WWF is working with a group of retailers and manufacturers who are committed to phasing out the sale of wood that does not come from independently certified, well-managed forests. With the strong recognition of WWF's name and logo, the organization has been able to generate substantial income from joint promotions with private companies wishing to promote the image of particular brands.

WWF also maintains links with other non-governmental organizations, both national and international. It makes a particular point of responding to local conservation needs and working with local people. More and more projects involve rural communities in making decisions as to how their environment should be both used and conserved, while providing economic incentives.

WWF has always recognized the importance of working in partnership with governments, other conservation organizations and local communities, or with the millions of people whose financial and moral support enables WWF to carry out conservation work throughout the world.

In 1993, the organization completed a two-year network-wide evaluation of its conservation work. On the strength of this critical study, which challenged the effectiveness of a number of WWF programmes, it resolved to focus its activities on three key areas: forests, freshwater ecosystems, and oceans and coasts. WWF believes that, in pursuing the new goals via carefully planned strategies, it will be able to make the best use of its resources.

Questions

1 With its widening remit, WWF changed its name from the World Wildlife Fund to the World Wide Fund for Nature in 1986. Following a major evaluation of its work, it was decided to re-focus on three core areas. What are the factors which should determine that the right strategy is to focus, and when it should diversify?

2 The WWF brand (name and logo) is recognized all over the world and associated with a positive attitude to the environment and to wildlife. As a result, WWF has been able to lucratively engage in joint promotions with producers of a wide range of products. To what extent do such joint promotions damage the name of the voluntary organization? And what limits should the organization set upon whom (and which products) it will engage in joint promotions with?

3 WWF collaborates closely with governments. To what extent does this restrict or enhance its effectiveness?

4 How would you describe the strategy of WWF in contrast to that of Greenpeace?

5 Write a mission statement for WWF.

6 What performance indicators should WWF use to assess whether it is successful or not?

Further reading

G. J. Medley (1986) 'Strategic planning for the World Wildlife Fund', reprinted in J. M. Bryson (ed.) (1999) *Strategic management in public and voluntary services – a reader*, Pergamon.

G. J. Medley (1988) 'WWF UK creates a new mission', reprinted in J. M. Bryson (ed.) (1999) *Strategic management in public and voluntary services – a reader*, Pergamon.

WWF websites: www.wwf-uk.org/, www.panda.org/, www.wwf.org/.

CARE

The beginning

CARE is one of the earliest and largest relief agencies in the USA. It was founded in 1945 when twenty-two American organizations formed a cooperative to rush lifesaving CARE Packages to survivors of World War Two. The first 20,000 food parcels, each the gift of an American who cared, reached the battered French port of Le Havre, on 11 May 1946.

Some 100 million more CARE Packages followed in the next two decades, reaching people in need, first in Europe and later in Asia and other regions of the developing world.

Over the years, CARE has adapted to meet changing human needs. In the 1950s, they expanded into emerging nations and used US surplus food to feed the hungry. In the 1960s, they pioneered primary healthcare programmes. In the 1970s, they responded to massive famines in Africa and helped prevent them with an innovation called agro-forestry, which integrated environmentally sound tree and land management practices with farming programmes.

The CARE name

The organization has always been known by its acronym – CARE – but the meaning behind the letters changed as their mission expanded. At its founding in 1945, CARE stood for the Cooperative for American Remittances to Europe. Now 'CARE' and 'CARE Package' are registered marks of the Co-operative for Assistance and Relief Everywhere, Inc. With headquarters in Atlanta, Georgia, CARE USA is one of ten member organizations of CARE International, whose secretariat is located in the Belgian capital, Brussels.

The CARE Package

In 1946, the first CARE Packages arrive at Le Havre, and shortly afterwards CARE airlifted food to Berlin when Soviet troops blockaded the city. A

CARE food truck was the first vehicle to enter Berlin after the blockade was lifted. The first CARE Packages were US Army surplus '10-in-1' food parcels originally intended to provide one meal for ten soldiers during the planned invasion of Japan. CARE obtained them at the end of World War Two and began a service that enabled Americans to send the parcels to friends and families in Europe, where food shortages were severe and millions were in danger of starvation. Ten dollars bought the Package and guaranteed that its addressee would receive it within four months. When the '10-in-1' parcels ran out, CARE began assembling its own food packages, greatly assisted by donations from American companies.

In 1949, CARE began work in the Philippines, launching its first programmes in the developing world. In the 1950s, CARE undertook a major relief operation in Korea as the war expanded; and shipped food to thousands of Hungarian refugees after the failed revolt. The US Congress also gave recognition to the work of CARE by passing Public Law 480, allowing CARE to use America's vast stocks of surplus food in the fight against hunger overseas.

In the 1960s, CARE expanded its relief work in Vietnam as the war created more civilian victims and refugees, and began phasing out the CARE Package as self-help projects gained importance. In this period governments started sharing project costs in their own countries.

In the 1970s, CARE brought food and emergency supplies to survivors of the Bangladesh war of independence and helped them to resume farming and re-establish schools, homes and health centres; provided food, relief kits and medical supplies to drought victims in Niger and Chad and launched agro-forestry efforts to help prevent drought and increase food production; and sent relief to refugees fleeing Cambodia's killing fields.

In the 1980s, the century's worst famine gripped Africa and more than a million people died. CARE delivered food to 6.3 million starving Africans. And in 1988, CARE became the first private development organization to work in the People's Republic of China and, as the Cold War waned, began operations in the former Soviet Union and the former Yugoslavia. In 1986 CARE began its small-business support programme.

In the 1990s, CARE continued its relief operations by delivering food to two million people during the Somali famine, despite widespread violence and instability; helped the Haitian people survive food shortages and economic collapse, with programmes giving aid to 10 per cent of the population; delivered food, water and sanitation to hundreds of thousands of Rwandan refugees; sent CARE Packages to Bosnian schoolchildren; and responded to emergencies such as Hurricane Mitch in Central America, cyclones in Orissa, India, and strife in Kosovo.

By 2000, CARE employed over 10,000 staff, most of whom are citizens of the countries in which CARE works, delivering a 'CARE Package' that encompasses programmes in emergency relief and rehabilitation, education, health and population (including maternal and child health, reproductive health and water and sanitation) and income development (which includes small economic activity development, agriculture and community development and the environment).

However, it also became clear that the organization faced a number of challenges (Henry 1999; Lindenberg 2001):

- A number of other organizations had become equally recognized for their relief activities, and CARE wasn't necessarily the agency of first choice.
- A number of other specialist agencies had grown up providing high quality specialized services in developing countries.
- Donors were increasingly questioning CARE's cost structure and were looking for evidence of programme impact in the face of persistent poverty and inequality.
- CARE's direct delivery approach was increasingly being questioned, as other agencies began to work more in partnership with indigenous organizations.
- CARE staff were struggling to deliver an ever-expanding programme with antiquated systems and procedures.
- CARE's confederation partners in other Western countries demand increased autonomy.
- There is a need to create a more functional international confederation, when 70 per cent of the programme is currently in the hands of one member (CARE USA).
- There is a need to become a global organization including southern member organizations.
- There is a need to create and project a common, shared vision and identity for the organization.
- There is a need to overcome funding vulnerabilities, particularly in light of changing priorities of institutional donors.
- There is a need for CARE to overcome its insularity and become a genuine learning organization that promotes innovation.

Questions

1 Identify the different kinds of strategies that CARE has adopted over its history.
2 To what extent should CARE specialize or diversify (in terms of its programmes and countries), and why?
3 How would you advise CARE on the development of an appropriate international structure?
4 How should CARE assess the impact of its programmes?

Further reading

K. M. Henry (1999) 'CARE International: Evolving to meet the challenges of the 21st century', *Nonprofit and Voluntary Sector Quarterly* 28(4) Supplement.

M. Lindenberg (2001) 'Are we at the cutting edge or the blunt edge? Improving NGO organisational performance with private and public sector strategic management frameworks', *Nonprofit Management and Leadership* 11 (3), Spring.

CARE International Annual Review 2000.

CARE USA 2000 Annual Report.

The CARE websites. CARE USA: www.care.org/; CARE International UK: www.careinternational.org.uk/

The Simon Community

The beginning

The Simon Community was founded in England in September 1963 by a former probation officer, Anton Wallich-Clifford. Its two main aims were:

1   to be an alerting body concerned nationally to draw the attention of the government and the public to a largely unrecognized and growing problem, i.e. the plight of the homeless and rootless in towns and cities;
2   to develop an experimental venture in care.

Wallich-Clifford was born in England in 1924, and after his father died when Anton was eighteen months old, he was brought up by his mother in their guest house on the south coast. His mother was an important influence, both in terms of his faith and his attitude to the underprivileged. He was always given a couple of pennies to share with 'a tramp', and the sight of the Jarrow marchers in 1933 had a major impact on him.

He originally trained to be a minister of religion but, when World War Two broke out, he enlisted in the RAF. After the war he was appointed as housemaster in Kent, working with young offenders in what was known then as an 'approved school'. The lack of places for many of these young people to go to after they left the school made a lasting impression on him.

It was a natural step to move into the newly formed Probation Service, working with offenders and ex-offenders of all ages, and after formal training and two initial posts he was attached to Bow Street Magistrates Court in London where he came into contact with many homeless men and women. He spent time getting to know many of those who were sleeping rough in London at that time, spending days and nights dressing shabbily and congregating with groups of homeless men and women on derelict sites in the area. He also operated an unofficial office in a Villiers Street café near the Embankment, which many homeless individuals frequented.

He was also influenced by experimental initiatives in other countries: Château D'Orblauisse and the Emmaus Community in France, Father Burelli's work with children in Naples, and Dorothy Day's work in America.

At that time Wallich-Clifford was described variously as remarkable, courteous, kind, firm and eccentric. A fellow probation officer, meeting him for the first time, described him as an 'eccentric looking...larger than life character' who was 'dressed for the part of Mr Micawber'. He could be very amusing, but also quiet and contemplative. His faith was clearly very important to him, as was his commitment to social action.

In 1962 he resigned from the Probation Service to become the first warden of Dismas House ('Dizzy', as it was nicknamed) for discharged prisoners in Southampton.

Along with many others in the early 1960s, Wallich-Clifford had become very interested in the concept of community and the possibility of living in community with others, particularly those who were the 'rejects' of society, the homeless and rootless.

The Simon Community is launched

On 1 September 1963 he made the decision to give up his job at Dismas House and form a community, which initially comprised himself, his mother and two men who had received extensive support from him ever since his days as a Probation Officer. The Community was based in a flat in St Leonard's-on-Sea in Sussex. In the following months Wallich-Clifford used his journalistic experience and wide range of contacts to generate enthusiasm and financial support for this experimental venture. At the beginning of 1964 the Simon Community Trust was legally registered as a charitable body.

In order to highlight the plight of the homeless in London, Wallich-Clifford organized a rally in Trafalgar Square at which he and a number of others spoke about the problem of homelessness. The event attracted substantial media attention. Wallich-Clifford was the kind of speaker who stirred the heart, and he obviously inspired Miss Margaret Handel, who, as a result of his speech, offered the fledgling community a house in Maldon Road, North London, which she had been running for 'vagrant alcoholics' for some time.

As a result the Simon Community opened its first house of hospitality, St Joseph's, for the homeless and rootless in March 1964 (St Joseph's is still a Simon house to this day).

It quickly became clear that this was an idea whose time had come. The commitment to egalitarian and communitarian principles found a ready audience in the 1960s, particularly with the young, many of whom also felt alienated from the society in which they lived. With Wallich-Clifford's infectious enthusiasm, charisma and promotional skills, the community rapidly began to expand and blossom, new houses were opened in Rochester and East London, and the Simonwell Farm was opened in Kent.

Within a few years new communities were also to be established in Liverpool, Glasgow, Edinburgh, Oxford, Cambridge and Exeter.

National movement

Wallich-Clifford's emphasis on being a national alerting movement derived from his own involvement with various initiatives and his awareness of the work of others. He saw that various individuals were doing excellent work, but that interest in their experimental approach was fairly localized. He became concerned about the problem in its overall context, and in linking this experimental knowledge. He felt that the campaign for the 'dropouts', as he originally called them, needed to be extended if the public were to be shaken out of their apathy and the stereotypical belief that 'the Welfare State takes care of those sort of people'.

Some of Simon's earliest pamphlets referred to these people as 'the submerged tenth' of the population, a statement taken from Charles Booth's study of life in London at the turn of the century, but equally applicable more than six decades later.

Basic aims

Wallich-Clifford saw the aims of his own experimental venture as 'acceptance of the needs and dependency of the inadequate, sometime life long, and the provision of care aimed at assimilation, protection, development and resettlement through:

- long-term, unpressurized and protected community life under specialized guidance;
- unit houses allowing for individual and family reintegration;
- estate maintenance work; work projects; and occupational experiments, redeveloping incentives and ability in shared labour, responsibility and recreation, based on the ordered pattern of the Community spiritual life.'

The key to the experiment lay in two fundamental tenets: the caring and the cared-for living and working together co-equally; and the use of a group structure within a communitarian format.

The Simon Community Trust

The Simon Community Trust was the administrative body which created and guided the early developments in Simon. Its initial plan had been to purchase a large manor house and farm in Sussex where, Wallich-Clifford envisaged, a basic community could be developed. However, the Trust was unable to do this because of opposition and public pressure from the local people of the area. Therefore, in Wallich-Clifford's view, 'the Simon Community started its active caring programme back to front'. Instead of an established community developing with further centres being developed provincially, the outer wheel of unit houses opened at the beginning, without a central community. This unplanned development caused come structural changes and administrative alterations, but the spirit and aim of the original plan remained.

Taking stock

By the autumn of 1965, the organization was forced to take stock of itself, its ideology and development. For two years, Simon had grown substantially and begun to make its voice heard. As a campaigning body its efforts were beginning to be successful. However, in the setting-up of its caring communities it had attempted to do too much, too early. It became clear that Wallich-Clifford's special skills were in innovation and challenge rather than in consolidation. He was an 'ideas man' rather than an administrator.

Because of the fragmented growth of the new communities, the administrative and organizational weakness of the parent body, and the irregularity of training courses for new volunteer workers due to insufficient finance, local communities tended to become isolated and defeated by internal problems. Some of the original houses were forced to close. It became clear that the movement and its organization as established could not function without some significant changes. The outcome of this crisis situation was an awareness of the need to decentralize on the part of the Exeter, Liverpool, Edinburgh, Glasgow, Canterbury and Oxford Communities, which started to become more independent of the parent body. These communities became increasingly financially self-supporting and were given greater freedom to accept, reject, or develop the various techniques, methodology and ideology given them by the parent organization.

However, this independence was initially given somewhat reluctantly by Wallich-Clifford.

> Without the full implementation of theory, there must remain a considerable danger that isolated units, pursuing policies suited to their own needs may, in fact, degenerate into conventional hostels, or at best watered down versions of the Simon houses. In place of community one is left with only a chain of caring establishments, having in common a name and one charity number. This is not 'community', nor is it the Simon way of life.

Such was the dilemma that the Simon Community Trust had to face at this time. Having a basic philosophy that it would not do what other people were doing adequately, it therefore acted on the basis that it would 'go in, set up, and move out', once other people come forward to carry on. However, this created a dilemma, because the organization could not guarantee that those who did carry the work forward would uphold the same philosophy. Yet it was felt that the organization must hand over if it was to direct its

energies towards other unmet needs in new areas. This remained a permanent situation, and introduced tension into the movement as a whole.

With the further expansion of Simon, a second re-assessment came at the
Simon Conference in 1969. At this conference Wallich-Clifford delivered a
paper which, he said, was 'the result of six years hard practical experience
with the Simon Venture in action'. The paper raised the following particular
issues:

- The justification of the continued need for Simon. One of the original
  aims had been a need to alert the public and the government to what
  Wallich-Clifford called 'social inadequacy' and its growing incidence.
  He felt happy that Simon and others had taken to this publicity fairly
  successfully. What was then (i.e. at the time Simon was founded)
  'unmentionable, hidden and of no interest to the media is now common-
  place and features regularly in the press and on radio and TV'. Therefore,
  while he felt a need to maintain campaigning pressures generally, the
  campaign should be one of support for Simon and in particular for
  expanded projects, recruitment and direct aid to those in need.
- He pointed out that Simon had lost support from previously helpful
  official quarters because:

  > [F]or no valid reason we have continued to run in competition
  > with, and in some cases campaign against progressively improving
  > statutory facilities instead of working in co-operation with them. It
  > is just this senseless spirit of competition and insular activity which
  > has brought our efforts to achieve co-ordinated care work to a
  > complete standstill, and I would strongly submit that unless we
  > improve our own image in this respect we shall ourselves be doing
  > the cause a grave disservice.

- Wallich-Clifford felt that the field of need had changed during the
  period of Simon's existence, and he gave the care of drug addicts as an
  example of a new need. Another changing need was in the field of after-
  care for people coming out of prison. 'During the first three years of our
  work we were inundated with court and after-care referrals. Today,
  because of the parole system, we are no longer so much in demand.'

Therefore, in his view, Simon needed both to look at itself as a movement,
and to look beyond too, if it was to survive in a useful form. He felt that to
try to maintain a unified centralized organization made up of the local
communities was unrealistic, and the local communities, locally supported
and serving local requirements, needed to be independent – as many already
were. Therefore he supported the idea of disbanding the Simon Community
Trust, with the substitution of a National Association of Simon
Communities incorporating independently registered, autonomous Simon

Communities and associated bodies offering similar caring or campaigning facilities. Within this structure Wallich-Clifford envisaged three separate 'wings'. These would consist of:

1   A section concerned with campaigning, and promotion of ideas and service. He felt this should be the work of a completely separate group, declaring:

> In retrospect I can see that it is quite impossible for a caring agency to be one and at the same time an alerting body. I know that we did it, but at what cost to our caring? At what cost to our promotional work?

During 1968 he had concentrated his energies on establishing REPs (Research Experimental Projects), as Simon's campaigning wing.

2   The Simon Communities, i.e. those ventures in care (community houses, etc.), subscribing fully to the Simon philosophy.
3   Associated and 'Beyond Simon' communities. He envisaged the associated communities would include groups undertaking similar work to Simon. A large number of such groups had sprung from Simon's roots, but later branched away as they developed their own ideas and ways of working.

Vision of community

Wallich-Clifford's vision of 'community' was that it should comprise in the main married couples and single persons drawn together and semi-permanently committed to undertaking a piece of work, offering where possible professional, trade or domestic skills and bound by a community discipline which, in the ideal, would be a lay religious group. Around this central 'core' could be developed the two circles which complete the community structure:

1   Carefully vetted, screened and selected volunteers offering, under the same conditions, up to two years short-term service.
2   Selected 'third tier' members (i.e. long-term) who, either through referral or direct application, or some form of service selection, live in the community and work an eight-hour day.

As the concept revolved round the idea of a 'worker community', Wallich-Clifford went on to suggest the workers 'should live in a community house around which (or from which) are served unit houses, offering specialized caring facilities'. He quoted the example of a community in London which offers a twenty-four-hour emergency short-term service to professional and other referring agencies.

He believed that such a community should be self-supporting, with a developed work programme, accepting gifts in kind, particularly food – but endeavouring to be independent of cash donations and emphatically opposed to any state aid. Such a community should have its roots in the country, and it should have as its objective the setting-up of a village or a similar project. In his view it followed that, in such a structure, a member of the community is not attached to a house but to a piece of work.

Expansion

During the next couple of years this policy was put into effect only partially. The Simon Community Trust remained as a campaigning and organizing parent body despite the plans to disband it. There was a further vigorous expansion of Simon Communities. Those newly set up included five in Ireland, in Dublin, Limerick, Waterford, Cork and Belfast. Consideration was given to starting Simon Community projects in South America, Kenya, Australia and India.

However, during this period Wallich-Clifford also turned his attention to the problem of homeless families, with the ideal of a Simon village always in his mind. As a starting point for the development of this work, a Families' Special Problems Bureau was set up. It was based at Simon Headquarters in the Ramsgate Community, and aimed to be an information service working closely with statutory and other voluntary agencies.

A number of the original Simon Communities, under the banner of the National Council of Companions of Simon, started discussions on the establishment of a decentralized National Association of Simon Communities which, as 'National Cyrenians', was eventually to become entirely independent of Simon in the early 1970s.

After the death of its founder, the development of the Simon Community in the Republic of Ireland, Northern Ireland and Britain, as well as in London, provides an interesting case study in organizational development. The main coherence in the Simon Movement came from the Simon principles that Wallich-Clifford had enunciated in several books. These principles included not accepting government funding (because, in his view, it inevitably had strings attached to it) and that everyone who worked with Simon should be a volunteer on the same income as the residents. Adhering to these radical principles had significant consequences. Leadership of each community, a very pressurized role, was to be in the hands of a volunteer who was often young and inexperienced and who in many cases quickly moved on to University or paid employment elsewhere. Management committees were made up entirely of co-workers, i.e. part-time volunteers. Not accepting government grants severely restricted the potential for development, in terms of new accommodation projects, the physical quality of existing projects and the development of new services.

The original Simon Community in London adhered the most closely to the founder's original principles, and it experienced a number of periods of retrenchment when funds ran out or the shortage of volunteers became too severe to continue managing the projects. The organization, while holding true to its principles, was also unable to respond to the dramatic increase in the level of homelessness in London. Much of this task, by default, was left to other agencies such as St Mungo's and Centrepoint.

Outside of central London the communities that had separated from Simon and formed the Cyrenian Federation adopted their own set of principles which, while allowing for paid staff and the acceptance of government funding, maintained the culture of volunteer-run 'communities'. The development of the member communities was very uneven, with some enthusiastically taking advantage of new funding sources to appoint paid staff and develop new projects and services, and others remaining closer to the original ethos. Some felt uncomfortable with the original religious ethos of the movement and changed their name to something that included neither Simon nor Cyrenian in it. To others this link with the past remained important. At the same time, many small-scale accommodation projects were being opened across the country by a variety of other organizations, to replace the closure of large institutional hostels.

A shortage of resources, and questions about the continuing role of the Cyrenian Federation, resulted in its eventual demise. An attempt to revive the Federation for like-minded organizations in Britain as 'Homes for Homeless People' was also short-lived. There is now no link between the organizations in Britain that began as Simon Communities, and most are now called something else.

In the Republic of Ireland the development of a Federation of Simon Communities was more successful. While not all the communities established in Ireland managed to survive, four (Dublin, Cork, Dundalk and Galway) survived and developed. While the local communities were originally volunteer-based, the principle of paid staff was established for the Federation at an early stage and eventually for the local communities as well. The Central Office played an important role in terms of the recruitment of volunteers, the support of local communities, the development of public policy and campaigning. As the proportion of paid staff in local communities increased, the relationship between the local communities and the National Office also changed, resulting in a number of conflicts around roles and authority, which eventually triggered a fundamental review in 2000 of the Federation in the Republic of Ireland, its strategy, principles and structures. This review resulted in a series of changes in the structure of the Federation and the role of the National Federation Office to reflect the increasing capabilities of the local communities, and work was undertaken for the first time on an integrated strategy for the Federation as a whole.

In Northern Ireland the incremental development of the Belfast Simon Community, which had been set up in 1971, by opening new accommodation projects around Northern Ireland led to a change of name to the Simon

Community Northern Ireland. There followed a fundamental review of the Simon Principles to create a set of values more appropriate to practice in the 1980s; the development of a strategic planning process to enable it to plan for the future in terms of new accommodation projects and services; continuously improving quality of existing services; and effective resource acquisition. By 1998 the organization, hierarchical in structure although participative in style, had over 200 paid staff, and accommodation projects in most of the major towns and cities of Northern Ireland, and had achieved ISO 9000, Investors In People and National Training Awards.

Questions

1   To what extent should a voluntary nonprofit organization remain true to its founding principles, and how much should it change to reflect the current environment in which it works? Use examples from the case study of the Simon Community.

2   To what extent should an organization decentralize decision-making, and why? Use examples from the Simon Community case study.

3   Is there a case for voluntary nonprofit organizations remaining small? What are some of the consequences of expansion?

4   What is organizational culture? How has it been changing in the Simon Community?

5   What are the pros and cons of voluntary nonprofit organizations adopting professionalized approaches to management? Use examples from the Simon Community case study.

6   For a multi-site movement like the Simon Community, what is the most appropriate structure, and why?

7   To what extent are the skills of a founder who creates a voluntary nonprofit organization different from those required to manage and develop the organization?

8   To what extent can, and should, a voluntary nonprofit organization engage in both service-provision and campaigning, or do both lose out?

Further reading

R. Courtney (1992) *Making a difference: The story of the Simon Community in Northern Ireland*, Simon Community Northern Ireland.
Anton Wallich-Clifford (1976) *Caring on skid row*, Simon Community.
Anton Wallich-Clifford (1989) *No fixed abode*, Simon Community Trust.
Simon Community websites: www.simoncommunity.com/, www.iol.ie/~dubsimon/.

Grameen Bank

The beginning

In 1974, Bangladesh fell into the grip of famine. Professor Yunus was head of the Economics Department at Chittagong University in the south-eastern extremity of Bangladesh. At first he and others at the university did not pay much attention to the newspaper stories of death and starvation in the remote villages of the north, until skeleton-like people began showing up in the railway stations and bus depots of the capital, Dhaka. Soon this trickle became a flood, and hungry people were everywhere.

Yunus's realization of the limited usefulness of the traditional economic theories he taught, for the poor of Bangladesh, led him to become a student again, with the people of the nearby village of Jobra as his teachers.

His repeated trips to the villages around the university campus led him to discoveries that were essential to establishing the Grameen Bank. The poor taught him an entirely new economics. He learned about the problems that they face from their own perspective. He realized that people were poor not because they were stupid or lazy. They worked all day long, doing complex physical tasks. They were poor because the financial institutions in the country did not help them widen their economic base. No formal financial structure was available to cater to the credit needs of the poor. This credit market, by default of the formal institutions, had been taken over by the local moneylenders who created a heavy rush of one-way traffic on the road to poverty. Yunus realized that, if someone lent the Jobra villagers just $27, they could sell their products to anyone at the best price and escape from the usurious practices of the traders and moneylenders which kept them in poverty. So Yunus gave one of the villagers the $27 and said to her, 'Lend this money to the forty-two villagers on the list. They can repay the traders what they owe them and sell their products at a good price.' 'When should they repay you?' she asked him. 'Whenever they can,' he replied; 'whenever it is advantageous for them to sell their products. They don't have to pay any interest.'

Yunus also tried to persuade the local banks to lend money to the poor. He argued that, if they borrowed money from a bank at commercial rates, they would be able to sell their products on the open market and make a decent profit that would allow them to live better lives. The banks, however, had a list of reasons why they couldn't lend to the poor, including the fact that the poor were illiterate so they couldn't fill in the forms, nor did they have security or collateral for the loans.

Finally, in December 1976, Yunus succeeded in taking out a loan from the Janata Bank and giving it to the poor of Jobra. However, the bank would only make the loan on the basis that he was the guarantor and approved all transactions. The bank would not deal with the poor who used their capital.

That was effectively the beginning of Grameen ('Grameen' derives from the word 'gram', meaning 'village'. Its adjectival form grameen means 'rural, of the village'). Yunus never intended to become a moneylender. All he really wanted was to solve an immediate problem. Out of sheer frustration, he had questioned the most basic banking premise of security/collateral. He did not know if he was right. He had no idea what he was getting himself into. He was walking blind and learning as he went along. His work became a struggle to 'show that the financial untouchables are actually touchable, even huggable'.

To his great surprise, the repayment rate by people who borrowed without security/collateral proved to be much better than those whose borrowings are secured by assets. Indeed, more than 98 per cent of the Grameen Bank's loans are repaid. The poor know that this credit is their only opportunity to break out of poverty. They do not have any cushion whatsoever to fall back on. If they default on this one loan, then they will have lost their one and only chance to get out of the rut.

Slowly Yunus and his colleagues developed their own delivery–recovery mechanism and, inevitably, made many mistakes along the way. They adapted their ideas and changed their procedures as they grew. For example, when they discovered that support groups of borrowers were crucial to the success of the operation, they required that each applicant join a group of like-minded people living in similar economic and social conditions. Convinced that solidarity would be stronger if the groups came into being by themselves, Yunus and his colleagues refrained from managing them, but created incentives that encouraged the borrowers to help one another succeed in their businesses. Group membership provided support and protection, making each borrower more reliable in the process. Peer pressure kept each group member in line with the broader objectives of the credit programme. A sense of inter-group and intra-group competition also encouraged each member to be an achiever. Shifting the task of initial supervision to the group not only reduced the work of the bank but also increased the self-reliance of individual borrowers. Because the group approved the loan request of each member, the group assumed moral responsibility for the loan. If any member of the group got into trouble, the group usually came forward to help.

It could take anything from a few days to several months for a group to be recognized or certified by Grameen Bank. To gain recognition, all the members of a group of prospective borrowers had to present themselves to the bank, undergo at least seven days of training on Grameen policies, and demonstrate their understanding of those policies in an oral examination administered by a senior bank official.

Early on, borrowers were encouraged to build up savings that they could fall back on in hard times or use for additional income-generating opportunities. They were required to deposit 5 per cent of each loan in a group fund. Any borrower could take an interest-free loan from the group fund, provided that all the other members of the group approved of the amount and its usage and that the loan did not exceed half of the fund's total. These loans made to group members from their group's funds staved off seasonal malnutrition, paid for medical treatments, purchased school supplies, recapitalized businesses affected by natural disasters, and financed modest but dignified family burials, etc.

Loans lasted one year and instalments were paid weekly. Repayment started one week after the loan and the interest rate was 20 per cent. Repayment amounted to 2 per cent of the loan per week for fifty weeks. If an individual was unable or unwilling to pay back the loan, the group risked becoming ineligible for larger loans in subsequent years until the repayment problem was brought under control.

As of 1998, the total amount in all the group funds exceeded $100 million, more than the net worth of all but a handful of Bangladeshi companies, but the loans are still paid in the same way, week by week, though now they are made to the frontline bank workers who meet weekly with borrowers in their villages. Despite serving the very poor in disaster-prone areas, the repayment rate has remained very high.

Grameen also tried to concentrate on loans to women, because money entering a household through the agency of a woman brings more benefits to the family as a whole. If the goals of economic development include improving the general standard of living, reducing poverty, creating dignified employment opportunities and reducing inequality, then it is natural to work through women. Not only do women constitute the majority of the poor, the under-employed, and the economically and socially disadvantaged, but they more readily and successfully improve the welfare of both children and men. However, opposition to this policy came from husbands, religious leaders and educated civil servants.

Expanding beyond Jobra into Tangail

In order to expand the work of Grameen into a second district of Bangladesh, the University of Chittagong granted Yunus a two-year leave of absence, and in June 1979 he officially joined the Grameen Bank Project in the District of Tangail near the capital, Dhaka. It was agreed that each national bank would make three branches available to Yunus, and one small bank offered one branch, giving Grameen a total of nineteen branches in Tangail, six branches in Chittagong, and the Agriculture Bank branch already created in Jobra. Suddenly, Grameen was twenty-five bank branches strong. By November 1982, Grameen Bank membership had grown to 28,000, from the 500 Jobra members they had in 1979.

However, Grameen was still not an independent bank at this stage. A new independent legal framework was drawn up, proposing that 40 per cent of shares go to the government and 60 per cent for borrowers. In late September 1983, the president signed the proclamation and the independent Grameen Bank was born. However, the balance of shares had been altered so that the majority of shares would be held by the government, not the borrowers.

The challenge of transforming Grameen from a pilot project operating inside a mostly hostile banking system to an independent bank for the poor thrilled everyone involved.

Independence allowed Grameen to grow, adding new branches at a breathtaking rate. Not only did they undergo quantitative growth, but many improvements were made to the methodology in the second half of the 1980s. Until then the staff had been recruited on a temporary basis and had continually to worry about whether the project would be terminated and they would be out of a job. When Grameen became an independent bank, they automatically became permanent staff of the new organization.

They also expanded the range of types of loans provided by offering integrated housing loans into the programme, experimenting with irrigation loans and other seasonal loan programmes, and they expanded their social development efforts. Though there were setbacks, such as the floods of 1987 and 1988 and a repayment crisis in the district of Tangail (the first), it was a time of growth, innovation and confidence. But the bank realized that for growth to be sustainable, they needed to resolve some governance issues that were left over from the campaign for independence. The most pressing issue was how to transform Grameen from a bank owned by the government to one owned primarily by the people who borrowed from it. The government eventually changed the ownership structure of Grameen by granting 75 per cent of the shares to the borrowers and keeping 25 per cent for the government, the government-owned Sonali Bank, and the Bangladesh Krishi (Agriculture) Bank.

Throughout the 1980s, Grameen's aggressive expansion programme saw them adding approximately one hundred new branches every year. These new branches were of very high quality, as six years of experimentation in Jobra and Tangail had taught them a great deal and allowed them to refine their methodology. By 1985, they had an impressive cadre of young professionals with several years of village experience behind them who were able to guide and manage hundreds, and later thousands, of new recruits. They experienced some problems in the oldest branches in Chittagong and

Tangail, where borrowers had been subjected to many changes in policies as Grameen went through a process of trial-and-error, but branches started during or after 1983 performed extremely well.

As they expanded, they watched borrowers progress through successive loan cycles. In most cases, the size of their loans increased as their businesses and their self-confidence grew. Some of the most dynamic borrowers used their profits to build new houses or repair existing homes.

Every time Yunus visited a village and saw a house built with profits from a Grameen-financed business, he felt a thrill, but regretted that more borrowers were not able to undertake such major investments. He began to think about how they could create a new programme that would offer dependable borrowers with perfect repayment records long-term loans for housebuilding or repairs. Grameen Bank applied to the Central Bank for help in introducing a housing programme to its borrowers. They explained that they were constrained by the modest circumstances of their borrowers, who could not repay large sums of money and only wanted a 5,000 taka ($125) housing loan. The Central Bank rejected the application. Its experts and consultants decided that whatever one built for $125 would not satisfy the structural definition of a house and that such a house would not add to the 'housing stock of the country'.

The success in Bangladesh led Yunus to hope that Grameen's micro-credit methodology could have near-universal applicability. During the late 1980s and early 1990s, they proved that the Grameen idea could improve the lives of poor people throughout the world. Pilot projects in Malaysia and the Philippines led the way.

Building a Grameen programme in Malaysia from scratch, and finding an appropriate legal framework to distance the programme from governmental control without losing financial support, was quite a balancing act. By the end of their two-year experimental phase, Grameen announced ambitious plans to expand to even less-developed regions of northern Malaysia. Today the pioneers of Grameen in Malaysia are ambassadors-at-large for Grameen, working night and day to jump-start Grameen programmes in more than a dozen Asian countries. They have been instrumental in forming an association of Grameen replication programmes called CASHPOR, and as a result of their efforts Amanah Ikhtiar Malaysia now reaches more than 36,000 poor families. The Malaysian repayment rate is even higher than that of borrowers in Bangladesh.

Even before the pilot phase of Project Ikhtiar in Malaysia was complete, serious Grameen replication projects began to crop up in a number of other countries, including three in the Philippines. At first, Yunus thought that operating a Grameen-type lending programme in the Philippines would be easier than doing so in Bangladesh, where the long-standing poverty, low status of women and frequent natural disasters are more extreme. But they ran into trouble in the Philippines when they set their sights on expansion. The leader of the project was skilled at working directly with borrowers, but had more difficulty managing his staff and board of directors. Once the action–research project was converted into an independent micro-credit organization, called Ahon Sa Hirop ('Rise Above Poverty'), or ASHI, they struggled to establish a dependable management structure. After several years of internal battles, the project leader left and a new chief executive was appointed. Within a surprisingly short time, things began to look up and ASHI is now one of the most successful Grameen replication programmes in the Philippines.

The third Filipino programme to emerge was the Landless People's Fund of the Center for Agriculture and Rural Development (CARD). CARD was established by a number of energetic people from an organization called the Philippine Business for Social Progress. After visiting Grameen in Bangladesh, the founders of this project decided to apply the Grameen methodology to rural development in the Philippines, and eventually became the leaders of a very successful network of more than thirty Grameen replication programmes in the Philippines. In 1997, by which time CARD had acquired more than nine thousand borrowers, an excellent repayment rate, and seven branches, the staff took steps to establish the CARD Bank, an independent financial institution. By February 1999, CARD had grown to 21,000 borrowers.

Despite its remarkable success, CARD did face some difficulties. In the early 1990s, it looked to the German government to provide it with expansion funding, but were told that, as a result of an evaluation, CARD was considered a failure. It transpired that a German evaluator had anonymously visited the head office and, without talking to any borrowers, written a negative evaluation report. In response, Grameen then commissioned an independent evaluator of impeccable credentials who, after many months' work, produced an objective report demonstrating the substantial value of Grameen's work for the poor in Jobra.

Application in other poor countries

Encouraged by the success of the programmes in Malaysia and the Philippines, new programmes continued to sprout up in India, Nepal, Vietnam and elsewhere. Even China launched three programmes in the mid-1990s. Then came Latin America and Africa. A programme in South Africa, called the Small Enterprise Foundation (SEF), has been particularly successful, reaching thousands of poor borrowers in rural villages.

The MacArthur Foundation's decision to support the Grameen Trust jump-started an ambitious new replication programme and encouraged other donors to follow suit. These included the Rockefeller Foundation, the World Bank, the US government, the UN Capital Development Fund and the German government. In total, the Grameen Trust has received more than $11 million, which has been used to support sixty-five Grameen replication projects in twenty-seven countries. As of late 1998, these organizations had granted more than $88 million in loans to some 280,000 poor people.

Grameen attracts potential replicators by inviting them to International Dialogue Programmes – two-week-long conferences hosted by Grameen in Bangladesh four times each year. They send these visitors in groups of two to far-flung branches throughout the country for five days to learn as much as possible about the branch, its workers, its borrowers and its socio-economic environment. This is followed by an in-depth interview with one Grameen borrower over several days to see the direct impact of Grameen on a very human level, and thus break down the myths and prejudices the participants may have about poor people. When the Dialogue participants return from the field, they are encouraged to debate the merits and limitations of the Grameen approach. Towards the end of the two-week period, they are shown how to apply to the Grameen Trust for seed money to get their own programme started.

Grameen sees a tremendous demand for new funding and hopes to reach 10 million borrowers through replication programmes funded by the Grameen Trust by 2005, which would require roughly $2.2 billion funding.

Wealthy countries

Today the Grameen Foundation USA (GF-USA), the Washington D.C.-based voluntary nonprofit organization, jump-starts Grameen-style micro-credit programmes in places such as Tulsa, Dallas and Harlem, and in Canada and Latin America. There are also many US programmes that have taken the micro-credit idea and adapted it in various ways. These organizations, some 250 of them, have formed a network called the Association for Enterprise Opportunity (AEO) to coordinate their activities. Fifty or so AEO member organizations operate on Grameen principles.

Setbacks in Bangladesh

With the continuing expansion of the micro-credit programme, Grameen was caught off-guard by a series of setbacks that would make 1991 one of its hardest years. The first of these hit when, ironically, the newly-elected Bangladeshi government decided to write off all loans from government banks that were under 5,000 taka (approximately $125 at the time). Though this policy may sound as though it would benefit the poor, in reality almost all of these loans made by government banks went to land-owning, wealthier members of the population. But because most Grameen loans were also under 5,000 taka, many Grameen borrowers thought that their loans had been written off. It was extremely difficult to explain to borrowers why the rich people in their villages were getting their loans written off while they were not. Yet Grameen had no choice. Grameen did not survive on government subsidies, and writing off all loans under $125 would have meant the end of Grameen. In the end, the borrowers accepted the arguments, but it was a bitter pill for them to swallow.

By 1994, Grameen had fully recovered from the challenges of the decade's beginning and was enjoying its best financial year ever, operating entirely on commercial terms. Two years later, in April 1996, the bank extended its billionth dollar in loans to one of its two million borrowers. A project that had started with a spontaneous twenty-seven-dollar loan by Professor Yunus had reached its billionth dollar. Just over two years later, Grameen loaned its two-billionth dollar.

Many of Grameen's borrowers had not only crossed the poverty line but left it far behind. In some cases their capacity to borrow, invest, and repay had increased fifty-fold in ten years.

To encourage successful borrowers, Grameen started a variety of new loan programmes in the 1990s. These included seasonal loans for borrowers who were sharecroppers or who had bought some land since joining Grameen. They also established a tube well loan programme for borrowers who needed $50–$100 to sink a hand-powered well to access safe drinking water. A new family loan programme enabled borrowers to take out loans for family members' income-generating projects. And an equipment- and cattle-leasing programme allowed borrowers to gradually purchase costly equipment and livestock through a lease-to-own agreement.

Grameen borrowers were constantly branching out into new, creative money-making schemes, and, though the bank wanted to encourage the most successful borrowers to take out bigger and bigger loans, Grameen did not abandon those who were still starting the struggle against poverty. Indeed, Grameen declared a new goal: to make every Grameen branch 'poverty-free' within an allotted period of time. How did the bank define 'poverty-free'? After interviewing many borrowers about what a poverty-free life meant to them, Grameen developed a set of ten indicators that staff and outside evaluators could use to measure whether a family in rural Bangladesh lived a poverty-free life. These indicators are based upon having:

1   a house with a tin roof;
2   beds or cots for all members of the family;
3   access to safe drinking water;
4   access to a sanitary latrine;
5   all school-age children attending school;
6   sufficient warm clothing for the winter;
7   mosquito nets;
8   a home vegetable garden;
9   no food shortages, even during the most difficult time of a very difficult year;
10 sufficient income-earning opportunities for all adult members of the family.

Grameen both monitors these criteria itself and invites local and international researchers to help track the successes and setbacks on the way to its goal of a poverty-free Bangladesh.

Grameen Bank has now extended the concept of collective resource management to meet a variety of needs: Grameen Phone to inexpensively lease cellular phones to the poor, Grameen CyberNet to provide cheap internet access, and Grameen Energy to provide solar and wind energy system to isolated or neglected communities. These extensions of the Grameen Bank model are equally revolutionary. The Grameen push is likely to further increase performance and reduce costs by expanding the market for these services and technologies. Grameen Bank has opened the door to these and other technologies and services which build synergistically with increased access to capital to spur locally controlled – not aid-driven – development.

The Grameen phenomenon is, however, not without problems. An emerging concern, ironically, may be a creature of the success of the Grameen Bank, and the tremendous interest that it has attracted. A recent Microcredit summit highlighted the new goal of 'expanding micro credit to 100 million of the world's poorest families'. This lofty but potentially realizable goal requires an initially daunting expansion in human capacity. Field experience has shown that one field worker can serve 200 borrowers. Assuming this staff–client ratio, 500,000 field workers will be needed in order to serve 100 million clients. If one assumes a drop-out rate during training of 15 per cent, the total intake of trainee field workers should be 575,000. This sort of capacity would be totally beyond the scope of traditional aid and development organizations, including the World Bank and other mega-lenders, due to the sheer size and in-the-village presence that is required. Yet the Grameen Bank grew over 20 years in Bangladesh in just such a fashion, and now works in tens of thousands of villages nationwide.

The Grameen Bank has drawn the interest, and the funding, of the World Bank, US, Japanese, and European Aid Agencies, and the largest commercial banks. The desire to inject hundreds of millions of dollars into the Grameen bandwagon may come without the patient two-decade build-up of human capacity, educational programmes and local accountability that characterized the original. Multinational funds too often come with demands of virtually instant returns and sound-bite successes, at a pace which violates the careful learning and training that makes the Grameen concept so successful.

The potential for problems is not confined to the big lenders, as many NGOs will need to dramatically change their approaches, capabilities and systems if they are to be successful in microcredit. Microcredit needs to be approached as a socially-responsible business, not as charity or social welfare. It is difficult to incorporate a successful microcredit programme into an institution that has a relief, social-service or paternalistic approach to helping the poor.

The Grameen Bank also faced a challenge from many organizations in Asia and worldwide when it announced a partnership with Monsanto, a major international agri-business company which has been heavily involved in efforts to promote the sale of genetically modified (GM) foods across the world, including in Bangladesh. As a result of the pressure from environmental groups, Grameen was forced to pull out of the $150,000 deal with Monsanto.

Questions

1   The majority of Grameen shares used to be in the hands of government and are now in the hands of the borrowers, with the government holding a minority stake. Funds for Grameen development are channelled through Grameen Foundations, with charitable status. Referring to the discussion in Chapter 2 of this book, which sector(s) is Grameen in?

2   What are the consequences of being closer to the public sector? The private sector? Or the voluntary nonprofit sector?

3   Can you identify the main strategies that Grameen has adopted, and at which point?

4   What are the advantages and disadvantages of continued geographical growth?

5   What might be the negative consequences of further rapid expansion?

6   What evidence is there of organizational learning in the development of Grameen?

7   What are Grameen's core or distinctive competencies/capabilities?

8   What is the most appropriate structure for Grameen?

9   To what extent can an organization be large and maintain a real understanding and sensitivity to the poor on the ground? How might a large organization maintain its close understanding of the needs of its beneficiaries?

10 Are there limits to whom voluntary nonprofit organizations should accept money from, or engage in partnerships with?

Further reading

B. Bornstein (2001) *The price of a dream: The story of the Grameen Bank*, Hummingbirdgreen.

Daniel M. Kammen *One view of Grameen Bank*. Kammen is Assistant Professor of Public and International Affairs, and Co-Chair, Science, Technology and Public Policy Program (STPP), Woodrow Wilson School of Public and International Affairs, Princeton University. Available online at: www.citechco.net/Grameen/.

M. Yunus (1999) *Banker to the poor: Micro-lending and the battle against world poverty*, BBS Public Affairs.

Grameen website: www.grameen-info.org/.

Homeline*

Background

Following the deaths of three homeless people on the streets of the city, a Freephone Helpline service was established for people who are homeless in a major city in Britain in November 1993, to ensure that any homeless person requiring accommodation in emergency circumstances would be provided with it and that nobody would need to go without shelter or spend a night on the street.

The local authority decided that the service should be contracted to one particular voluntary nonprofit organization, because of the high level of expertise which the organization had developed and because it was already providing a range of services to homeless people.

The service is provided between 5pm and 1am Monday to Friday and 10am to 1am on Saturdays and Sundays by staff who work in the organization. The Freephone Helpline service is provided from a small room, away from the provision of other services.

The purpose of the 'Night Service' as proposed was 'to be available to those who found themselves in need of emergency accommodation, so as to ensure that no family or individual had any reason, other than their own choice, to spend a night on the street'. And 'to be available to those who needed support until day service recommenced operations'. The proposal to establish the service considered the deployment of two additional staff to the organization 'would meet virtually all emergency needs'.

The service would 'continue to use hostel accommodation where possible and bed and breakfast accommodation when hostels are not available'. In emergency circumstances, homeless applicants could be transported to their destinations using taxis; 'where it is deemed necessary to meet a client, an appropriate arrangement would be made. It is envisaged that this element of the service would be used more frequently at weekends than in the evenings.'

Practical operation

In 1997 the service dealt with a total of 12,260 calls (an average of 34 per day), 68 per cent of which were from single men and 16 per cent from single women. Eleven per cent of calls involved a total of 1,427 children. Almost two thousand of the calls were new cases. Two-thirds of new cases were from within the local authority area. One-third of new cases were aged 25 or under; 42 per cent were aged 26–40; and 22 per cent were over 40.

In practice, at any one time, there is one staff member or volunteer who, on a rota basis, staffs the Freephone Helpline service from 5pm to 1am Monday to Friday and 10am to 1am on Saturday and Sunday. The staff and volunteers are entitled to a break of 1 hour 20 minutes during their period of duty. During this break an answering machine is operated, telling callers to call back later. There are two incoming lines for the Helpline number and four outgoing lines. If the second line rings while the first one is engaged, some staff and volunteers will put the first caller on hold to clarify the nature of the second call and usually to ask them to hold until the first call is dealt with or to call back. Other staff will wait until they have dealt with the first call before answering the second line. There is also a mobile phone which can be used if necessary.

The manager of the service is always available on his pager/mobile phone if the staff or volunteers require advice or guidance on a particular case or issue.

Brief details of each call and where the person is referred to are put into a log book and card index.

Evaluation

Because the service had not been evaluated since it was established in November 1993, it was decided by the local authority to commission an external evaluation of the Freephone Helpline.

In August 1996 the local authority stated that 'In 1995 the service has operated to good effect and has been able to meet [the] objective' of ensuring 'that any person who has been rendered homeless in the region, without the resources to provide for their need, will be offered emergency accommodation to meet that need'. They estimated that only on 17 occasions out of 8,173 calls was it not possible to meet the need because all hostels were full. However, by 1998 this figure had increased to 737.

The purpose of the recent evaluation was specified in the brief as the following:

*   to clarify the aims of the service;
*   to explore to what extent these aims are still legitimate;
*   to examine to what extent these aims are being achieved;
*   to make recommendations on the future of the Freephone Helpline service, in the context of current and anticipated need of homeless people.

In order to gain information about the service and the views of various stakeholders, a survey was undertaken of the various statutory and voluntary agencies who are regularly in touch with the Freephone Helpline service, or who have clients who are in touch with the Freephone Helpline service. Meetings were also held with the staff and volunteers who operate the service and with the manager, and the service was viewed in operation on one evening.

Because there are no formally established quality standards for the service by the organization or the local authority, other Freephone Helpline services were consulted. Particularly useful information was provided by the Telephone Helpline Association.

Accessibility

The survey of stakeholders asked a number of questions about accessibility. Generally 60 per cent of respondents considered that the service was easy to access, while 40 per cent disagreed or strongly disagreed. The answers to the remaining questions about accessibility help to clarify this divergence of responses.

Half of the respondents felt that the telephone number itself is not well enough promoted. It was suggested that 'the phone number needs greater continuous promotion' and 'the Freephone number should be clearly displayed in all call boxes and other public phones in pubs, clubs, etc.'.

Less than one-third of respondents felt that the service is available during the hours it is needed; half disagreed or strongly disagreed. 'Longer hours' were suggested, and it 'should be a 24-hour service if at all possible'. In the view of the staff and volunteers, however, this issue is linked to the availability of emergency accommodation. They would be in favour of providing a 24-hour service if the accommodation resources are available throughout the night, but if there are no beds available after 1am, either because of the number of beds or the acceptance policies of the hostels and BandBs, there is little value in extending the opening hours at present. Offering the service over a greater time period would also require additional staff resources.

The strongest views concerned the question of how easy it is to get through to the service, when it is operated by only one person who is entitled by European law to decent breaks. The majority (60 per cent) of respondents felt that it is not easy to get through. Respondents recognized that 'one person can only deal with one call at a time' and that it is 'overstretched for the person on duty'. It was also suggested that 'phones need to be covered at all designated times. Have a call-waiting message service if phones cannot be answered.' The Telephone Helpline Association produce particular guidelines on how to use modern telephone technology to best advantage.

The difficulty of having no cover when the staff member or volunteer needs to take a break was also problematic. They try to take a break when there appears to be a lull in the calls, but this was no guarantee that there weren't going to be a significant number of calls during this period. When there was limited supply of accommodation, many callers are encouraged to call back later to see if any beds have become available, substantially increasing the number of repeat callers. Technology is also currently not used to track the number of calls which are unanswered or how long it takes on average to get a call answered. A number of respondents referred to the problem caused by the variable timing of the breaks and the message on the answering machine not always giving an indication of when the service will be available again.

Staff skills and attitudes

Most respondents (60 per cent) felt the staff and volunteers had the knowledge to give relevant and accurate advice, although 40 per cent were neutral on the question. Comments were 'considerable on-the-ground experience built up' and 'formal training in the unit is non-existent', a comment which was confirmed by the staff and volunteers who stated that, apart from generic organizational training, there was neither induction training for new staff or volunteers into the Freephone Helpline service (apart from a 'sitting with Nellie' approach), nor on-going training on relevant issues related to homelessness or the Freephone Helpline service. There is also no regularly up-dated manual of relevant information available to the staff on the Helpline.

Views on whether the staff and volunteers have the skills to deal with callers in crisis were very wide, ranging from 'strongly agree' to 'strongly disagree'. Thirty per cent agreed or strongly agreed; 40 per cent were neutral; and 30 per cent disagreed or strongly disagreed. Comments included 'staff need training in dealing with people sensitively, particularly people in crisis or people with mental health issues', and 'a personal contact through a central drop-in location would better facilitate the assessment of the person's need' (a view shared by the staff and volunteers).

There was also a close link with the next question as to whether the staff treated the callers with dignity and respect. Again there were widely varying views. Forty-five per cent did feel the staff treated callers with dignity and respect; 36 per cent disagreed. Comments included the following:

- 'Adequate staffing is needed so that staff and volunteers don't get over-worked/stressed.'
- 'Needs to be a more friendly, less official service.'
- 'Staff do not treat them respectfully and don't take into account concerns they may have.'

The staff and volunteers felt that they do treat the callers with dignity and respect, but that this is often made difficult by the lack of options they have to offer callers and the anger that is often expressed by the callers who may have been trying to get through for some time and who may be offered nothing at the end of it. The facts that the staff and volunteers work on their own, feel they are over-stretched, work in very poor physical surroundings during the day and out-of-hours (described by the staff as 'quite Dickensian'), receive little induction or training, have no quality standards to work to, and do not get the opportunity for effective formal debriefing after a difficult situation, all make the position of the staff and volunteers very difficult.

Referral to appropriate accommodation

This question generated most comments and most concern from the staff and volunteers, who understandably feel themselves to be in an impossible situation in being responsible for referring callers to emergency accommodation options that often do not exist.

Clearly, however, the respondents understand the constraints under which the staff are operating, as 60 per cent of respondents agreed or strongly agreed that callers are referred to appropriate emergency accommodation when required. Thirty per cent disagreed or strongly disagreed. Comments included the following:

- 'The staff are trying to work miracles with the limited options available.'
- 'Appropriate emergency accommodation isn't always available and people haven't been offered anything and are left to sleep rough.'
- 'Staff are not responsible if there are no beds available.'

A related question, which was particularly significant in light of the background to how and why the service was set up, was whether staff and volunteers made every effort to ensure that callers didn't have to sleep rough that night. Almost two-thirds of respondents felt they do, with only 18 per cent disagreeing or strongly disagreeing. The only comment was 'staff frustration is high due to the lack of proper and appropriate crisis accommodation services'. This was confirmed by the staff and volunteers.

There was a wide variation of views as to whether the staff informed callers where they could get the most appropriate help the next morning or on the following Monday. Forty-five per cent agreed or strongly agreed that they did; 19 per cent were neutral; and 36 per cent disagreed or strongly disagreed. It depends on what is considered to be the most appropriate help. Nearly all callers are referred to the Homeless Person's Unit the next day. One respondent commented that 'the service could be improved by a better follow-up of people who phone the service, by linking in to other agencies and ensuring that people who don't get a bed are interviewed by staff to ensure follow-up'.

Liaison with other agencies

Respondents were equally divided about the extent that there is effective liaison between the staff operating the Freephone Helpline service and other relevant agencies working with homeless people. Thirty-six per cent agreed or strongly agreed that there is, 36 per cent disagreed or strongly disagreed. Comments included the following:

- 'There needs to be increased liaison with other organizations and service providers.'
- 'There needs to be more link with other agencies.'

There was clearly extensive contact with other agencies in relation to referrals of individual clients. However, as the last comment above suggests, there was limited opportunity for wider discussions and liaison with these other agencies about issues of common concern or how to improve the way the various agencies work together. The opportunity for increased liaison would be welcomed by the staff and volunteers.

Efficiency and effectiveness

Respondents were asked the extent to which they felt that the after-hours service provided an effective and efficient service to homeless people. No-one strongly agreed that it did; 27 per cent agreed that it did; 18 per cent were neutral; and 54 per cent disagreed or strongly disagreed. Comments included the following:

- 'The service operates from appalling premises that are inadequate in space.'
- 'The service should be adequately resourced in terms of staff.'
- 'The service is poorly managed.'
- 'No monitoring occurs.'

The staff and volunteers would concur with the comments about the resources and conditions. It was difficult to see how staff and volunteers could be expected to provide an efficient and effective service when it was so under-resourced in terms of staffing, documentation, physical conditions, training, IT and access to appropriate emergency accommodation.

Importance of the service

Respondents were asked how important the Freephone Helpline after-hours service was in providing advice and information to homeless people. Seventy per cent strongly agreed that it was crucially important; 80 per cent either agreed or strongly agreed.

Other quality issues

The Telephone Helpline Association suggested a number of additional areas that any evaluation should cover but which are not included in the above survey, as follows:

Documentation/monitoring

The system for documenting and monitoring calls was a manual system based on a card index and basic statistics forms. The record keeping was very rudimentary. There was no database or computer. In the context of what information technology can now provide, the system was completely inadequate in recording or monitoring the use of the service, the callers and the outcomes.

Quality assurance

To ensure that the Freephone Helpline provides a consistent service to its clients, it is necessary to establish some clear quality standards and operating procedures for the staff and volunteers to follow, with training in these standards and procedures. The staff and volunteers are not currently provided with any standards or procedures to follow, or sufficient appropriate training. Staff and volunteers simply try to follow established custom and practice and use their own experience and judgement.

Confidentiality

Confidentiality of personal information is crucially important and enshrined in legislation. The Freephone Helpline service is in accommodation shared with staff of another agency. Although there is no evidence of breaches of confidentiality, current arrangements in the shared office fail to provide the appropriate level of security and confidentiality of records. Staff and volunteers are not provided with any particular guidance or training in relation to the difficult issues that can arise in applying the principle of confidentiality in relation to this particular kind of service, beyond the basic expectation of a public servant dealing with the public.

Equal opportunities

Staff and volunteers were unaware of an agency equal opportunities policy and felt that such a policy would need to address the needs of those with hearing impairment or whose first language isn't English. There is no evidence that these issues have been given consideration or that there is any equal opportunities monitoring.

Planning

In achieving the aims of any organization, it is increasingly the norm to put in place a strategic and operational planning process which involves considering the needs and expectations of the organization's stakeholders and how the process can be continuously improved. Such a process would also establish performance indicators by which the service could be continuously and transparently evaluated. The organization or the local authority had not put in place such a planning process for the Freephone Helpline service.

Key evaluation issues

Returning to the brief for the evaluation, the above findings and discussion provide some very important data in evaluating the service and suggesting recommendations for the future.

Aims of the service

It is clear that the main purpose of the Freephone Helpline service is to prevent homeless people from having to sleep rough by acting as a bed bureau referring homeless people to emergency accommodation. Secondary aims include referring callers to other services and providing an emergency welfare allowance in exceptional circumstances when it could not wait until the next morning or on the following Monday.

The extent to which these aims are still legitimate

There was considerable support from the vast majority of agencies working with people who are homeless for a Freephone Helpline service providing after-hours advice and information. There was no change in the perception that such a service is crucial in facilitating access to the emergency accommodation that is available. The very large number of calls to the service also testifies to the continuing need for such a service.

The extent to which these aims are being achieved

All the various stakeholders recognized that the service is not currently achieving the agreed aim of preventing homeless people from having to sleep rough. However, it is clear that the need for accommodation for homeless people far outstrips the supply, and that emergency accommodation that is supposed to be providing short-stay beds has become silted up with long-stay residents who cannot obtain the longer-term housing they need. The inevitable consequence has been that the number of people who are homeless has been increasing rather than decreasing and there is less emergency accommodation available for those who do become homeless.

The current referral policies and procedures of some hostels also make it particularly difficult to obtain accommodation for some groups of homeless people.

With this background, the staff of the Freephone Helpline service have an impossible task in trying to access emergency accommodation for homeless people when it frequently isn't available.

Conclusions

The evaluation came to the following conclusions:

- The service is failing to achieve the aim it was established to meet because of problems with the availability of emergency and long-term accommodation.
- The current service is under-resourced to meet the needs of people who are homeless.
- The organization and the local authority have, even given any resource constraints, failed to ensure that the service is effective and efficient. The very basics of documentation, policies, monitoring, staff induction and training, IT, equipment and physical premises are well below any acceptable standard.

Recommendations

In light of the findings and discussion above, the following were recommended in relation to the future of the service:

- Local authority housing policy needs to urgently address the long-term housing needs of those people least able to compete in the current highly competitive housing market.
- A strategy urgently needs to be put in place to tackle the needs of people sleeping rough in the area, combining emergency accommodation, semi-independent accommodation and affordable housing for rent.
- Greater effort needs to be put into settlement in relation to all hostels to help people who are homeless and in emergency accommodation to move to longer-term accommodation.
- The availability of a night-time drop-in centre which could provide advice, information and counselling, as well as warmth and refreshments all the year round, would help prevent deaths from rough sleeping and improve access to, and assessment for, services on a face-to-face basis.
- An after-hours Freephone Helpline service should continue to be one part of this strategy to tackle rough sleeping in the area.
- The Freephone Helpline should have a close link to an all-night drop-in centre which is open all the year round.

- The Freephone Helpline should be available all night and be properly resourced, with two staff members available at any one time.
- The physical premises of the staff who answer calls should be dedicated, and be of a sufficient standard and size.
- All records should be kept confidentially and securely and a computerized database and recording and monitoring system put in place to ensure that all appropriate data is gathered and regularly analysed.
- Information technology should also be used to link the Freephone Helpline with accommodation providers.
- Modern telephone technology should also be used to improve access to the service, the monitoring of unsuccessful calls and the length of time it takes someone to get through.
- A system for regularly obtaining the views of users of the service should be put in place.
- Consideration should be given to regular 'mystery shopper' evaluations of the service against agreed standards.
- An information database that is frequently updated should be continuously available to those operating the Freephone Helpline service.
- The staff of the Freephone Helpline should be involved in a forum that meets regularly with other providers of services to people who are homeless, to ensure effective coordination.
- The Freephone Helpline service should put in place a strategy and operational planning process that involves the other stakeholders in continuously improving the service and establishes clear objectives and performance indicators.
- The Freephone Helpline service should put in place a set of agreed quality standards and policies to ensure that good practice is clearly identified and maintained.
- All new staff and volunteers of the service should receive a thorough induction into the standards and procedures guiding the service before having the responsibility of dealing with callers.
- All staff and volunteers of the service should regularly be involved in identifying their specific training needs in relation to the Freephone Helpline, and should undertake regular training to update their skills and knowledge.
- All staff and volunteers of the service should have specific job/role descriptions that clarify their responsibilities.
- All staff and volunteers of the service should receive regular supervision and the opportunity to discuss issues arising from dealing with calls.
- There should be regular meetings of all the staff operating the Freephone Helpline service to discuss its operation and how it could be improved.
- A strategy should be put in place for pro-actively promoting the service.
- All referrals should be followed up with the agency to whom the homeless person was referred, to monitor the outcome.

Questions

1 From the information in the case study, carry out a SWOT analysis of Homeline.
2 Who are the stakeholders of Homeline? What are their expectations and aspirations of Homeline?
3 Assume you have just been asked to take over the management of Homeline; list the strategic issues that you need to deal with.
4 What should be the performance indicators of Homeline?
5 What are the lessons for the local authority in relation to the contracting of services?

Note

* This is not the real name of the organization.

NSPCC

The beginning

The National Society for the Prevention of Cruelty to Children (NSPCC) was founded in 1884 to protect children from abuse and neglect and to support vulnerable families. It has pioneered the development of child protection in the UK.

Despite the economic successes of the Victorian era, life in the late nineteenth century was extremely harsh for a large number of children. Social deprivation and brutal attitudes meant that many of them experienced cruelty and neglect from uncaring or desperate parents. They were forced to work exhaustingly long hours or left to beg in the streets, often starving and in need of medical attention.

Inspiration from the USA

In the USA, children were also suffering – so much so that a New York Society for the Prevention of Cruelty to Children was founded in 1875, after the highly publicized case of a young girl, Mary Ellen McCormack, who was subject to vicious daily beatings by her adoptive parents. She could not be given legal protection as no appropriate law existed on the statute book. Henry Bergh, founder of the New York Society for the Prevention of Cruelty to Animals, successfully petitioned the US Supreme Court on Mary Ellen's behalf. He argued that, as she was a 'human animal', she was legally entitled to protection comparable to that given to animals.

The development of child protection in Britain began shortly after a Liverpool banker, Thomas Agnew, visited New York in 1881. He was greatly impressed by the city's pioneering children's charity and returned home in 1882 determined to provide similar help for the children of Liverpool. Agnew gained the support of Samuel Smith, a local Liberal MP. Together they founded the Liverpool Society for the Prevention of Cruelty to Children in 1883, which remained independent of the NSPCC until 1953.

The London Society for the Prevention of Cruelty to Children

News of Agnew's work reached London, where he was invited to meet a number of like-minded and influential individuals. As a result, the London Society for the Prevention of Cruelty to Children was formed on 8 July 1884, with Lord Shaftesbury as President and the Reverend Edward Rudolph and Reverend Benjamin Waugh as joint Honorary Secretaries. Waugh later became the first Director of the NSPCC. Born in 1839 in Yorkshire, his work as a Congregational minister led him to the slums of Greenwich in East London, where he was appalled by the scenes of deprivation and cruelty to children that surrounded him there and began working on behalf of local children. He stood bail for them at the local police court so frequently that officers began to send young offenders straight to him rather than to prison.

A powerful character who abhorred social injustice, Waugh's urgent priority was to draw public and government attention to the plight of children who had no-one to speak for them. The London Society published detailed reports of the widespread cruelty it uncovered, thereby offering the irrefutable proof needed to stir the public and official conscience.

The formation of the NSPCC

By 1889 the London Society for the Prevention of Cruelty to Children had thirty-two branches, known as 'aid committees', throughout England, Wales and Scotland. At the 1889 Annual General Meeting the Society resolved to revise its constitution and to change its name to the National Society for the Prevention of Cruelty to Children. Queen Victoria became Royal Patron, and Waugh was appointed Director. In the same year, the NSPCC established its first Irish aid committee in Dublin. The (independent) Royal Scottish Society for the Prevention of Cruelty to Children was also founded in 1889 and co-existed with the NSPCC until the NSPCC ceased operating in Scotland in July 1907.

The NSPCC was by then employing twenty-nine Inspectors. In 1889 alone they dealt with 3,947 cases of child abuse and neglect, many of which involved extreme brutality.

The Children's Charter: a landmark in child protection

The year 1889 was to prove momentous for children. In addition to the emergence of the NSPCC, it saw the passing of the first Act of Parliament for the Prevention of Cruelty to Children, popularly known as 'the Children's Charter'. This crucial landmark in child protection was the result of five years' lobbying by the Society and its supporters to convince Parliament of the need for laws governing the treatment of children.

The Children's Charter enabled British law to intervene, for the first time, in relations between parents and children. The police could now arrest anyone found ill-treating a child and obtain a warrant to enter a home if a child was thought to be in danger. The Children's Charter also included guidelines on the employment of children, and it outlawed begging. After five years' implementation it was evaluated and in 1894 was amended and extended with the help of the NSPCC. Children were now allowed to give evidence in court, mental cruelty was recognized and it became an offence to deny a sick child medical attention.

The NSPCC in the early years

By the beginning of the twentieth century the NSPCC had grown consider-ably in size, reflecting increasing public recognition of the importance of its work. In 1900 the Society had 163 Inspectors, a six-fold increase in the number employed just ten years earlier. Informally known as the 'Cruelty Men', these uniformed Inspectors gained a unique status. The 1904 Prevention of Cruelty to Children Act allowed them to remove children from abusive or neglectful homes without the involvement of the police, but with the consent of a Justice of the Peace. By 1905 the NSPCC had helped more than one million children.

In 1907 the Probation Offenders Act was passed, which enabled petty offenders to serve probation rather than imprisonment. The Act aimed to prevent the economic deprivation that resulted from the imprison-ment of a family's wage-earner. NSPCC Inspectors were often made responsible for supervising probations relating to child abuse or neglect offences.

In the following year, the 1908 Children Act introduced further valu-able legislation. It established juvenile courts and addressed the issue of child life insurance. Foster-parents now had to be registered and could no longer insure the lives of foster-children, a move designed to stamp out 'baby farming' and profit-motivated child killings. The Punishment of Incest Act was also passed in 1908, making sexual abuse within families a matter for state jurisdiction rather than intervention by the clergy.

Early fundraising

In 1889 the NSPCC had a total income of £8,835, raised by its thirty-two local aid committees. Two years later Princess Mary of Teck (later to be Queen Mary) took out a subscription to the Society for herself and her younger brothers. Her interest inspired the formation of the Children's League of Pity in 1891. The League was the forerunner of today's NSPCC Schools, which enabled children of all ages to learn about the NSPCC's work and to become involved in fundraising activities.

A Royal Charter

On 28 May 1895 Queen Victoria granted the NSPCC a Royal Charter of Incorporation, which allowed the Society to hold property in its own right. The Charter stated that the objectives of the NSPCC were:

- To prevent the private and public wrongs of children and the corruption of their morals.
- To take action for the enforcement of laws for their protection.

The first female Inspectors

Until the outbreak of World War One in 1914, all NSPCC Inspectors were male. During the war years many were called up for military service. Their wives, who had traditionally supported the Inspectors from behind the scenes, stepped in to fill vacant posts.

In 1920 the NSPCC began providing specialist services to meet specific social needs. Four female Inspectors were appointed to a medical branch in London, set up to deal with health problems caused by poor nutrition and living conditions. It also ran the NSPCC children's ambulance, which transported sick children to and from hospital. In the same year, an Inspector was appointed to help canal-boat children, who lived in appalling conditions and received no education.

New ideas in fundraising and promotion

Charity street collections gained a dubious reputation during World War One. Bogus fundraisers were discovered to be fraudulently collecting in aid of the families of those killed or injured in action. The NSPCC, therefore, avoided street collections until the War Charities Act of 1916 introduced regulations to protect and guide collectors. After the Act, many branches began to hold annual NSPCC Flag Days. These quickly proved to be a highly effective means of supplementing the income raised through subscriptions, regular donations and legacies.

In 1909 the NSPCC's branch in Preston, Lancashire, pioneered two fundraising innovations which were later adopted throughout the NSPCC. The first, Children's Sunday, was an annual event through which the branch promoted the Society's work in churches and meeting-places. Children's Sunday aroused considerable public interest in the NSPCC, and was in effect a forerunner of the present-day NSPCC Children's Day. The second innovation, the Workpeople's Committee, was an employee fundraising scheme run by companies local to the branch.

The emerging media of radio and cinema presented the NSPCC with exciting new opportunities for campaigning. The Prince of Wales, later to be King Edward VIII, spoke on behalf of the NSPCC in a 1926 radio appeal, the first of many such appeals by the Society. By the early 1930s the NSPCC was one of the first charities to screen appeal films to cinema audiences. During the years following World War Two it increasingly used television to show such films, and in 1959 the new ITV channel broadcast an interview with NSPCC Director the Reverend Arthur Morton.

Further legislation

The 1930s was a time of increased legislation to improve child protection in Britain, and the Children and Young Persons Act of 1932 broadened the powers of the juvenile courts and introduced supervision orders for children at risk.

World War Two and the post-war years

By the outbreak of World War Two in 1939, there was widespread public acceptance of the need for the Society's work. Parents and relatives of children began to approach the NSPCC directly for help.

Although eighty-seven of its Inspectors were called to active war service, the NSPCC continued to maintain and develop its work. The Society also gave the government advice and practical help on various wartime issues that affected children. For example, the Society was instrumental in the evacuation of city children to homes in country areas, where the danger of air raids was sometimes replaced by those of physical violence and neglect.

The aftermath of war

The experience of World War Two reinforced the vital necessity of protecting the nation's most important asset – the future generation. The post-war Labour Government began developing Britain's pioneering Welfare State (see Chapter 2). In 1945 the Parliamentary Care of Children Committee was set up after the death of 13-year-old Dennis O'Neill at the hands of foster-parents. The NSPCC contributed to the Committee's report of 1946 which demonstrated the need for both more foster parents and the establishment of a Children's Committee and a Children's Officer in each local authority area. Both recommendations were incorporated into the Children Act of 1948.

The trend for parents and carers to seek advice directly from the Society continued to grow. 'Advice sought' cases numbered over 10,000 a year, a quarter of all NSPCC cases. But increasingly heavy workloads prevented Inspectors from providing the follow-up support required by such families. To meet this need, the NSPCC set up a Women Visitors' Scheme in 1948, whereby female staff visited families with practical help and advice. Local authorities welcomed the scheme and soon were helping to finance it. By 1953, the NSPCC was employing twenty-six Women Visitors.

The 1950s brought a number of important organizational changes. In 1953 the NSPCC enlarged its operation in the north-west of England by absorbing the last of England's independent child protection societies: the Liverpool Society for the Prevention of Cruelty to Children and the Birkenhead and Wirral Society for the Prevention of Cruelty to Children. Meanwhile, the NSPCC's seventy-year-long operation in the Republic of Ireland ended in March 1956, following the founding of the independent Irish Society for the Prevention of Cruelty to Children. In Northern Ireland, however, the NSPCC continued (and continues) to operate.

As the Welfare State became part of the fabric of British life, state-run child protection services started to overlap with those provided by the NSPCC. Although the aim was close cooperation between the voluntary and public sectors, in reality this working relationship proved far from easy. The government's Ingleby Report of 1960 made a number of recommendations intended to ease this professional tension, including one whereby the NSPCC would consult with government case-coordinating committees before taking action over children. While the NSPCC agreed to this, it objected strongly to the recommended withdrawal of its status of 'authorized person' and its power to intervene. The Society promptly launched a successful campaign to challenge the withdrawal. As a result the NSPCC retained this important legal power.

The innovations of the 1960s

The 1960s was a decade of unprecedented change for the NSPCC. By 1963 it had a child protection staff of 325, who helped 121,565 children in that year alone. However, the Children and Young Persons Act of the same year gave many local authorities responsibility for providing support to families at home, in order to reduce the number of children being placed in care. The subsequent increase in local authority preventive work reduced the number of vulnerable families dealt with by the NSPCC. This release of resources enabled the Society to develop other, more specialized services, such as child and family therapies, child protection training, and research to aid policy-makers.

Increasing professionalism

The social work profession generally was growing and gaining increasing recognition. Universities and further education colleges began to provide courses leading to accredited qualifications for the profession. In 1961 the NSPCC introduced a six-month social work training course, the duration of which was eventually extended to fourteen months; Inspectors could obtain secondment leave to study for external professional qualifications.

The professional status of the NSPCC Inspector was improving in other ways. Uniforms were abolished in 1969, as was the requirement for

Inspectors to live in tied houses. Salary levels were increased. The distinction in title and authority between Inspectors and Women Visitors was removed.

Research into violence to children

The NSPCC introduced three major innovations in the 1960s. The first was the development of the NSPCC's Battered Child Research Department. It was to prove influential in shaping government policy and practice, including the setting up of child protection registers nationwide.

Second, with the aid of government funding, the NSPCC set up a network of pre-school playgroups, a large number of which were based in Northern Ireland. This pioneering scheme provided socially isolated children aged between thirty months and five years with a safe environment in which to build relationships with their peers and adults. Initially set up for children at risk, the scheme was later extended to include those living in deprived communities.

The group system develops

The NSPCC's third innovation of the decade was to modernize the structure of its child protection network. Inspectors traditionally worked alone, responsible to local NSPCC branches. In the late 1960s the NSPCC decided to amalgamate more than 217 branches into groups of between four and ten units, each led by a group officer. No longer isolated in their work, Inspectors could enjoy the benefits of teamwork, share specialist skills and receive direct support and supervision. For the public, the group system ensured improved quality and continuity. By 1971 this new system was in place throughout England, Wales and Northern Ireland, with forty-three groups in operation.

Creating a safe environment

The NSPCC had long been aware that a child could be as much at risk from his or her environment as from ill-treatment at the hands of adults. In the 1960s it placed renewed emphasis on raising public awareness of accident prevention in the home, for accidents were continuing to be a major cause of death and injury among children. Furthermore, the 1960s' architectural fashion for tower-block housing presented new hazards, particularly as children often played without supervision in communal spaces at ground level.

The challenges of the 1970s

Despite financial difficulties stemming from Britain's chronic inflation, the NSPCC continued to develop and expand in the 1970s, with only a temporary cut in staffing levels in 1975. When Sir Keith Joseph, then Secretary of State for Social Services, spoke at the Society's Annual Council Meeting of 1971, he referred to Britain's 'veritable avalanche of social need' and the fact that 'something like a quarter of child referrals in England and Wales come through the NSPCC'.

The 1970s proved to be a time of intense public and media scrutiny of social work practice. In 1974, a report into the tragic and preventable death of Maria Colwell at the hands of her stepfather highlighted a serious lack of coordination within child protection services. During the next ten years there were a further twenty-seven inquiries into child deaths through physical abuse and severe neglect. The NSPCC Battered Child Research Department completed and published pioneering research into physical abuse in 1976.

The first NSPCC Special Unit

In the search for more effective methods of dealing with child abuse, the NSPCC set up the first of its Special Units in Manchester in 1973, with funding from the City Council. The Unit Team was on call twenty-four hours a day and services included child counselling, professional consultation and training, a case conference service, and a central register of children at risk of physical abuse. In 1976 the NSPCC opened a Family Day Centre at the Unit, the Society's first. Such was the success of the Manchester Special Unit that a further thirteen were developed in close cooperation with the Department of Health and local authorities, who also helped with funding.

At the end of the 1970s the largest study into child abuse ever produced for England, Wales and Northern Ireland showed that, each year, at least 7,700 children were suffering physical abuse, which included 110 deaths.

National Advisory Centre on the Battered Child

In 1974 the NSPCC added a new dimension to its work on the battered child with the setting up of the Battered Child Advisory Centre. The Centre had staff on call twenty-four hours a day, and provided a full range of services for children in need of protection and their families. Services included a psychiatric and psychotherapeutic facility, as well as paediatric assessment, treatment and nursery care. It also offered education and consultative facilities to professionals nationwide, including general practitioners, hospital staff, healthcare workers and social workers.

The NSPCC in the 1980s

The NSPCC entered the 1980s faced with considerable difficulties as an organization. Against a background of worldwide recession, the Society was beset with financial problems. It was receiving little government assistance and insufficient income from public donations. Declining funds meant that the number of Inspectors fell from its 1962 peak of 325 to 230 in 1984. The pressures created by the need to maintain a high standard of work with reduced resources were enormous.

The NSPCC faced two major challenges. It needed to take radical steps to ensure that children received the best services the NSPCC could offer, and that these services utilized the Society's resources to the full. And there was also an urgent need to remedy the NSPCC's financial situation and to establish it on a solid footing.

The Centenary Charter

In 1983 the NSPCC drew up a new Charter to mark its 1984 Centenary and outline the Society's new priorities for the future. The Centenary Charter emphasized the NSPCC's commitment to supporting children who had been abused and to preventing further abuse. To further this aim, it pledged to replace the group working system with a nationwide network of child protection teams. The Charter stressed that the NSPCC should maintain its pioneering role, and further develop its training and consultative activities.

The Centenary Appeal

The Charter's first aim was to establish sixty child protection teams across the country. Faced with such an ambitious goal alongside falling income, the NSPCC needed to raise a large amount of money as quickly as possible. In 1983 it launched the Centenary Appeal, led by the Duke of Westminster. A series of high-profile fundraising events followed from 1984, which stimulated enormous public, corporate and media interest. The Appeal was phenomenally successful, raising over £14 million.

Child protection teams

The 1980s saw a growing awareness of the scale and complexity of child abuse. In order to ensure the high level of professionalism required to combat abuse, the NSPCC decided to completely integrate its services for children from 1984 onwards. Over the next five years, thirteen special units, twenty-four family centres, sixty-five therapeutic playgroups and various student units were brought together to create a national network of child protection teams. Together these provided a range of investigation, treatment, training, consultation and case-conferencing services in collaboration with local authorities.

Professional training

By the early 1980s, external social work training had improved to the extent that the NSPCC could attract ready-qualified staff for all its vacancies. In addition, training secondment ensured that existing staff remained equally well qualified. Therefore, in 1981 the Society discontinued its social work course, which it had run since the early 1960s. This freed trainers to develop a comprehensive programme of specialized courses in child protection and management, for the benefit of NSPCC staff and those working in related professions. In May 1989 the NSPCC opened its purpose-built National Child Protection Training Centre in Leicester.

Campaigning for change

In 1980 the NSPCC set up its first public affairs department, which gave added impetus to the Society's political campaigning. The public could also now be targeted with renewed vigour, as was proved by the success of the NSPCC's first major multimedia public awareness campaign in Autumn 1986. Entitled 'The Forgotten Children', the campaign used television, cinema and radio advertising, posters and publications to educate parents, professionals and the public at large about the dangers and long-term consequences of physical and emotional neglect. Subsequent NSPCC campaigns have included 'Protect Your Child' (prevention of sexual abuse, 1987–88); 'Putting Children First' (promoting the needs and rights of children, 1988–89); 'Listen to Children' (listening and responding to children's needs, 1989–90); 'Make a Difference for Children' (promoting volunteer fundraising, 1993); 'Justice for Children' (lobbying for a child-friendly criminal justice system, ongoing since 1993); and 'A Cry for Children' (to increase public awareness and action against abuse, 1994–97).

The 1990s: a regional focus

The very significant Children Act of 1989 prompted a further increase in local authority childcare provision in the UK. Following this Act and the appointment of a new Director, Christopher Brown, NSPCC carried out a fundamental review of the Society's services, which also sought to identify any existing unmet need for child protection services. The subsequent strategy for the 1990s outlined how the NSPCC could best use its resources and expertise to protect children in 1990s Britain. One important innovation was the move to devolve decision-making to eight regions throughout England, Wales and Northern Ireland. This ensured that the NSPCC's services could be designed and funded to meet specific local need.

By the end of 1991, the NSPCC had over 120 Child Protection Teams and Projects carrying out protective and preventive work throughout the regions. Some offered highly specialized services; e.g. treatment of young people who sexually abuse other children, and specialist assessments for courts and other professional agencies.

The NSPCC Child Protection Helpline

Another major innovation was the launch of the NSPCC Child Protection Helpline in 1991. This free, twenty-four-hour, nationwide service was the first of its kind in Europe, enabling anyone concerned about a child at risk to obtain advice quickly and easily from an experienced telephone counsellor at any time of the day or night. The effectiveness of the Helpline service meant that there was no longer a need for project team workers to be on call twenty-four hours a day.

In 1999 the Helpline's counsellors dealt with 74,000 calls. The service is constantly being developed to give access to as many people as possible. For example, in July 1997 a Textphone line was introduced for hearing-impaired adults and children.

The National Commission of Inquiry into the Prevention of Child Abuse

Throughout the 1990s, campaigning and parliamentary work played a major role in the NSPCC's mission to ensure better protection of children. The Society entered the decade feeling increasingly concerned that far greater resources were used to deal with the aftermath of abuse than were used to prevent its occurrence in the first place. As a first step towards a solution, it set up and funded the National Commission of Inquiry into the Prevention of Child Abuse in 1994, under the chairmanship of Lord Williams of Mostyn QC. This was the most thorough investigation of child abuse ever seen in the UK. More than 10,000 people contributed to the work of the Commission, which published the report of its findings, *Childhood Matters*, in 1996.

The National Commission was asked to address the question 'Can you identify all the causes of child abuse and put an end to each one?'. It reached the clear conclusion that '...child abuse and neglect can almost always be prevented – provided the will to do so is there'.

Ending cruelty to children

The NSPCC carried out a lengthy appraisal of services in the light of the National Commission's findings, and also analysed the opportunities for change from the broader political, economic and social perspectives. They concluded that cruelty to children can be eliminated in the UK, and developed an innovative long-term strategy for the organization.

The NSPCC 'FULL STOP' Campaign

As a result, in March 1999 the NSPCC launched the FULL STOP Campaign, which invited the people of Britain and Northern Ireland to support the NSPCC in its aim of 'ending cruelty to children'. The campaign aims to end child cruelty within twenty years by radically increasing awareness of the issues surrounding child abuse, to bring about fundamental changes in attitudes and behaviour towards children.

The NSPCC recognizes that it cannot end cruelty to children on its own but requires the involvement of organizations and individuals across all sectors of society, cooperating in five action programmes led by the NSPCC:

1   Protecting the child
2   The child in the family
3   The child in school
4   The child in the community
5   The child in society

The Society argues that many of the great movements in history that have radically improved the quality of life for future generations, such as the abolition of slavery, started with the conviction that certain practices were morally and socially unacceptable.

However, this high-profile campaign has not been without criticism, on two grounds. The first is that the NSPCC has established a mission, 'To end child cruelty', which is bound to fail. However, the organization has responded robustly by saying that the campaigners for the abolition of slavery did not campaign for improved services to slaves, but for an end to slavery, and they were successful.

The second criticism has concerned the costs of campaigning, administration, education and fundraising work, which comprised 60 per cent of the organization's total costs in 2000. This has received considerable criticism in the media, for 'wasting' money on 'administration' rather than on services to children.

Questions

1   To what extent is the NSPCC's mission statement achievable? Should a mission statement be achievable?
2   Is it legitimate for a children's charity to spend the majority of its money on other things than services to children?

3   If the state had taken over complete responsibility for child protection work after World War Two, to what extent would that have been a success or failure for the NSPCC?
4   What are the main strategies adopted by the NSPCC since it was founded?
5   What are the advantages and disadvantages of maintaining a focus on the one core issue, cruelty to children?

Further reading

The NSPCC website: www/nspcc.org.uk/
NSPCC annual report and The 'FULL STOP' campaign pack (available from NSPCC, 42 Curtain Road, London, EC2A 3NH. Tel: 020 7825 2500)

Oxfam

In the beginning

During World War Two, Greece was occupied by the German army. In 1941, the Allies imposed a naval blockade and scarcely any food or medical supplies could get through, even to civilians. Famine quickly took hold, and by the end of January 1942 more than 2,000 people were dying of starvation every day in Athens and Piraeus alone.

A national Famine Relief Committee was set up in May 1942 and support groups were formed throughout the UK. They tried to persuade the British government to allow essential supplies through the blockade, and raised funds for war refugees and displaced people across Europe. The Oxford Committee for Famine Relief met for the first time on 5 October 1942.

Many of the Relief Committees were wound down after the war, but the Oxford Committee saw a continuing need and enlarged its objectives to include 'the relief of suffering in consequence of the war'. Activity then centred on the provision of food parcels and clothing to Europe.

From 1948, grants were made to projects in Europe and elsewhere, and in 1949 the Committee's objectives were again broadened to 'the relief of suffering arising as a result of wars or of other causes in any part of the world'. The Committee gradually became known by its abbreviated telegraph address, Oxfam (this name was formally adopted in 1965).

In 1951, Howard Leslie Kirkley was appointed General Secretary of the Committee. Registered as a conscientious objector in 1939, Kirkley had helped found and run the Leeds Famine Relief Committee. He remained with Oxfam for 24 years, latterly as Director, and his own presence in disaster situations, the swift response of his organization and his work as Chairman of the UK Publicity Committee for the UN World Refugee Year in 1959–60 brought Oxfam to the attention of a wide audience.

During the 1950s the Committee responded to famine in Bihar, India, by raising £3,500 for its first response to a natural disaster in what would later be known as a 'developing country'. The Committee then turned its attention to those left homeless, hungry or orphaned at the end of the Korean war, and had raised £60,000 by the end of 1956.

Over this period the Committee's fund-raising and publicity work transformed it from a small local charity into one with national and international status.

Growing and developing: the 1960s

At the beginning of the 1960s Oxfam took a lead role in the international Freedom from Hunger campaign. Launched by the United Nations Food and Agriculture Organization, in collaboration with other organizations it aimed to combat food shortages by enabling people to grow enough to feed themselves, rather than by food aid. By 1965, hundreds of local Freedom from Hunger groups had raised £7 million in the UK alone.

The 1960s brought great changes. Concern for the world's poor grew among the general public and the charity's income trebled over the course of the decade. The organization worked to present a different picture of poor people in the Third World: one in which they were portrayed as human beings with dignity, not as passive victims. Education and information materials explained the root causes of poverty and suffering, the connections between North and South, and the role of people in the North in creating, and potentially solving, poverty in the developing world.

The major focus of Oxfam's overseas operations, managed by a growing network of Oxfam Field Directors (the first one in South Africa), became support for self-help schemes whereby communities improved their own water supplies, farming practices and health provision.

As well as providing aid, Oxfam began marketing handcrafts from the South, giving small-scale producers fair prices, training, advice and funding. This 'Bridge Programme' later became the Oxfam Fair Trade Company.

By the mid-1960s, the provision of village water supplies was established as a main plank of aid to India. Water and sanitation facilities were to become Oxfam's great specialist technical strength.

The famine in Bihar, India, recurred and Oxfam sent volunteers to help run a major feeding programme, the first time it became directly involved in a long-term emergency rather than sending funds and supplies.

During the 1960s the first Oxfam outside the UK was formed, in Canada.

Expansion: the 1970s

As Oxfam continued to expand its work through the 1970s, many new ideas and theories were put forward about development and poverty, including the decision to employ local people to run and work on projects. Oxfam's relief work in the African Sahel in the late 1970s looked at the traditional ways in which communities survived – helping them to improve and refine their survival techniques, and making sure that the local people kept control of the schemes they were involved in. The same principles of community involvement and control are still behind Oxfam's work today.

By 1971 Oxfam was working with 800 community projects in nineteen countries.

The Bangladesh war of independence drove millions of refugees into India. Oxfam responded by employing local people and the refugees themselves rather than outsiders.

In 1979 Oxfam hit the headlines for its work in Cambodia, where Pol Pot's brutal regime had laid waste to the country and left more than one million people dead. Oxfam led a group of agencies which mounted the largest voluntary relief effort at that time, importing supplies of rice, seeds, tools, water pumps and fertilizers for cities and rural areas alike.

Lobbying

During this period, it became clear that many of the problems associated with poverty required government and international action. Oxfam started – within the bounds set by charity law – to campaign on behalf of the people it worked with overseas and to talk to decision-makers who shaped policy on relevant issues. Oxfam's Public Affairs Unit (PAU) was set up to provide research into and analysis of the causes of poverty. By the mid-1980s the PAU was lobbying on a range of issues including pesticides, food aid and Third World debt.

Retail success

Oxfam's network of shops run by volunteer groups around the country became one of the main sources of income in the late 1960s, selling donated items and handcrafts from overseas. They are now a familiar sight on most high streets. Approximately 22,000 volunteers work in more than 830 Oxfam shops in the UK, making it one of the largest retailers in the UK.

In 1974, Oxfam established the 'Wastesaver Centre' in Huddersfield, with pioneering facilities for recycling. Today, Wastesaver processes around 80 tonnes of used clothing every week.

Oxfam Trading rapidly expanded its Bridge programme, with sales of fair trade products, during the 1970s and 1980s. A mail-order catalogue was also started, which boosted annual sales above £1 million by the early 1980s. The programme took the name Fair Trade in 1996 (trading under the name Oxfam Fair Trade Company) to bring it in line with the wider Fair Trade movement, which included campaigning for improvements in the terms of trade and conditions of workers.

Responding to change: the 1980s

In October 1984, TV footage of famine in Ethiopia (especially a BBC news report by Michael Buerk) prompted unprecedented public generosity. High-profile initiatives like Band Aid and Comic Relief followed, and contributed to Oxfam's income, which more than doubled in one year to £51 million.

Oxfam's 'Hungry for Change' campaign was launched. It captured public indignation at the obscenity of famine in the Third World set agaisnt the food mountains of the First World. Oxfam raised £1m to send a shipment – the 'Grain of Hope' – to feed 350,000 people in Ethiopia and Sudan for a month.

The first move was made at this time towards a more independent Oxfam in India, with the appointment of a Regional Director to manage the programme towards greater autonomy.

Tackling conflict: the 1990s

With the escalating number of conflicts following the collapse of the Soviet Union and the Eastern bloc, Oxfam began emergency and rehabilitation work in this region. During the 1990s, Oxfam supplied humanitarian aid to affected civilians on all sides of the wars in the former Yugoslavia.

Oxfam's largest-ever response to a humanitarian disaster was in the Great Lakes region of Central Africa in the mid-1990s, although aid alone could not provide solutions to the political, economic and social problems of the region. The work on the ground was matched by international lobbying and campaigning aimed at the UN, the Organization of African Unity, and powerful governments, in an effort to build a lasting peace.

In 1994 the genocide of an estimated 800,000 people in Rwanda, and the ensuing exodus of more than 1.7 million refugees, precipitated Oxfam's largest-ever humanitarian response. In the camps around Goma in Eastern Zaire, Oxfam rapidly installed clean water and sanitation for 700,000 refugees. The same year Oxfam UK and Ireland joined with nine other relief and development agencies based in Australia, New Zealand, America, Canada, Quebec, Hong Kong, Holland and Belgium to form Oxfam International, and this was followed by the first international launch of an Oxfam campaign, the 'Campaign for Basic Rights', simultaneously in UK, Ireland, South Africa, Zimbabwe, Zambia, Uganda and the USA.

An Oxfam International advocacy office opened in Washington DC to lobby international bodies like the World Bank, the International Monetary Fund, and the United Nations.

In 1996, for the first time Oxfam began to address poverty issues in the UK, with a £500,000 award from lottery funds.

Collaboration

The importance of working together with other world development organizations was particularly highlighted in the 1990s with the setting up of the Fairtrade Foundation by Oxfam, CAFOD, Christian Aid, New Consumer, Traidcraft Exchange and the World Development Movement, to tackle exploitation of workers in the Third World. Oxfam was also involved in the Disasters Emergency Committee (DEC) which, in its first year alone, launched four separate appeals – for people whose lives were devastated by floods in Bangladesh, Hurricane Mitch in the Caribbean, and wars in South Sudan and Kosovo. Oxfam also participated actively in the Jubilee 2000 Campaign, a coalition of organizations campaigning for debt relief at demonstrations in London, Edinburgh and Cardiff, and at the G7 (world leaders') meeting in Cologne.

In the 1990s, Oxfam UK and Ireland became two separate bodies, Oxfam GB and Oxfam Ireland. By the time of the Millennium there were eleven members of Oxfam International (of which Britain and Holland are the largest members in terms of income). Oxfam International, in order to develop greater international coherence, adopted a new strategic plan (2001–2004) under the title 'Towards global equity', which adopted a strongly rights-based approach.

Questions

1 How many different strategies can you identify during Oxfam's history? Give examples.
2 Does Oxfam's charitable status restrict its ability to tackle the root causes of poverty?
3 What are the pros and cons of Oxfam funding projects in the UK?
4 Should Oxfam employ expatriate staff overseas?
5 Should Oxfam's priority be responding to disasters or long-term development work? What are the strategic consequences of each approach?
6 Should Oxfam's priority be campaigning to prevent poverty or supporting projects to help poor people? Can they do both effectively? What are the consequences of prioritizing one over the other?
7 Oxfam is one of the largest retailers in the UK. Does selling cheap second-hand clothing which has been donated do no more than put poor small clothing retailers out of business?
8 Selling donated second-hand clothes makes much more profit than selling goods produced by Oxfam's overseas partners. How much of its retail space should be given over to fair-traded goods?
9 Write a mission statement for Oxfam.
10 What should Oxfam's performance indicators be?

11   Has Oxfam become more, or less, effective by becoming decentralized?
12   To what extent should Oxfam consider other world development agencies to be competitors for scarce funds, or allies and potential collaborators?

Further reading

Towards global equity, Oxfam International's strategic plan for 2001–2004.
Oxfam GB annual report, 1999–2000.
Oxfam Ireland/Northern Ireland annual report, 1999–2000.
Oxfam websites: www.oxfam.org.uk/ and www.oxfamireland.org/

References

AA (AccountAbility) (2000) *AccountAbility 1000 standard*, available from Account-Ability, Thrale House, 44–6 Southwark Street, London SE1 1UN, or from their website: www.accountability.org.uk/

Acar, W. (1987) 'Organisational processes and strategic postures: Cross-classification or continuous', *Proceedings of the General Systems Society*, J70–J84.

Adams, J. S. (1965) *Inequity in social exchange*, Academic Press.

Alderfer, C. P. (1972) *Existence, relatedness and growth: Human needs in organisational settings*, The Free Press.

Aldrich, H. (1979) *Organisations and environments*, Prentice-Hall.

Allison, M. and Kaye, J. (1997) *Strategic planning for nonprofit organisations*, Wiley.

Anderson, T. J. (2000) 'Strategic planning, autonomous actions and corporate performance', *Long Range Planning* 33(2).

Andrews, G., Peters, L. and Teesson, M. (1994) *The measurement of consumer outcome in mental health: A report to the national mental health information strategy committee*, Clinical Research Unit for Anxiety Disorders.

Andrews, K. R. (1971) *The concept of corporate strategy*, Richard D. Irwin.

Anheier, H. K. (2000) *Managing nonprofit organisations: Towards a new approach*, Civil Society working paper 1, Centre for Civil Society, London School of Economics and Political Science.

Ansoff, H. I. (1965) *Corporate strategy*, Pelican.

Ansoff, I., Avner, J., Brandenberg, R. C. *et al.* (1970) 'Does planning pay?', *Long Range Planning* 3(2).

Ansoff, I. and McDonnell, E. (1990) *Implanting strategic management*, Prentice-Hall.

Anthony, R. and Young, D. (1984) *Management control in nonprofit organizations*, Irvin.

Argenti, J. (1965) *Corporate planning*, Allen & Unwin.

Argenti, J. (1997) 'All things to all men', *Strategy*, March: 5–6.

Argyris, C. (1964) *Integrating the individual and the organisation*, Wiley.

Argyris, C. and Schon, D. A. (1974) *Theory in practice: Increasing professional effectiveness*, Jossey-Bass.

Argyris, C. and Schon, D. A. (1978) *Organisational learning: A theory of action perspective*, Addison-Wesley.

Argyris, C. and Schon, D. A. (1996) *Organisational learning II: Theory, method and practice*, Addison-Wesley.

Armstrong, J. S. (1991) 'Strategic planning improves manufacturing performance', *Long Range Planning* 24(4).

Au, C.-F. (1996) 'Rethinking organisational effectiveness: Theoretical and method-ological issues in the study of organisational effectiveness for social welfare organisations', *Administration in Social Work* 20(4): 1–17.

Aupperle, K. E., Acar, W. and Booth B. E. (1986) 'An empirical critique of "In search of excellence": How excellent are excellent companies?', *Journal of Management* 12(4): 127–9.

Ayal, I. (1986) 'Planning for a professional association', *Long Range Planning* 19(3): 51–8.

Baden-Fuller, C. and Stopford, J. M. (1992) *Rejuvenating the mature business: The competitive challenge*, Harvard Business School Press.

Ball, M. (1989) *Multiple funding in the voluntary sector*, Home Office Voluntary Services Unit.

Barnard, C. (1938) *The functions of the executive*, Harvard University Press.

Barnard, H. and Walker, P. (1994) *Strategies for success*, NCVO.

Barr, A., Hashhagen, S. and Purcell, R. (1996) *The monitoring and evaluation of community development*, Scottish Community Development Centre/VAU.

Barry, B. W. (1986) *Strategic planning for non-profit*, Amherst Weider Foundation.

Bart, C. K. and Tabone, J. C. (1998) 'Mission statement rationales and organisa-tional alignment in the not-for-profit health care sector', *Health Care Management Review* 23(4): 54–69.

Bartlett, C. A. and Ghoshal, S. (1989) *Managing across borders*, Harvard Business School Press.

Bartlett, C. A. and Ghoshal, S. (1998) 'Beyond strategic planning to organisational learning: Lifeblood of the individual corporation', *Strategy and Leadership* Jan/Feb: 34–9.

Basini, S. and Buckley, F. (1999) *The meaning of work in the Irish voluntary sector*, AVARI/University of Ulster.

Bass, B. M. (1970) 'When planning for others', *Journal of Applied Behavioural Science* VI(2): 1551–71.

Batsleer, J. (1995) 'Management and organisation', in J. Davis Smith, C. Rochester and R. Hedley (eds) *An introduction to the voluntary sector*, Routledge.

Batsleer, J., Cornforth, C. and Paton, R. (eds) (1992) *Issues in voluntary and nonprofit management*, Addison-Wesley in association with the Open Univeristy Press.

Beckford, J. (1991) 'Great Britain: voluntarism and sectoral interests', in R. Wuthnow (ed.) *Between states and markets: The voluntary sector in comparative perspec-tive*, Princeton University Press.

Bennis, W. G. (1966) *Changing organisations*, McGraw-Hill.

Bennis, W. and Nanus, B. (1985) *Leaders: The strategies for taking charge*, Harper & Row.

Berger, P. and Luckmann, T. (1967) *The social construction of reality*, Doubleday.

Beveridge, W. (1948) *Voluntary action*, Allen & Unwin.

Bigelow, B., Stone, M. S. and Arndt, M. (1996) 'Corporate political strategy: A framework for understanding nonprofit strategy', *Nonprofit Management and Lead-ership* 7(1).

Billis, D. (1984) 'The missing link: Some challenges for research and practice in voluntary sector management', in B. Knight (ed.) *Management in voluntary organi-sations*, ARVAC occasional paper No. 6.

Billis, D. (1993) *Organising public and voluntary agencies*, Routledge.

Billis, D. and Harris, M (eds) (1996) *Voluntary agencies: Challenges of organisation and management*, Macmillan.

Blau, P. M. and Scott, W. R. (1962) *Formal organisations*, Routledge & Kegan Paul.

Bluedorn, A. C. (1980) 'Cutting the Gordian knot: A critique of the effectiveness tradition in organisational research', *Sociology and Social Research* 64: 447–96.

Blumberg, P. (1968) *Industrial democracy: The sociology of participation*, Schocken.

Bolman, L. G. and Deal, T. E. (1991) *Reframing organisations*, Jossey-Bass.

Bornstein, D. (2001) *The price of a dream: The story of the Grameen Bank*, Hummingbirdgreen.

Boschken, H. L. (1988) *Strategic design and organisational change*, University of Alabama Press.

Bovaird, T. and Rubienska, A. (1996) 'Marketing in the voluntary sector', in S. P. Osborne (ed.) *Managing in the voluntary sector – a handbook for managers in charitable and non-profit organisations*, International Thomson Business Press.

Bowman, C. and Asche, D. (1987) *Strategic management*, Macmillan.

Boyd, B. K. (1991) 'Strategic planning and financial performance', *Journal of Management Studies* 28(4): 353–74.

Bozzo, S. (2000) *Evaluation resources for nonprofit organisations: Usefulness and applicability*, Canadian Center for Philanthropy.

Bracker, J. S. and Pearson, N. J. (1986) 'Planning and finanacial performance of small, mature firms', *Strategic Management Journal* 7: 503–22.

Bradshaw, P., Murray, V. V. and Wolpin, J. (1992) 'Do nonprofit boards make a difference? An exploration of the relationships among board structure, process and effectiveness', *Nonprofit and Voluntary Sector Quarterly* 21(3).

Brenton, M. (1985) *The voluntary sector in British social services*, Longman.

Bresser, R. K. and Bishop, R. C. (1983) *Dysfunctional effects of formal planning*, Academy of Management.

Brown, L. D. and Covey, J. (1987) *Organising and managing private development agencies*, PONPO working paper No. 129, Yale University Press.

Bruce, I. and Leat, D. (1993) *Management for tomorrow*, Volprof City University Business School.

Brudney, J. L. and Golec, R. R. (1997) 'Organisational benchmarks, impact, and effectiveness assessments: Closing the measurement circle', in *The changing social contract*, Independent Sector.

Bryson, J. M. (1988) *Strategic planning for public and non-profit organisations: A guide to strengthening and sustaining organisational achievement*, Jossey-Bass.

Bryson, J. M. (1995) *Strategic planning for public and nonprofit organizations* (2nd edn), Jossey-Bass.

Bryson, J. M. (ed.) (1999) *Strategic management in public and voluntary services – a reader*, Pergamon.

Bunker, B. B. and Alban, B. T. (1997) *Large group interventions: Engaging the whole system for rapid change*, Jossey-Bass.

Burgelman, R. A. (1980) *Managing innovating systems: A study of the process of internal corporate venturing*, PhD dissertation, Columbia University.

Burgelman, R. A. (1988) 'Strategy making as a social learning process: The case of internal corporate venturing', *Interfaces* 18(3).

Burgoyne, J., Pedlar, M. and Boydell, T. (1994) *Towards the learning company*, McGraw-Hill.

Burkhart, P. J. and Reuss, S. (1993) *Successful strategic planning: A guide for nonprofit agencies and organisations*, Sage.

Burns, T. (1961) 'Micropolitics: Mechanisms of organisational change', *Administrative Science Quarterly* 6: 257–81.

Burns, T. and Stalker, G. M. (1961) *The management of innovation*, Oxford University Press.

Bush, R. (1992) 'Survival of the nonprofit sector in a for-profit world', *Nonprofit and Voluntary Sector Quarterly* 21(4).

Butler, R. J. and Wilson, D. C. (1990) *Managing voluntary and non-profit organisations*, Routledge.

Byington, D., Martin, P., Maxwell, M. *et al.* (1991) 'Organisational affiliation and effectiveness: The case of rape crisis centers', *Administration in Social Work* 15: 83–103.

Cameron, K. (1982) 'The relationship between faculty unionism and organisation effectiveness', *Academy of Management Journal* 25: 6–24.

Carr, C. (1996) *Choice. Chance and organisational change*, AMACOM.

Carr, W. and Kemmis, S. (1986) *Becoming critical*, Falmer.

Carroll, D. (1983) 'A disappointing search for excellence', *Harvard Business Review* 61(6).

Champy, J. and Hammer, M. (1993) *Re-engineering the corporation*, HarperBusiness.

Chanan, G. (1991) *Taken for granted*, Community Development Foundation.

Chandler, A. D. Jr (1962) *Strategy and structure*, MIT Press.

Chauhan, Y. (1998) *A planned journey into the unknown*, Centre for Voluntary Organisations working paper 20, LSE.

Chesterman, M. (1979) *Charities, trusts and social welfare*, Weidenfeld & Nicolson.

Cialdini, R. B. (1984) *Influence: Science and practice*, Longman Higher Education.

Clausewitz, K. von (1984) *On war*, Princeton University Press.

Clutterbuck, D. and Dearlove, D. (1996) *The charity as business*, Directory of Social Change.

Coghlan, D. (1987) 'Corporate strategy in Catholic religious orders', *Long Range Planning* 20(1): 44–51.

Cole, G. D. H. (1945) 'A retrospect of the history of voluntary social service', in A. F. C. Bourdillon (ed.) *Voluntary social services: Their place in the modern state*, Methuen.

Collins, J. C. and Porras, J. I. (1994) *Built to last: Successful habits of visionary companies*, Random House.

Connoly, T., Conlon, E. and Deutsch, S. (1980) 'Organisational effectiveness: A multiple constituency approach', *Academy of Management Review* 5: 211–17.

Cooke, R. A. and Rousseau, D. M. (1988) 'Behavioural norms and expectations: A quantitative approach to the assessment of organisational culture', *Group and Organisation Studies* 13: 245–73.

Coopey, J. (1995) 'The learning organisation, power, politics and ideology', *Management Learning* 26(2).

Cornforth, C. and Edwards, C. (1998) *Good governance: Developing effective board–management relations in public and voluntary organisations*, CIMA.

Courtney, R. B. (1992) *Making a difference: The story of the Simon Community in Northern Ireland*, Simon Community Northern Ireland.

Courtney, R. B. (1995) *Planning a fundraising strategy*, 2nd edn, NICVA.

Courtney, R. B. (1996) *Managing voluntary organisations: New approaches*, ICSA.

Craig, J. C. and Grant, R. M. (1993) *Strategic management*, Kogan Page.

Crittenden, J. C. (2000) 'Spinning straw into gold: The tenuous strategy, funding and financial performance linkage', *Nonprofit and Voluntary Sector Quarterly* 29(1) Supplement.

Crittenden, W. F., Crittenden, V. L. and Hunt, T. G. (1988) 'Planning and stakeholder satisfaction in religious organisations', *Journal of Voluntary Action Research* 17: 60–73.

Cummings, S. (1993) 'The first strategists', in B. de Wit and R. Meyer (eds) *Strategy process, concepts, context, cases*, Prentice-Hall.

Cutt, J. (1998) 'Performance measurement in non-profit organisations: A note on integration and focus within comprehensiveness', in G. Dinsdale, J. Cutt and V. Murray (eds) *Performance and accountability in non-profit organisations*, University of Victoria School of Public Administration Papers in Public Policy No. 4.

Cyert, R. M. (1975) *The management of nonprofit organisations*, D. C. Heath.

Cyert, R. M. and March, J. G. (1963) *A behavioural theory of the firm*, Prentice-Hall.

D'Aunno, T. (1992) 'The effectiveness of human service organisations: A comparison of models', in Y. Hasenfield (ed.) *Human services as complex organisations*, Sage.

D'Aunno, T. A., Sutton, R. I. and Price, R. H. (1991) 'Isomorphism and external support in conflicting institutional environments: The case of drug abuse treatment units', *Academy of Management Journal* 34(3): 636–78.

Davis, R. C. (1928) *The principles of factory organisation and management*, Harper & Row.

Davis, R. C. (1951) *The fundamentals of top management*, Harper & Row.

Davis Smith, J. (1992) 'An uneasy alliance', in R. Hedley and J. Davis Smith (eds) *Volunteering and society: Principles and practice*, Bedford Square Press.

Davis Smith, J. (1995) 'The voluntary tradition: Philanthropy and self-help in Britain 1500–1945', in J. Davis Smith, C. Rochester and R. Hedley (eds) *An introduction to the voluntary sector*, Routledge.

Davis Smith, J., Rochester, C. and Hedley, R. (eds) (1995) *An introduction to the voluntary sector*, Routledge.

Deakin, N. (1995) 'The perils of partnership: The voluntary sector and the state 1945–1992', in J. Davis Smith, C. Rochester and R. Hedley (eds) *An introduction to the voluntary sector*, Routledge.

Deakin, N. (1996) *Meeting the challenge of the future: The report of the commission on the future of the voluntary sector*, NCVO.

De Geus, A. (1988) 'Planning as learning', *Harvard Business Review* March/April: 70–4.

De Vagal, S. H. (1995) *Ethics in O. D.*, Peiffer.

Dierickx, I. and Cool, K. (1989) 'Asset stock accumulation and the sustainability of competitive advantage', *Management Science* 34(12).

Dierkes, M. and Bauer, R. A. (eds) (1973) *Corporate social accounting*, Praeger.

Doane, D. (2001) *Corporate spin: The troubled teenager years of social reporting*, Central Books.

Donnelly-Cox, G. and O'Regan, A. (1999) *Resourcing organisational growth and development: A typology of third sector service delivery organisations*, paper presented to IRSPSM Aston.

Drucker, P. F. (1954) *The practice of management*, Harper & Row.

Drucker, P. F. (1964) *Management by results*, Harper & Row.

Drucker, P. F. (1980) *Managing in turbulent times*, Pan.

Drucker, P. F. (1990) *Managing the nonprofit organisation – Principles and practices*, HarperBusiness.

Dunnette, M. D., Campbell, J. P. and Hakel, M. D. (1967) 'Factors contributing to job satisfaction and dissatisfaction and in six occupational groups', *Organisational Behaviour and Human Performance* 2: 143–74.

Eccles, R. and Nohria, N. (1992) *Beyond the hype: Rediscovering the essence of management*, Harvard Business School Press.

Eccles, R. and Nohria, N. (1997) 'Strategy as a language game', in S. Segal-Horn (ed.) *The strategy reader*, Blackwell.

Edwards, R. L. and Eadie, M. S. (1994) 'Meeting the change challenge: Managing growth in the nonprofit and public human services sectors', *Administration in Social Work* 18(2): 107–23.

Edwards, R. L., Yankey, J. A. and Altpeter, M. A. (eds) (1998) *Skills for effective management of nonprofit organisations*, NASW Press.

Egan, G. (1985) *Change agent skills*, Brooks/Cole.

Elliot, J. (1992) *Action research: A framework for self evaluation in schools*, Schools Council.

Elmore, R. F. (1978) 'Organisational models of social program implementation', *Public Policy* 26: 185–228.

Emery, M. and Purser, R. E. (1996) *The search conference: Theory and practice*, Jossey-Bass.

Erez, M. and Arad, R. (1986) 'Participative goal-setting: Social, motivational and cognitive factors', *Journal of Applied Psychology* 71: 591–7.

Erez, M. and Zidon, I. (1984) 'Effect of goal acceptance on the relationship of goal difficulty to performance', *Journal of Applied Psychology* 69: 69–78.

Etzioni, A. (1964) *Modern organisations*, Prentice-Hall.

Evered, R. (1985) *So what is strategy?*, Naval Post-Grad School.

Falk, N. and Lee, J. (1978) *Planning the social services*, Saxon House.

Fayol, H. (1916) *General and industrial management*, English trans. by Constance Storrs (1949), Pitman.

Firstenberg, P. B. (1979) 'Profitminded management in the nonprofit world', *Management Review* 68: 8–13.

Flynn, N. and Talbot, C. (1996) 'Strategy and strategists in UK local government', *Journal of Management Development* 15: 24–37.

Follett, M. P. (1941) *Dynamic administration* (E. Fox and L. Lyndall, eds), Harper & Row.

Forbes, D. P. (1998) 'Measuring the unmeasurable: Empirical studies of non-profit organisation effectiveness', *Nonprofit and Voluntary Sector Quarterly* 27(2): 159–82.

Ford, J. D. and Ford, L. W. (1990) *Designing organisations for growth*, unpublished working paper, Ohio State University.

Fredrickson, J. W. (1984) 'The comprehensiveness of strategic decision processes: Extension, observations and future directions', *Academy of Management Journal* 27: 445–66.

Fredrickson, J. W. and Iacquinto, A. L. (1989) 'Intention and creeping rationality in strategic decision processes', *Academy of Management Journal* 32: 516–42.

Fredrickson, J. W. and Mitchell, T. (1984) 'Strategic decision processes: Comprehensiveness and performance in an industry with an unstable environment', *Academy of Management Journal* 27: 399–423.

Freeman, R. E. (1984) *Strategic management: A stakeholder approach*, Pitman.

Frumkin, P. and Andre-Clark, A. (2000) 'When missions, markets and politics collide: Values and strategy in the nonprofit human services', *Nonprofit and Voluntary Sector Quarterly* 29(1) Supplement: 141–63.

Fulton, Lord (1968) *The Report of the Committee on the Civil Service*, HMSO.

Gable, M. and Topol, M. T. (1987) 'Planning practices of small-scale retailers', *American Journal of Small Business* 12: 19–32.

Galbraith, J. R. (1977) *Organisation design*, Addison-Wesley.

Gann, N. (1996) *Managing change in voluntary organisations: A guide to practice*, Open University Press.

Garrick, J. and Rhodes, C. (1998) 'Deconstructing organisational learning: The possibilities for a post-modern epistemology of practice', *Studies in the Education of Adults* 30(2).

Georgopoulos, B. S. and Tannenbaum, A. S. (1971) 'A study of organisational effectiveness', in J. Ghorpade (ed.) *Assessment of organisational effectiveness: Issues, analysis and readings*, Goodyear.

Gerard, D. (1983) *Charities in Britain: Conservatism or change?*, Bedford Square Press.

Gherardi, S. (1999) 'Learning in the face of mystery', *Organisation Studies* 20(1).

Ghobadian, A. and Woo, H. S. (1994) 'Characteristics, benefits and shortcomings of our major quality awards', *International Journal of Quality and Reliability Management* 1392: 10–44.

Gilbert, X. and Strebel, P. (1988) 'Developing competitive advantage', in J. B. Quinn, H. Monteberg abd R. James (eds) *The strategy process*, Prentice-Hall.

Glisson, C. and Martin, P. (1980) 'Productivity and efficiency in human service organisations as related to structure, size and age', *Academy of Management Journal* 23: 21–37.

Gluck, F. W., Kaufman, S. P. and Wolleck, A. S. (1980) 'Strategic management for competitive advantage', *Harvard Business Review* July/August: 154–61.

Gnaerig, B. and MacCormack, C. F. (1999) 'The challenges of globalization: Save the Children', *Nonprofit and Voluntary Sector Quarterly* 28(4) Supplement.

Goldsmith, W. and Clutterbuck, D. (1984) *The winning streak*, Weidenfeld & Nicolson.

Goldsmith, W. and Clutterbuck, D. (1997) *Winning streak – Mark II*, Orion Business Books.

Gonella, C., Pilling, A. and Zadek, S. (1998) *Making values count: Contemporary experience in social and ethical accounting, auditing and reporting*, ACCA.

Goold, M. (1997) 'Institutional advantage: A way into strategic management in not-for-profit organisations', *Long Range Planning* 30(2).

Gosden, P. (1973) *Voluntary associations in nineteenth century Britain*, Batsford.

Gouldner, A. W. (1971) 'Organisational analysis', in J. Ghorpade (ed.) *Assessment of organisational effectiveness: Issues, analysis and readings*, Goodyear.

Grant, R. (1997) 'The resource-based theory of competitive advantage: Implications for strategy formulation', in S. Segal-Horn (ed.) *The strategy reader*, Blackwell.

Green, J. and Griesinger, D. (1996) 'Board performance and organisational effectiveness in nonprofit social services organisations', *Nonprofit Management and Leadership* 6: 381–402.

Greenberg, E. (1982) 'Nonprofit agencies: Competing for scarce resources', *Journal of Business Strategy* 2(3).

Greenley, G. E. (1986) 'Does strategic planning improve performance?', *Long Range Planning* 19(2).

Grewe, T., Marshall, J. and O'Toole, D. (1989) 'Participative planning for a public service', *Long Range Planning* 22(1): 110–17.

Grossman, A. and Rangman, V. K. (2001) 'Managing multi-site nonprofits', *Nonprofit Management and Leadership* 11(3).

Gruber, R. E. and Mohr, M. (1982) 'Strategic management for multiprogramme nonprofit organisations', *California Management Review* 24(3): 15–22.

Gutch, R. (1992) *Contracting lessons from the US*, NCVO.

Gutch, R., Kunz, C. and Spencer, K. (1990) *Partners or agents*, NCVO.

Gyford, J. (1985) *The politics of local socialism*, Allen & Unwin.

Haberberg, A. (2000) 'Swotting SWOT', *Strategy* Sept.

Hackman, J. R. and Lawler, E. E. (1971) 'Employee reactions to job characteristics', *Journal of Applied Psychology* 55: 259–86.

Hackman, J. R. and Oldham, G. R. (1975) 'Development of the job diagnostic survey', *Journal of Applied Psychology* 60: 159–70.

Hackman, J. R. and Oldham, G. R. (1979) *Work redesign*, Addison-Wesley.

Hadley, R. and Hatch, S. (1981) *Social welfare and the failure of the state*, Allen & Unwin.

Hailey, J. (1999) *Strategic indicators of NGO values*, Paper presented to the European conference on the challenges of managing the Third Sector, University of Edinburgh, June.

Hailey, J. (2001) 'Indicators of identity: NGOs and the strategic imperative of assessing core values', in D. Eade and E. Ligteringen (eds) *Debating development*, Oxfam Publications.

Hain, P. (1975) *Radical regeneration: Protest. direct action and community politics*, Quartet.

Hall, P. D. (1994) 'Historical perspectives on nonprofit organisations', in R. D. Herman and Associates (eds) *The Jossey-Bass handbook of nonprofit leadership and Management*, Jossey-Bass.

Hall, S. (1989) *The voluntary sector under attack...?*, Islington Voluntary Action Council.

Hamel, G. (2000) *Leading the revolution*, Harvard Business School Press.

Hamel, G. and Prahalad, C. K. (1994) *Competing for the future*, Wiley.

Hamel, G. and Prahalad, C. K. (1997) 'Strategy as stretch and leverage', in S. Segal-Horn (ed.) *The strategy reader*, Blackwell.

Hammer, M. and Champy, J. (1993) *Re-engineering the corporation*, Nicholas Brealey.

Hammer, W. C. (1974) *Reinforcement theory and contingency management in organisational settings*, St Clair Press.

Handy, C. (1981) *Improving the effectiveness of the voluntary sector*, NCVO.

Handy, C. (1988) *Understanding voluntary organisations*, Penguin.

Hannan, M. T. and Freeman, J. (1977) 'Obstacles to comparative studies', in P. S. Goodman and J. M. Pennings (eds) *New perspectives on organisational effectiveness*, Jossey-Bass.

Harlow, J. (1998) *The nature and scope of changes effected by the utilization of strategic management in volunteer-managed nonprofit organisations*, Dissertation Abstracts International 59/05A 1775.

Harris, M. (1993) *The power and authority of governing bodies: Three models of practice in service providing agencies*, working paper, Centre for Voluntary Organisations, LSE.

Harris, M. (1997) *Voluntary associations: Five organisational challenges*, LSE.

Harris, M. and Billis, D. (1986) *Organising voluntary agencies*, NCVO.

Harvey-Jones, J. (1987) 'Introduction', in I. Ansoff, *Corporate strategy*, Penguin.

Hasenfield, Y. and Gidron, B. (1993) 'Self-help groups and human service organisations: An interorganisational perspective', *Social Services Review* June: 217–36.

Hatch, S. (1980) *Outside the state*, Croom Helm.

Hatten, M. L. (1982) 'Strategic management in not-for-profit organisations', *Strategic Management Journal* 3: 89–104.

Hayward, S. (1996) *Applying psychology to organisations*, Hodder & Stoughton.

Heffron, F. (1989) *Organisation theory and public organisations: The political connection*, Prentice-Hall.

Heijden, K. van der (1996) *Scenarios: The art of strategic conversation*, Wiley.

Heimovitics, R. D., Herman, R. D. and Jurkiewicz, C. L. (1993) 'Executive leadership and resource dependence in nonprofit organisations: A frame analysis', *Public Administration Review* 53(5): 419–27.

Heimovitics, R. D., Herman, R. D. and Jurkiewicz, C. L. (1995) 'The political dimension of effective nonprofit leadership', *Nonprofit Management and Leadership* 5(3): 233–48.

Heller, R. (1997) *In search of European excellence*, HarperCollins.

Henderson, B. (1970) *The product portfolio*, Boston Consulting Group.

Henderson, B. (1979) *Henderson on corporate strategy*, Abt Books.

Henderson, B. (1984) *The logic of business strategy*, Ballinger.

Henry, K. M. (1999) 'CARE International: Evolving to meet the challenges of the 21st century', *Nonprofit and Voluntary Sector Quarterly* 28(4) Supplement.

Herman, R. D. (1994) 'Conclusion: Preparing for the future of nonprofit management', in R. D. Herman and Associates (eds) *The Jossey-Bass handbook of nonprofit leadership and management*, Jossey-Bass.

Herman, R. D. and Heimovitics, R. D. (1994) 'A cross-national study of a method for researching non-profit organisational effectiveness', *Voluntas* 5(1): 86–100.

Herman, R. and Renz, D. (1996) 'Thesis on nonprofit organisational effectiveness', *Nonprofit and Voluntary Sector Quarterly* 28(2).

Herman, R. and Renz, D. (1998) 'Nonprofit organisational effectiveness: Contrasts between especially effective and less effective organisations', *Nonprofit Management and Leadership* 9: 23–38.

Herman, R. and Renz, D. (1999) 'Multiple constituencies and the social construction of nonprofit organisational effectiveness', *Nonprofit and Voluntary Sector Quarterly* 19: 293–306.

Herman, R. and Tulipana, F. (1985) 'Board–staff relations and perceived effectiveness in nonprofit organisations', *Journal of Voluntary Action Research* 14: 48–59.

Herold, D. M. (1972) 'Long range planning and organisational performance', *Academy of Management Journal*, March: 91–102.

Hertzberg, F. (1968) 'One more time: How do you motivate employees?', *Harvard Business Review* 52–62.

Hill, C. P. (1970) *British economic and social history 1700–1964*, 3rd edn, Edward Arnold.

Hind, A. (1995) *The governance and management of charities*, Voluntary Sector Press.

Hofer, C. W. (1976) 'Research on strategic planning: A survey of past studies and suggestions for future efforts', *Journal of Economic Business* 28(3).

Home Office (1990) *Efficiency scrutiny of government funding of the voluntary sector*, HMSO.

Howard, R. J. (1982) *Three faces of hermeneutics*, University of California Press.

Hudson, M. (1995) *Managing without profit*, Penguin.

Imai, M. (1986) *Kaizen: The key to Japan's competitive success*, McGraw-Hill.

Jain, S. C. and Surendra, S. S. (1977) 'Environmental forecasting and nonprofit professional organisations', *Long Range Planning* 10 (June).

James, B. G. (1985) 'Reality and the fight for market position', *Journal of General Management* Spring: 45–57.

Janis, I. L. (1972) *Victims of Groupthink*, Houghton Mifflin.

Janis, I. L. (1982) *Groupthink: Psychological studies of policy decisions and fiascos*, Houghton Mifflin.

Jansson, B. S. and Taylor, S. H. (1978) 'The planning contradiction in social agencies: Great expectations versus satisfaction with limited performance', *Administration in Social Work* 2(2).

Jay, A. (1987) *Management and Machiavelli*, Business Books.

Jeavons, T. H. (1992) 'When the management is the message: Relating values to management practice in nonprofit organisations', *Nonprofit Management and Leadership* 2(4): 403–17.

Jenkins, J. C. (1977) 'Radical transformation of organisational goals', *Administrative Science Quarterly* 22(4): 568–86.

Jenster, P. V. and Overstreet, G. A. (1990) 'Planning for a non-profit service', *Long Range Planning* 23(2): 103–11.

Jobson, J. and Schneck, R. (1982) 'Constituent views or organisational effectiveness: Evidence from police organisations', *Academy of Management Review* 25: 25–46.

Johnson, G. and Scholes, K. (1993) *Explaining corporate strategy*, Prentice-Hall.

Johnson, N. (1981) *Voluntary social services*, Martin Robertson.

Jones, I. W. and Pollitt, M. G. (1998) *The role of business ethics in economic performance*, Macmillan.

Jordan, W. K. (1959) *Philanthropy in England: 1480–1660*, George Allen & Unwin.

Joyce, P. (1999) *Strategic management for the public services*, Open University Press.

Joyce, P. and Woods, A. (1996) *Essential strategic management*, Butterworth–Heinemann.

Kanter, R. M. (1989) *When giants learn to dance: Mastering the challenges of strategy, management and careers in the 1990s*, Simon & Schuster.

Kanter, R. M. and Brinkerhoff, D. (1981) 'Organisational performance: Recent developments in measurement', in R. H. Turner and J. F. Short, Jr (eds) *Annual Review of Sociology*: 321–49.

Kanter, R. M. and Summers, D. V. (1987) 'On doing well while doing good: Dilemmas of performance measurement in nonprofit organizations and the need for a multi-constituency approach', in W. W. Powell (ed.) *The nonprofit sector: A research handbook*, Yale University Press.

Kaplan, R. S. (2001) 'Strategic performance measurement and management in nonprofit organisations', *Nonprofit Management and Leadership* 11(3): Spring.

Kaplan, R. S. and Norton, D. P. (1992) *The balanced scorecard: Measures that drive performance*, Harvard Business Review.

Kaplan, R. S. and Norton, D. P. (1996) *The balanced scorecard*, Harvard Business School Press.

Kare-Silver, M. de (1997) *Strategy in crisis*, Macmillan.

Karger, D. W. and Malik, Z. A. (1975) 'Long range planning and organisational performance', *Long Range Planning* Nov/Dec (6): 60–4.

Katsioloudes, M. L. and Butler, L. M. (1996) 'The importance of strategic planning activities in nonprofit organizations', unpublished paper presented to the 1986 ARNOVA annual conference, New York.

Katz, D. and Kahn, R. L. (1966) *The social psychology of organisations*, Wiley.

Katz, R. (1978) 'Job longevity as a situational factor in job satisfaction', *Administration Science Quarterly* 23: 204–23.

Katzell, R. A. and Yankelovich, D. (1975) *Work, productivity and job satisfaction*, Psychological Corporation.

Kaufman, R. (1991) *Strategic planning plus*, Scott Foresman.

Kay, J. (1994) *Foundations of corporate success*, Oxford University Press.

Kearns, K. P. (2000) *Private sector strategies for social sector success*, Jossey-Bass.

Kearns, K. P. and Scapino, G. (1996) 'Strategy planning research', *Long Range Non-Profit Management and Leadership*.

Kearns, K. P. and Scapino, G. (1996) 'Strategic planning research: Knowledge and gaps', *Nonprofit Management and Leadership* 6(4).

Keating, B. P. (1979) 'Prescriptions for efficiency in nonprofit firms', *Applied Economics* 11: 321–32.

Kendall, J. and 6, P. (1994) 'Government and the voluntary sector', in S. Saxon-Harold and J. Kendall (eds) *Researching the voluntary sector*, vol. 2, CAF.

Kendall, J. and Knapp, M. (1995) 'A loose and baggy monster: Boundaries, definitions and typologies', in J. Davis Smith, C. Rochester and R. Hedley (eds) *An introduction to the voluntary sector*, Routledge.

Kendall, J. and Knapp, M. (1996) *The voluntary sector in the UK*, Johns Hopkins Nonprofit Sector Series, Manchester University Press.

Kendall, J. and Knapp, M. (1998) 'Evaluation and the voluntary nonprofit sector: Emerging issues', in D. Lewis (forthcoming).

Kendall, J. and Knapp, M. (1999) *Measuring the outcomes of voluntary activity*, VAU.

Kendall, J. and Knapp, M. (2000) 'Measuring the performance of voluntary organisations', *Public Management* 2(1).

King, W. R. (1979) 'Strategic planning in nonprofit organisations', in G. Zaltman (ed.) *Management principles for nonprofit agencies and organisations*, AMACOM.

Klausen, K. K. (1995) 'On the malfunction of the generic approach in small voluntary associations', *Nonprofit Leadership and Management* 5(3): 275–90.

Klien, H. A. (1981) 'The impact of planning on growth and profit', *Journal of Small Business* 12: 19–32.

Knapp, M. R. J. (1984) *The economics of social care*, Macmillan.

Knauft, B., Berger, R. A. and Gray, S. T. (1991) *Profiles of excellence: Achieving success in the profit sector*, Jossey-Bass.

Knight, B. (1993) *Voluntary action*, HMSO.

Kohjasten, M. (1993) 'Motivating private versus public sector managers', *Public Personnel Management* 22(3): 391–401.

Kohl, J. P. (1984) 'Strategies for growth: Intervention in a church', *Long Range Planning* 17(6): 76–81.

Koteen, J. (1989) *Strategic management in public and nonprofit organisations*, Praeger.

Kramer, R. M. (1981) *Voluntary agencies in the welfare state*, University of California Press.

Kramer, R. M. (1992) 'Voluntary organizations: Contracting and the welfare state', in Batsleer, J., Cornforth, C. and Paton, R. (eds) *Issues in voluntary and nonprofit management*, Addison-Wesley.

Kudla, R. J. and Cesta, J. R. (1982) 'Planning and financial performance: A discriminant analysis', *Akron Business and Economic Review* Spring: 30–6.

Kushner, R. and Poole, P. (1996) 'Exploring structure effectiveness relationships in nonprofit arts organisations', *Nonprofit Management and Leadership* 7: 119–36.

Lan, Z. and Rosenbloom, D. (1992) 'Editorial', *Public Administration Review* 52(6).

Landry, C., Morley, D., Southwood, R. and Wright, P. (1985) *What a way to run a railroad*, Comedia.

Lawler, E. E. III (1986) *High-involvement management*, Jossey-Bass.

Lawrie, A. (1994) *The complete guide to business and strategic planning for voluntary organisations*, Directory of Social Change.

Learned, E. P., Christensen, C. R., Andrews, K. R. and Guth, W. D. (1965) *Business policy: Text and cases*, Irwin.

Leat, D. (1993) *Managing across sectors: Similarities and differences between for-profit and nonprofit organisations*, VOLPROF, City University Business School.

Leat, D. (1995) *Challenging management*, VOLPROF, City University Business School.

Leavitt, H. J. (1963) *The social science of organisations*, Prentice-Hall.

Letts, C. W., Ryan, W. P. and Grossman, A. S. (1998) *High performance nonprofit organisations: Managing upstream for greater impact*, Wiley.

Lewin, K. (1946) 'Action research and minority problems', *Journal of Social Issues* 2(4): 34–46.

Lewin, K. (1957) *Field theory in social science*, Harper.

Lewin, K., Lippit, R. and White, R. (1939) 'Patterns of aggressive behaviour in experimentally created "social climates"', *Journal of Social Psychology* 10: 271–99.

Lewis, J. (1996) 'What does contracting do to voluntary agencies?', in D. Billis and M. Harris (eds) *Voluntary agencies: Challenges of organisation and management*, Macmillan.

Likert, R. (1967) *The human organisation*, McGraw-Hill.

Lillis, C. and Shaffer, P. (1977) 'Economic output as an organisational effectiveness measure for universities', *Academy of Management Journal* 20: 76–482.

Lindblom, C. E. (1959) 'The science of muddling through', *Public Administration Review* 19(2).

Lindenberg, M. (2001) 'Are we at the cutting edge or the blunt edge? Improving NGO organisational performance with private and public sector strategic management frameworks', *Nonprofit Management and Leadership* 11(3), Spring.

Lippitt, R., Watson, J. and Westlet, B. (1958) *Dynamics of planned change*, Jossey-Bass.

Locke, E. A. (1968) 'Towards a theory of task motivation and incentives', *Organisational Behaviour and Human Performance* 3: 157–89.

Locke, E. A., Shaw, K. N., Saari, L. M. and Latham, G. P. (1981) 'Goal setting and task performance: 1969–1980', *Psychological Bulletin* 90: 125–52.

Lowe, R. (1993) *The welfare state in Britain since 1945*, Macmillan.

Lubelska, A. (1996) *Strategic management challenges for the nonprofit sector*, Aston University.

Lyons, M. (1996) 'On a clear day...: Strategic management for VNPOs', in S. P. Osborne (ed.) *Managing in the voluntary sector – a handbook for managers in charitable and non-profit organisations*, International Thomson Business Press.

McClelland, D. C. (1961) *The achieving society*, Van Nostrand.

McConkey, D. D. (1975) *MBO for nonprofit organisations*, AMACOM.

McGahan, A. and Porter, M. E. (1997) 'How much does industry matter, really?', *Strategic Management Journal* 18, Summer Special Issue: 15–30.

McGrath, J. E. (1984) *Groups' interaction and performance*, Prentice-Hall.

McGregor, D. M. (1960) *The human side of enterprise*, McGraw-Hill.

Machiavelli, N. (1950) *The prince and discourses*, Modern Library.

McLaughlin, C. (1986) *The management of non-profit organisations*, John Wiley.

MacMillan, I. C. (1983) *Competitive strategies for not-for-profit organisations: Advances in strategic management*, vol. 1, JAI Press.

Maier, N. R. F. (1967) *Psychology in industrial organisations*, Houghton Mifflin.

March, J. G. and Simon, H. A. (1959) *Organisations*, Wiley.

Marshall, T. F. (1996) 'Can we define the voluntary sector?', in D. Billis and M. Harris (eds) *Voluntary agencies: Challenges of organisation and management*, Macmillan.

Martin, A. O. and Peterson, M. (1987) 'Two-tier wage structures: Implications for equity theory', *Academy of Management Journal* 30(2).

Maslow, A. (1970) *Motivation and personality*, 2nd edn, Harper.

Mason, D. (1984) *Nonprofits well-managed*, Supportive Services Inc.

Mastrofski, S., Ritti, R. and Snipes, J. (1994) 'Expectancy theory and police productivity', *Law Society Review* 28(1): 113–48.

Matthews, D. (1996) *Can public life be regenerated?*, paper to Independent Sector conference on 'Measuring the impact of the not-for-profit sector on society', Independent Sector Conference, Washington DC.

Mayo, E. (1945) *The social problems of an industrial civilisation*, Harvard University Press.

Medley, G. J. (1986) 'Strategic planning for the World Wildlife Fund', *Long Range Planning* 21(1).

Medley, G. J. (1988) 'WWF creates a new mission', *Long Range Planning* 25(2).

Meyer, J. and Rowan, B. (1991) 'Institutionalised organisations: Formal structure as myth and ceremony', in W. Powell and P. diMaggio (eds) *The new institutionalism in organisational analysis*, University of Chicago Press.

Meyer, M. and Zucker, L. (1989) *Permanently failing organisations*, Sage.

Meyer, M. W. and Gupta, V. (1994) 'The performance paradox', in B. W. Shaw and L. L. Cummings (eds) *Research in organisation behaviour* 16: 309–69, JAI Press.

Micklethwaite, J. and Wooldridge, A. (1996) *The witch doctors*, Heinemann.

Miles, R. E. and Snow, C. C. (1978) *Organisational strategy, structure and process*, McGraw-Hill.

Miller, C. C. and Cardinal, L. B. (1994) 'Strategic planning and firm performance: A synthesis of more than two decades of research', *Academy of Management Journal* 37: 1649–65.

Miller, D. (1976) *Strategy making in context: Ten empirical archetypes*, PhD thesis, McGill University, Montreal.

Miller, D. (1979) 'Strategy, structure and environment', *Journal of Management Studies* 16: 294–316.

Miller, D. (1986) 'Configurations of strategy and structure: Towards a synthesis', *Strategic Management Journal* 7: 233–49.

Miller, D. (1992) 'The generic strategy trap', *Journal of Business Strategy* 13(1).

Miller, D. (1997) 'Configurations of strategy and structure: Towards a synthesis', in S. Segal-Horn (ed.) *The strategy reader*, Blackwell.

Miner, J. B. (1984) 'The unpaved road over the mountain: From theory to applications', *The Industrial/Organisational Psychologist* 21: 9–20.

Mintzberg, H. (1979) *The structure of organisations: A synthesis of research*, Prentice-Hall.

Mintzberg, H. (1987) 'Crafting strategy', *Harvard Business Review* 66–75.

Mintzberg, H. (1994) *The rise and fall of strategic planning*, Prentice-Hall.

Mintzberg, H. and Waters, J. (1997) 'Of strategies, deliberate and emergent', in S. Segal-Horn (ed.) *The strategy reader*, Blackwell.

Mintzberg. H. and Westley, F. (1992) 'Cycles of organisational change', *Strategic Management Journal* 13: 39–59.

Mintzberg, H., Ahlstrand, B. and Lampel, J. (1998) *Strategy safari: A guided tour through the wilds of strategic management*, Prentice-Hall.

Mitchell, J. C. (1983) 'Case and situational analysis', *Sociological Review* 31: 187–211.

Moore, J. I. (1992) *Writers on strategy and strategic management*, Penguin.

Moore, M. H. (2000) 'Managing for value: Organisational strategy in for-profit, nonprofit and governmental organisations', *Nonprofit and Voluntary Sector Quarterly* 29(1) Supplement: 183–204.

Morales, H. R. Jr (1997) 'Earning income through trade and exchange', in L. M. Fox and S. B. Schearer (eds) *Sustaining civil society: Strategies for resource mobilisation*, Civicus.

Morgan, G. (1983) *Beyond method*, Sage.

Morgan, G. (1986) *Images of organisations*, Sage.

Mulhare, E. M. (1999) 'Mindful of the future: Strategic planning ideology and the culture of nonprofit management', *Human Organisation* 58(3): 323–30.

Murray, V. and Balfour, K. (1999) *Evaluating performance improvement in the non-profit sector: Challenges and opportunities*, Altruvest.

Murray, V., Bradshaw, P. and Wolpin, J. (1992) 'Power in and around nonprofit boards: A neglected dimension of governance', *Nonprofit Management and Leadership* 3(2).

Murray, V. and Tassie, B. (1994) 'Evaluating the effectiveness of nonprofit organisations', in R. D. Herman and Associates (eds) *The Jossey-Bass handbook of nonprofit leadership and management*, Jossey-Bass.

Lord Nathan (1990) *Effectiveness and the voluntary sector*, NCVO.

Nelson, R. and Winter, S. (1982) *An evaluation theory of economic change*, Harvard University Press.

Newman, W. H. and Wallender, H. N. III (1978) 'Managing nonprofit enterprises', *Academy of Management Review* 3: 24–31.

Nonaka, I. (1991) 'Toward middle-up-down management', *Sloan Management Review* 29(3).

Nutt, P. C. and Backoff, R. W. (1992) *Strategic management of public and third-sector organizations*, Jossey-Bass.

Odiorne, G. S. (1987) *The human side of management*, Lexington Books.

Odom, R. Y. and Boxx, W. R. (1988) 'Environmental, planning processes and organisational performance of churches', *Strategic Management Journal* 9: 197–205.

Ohmae, K. (1982) *The mind of the strategist*, McGraw-Hill.

O'Neill, M. and Young, D. R. (1988) *Educating managers of nonprofit organisations*, Praeger.

Osborne, D. and Graebler, T. (1992) *Reinventing government: How the entrepreneurial spirit is transforming the public sector*, Addison-Wesley.

Osborne, S. P. (ed.) (1996) *Managing in the voluntary sector – a handbook for managers in charitable and non-profit organisations*, International Thomson Business Press.

Osborne, S. P. (1998) *Voluntary organisations and innovation in public services*, Routledge.

Osborne, S. P. and Tricker, M. (1995) 'Researching non-profit effectiveness', *Voluntas* 6(1): 93–100.

Oster, S. (1992) 'Nonprofits as franchising operations in nonprofit management and leadership', *Spring* 2: 223–38.

Oster, S. M. (1995) *Strategic management for nonprofit organizations: Theory and cases*, Oxford University Press.

O'Toole, J. (1986) 'Why good companies get into trouble', *New Management* Summer: 60–4.

Ouchi, W. G. (1981) *Theory Z: How American business can meet the Japanese challenge*, Addison-Wesley.

Owen, D. (1964) *English philanthropy: 1660–1960*, Harvard University Press.

Palmer, R. E. (1969) *Hermeneutics*, Evanston.

Pascale, R. T. (1990) *Managing on the edge*, Viking Penguin.

Pascale, R. and Athos, A. (1981) *The art of Japanese management*, Penguin.

Paton, R. (1992) 'The social economy: Value-based organisations in the wider society', in J. Batsleer, C. Cornforth and R. Paton (eds) *Issues in voluntary and nonprofit management*, Addison-Wesley.

Paton, R. and Cornforth, C. (1992) 'What's different about managing in voluntary and non-profit organisations?', in J. Batsleer, C. Cornforth and R. Paton (eds) *Issues in voluntary and nonprofit management*, Addison-Wesley in association with the Open University Press.

Patton, M. (1996) *Utilization-focused evaluation: The new century text*, 3rd edn, Sage.

Pearce, J. A. and David, F. (1987) 'Corporate mission statements: The bottom line', *Academy of Management Executive* 1(2): 109–16.

Pearce, J. A., Robbins, K. and Robinson, R. B. (1987) 'The impact of grand strategy and planning formability on financial performance', *Strategy Management Journal* 8(2).

Pekar, P. Jr and Abraham, S. (1995) 'Is strategic management living up to its promise?', *Long Range Planning* 28(5): 32–44.

Perlmutter, F. D. and Gummer, B. (1994) 'Managing organisational transforma-tions', in R. D. Herman and Associates (eds) *The Jossey-Bass handbook of nonprofit leadership and management*, Jossey-Bass.

Perry, L. (1993) 'Effects of inequity on job satisfaction and self-evaluation in a national sample of African-American workers', *Journal of Social Psychology* 133(4).

Perry, L. T., Stott, R. G. and Smallwood, W. N. (1993) *Real-time strategy*, John Wiley.

Peteraf, M. (1993) 'The cornerstones of competitive advantage: A resource-based view', *Strategic Management Journal* 14: 179–91.

Peters, T. and Austin, N. (1985) *A passion for excellence*, Collins.

Peters, T. and Waterman, R. H. Jr (1982) *In search of excellence: Lessons from America's best run companies*, Harper & Row.

Peters, T. J. (1987) *Thriving on chaos*, Alfred A. Knopf.

Pettigrew, A. and Whipp, R. (1993) 'Managing the twin processes of competition and change: The role of intangible assets', in P. Lorange *et al.* (eds) *Implementing strategic processes: Change learning and co-operation*, Blackwell.

Pfeffer, J. (1981) *Power in organisations*, Pitman.

Pfeffer, J. (1982) *Organisations and organisation theory*, Pitman.

Pfeffer, J. and Salancik, G. R. (1978) *The external control of organisations: A resource dependence perspective*, Harper & Row.

Philips, T. R. (1940)/(1989) *Roots of strategy*, 1st edn/2nd edn, Military Service Publishing.

Pinchot, G. III (1985) *Intrapreneuring*, Harper & Row.

Pollitt, C. (1990) *Managerialism and the public services: The Anglo-American experience*, Blackwell.

Porter, M. E. (1980) *Competitive strategy*, The Free Press.

Porter, M. E. (1985) *Competitive advantage: Creating and sustaining superior performance*, The Free Press.

Porter, M. E. (1997) 'What is strategy?', in S. Segal-Horn (ed.) *The strategy reader*, Blackwell.

Powell, C. T. (1992) 'Strategic planning as competitive advantage', *Strategic Management Journal* 13: 551–8.

Prashar, U. (1991) 'Introduction' to *The voluntary agencies directory*, Bedford Square Press.

Prochaska, F. (1988) *The voluntary impulse*, Faber & Faber.

Prochaska, F. (1990) 'Philanthropy', in F. M. L. Thompson (ed.) *The Cambridge social history of England 1750–1950*, vol. 3, Cambridge University Press.

Pruzen, P. and Thyssen, O. (1990) 'Conflict and consensus: Ethics as a shared value horizon for strategic planning', *Human Systems Development* 9: 134–52.

Public Services Management (1991) *Managing public services*, Open University.

Quality Standards Task Group (QSTG) (2000a) *Excellence in view*, NCVO.

Quality Standards Task Group (QSTG) (2000b) *Self-assessment workbook: Measuring success*, NCVO.

Quinn, J. B. (1980) *Strategic change: Logical incrementalism*, Richard D. Irwin.

Quinn, R. and Rohrbaugh, J. (1983) 'A spatial model of effectiveness criteria: Towards a competing values approach to organisational analysis', *Management Science* 29: 363–77.

Ramanathan, K. V. (1982) *Management control in nonprofit organisations*, Wiley.

Rapaport, R. N. (1970) 'Three dilemmas in action research', *Human Relations* 23.

Rapp, C. and Poertner, J. (1992) *Social administration: A client centred approach*, Longman.

Rauschenberger, J., Schmitt, J. and Hunter, J. E. (1980) 'A test of the need hierarchy concept by a Markov model of change in need strength', *Administrative Science Quarterly* 25: 654–70.

Raynard, P. and Murphy, S. (2000) *Charitable trust? Social auditing with voluntary organisations*, NEF/ACEVO.

Reimann, B. C. (1975) 'Organisational effectiveness and management's public values: A canonical analysis', *Academy of Management Journal* 18(2): 224–41.

Rhyne, L. C. (1986) 'The relationship of strategic planning to financial performance,' *Strategic Management Journal* 7: 423–36.

Rhyne, L. C. (1987) 'Contrasting planning systems in high, medium and low performing companies', *Journal of Management Studies* 24: 363–85.

Rice, J. J. (1997) 'Strategic vision in non-profit organisations: Providing a clear direction for the future', *The Journal of Volunteer Administration* 15(4): 30–9.

Richardson, A. and Goodman, M. (1983) *Self-help and social care: Mutual aid organisations in practice*, Policies Studies Institute.

Ring, P. S. and Perry, J. L. (1985) 'Strategic management in public and private organisations: Implications of distinctive contexts and constraints', *Academy of Management Review* 10: 276–86.

Robbins, S. P. (1990) *Organisation theory: Structure, design and applications*, 3rd edn, Prentice-Hall.

Robinson, R. B. (1982) 'The importance of outsiders in small firm strategic planning', *Academy of Management Journal* March: 80–93.

Robinson, R. B. and Pearce, J. A. II (1983) 'The impact of formalized strategic planning on financial performance in small organizations', *Strategic Management Journal* 4(3).

Robinson, R. B. and Pearce, J. A. II (1988) 'Planned patterns of strategic behaviour and their relationship to business-unit performance', *Strategic Management Journal* 9: 43–60.

Rochester, C. (1995) 'Voluntary agencies and accountability', in J. Davis Smith, C. Rochester and R. Hedley (eds) *An introduction to the voluntary sector*, Routledge.

Rodgers, B. (1949) *Cloak of charity: Studies in eighteenth century philanthropy*, Methuen.

Roller, R. H. (1996) 'Strategy formulation in nonprofit social services organisations: A proposed framework', *Nonprofit Management and Leadership* 7(2): 137–53.

Rubin, M. (1988) *Charity and community in mediaeval Cambridge*, Cambridge University Press.

Rule, E. G. (1984) 'What's happening to strategic planning in Canadian business?', *Business Quarterly* 51(4).

Rumelt, R. P. (1991) 'How much does industry matter?', *Strategic Management Journal* 12(3).

Salamon, L. M. and Anheier, H. K. (1993) 'A comparative study of the non-profit sector: Purposes, methodology, definition and classification', in S. Saxon-Harold and J. Kendall (eds) *Researching the voluntary sector*, vol. 1, CAF.

Salamon, L. M. and Anheier, H. K. (1994) *The emerging sector – an overview*, Johns Hopkins University Press.

Salamon, L. S. (1987) 'Partners in public service: The scope and theory of government–nonprofit relations', in W. W. Powell (ed.) *The nonprofit sector: A research handbook*, Yale University Press.

Salancik, G. R. and Pfeffer, P. (1978) 'A social information processing approach to job attitudes and task design', *Administrative Science Quarterly* 23: 224–53.

Salipante, P. F. and Golden-Biddle, K. (1995) 'Managing traditionality and strategic change in nonprofit organisations', *Nonprofit Management and Leadership* 6(1): 3–20.

Savas, E. S. (1977) 'Organisational strategy, performance and management technology', *Administration in Social Work* 1(2): 149–60.

Schein, E. H. (1988) *Organisational psychology*, Prentice-Hall.

Schein, E. H. (1988) *Process consultation*, Addison-Wesley.

Schein, E. H. (1992) *Organisational culture and leadership*, Jossey-Bass.

Schneider, J. and Locke, E. A. (1971) 'A critique of Hertzberg's incident classification system and a suggested revision', *Organisation Behaviour and Human Performance* 6: 441–57.

Schumaker, P. (1980) 'The effectiveness of militant tactics in contemporary urban protest', *Nonprofit and Voluntary Sector Quarterly* 9: 131–48.

Schwartz, P. (1992) *The art of the long view: scenario planning: Protecting your company against an uncertain future*, Century Business.

Scott, W. R. (1977) 'Effectiveness of organisational effectiveness studies', in P. S. Goodman and J. M. Pennings (eds) *New perspectives on organisational effectiveness*, Jossey-Bass.

Scott, W. R. (1992) *Organisations' rational, natural and open systems*, 3rd edn, Prentice-Hall.

Seashore, S. E. and Yuchtman, E. (1968) 'Factorial analysis of organisational performance', *Administrative Science Quarterly* 12: 377–95.

Seashore, W. R. (1983) 'A framework for an integrated model of organisational effectiveness', in K. S. Cameron and D. A. Whetten (eds) *Organisational effectiveness: A comparison of multiple models*, Academic Press.

Seebohm Report (1968) *Report of the committee on local authority and allied personal social services*, HMSO.

Seeger, J. A. (1991) 'Reversing the images of BCG's growth/share matrix', in H. Mintzberg and J. B. Quinn (eds) *The strategy process: Concepts, contexts and cases*, Prentice-Hall.

Selby, C. C. (1978) 'Better performance from nonprofits', *Harvard Business Review* Sept/Oct: 92–8.

Selznick, P. (1957) *Leadership in administration: A sociological interpretation*, Row, Peterson.

Senge, P. (1990) *The fifth discipline: The art and practice of the learning organisation*, Doubleday.

Setterberg, F. and Schulman, K. (1985) *Beyond profit*, Harper & Row.

Setterberg, F. and Schulman, K. (1991) *Beyond profit: The complete guide to managing the non-profit organisation*, Lutterworth Press.

Sheehan, R. M. Jr (1996) 'Mission accomplishment as philanthropic organisation effectiveness: Key findings from the Excellence in Philanthropy project', *Nonprofit and Voluntary Sector Quarterly* 25: 110–23.

Siciliano, J. I. (1997) 'The relationship between formal planning and performance in nonprofit organisations', *Nonprofit Management and Leadership* 7(4).

Siciliano, J. I. and Floyd, S. W. (1993) *Nonprofit boards, strategic management, and organisational performance: An empirical study of YMCA organisations*, PONPO working paper no 183, Yale University.

Simon, H. A. (1947) *Administrative behaviour: A study of decision-making processes in administrative organisations*, Macmillan.

Singh, K. K. (1996) *The impact of strategic planning process variation on mission performance in nonprofit mental health service organisations*, ARNOVA conference paper.

Sipel, G. A. (1984) 'Putting "In search of Excellence" to work in local government', *Public Management Magazine* 66(4).

Skinner, B. F. (1938) *Science and human behaviour*, Macmillan.

Slatter, S. (1980) 'Common pitfalls using the BCG Product Portfolio Matrix', *London Business School Journal* Winter.

Slatter, S. (1994) *Corporate recovery: Successful turnaround strategies and their implementation*, Harvard University Press.

Smircich, L. (1983) 'Concepts of culture and organisational analysis', *Administration Science Quarterly* 28: 339–58.

Smith, A. (1979) *An enquiry into the nature and causes of the wealth of nations*, R. H. Campbell and A. S. Skinner (eds), Oxford University Press.

Smith, Bucklin and Associates (1994) *The complete guide to nonprofit management*, Wiley.

Smith, D. and Shen, C. (1996) 'Factors characterising the most effective nonprofits managed by volunteers', *Nonprofit Management and Leadership* 6: 271–89.

Smith, D. H. (1991) 'Four sectors or five: Retaining the member-benefit sector', *Nonprofit and Voluntary Sector Quarterly* 20(2): 137–50.

Smith, R. J. (1994) *Strategic management and planning in the public sector*, Longman.

Smith, S. R. (1992) *Nonprofit organisations in the age of contracting*, working paper presented to NCVO conference.

Smith, S. R. and Lipsky, M. (1993) *Nonprofits for hire: The welfare state in the age of contracting*, Harvard University Press.

Smith, T. (1992) *Accounting for growth*, Century.

Spencer, L. J. (1989) *Winning through participation*, Kendall–Hunt.

Stacey, R. D. (1993) *Strategic Management and Organisational Dynamics*, Pitman.

Standley, A. P. (2001) 'Reinventing a large nonprofit: Lessons from four voluntary health associations', *Nonprofit Management and Leadership* 11(3) Spring.

Steers, R. M. and Porter, L. W. (1983) *Motivation and work behaviour*, McGraw-Hill.

Steiner, G. (1979) *Strategic planning: What every manager should know*, The Free Press.

Steiner, J. R., Gross, G. M., Ruffolo, M. C. and Murray, J. J. (1994) 'Strategic planning in non-profits: Profit from it', *Administration in Social Work* 18(2): 87–106.

Stone, M. M. (1989) 'Planning as strategy in nonprofit organisations: An exploratory study', *Nonprofit and Voluntary Sector Quarterly* 18(4).

Stone, M. and Crittenden, W. (1993) 'A guide to journal articles on strategic management in non-profit organisations, 1977 to 1992', *Nonprofit Management and Leadership* 4(2).

Stone, M. M., Bigelow, B. and Crittenden, W. (1999) 'Research on strategic management in nonprofit organisations: Synthesis, analysis, and future directions', *Administration and Society* 31(3).

Summers, H. G. Jr (1981) *On strategy: The Vietnam war in context*, GPO Strategic Studies Institute, US Army War College.

Szabat, K. and Simmons, K. (1996) *Nonprofit organisations and their strategic planning practices*, working paper presented to 1996 ARNOVA conference.

Szabat, K., Smither, J., Simmons, K. and Seltzer, J. (1996) *The relation between strategic planning practices and effectiveness in nonprofit organisations*, working paper presented to 1996 ARNOVA conference.

Taylor, F. W. (1911) *The principles of scientific management*, Harper & Row.

Taylor, M. (1992) 'The changing role of the non-profit sector in Britain: Moving towards the market', in B. Gidron, R. Kramer and L. Salamon (eds) *Government and the third sector: Emerging relationships in welfare states*, Jossey-Bass.

Taylor, S. J. and Bogdan, R. (1984) *Introduction to qualitative research methods*, John Wiley.

Thane, P. (1982) *The foundations of the welfare state*, Longman.

Thompson, A. A and Strickland, A. J. III (1990) *Strategic management: Concepts and cases*, Richard D. Irwin.

Thompson, J. L. (1997) *Strategic management: Awareness and change*, 3rd edn, Thomson Business Press.

Thune, S. S. and House, R. J. (1970) *Where long range planning pays off*, Business Hemsons.

Tober, J. (1991) *Strategic planning in organisations and environments*, PONPO working paper no. 165, Yale University.

Tsui, A. S. (1990) 'A multiple constituency model of effectiveness: An empirical examination at the human resource subunit level', *Administrative Science Quarterly* 35: 458–83.

Tzu, S. (1963) *The art of war*, Oxford University Press.

United Way of America (1996) *Measuring program outcomes: A practical approach*, available online at www.unitedway.org/outcomes/

Unterman, I. and Davies, R. H. (1982) 'The strategy gap is not for profits', *Harvard Business Review*.

Unterman, I. and Davies, R. H. (1984) *Strategic management for not-for-profit organisations: From survival to success*, Praeger.

Uphoff, N. (1995) 'Why NGOs are not a third sector: A sectoral analysis with some thoughts on accountability, sustainability and evaluation', in M. Edwards and D. Hulme (eds) *Non-governmental organisations – performance and accountability: Beyond the magic bullet*, Earthscan.

Urwick, L. (1943) *The elements of administration*, Pitman.

Urwick, L. (1956) *The golden book of management*, Newman Neame.

Vaill, P. B. (1990) *Management as a performance art*, Jossey-Bass.

Van de Ven, A. H. (1980) 'Problem solving, planning and innovation', *Human Relations* 33(10): 711–40.

Van Wijck, P. (1994) 'Evaluating income distributions', *Journal of Economic Psychology* 15(1).

Vroom, V. H. (1964) *Work and motivation*, Wiley.

Waalewijn, P. and Segaar, P. (1993) 'Strategic management: The key to profitability in small companies', *Long Range Planning* 26(2): 24–30.

Walker, J. M. (1983) 'Limits of strategic management in voluntary organisations', *Journal of Voluntary Action Research* 12(3).

Warr, P. (ed.) (1996) *Psychology at work*, Penguin.

Wasdell, D. (1980) 'Long range planning and the church', *Long Range Planning* 13.

Watson, T. Jr (1963) *A business and its beliefs*, McGraw-Hill.

Web, S. (1990) *Planning strategy for voluntary organisations*.

Webster, S. A. and Wylie, M. L. (1988) 'Strategic planning in competitive environments', *Administration in Social Work* 12(3): 25–43.

Weeden, C. (1998) *Corporate social investing: The breakthrough strategy for giving and getting corporate contributions*, Berret-Koehler.

Weisbrod, B. A. (1988) *The nonprofit economy*, Harvard University Press.

Weisbrod, M. R. and Janoff, S. (1995) *Future search*, Berret-Koehler.

Weiss, C. H. (1998) *Evaluation*, 2nd edn, Prentice-Hall.

Welch, J. B. (1984) 'Strategic planning could improve your share price', *Long Range Planning* April.

Wernerfelt, B. (1984) 'A resource-based view of the firm', *Strategic Management Journal* April–June: 171–80.

Whitehead, D. D. and Gup, B. E. (1985) 'Bank and thrift probability: does strategic planning really pay?', *Economic Review*, Reserve Bank of Atlanta.

Whittington, R. (1993) *What is strategy – and does it matter?*, Routledge.

Wiesendanger, B. (1994) 'Profitable pointers from non-profits', *Journal of Business Strategy* 15(4): 32–9.

Williams, I. (1989) *The alms trade*, Unwin Hyman.

Wolch, J. (1990) *The shadow state: Government and voluntary sector in transition*, The Foundation Centre.

Wolfenden, Lord (1978) *The future of voluntary organisations*, Croom Helm.

Wortman, M. (1981) 'A radical shift from bureaucracy to strategic management in voluntary organisations', *Journal of Voluntary Action Research* 10: 62–81.

Wortman, M. S. Jr (1979) *Strategic management in not-for-profit organisations*, Little, Brown.

Wortman, M. S. Jr (1979) *Current concepts and theories of strategic management in not-for-profit organisations in the 1980s*, paper given at the American Institute for Decision Sciences, November.

Wylie, M. Z. and D. (1974) 'Collated organisation', *Journal of Applied Behavioural Science* 12(3): 25–43.

Young, D. (1989) 'Beyond tax exemption: A focus on organisational performance versus legal status', in V. Hodgkinson, R. W. Lyman and Associates, *The future of the nonprofit sector*, Jossey-Bass.

Young, D. R. (1985) 'What business can learn from nonprofits', in *Models of health and human service in the nonprofit sector*, University Park Association of Voluntary Action Scholars.

Yuchtman, E. and Seashore, S. E. (1967) 'A system resource approach to organisational effectiveness', *American Sociological Review* 32: 891–903.

Yunus, M. (1999) *Banker to the poor: Micro-lending and the battle against world poverty*, BBS Public Affairs.

Zammuto, R. F. (1984) 'A comparison of multiple constituency models of organisational effectiveness', *Academy of Management Review* 9: 606–16.

Zerubavel, E. (1991) *The fine line*, University of Chicago Press.

Zimbardo, P. G. and Leippe, M. R. (1991) *The psychology of attitude change and social influence*, McGraw-Hill.

Index

Abraham, S. 141
Abyssinia 224; *see also* Ethiopia
'accommodation' strategy 201
accountability 28, 121–2
Accountability 1000 standard 161
action planning 213
active citizenship 30
Adams, J. S. 85–6
Agnew, Thomas 276–7
Ahon Sa Hirop 260
AIDS *see* HIV/AIDS
Aineias the Tactician 58
Albania 223
Alcoholics Anonymous 39
Alderfer, C. P. 84
Alexander the Great 58
Allen, Godfrey 23
Amanah Ikhtiar Malaysia 259
Amnesty International 19–21, 37–40,
    181–2
'analyser' strategy 198
Andrews, G. 192
Andrews, K. 7, 64–5
Anheier, H. K. 43, 46–7, 197
Ansoff, Igor 63, 67–8, 102
Ansoff's matrix 68, 113, 196
Apex Trust 22–3
Argenti, J. 46
Argyris, C. 87, 99, 101
Asche, D. 7–8
Association of Chief Executives of
    National Voluntary Organizations
    115, 160
Association for Enterprise Opportunity
    261
Athos, A. 48, 76, 183

'Attributes of Excellence' school 60, 73,
    79–80
autonomy of workers 87
Ayal, I. 110

'B'Hags' 189
Babbage, Charles 61
Backoff, R. W. 199–200
balanced scorecard model 134–5, 170
Baldridge Quality Award 79
Balfour, K. 135, 169–70
Bangladesh 243, 255–64, 291
Barnard, Chester 187
Barnardo's 15–17, 186, 202
Barry, B. W. 202
Bartlett, C. A. 186
Bass, B. M. 89
Batsleer, J. 30, 33
benchmarking 126
beneficiaries of voluntary activity 42–3
Benenson, Peter 19
Bennis, Warren 75, 182
Bergh, Henry 276
Bernhard, Prince 237
'Best Value' process 28
Bevan, Aneurin 17
Beveridge, William 17–18, 39
Bigelow, B. 128
Billis, D. 31, 39, 114
'bite-sized management' 213
Blau, P. M. 42
Bolman, L. G. 78, 129
Booth, Charles 15, 248
Boschken, H. L. 198
Boston Consulting Group 70, 113,
    151–3

Bowman, C. 7–8
Boxx, W. R. 144
Boyd, B. K. 141
Brenton, M. 28, 39–40, 44
British Quality Foundation 135, 165
Brown, Christopher 285
Bryson, J. M. 7–8, 74, 113, 150, 183, 185, 210–13
budgeting 211–12
Buerk, Michael 292
Bulgaria 223
'bureaucrat' strategy 201
Burelli, Father 246
Burgelman, R. A. 98
Burns, Tom 101
business planning 213
business process re-engineering 62, 70
Business Week 103
Buxton, Dorothy 221–2

Cadbury Report (1992) 49
Cambodia 291
campaigning 39–40
Canadian Comprehensive Auditing Foundation system 135, 170
cancer charities 175–6, 203–4
Cancer Research Campaign 204
CARD Bank 260
CARE 202, 242–4
Care In The Home (CITH) 27, 198, 204, 230–4
Carr, C. 95
case studies 219 *et seq*
'Cash Cow' programmes 152
central planning 96–9
Centrepoint 181–2, 184, 190, 253
Chandler, D. Jr 7, 60, 63–4, 92
charitable status 37, 40
Charities Act (1992) 122
Charities Evaluation Service 165
Charities Review Council of Minnesota 79
Charity Commissioners 37, 43
Chesterman, M. 13
Chi-Chi 235–6
Chief Executive Officers 64, 67, 89, 97–8, 116, 118, 214
Child Poverty Action Group 39
Childline 181–2

Children Act (1908) 278
Children Act (1948) 280
Children Act (1989) 285
Children and Young Persons Act (1932) 280
Children and Young Persons Act (1963) 281
Children's Charter (1889) 277–8
Children's Sunday 279
civil society organizations 38
Clark Whitehill study 115, 118
Clausewitz, Carl von 58–60
cloning 206
Clutterbuck, D. 77–8
code of practice for the voluntary sector 167–8
Cole, G. D. H. 18
Collins, J. C. 48, 78, 179, 185, 189
Colwell, Maria 283
'command and control' 82
'community', vision of 251
community empowerment 158
'compact' strategy 202
competing-values model 133–4
competition between organizations 32, 48, 176, 250
competitive advantage 69, 91
Conservative Party 29–30
constituency accounting 129
'consumers' of welfare 18
contingency approach to effectiveness 130–1
Contingency school of strategic management 102
continuous improvement 79, 159–60
continuous learning 95
contract culture 27–9, 42
contracting-out 29
Cooke, R. A. 185
Coopey, J. 101
core competencies 74, 91–2, 154
Cornforth, C. 45
corporate culture 76
corporate strategy 64, 128
cost-benefit analysis 116
cost-effectiveness 125
cost leadership 197, 200
Craig, J. C. 7, 71
critical success factors 188

Crittenden, J. C. 196
Crittenden, W. 143–4
Crossman, Richard 18
Cultural Revolution 207
culture, definitions of 185
'custodian' strategy 199
Cyert, R. M. 99
Cyrenian Federation 253

D'Aunno, T. 130
Davis, R. C. 61–2
Davis, R. H. 110
Day, Dorothy 246
'Dead Dog' programmes 152
Deakin, N. 29
Deal, T. E. 78, 129
decision-process model 128
'defender' strategy 198–9
dependency 30
Design school of strategic management 64–5, 73, 153
'developer' strategy 199
differentiation of service 197–8
'director' strategy 200
distinctive competencies 64, 154–5
dominant firms 199
Donnelly-Cox, G. 42
double-loop learning 99, 101
Drucker, P. F. 30–1, 46–7, 60, 63, 123, 180
Dunnette, M. D. 83

Earth Summit (Rio, 1992) 239
Eccles, R. 99
economy, assessment of 125
Edinburgh, Duke of 236, 238
Edward, Prince of Wales 279
effectiveness, organizational 88–9, 121–7, 130–3, 157; impact of strategic planning on 143–4
efficiency as distinct from effectiveness 125
emergent learning 98–9
'entrepreneur' strategy 199
environmental scanning 172–3
Epaminondas 58
equity 125
ERG theory 84
ethical accounting 129
Ethiopia 224, 227, 292

European Foundation for Quality Management (EFQM) excellence model 79, 135–7, 60–5
evaluation 156–8
'Evolutionary' perspective on management 70
'excellent' organizations 9, 74–5; *see also* 'Attributes of Excellence' school; European Foundation for Quality Management
ex-offenders 22–3, 184
expectation theory of motivation 86

Fayol, Henri 61–3
'first mover' advantage 155
focus strategies 198
Follett, M. P. 183
force field analysis 118, 177–8
France 4, 37
franchising 216
Frederick the Great 59
Freeman, R. E. 150
Frontinus 58
Fulton Report (1968) 24
Fundación Social 204–5
fundraising groups 42

Galápagos Islands 236
Gandhi, Indira 237
Gann, N. 27
gap analysis 68, 116
Gee, E. P. 236
generic strategies 195–8, 208–9
Gerard, D. 40–1, 111
Germany 4, 260
Gherardi, S. 101
Ghoshal, S. 186
Gidron, B. 39, 41
goal-setting theory 87, 124
Golden-Biddle, K. 111–12
Goldsmith, W. 77–8
Goold, M. 177
governance 49
Graebler, T. 27, 75–6
Grameen Bank 51, 202, 255–64
Grant, R. 7, 71, 154–5
grant-giving organizations 42
Greenley, G. E. 141
Grewe, T. 90

group dynamics 88
Guide Dogs for the Blind 46, 181, 184
guilds 13
Gutch, R. 29, 40
Gyford, J. 29

Hackman, J. R. 87
Hailey, John 126–7
Haiti 243
Hall, P. D. 37
Hall, S. 30
Hamel, G. 91–2, 97, 186–9
Hammer, M. 82
Handel, Margaret 247
Handy, Charles 30–2, 82
Handy Report (1981) 30
Harlow, J. 34
Harris, M. 39, 114
Harvey-Jones, J. 95–6
Hasenfield, Y. 39, 41
Hatch, S. 41, 44
Hawthorne experiments 62
'headless giants' 199
hedging strategy 202
Heffron, F. 130
Heijden, K. van der 103
Heimovitics, R. D. 129
Heller, Robert 76
Henderson, Bruce 70
Herman, R. 122–3, 128, 134
Hertzberg, F. 83
HIV/AIDS 202–3, 228
Hofer, Charles 109
Homeline 265–74
Hudson, M. 27, 38, 90, 101–2, 185
Human Resources school 9, 62, 81, 84,
    90–2
human rights 20–1
Human Rights Act (2000) 28
Hungary 4, 223, 243
Huxley, Sir Julian 235
'hygiene factors' 83, 88

IBM 30
ICA Strategic Planning Process 90
Imai, M. 77
Imperial Cancer Research Fund 204
implementation of strategic plans
    210–13

Incremental school of strategy formation
    see Learning school
Industrial Revolution 14–15
Ingleby Report (1960) 281
Inland Revenue 37
innovation 45, 98, 197–200
instrumental conditioning 82
International Classification of Non-
    profit Organizations (ICNPO) 43
Investors In People 160–4
Ireland 42, 253–4
issues impact analysis grid 173
Italy 4

James, B. G. 60
Janis, I. L. 88
Japan 4, 76–7, 80, 183
Jeavons, T. H. 38
Jebb, Eglantyne 221–4
Jenster, P. V. 144
job factor theory 87
Johnson, G. 7
Johnson, N. 44
Joseph, Sir Keith 283
Joseph Rowntree Foundation 167
Joseph Rowntree standards 79
Joyce, P. 102

Kaizen 77
Kalkas Group 97
Kanter, R. M. 124, 127
Kaplan, R. S. 134–5
Kare-Silver, M. de 97
Karger, D. W. 110
Katz, R. 88
Kay, John 91
Kearns, K. P. 144, 195–6, 207
Kendall, J. 12, 38, 40–1, 44–5, 133
Kirkley, Howard Leslie 289
Kleisthenes 57
Knapp, M. 12, 38, 40–1, 44–5, 133
Knauft, B. 180
Knight, B. 30, 40
Kohjasten, M. 83
Korea 225–6, 243
Koteen, J. 213
Kramer, R. M. 39
Kushner, R. 132–3

Landry, C. 33
Lawler, E. E. 88
leadership roles 100
leadership styles 89
learning organizations 99–101
Learning school of strategy formation
    97–101, 142
learning systems 99
Leat, D. 32–3, 45, 47–8, 74–5
Leavitt, H. J. 84
Lenin, V. I. 60
Letts, C. W. 90, 126, 170
leveraging strategy 202
Lewin, Kurt 89, 177
Likert, R. 85
Lindblom, C. E. 97–8
Lindenberg, M. 126, 176
Lipsky, M. 42
Liverpool Society for the Prevention of
    Cruelty to Children 276, 281
livery companies 13
lobbying 39
Locke, E. A. 87
logical incrementalism 98
London Lighthouse 203
London Society for the Prevention of
    Cruelty to Children 277
long-term aims 188–9
Loudon, John 238
Lowe, R. 18
Lubelska, A. 29, 143
Lyons, M. 32

MacArthur Foundation 260
McClelland, D. C. 85
McConkey, D. D. 110
McCormack, Mary Ellen 276
McDonnell, E. 102
McGrath, J. E. 88
McGregor, D. M. 82–3
Machiavelli, Niccolò 59
MacMillan, I. C. 153
Macmillan Cancer Relief 203
Maier, N. R. F. 89
Malaysia 259
Malik, Z. A. 110
Management By Objectives (MBO)
    62–3, 110
management style 40–1

management techniques, arguments for
    and against use of 33–4
mandate analysis 114, 150
Manpower Services Commission 21–4
Mao Tse-tung 60, 207
March, J. G. 99, 123
Marie Curie Cancer Care 203
market extension 196
Mary of Teck, Princess 278
Maslow, A. 82–4
Mason, D. 31, 45
Mastrofski, S. 86
Matthews, D. 122
Mayo, Elton 62, 84
membership organizations 40, 50
Mencap 181, 183–4
mergers of voluntary nonprofit
    organizations 203
Meyer, J. 132
Meyer, M. 127
microcredit programmes 263
Miles, R. E. 198
military strategy 57–60, 79
Miller, Danny 199–200
Minnesota principles of nonprofit
    excellence 168–9
Mintzberg, Henry 6, 8, 66–7, 70–1, 79,
    89, 94–9, 140, 182, 206, 211
mission and mission statements
    179–82, 187–8
models of strategic management
    109–10, 140–2
monitoring of progress 212
Monsanto 264
Morales, Horacio B. 205
Morton, Arthur 280
motivation 82–6
Moyer, Mel 34
multiple constituency approach 128–9
Murray, V. 135, 169–70
mutual aid organizations 39–42
'mutualist' strategy 201

Napoleon 59
National Association for the Care and
    Resettlement of Offenders (NACRO)
    184
National Childbirth Trust 181, 184

National Council for Voluntary Organizations 137, 161–5
National Health Service 4, 17, 203
National Lottery Board 23
National Society for the Prevention of Cruelty to Children (NSPCC) 27, 181–2, 184, 206, 276–87
National Westminster Bank 30
needs, satisfaction of 83–4
Netherlands 28
New Economics Foundation 129, 158, 160
new managerialism 29–30
'new modernist' approach 103
Newman, W. H. 110–11
niche marketers 200
Nicholson, Max 235
Nohria, N. 99
non-governmental organizations (NGOs) 38, 50, 263
Northern Ireland 253–4
Norton, D. P. 134
Nutt, P. C. 199–200

Odiorne, G. S. 85
Odom, R. Y. 144
Ohmae, K. 48, 77, 96
O'Neill, Dennis 280
operational plans 213
O'Regan, A. 42
organizational mapping 176
Osborne, D. 27, 75–6
Osborne, S. P. 37, 45, 51, 125, 133, 196–8
Oster, S. M. 156, 177, 180
Ouchi, W. G. 76–7
Overstreet, G. A. 144
Oxfam 39–40, 202, 289–93

'parlay' orientation 202
participant satisfaction approach 129
participation in planning process 87–91, 103, 117–18, 214–15
Pascale, R. 48, 76, 79, 183
Paton, R. 45, 51
Patton, George 58
Patton, M. 191
Pearce, J. A. 141
Pekar, P. Jr 141

performance appraisal for workers 214
performance indicators for organizations 190–3
PEST analysis 113, 116–17, 174
Peters, T. 9, 73, 79–80, 140, 173, 185
Pettigrew, A. 171
philanthropy 30, 39, 14–18
Philippines, the 259–60
'piggybacking' 204
PLANET DEFOE 174
planning departments and processes 95–7
Planning school of strategic management 67–8, 73, 196
Poertner, J. 191
Pol Pot 291
political parties 50
Political school of strategic management 101–2, 129–30
Poole, P. 132–3
Poor Law 13–14
Porras, J. I. 48, 78, 179, 185, 189
Porter, L. W. 82
Porter, M. E. 69–70, 176–7, 182, 197–8
portfolio analysis 70, 113, 151–3
Positioning school of strategic management 69–73, 151, 197
post-modernism 131–2
power-broking 101, 103
power equalisation 84–5
Practical Quality Assurance System for Small Organizations (PQASSO) 79, 165–7
Prahalad, C. J. 91–2, 97, 189
pressure groups 39
Prevention of Cruelty to Children Act (1904) 278
Princess Royal 227
private sector compared with voluntary nonprofit sector 45–9
Probation Offenders Act (1907) 278
Prochaska, F. 15
professionalization 29
profit-making 46
'prospector' strategy 198–9
psychological contract 86
Punishment of Incest Act (1908) 278
purchaser–provider split 27

purposive-rational model of organizations 123

quality leadership 197
quality of life, evaluation of 158
quangos 44
'Quest' orientation 201–2
'Question Mark' programmes 152
Quinn, J. B. 7–8, 60, 78–9, 94–8, 202
Quinn, R. 131, 133

Rapp, C. 191
'rational' perspectives 61–2, 110–12, 133–4
'reactor' strategy 198
Reaganism 24
religious institutions 13, 24, 27, 45, 50–1, 144, 206
Rensselaerville Institute 170
Renz, D. 122–3, 128
replicability of resources and capabilities 156
reputation 129
resource-based theory of strategy 91–2, 154–5
resourcing of plans 211–12
Rice, J. J. 183
'Rising Star' programmes 152
Rockefeller Foundation 260
Rodgers, B. 14
Rohrbaugh, J. 131, 133
Rommel, Erwin 58
Rousseau, D. M. 185
Rowan, B. 132
Rowntree, Seebohm 15
'rubber band' theory of organizational development 149
Rubin, M. 201
Rudolph, Edward 277

'saga' orientation 201
Salamon, L. M. 43
Salamon, L. S. 30
Salipante, P. F. 111–12
Save the Children Fund 202, 221–9
scenario analysis 118, 172–3
Schein, E. H. 86
Scholes, K. 7
Schon, D. A. 99, 101

scientific management 61–3, 82, 89
Scott, Peter 235
Scott, W. R. 42, 132
'Scrutiny' initiative 156
Seashore, W. R. 128
sectors, concept of 49–52
Seebohm Report (1968) 21
Segaar, P. 141
self-help groups 41, 48
Selznick, Philip 64
Senge, Peter 99–100
Shaftesbury, Lord 277
Shelter 39
Siciliano, J. I. 144
'silo' effect 216
Simmons, K. 119
Simon, H. A. 79, 123
Simon Community 187, 190, 206–7, 246–54
Singh, K. K. 143
single-loop learning 99
Sipel, G. A. 75
Skinner, B. F. 82
SMART objectives 213
Smircich, L. 185
Smith, Adam 61
Smith, David 38–9
Smith, S. R. 42
Smith, Samuel 276
Snow, C. C. 198
social auditing 128–9, 151, 158–61
social constructionist approach 131, 134
social economy concept 37
social exchange concept 85–6
Socrates 58
spin off of new organizations 206–7
'stabilizer' strategy 199
Stacey, R. D. 95, 97
stakeholder analysis 114, 150–1
stakeholders: management of 128; multiplicity of 46–7, 111, 128
Steers, R. M. 82
Steiner, G. 96
Stolan, Victor 235
Stone, M. M. 114, 116, 143, 211
strategic analysis 149–70
strategic conversations 103
strategic drift 100–1, 182
strategic formulation 195–209

strategic objectives 188
strategic planning, elements of 119
strategic planning pyramid 189–90
strategic types 198
strategy: components of 65; concept and
    definitions of 5–8, 57–8, 189; as
    distinct from tactics 60
stretch, concept of 189
Strickland, A. J. III 7
structural–rational paradigm 125
structure, organizational 215–17
success, criteria for and indicators of 46,
    127, 140
Summers, D. V. 124, 127
Summers, H. G. Jr 59
Sun Tzu 58
survivability 127
sustainability 155
SWOT analysis 66, 113, 116, 153–4,
    172
symbolic frame for an organization 132
synergy, concept of 68
system–resource approach 127
Szabar, K. 119

tactics 60
'target' strategy 202
Taylor, Frederick W. 61–3
Taylor, M. 28
Telephone Helpline Association 267,
    271
Terence Higgins Trust 203
Thatcherism 24, 29
Theory X 82–3
Theory Y 83–4
Theory Z 76
'third sector' 37
Thompson, A. A. 7
time-in-job theory 88
Total Quality Management 70, 79
trade unions 50–1
transferability of resources and
    capabilities 155–6
'trial' strategy 202
trial-and-error approaches to planning
    74
Tricker, M. 125, 133
triple bottom line 135

United Nations: Capital Development
    Fund 260; Children's Fund
    (UNICEF) 181–3; Convention on
    the Rights of the Child 223; Food
    and Agriculture Organization 290
United States 3–4, 28, 30, 38, 42, 51,
    134, 260
United Way of America 170, 191–2
Unterman, I. 110
Urwick, L. 62

Vajkai, Julie Eve 223
valence concept 86
value chain concept 69–70
value statements 187–8
values 32, 38, 184–8; compliance with
    126–7; in theory and in practice
    185–6; *see also* Victorian values
Van de Ven, A. H. 143
'venture' orientation 202
Victoria, Queen 277, 279
Victorian values 30, 186
Vietnam 243
Vincent, Neville 22
vision statements 182–4, 187–9
Voluntary Action Unit 158
voluntary nonprofit sector: expectations
    of 30–4; definition of 38–9, 44;
    distinctive features of 45–6; fields of
    activity 43; functions 38–40; history
    5, 12–24; importance 3–4; matrix of
    strategic choices for 207–8; use of
    strategic planning tools by 115–20
Voluntary Service Overseas 181, 188
'voluntaryism', 'volunteerism' and
    'voluntarism' 37
Vroom, V. H. 86

Waalewijn, P. 141
Walker, J. M. 111
Wallender, H. N. III 110–11
Wallich-Clifford, Anton 246–52
War Charities Act (1916) 279
Waterman, R. H. Jr 9, 73–6, 79–80,
    140, 185
Watson, Thomas Jr 184–5
Waugh, Benjamin 277
Weardale, Lord 222

Weber, Max 63
Webster, S. A. 91, 143
Weisbrod, M. R. 214
Weiss, C. H. 156
welfare, production of 133
welfare state 17, 39, 280
Westley, Frances 206
Westminster, Duke of 284
Whipp, R. 171
Whittington, R. 70
Williams, I. 15

Williams of Mostyn, Lord 286
Wolfenden Report (1978) 23–4
Woods, A. 102
'worker communities' 251–2
World Bank 260, 263
World Wide Fund for Nature 235–40
Wylie, M. L. 91, 143

Yunus, M. 255–9, 262

Zucker, L. 12